Constantine Andoniou

Fractal Fetishes

Constantine Andoniou

Fractal Fetishes

Essays on the Organization of the System of Information

VDM Verlag Dr. Müller

Imprint

Bibliographic information by the German National Library: The German National Library lists this publication at the German National Bibliography; detailed bibliographic information is available on the Internet at http://dnb.d-nb.de.

Cover image: www.purestockx.com

Publisher:
VDM Verlag Dr. Müller Aktiengesellschaft & Co. KG, Dudweiler Landstr. 125 a, 66123 Saarbrücken, Germany,
Phone +49 681 9100-698, Fax +49 681 9100-988,
Email: info@vdm-verlag.de

Produced in USA and UK by:
Lightning Source Inc., La Vergne, Tennessee, USA
Lightning Source UK Ltd., Milton Keynes, UK
BookSurge LLC, 5341 Dorchester Road, Suite 16, North Charleston, SC 29418, USA

ISBN: 978-3-8364-9704-6

DEDICATION

For my Mother, Katrina & Mia Belle

BRIEF CONTENTS

LIST OF ILLUSTRATIONS

CHAPTER 7

DIGITAL COMPONENT

DOWNLOAD/INSTALLATION

There is an additional component to be viewed with this book which at the time of printing can be downloaded from the following links:

http://rapidshare.com/files/93141132/VP_CAndoniou.part1.rar

http://rapidshare.com/files/93144408/VP_CAndoniou.part2.rar

Once downloaded, please extract all files in the same folder using WinRar or similar program. All presentations are made in Macromedia Flash and open in full screen. Press the ESC button to minimize full screen and CTRL+F to change back to full screen. Press ALT+F4 at any time to exit and return to Windows.

CONTENT

This digital component contains additional audiovisual material related to the theoretical discussions in the book: a 20-min virtual poster presentation of the main hypotheses and theoretical approximations proposed, and individual audiovisual presentations segments of the proposed theoretical approximations: Hypotheses, Infotypes, Virtual Implosion, Fractal Dynamics, Inforgrams, Endogenesis/Exogenesis, and Inforgramic Analysis (examples of).

REQUIREMENTS

Macromedia FLASH plugin (www.adobe.com)

Best viewed with 800x600 resolution

Sound ON

PROLOGUE

PROLOGUE

F ractal Fetishes is a philosophical investigation of the nature and organization of the *system of information*. It is my premise that this system of information comprises our knowledge of the social and defines individual and collective existence. At the same time, in a digital world where 'everything is, everything is not, or everything can be at the same time', the quest for true and absolute realities generates confusion and disillusion. Such a quest simply adds more fuel to the recycling procedure of already inadequate and insufficient justifications and conclusions to explain the contemporary world.

This book calls for a fresh new perspective, accepting that there can only be variations of given facts and realities. It begins from a Lefebvrian view that there can be only theoretical approximations to the true or the real. If truth and reality themselves have become at best ambiguous, the priority is rather to reset world views and analyses in relation to the fluid new bodies of knowledge in a global context. The challenge is to reconsider the value of available information and knowledge in their contexts of global electronic communication and digital technologies. This involves a reexamination of our ways of analyzing and processing information to reach a sufficient degree of understanding of our construction within our daily digital environments and informational landscapes. This must proceed from an in-depth analysis and a 'framing' of the organization of the system of information that comprises these digital environments, and which in effect organize our existence within them.

The book is divided in three parts focusing on the four hypotheses stated further below (Figures 0.1- 0.4). These are:

1. **The Information Flow hypothesis:** that mediated flows of information provide a way of describing contemporary history, politics, economy and culture. The discourses of representational information construct our social knowledge at different levels of

1

human information processing. Informational representations are language and visual images, which in turn shape ideology and are expressed through responsive patterns of social communication and action.

2. **The Social Knowledge hypothesis:** that these technologically mediated flows construct social knowledge, identity, and action. Social knowledge is to a great extent controlled and shaped by global communication media. In their spatial environment of operation, that of hyperspace, human/machine information processing and exchange, there are fractal levels of distortion of the system of information.

3. **The Code of Information hypothesis:** that these flows have specific structures, channels and processes that effect society and knowledge. The structure and organization of the system of information can be analysed to its distinct code. Isomorphies and analogies can be identified among information systems of social knowledge. The line between 'generic' human information processing, and 'external' cybernetic interference is thin, challenging authenticity and free expression in human communication.

4. **The System of Information hypothesis:** That there is a distinctive, contemporary epochal organization of information in space and time that influences cognition, everyday life and society. The system of information is characterized by three levels of spatial organization across time: the era of Romanticism, the epoch of Ersatz, and, the age of Chimera, representing, freedom, exploitation and domination of the system of information, respectively. Their levels of intensification regulate the relations of meaning, and consequently the organization of the social.

The first part of the book, titled *the Digital Labyrinth*, examines theoretical accounts on the contemporary social organization and structure, discourses and cultural environment. The aim is to establish and examine the first two hypotheses. Looking at the Information Flow hypothesis, I establish the historical and socio-cultural conditions within which this book is located. Turning to the Social Knowledge hypothesis, I identify specific informational patterns of organization in structures, discourses, ideological systems, and cultural trends, which can be reflexively applied to describe the organization of the dominant system of information.

The second part of the book, *Terra Incognita*, first focuses on establishing a theoretical framework which can account for diverse aspects of the organization of the system of information. This builds the Code of Information hypothesis. To this end I describe systemic properties, and interdisciplinary analogies and isomorphies, as well as principles of information theory, cybernetic control and human communication.

The third and last part of the book, titled *Fractal Fetishes*, offers a new philosophic description of the current epoch: which I term the space and time of the *System of Information.* This section consists of theoretical approximations, more speculative and futures-oriented, regarding the organization and implication of the system of information in the era of global electronic communication and digital technologies.

[Hypothesis 1] **The Information Flow hypothesis:** Our view and perception of the social, the world out there, are shaped by our accumulated life experiences, which exponentially add up to our banks of social knowledge. The discourses of history, politics, economy and culture, as separate, though inseparable to each other, as discourses of representational information, construct a real and imagined at the same time vision of this world within the human mind. Social knowledge is constructed at the subjective and collective levels of human information processing, and is therefore dependent on the organization of the system of information within which it is produced. Informational representations take form and shape in language and visual images, are reflected and manipulated in ideology, and finally they are expressed though patterns of social communication and action as a response to historical, political, economic and cultural conditions (Figure 0.1)

In this context, **Chapter One** looks into contemporary social theory on the emerging societies at the end of the second millennium. The chapter provides an account of the dominant historical, political, and socio-economic attributes of the world society, through theories of the information society, the post-industrial society, the public sphere, flexible specialization, heightened surveillance, the network society, and digital capitalism. The concept of information is identified as a key form of representation, which is structuring and organizing social knowledge, consequently social life, at different levels and geographical locations. The concept of information emerges as

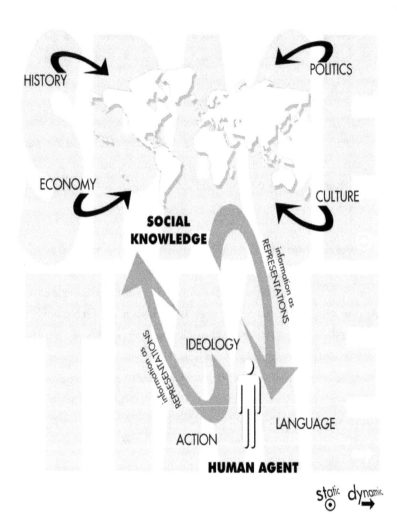

Figure 0.1: [Hypothesis 1] The Information Flow hypothesis: That mediated flows of information provide a way of describing contemporary history, politics, economy and culture. The discourses of representational information construct our social knowledge at different levels of human information processing. Informational representations are language and visual images, which in turn shape ideology and are expressed through responsive patterns of social communication and action.

the defining feature of our contemporary society. It has always been a defining characteristic of industrial modernity, but the technological innovations in the late 20th century have led to the intensification of its volume and usage. This intensification is conducive to an emerging global social experience. This in turn has been traced to mixed effects, ranging from the radical reorganization of advanced, developing, and under-developed world economies and practices of everyday life, to the growth of a global youth consciousness and understanding among people.

In this regard, social 'reality' is now an informational product, generated by the processing and management of the dominant system of information, through means of electronic communication and advances and applications of digital technologies. Therefore, the organization of social structure and associated processes can be seen as a reflexive reflection of the organizational patterns of the system of information. Chapter One sets the stage for multi-perspectival, inter-disciplinary and in-depth micro-analytical conceptualizations and theorizations, based on the concept of information. These theorizations can become one of many starting points for a reconstruction of social theory dealing with human and/or machine (computer) communication in the era of intensified digital technologies and applications – the aims of subsequent chapters.

Chapter Two focuses on elements of social practice and discourse: more specifically, the cultural imperialism thesis, globalization arguments and the McDonaldization project. The chapter aims to define the characteristic processual attributes of social configurations and to establish the dominant social trends and tensions prevalent in our information world. The arguments of cultural imperialism signal the onset of the trans-national expansion of global media worldwide, and raise concerns over the control and effects of media imperialism on social organization and social control and change. The account of cultural imperialism also points to the power of the system of information in affecting and intruding worldwide cultural systems. Behind the power of media or cultural imperialism, stands though, a powerful global system of information that produces and organizes dominant reflections of social reality and life. These reflections are evident in the culturization of social life, as the globalization proposals would argue. Globalization arguments, briefly discussed in this chapter, indicate the importance of symbolic communication and of culture, which realize the project of globalization. By contrast, arguments of McDonaldization of the world society point towards the existence and persistence of higher forms of rationalization, consumerism, homogeneity and uniformity. As argued in the first chapter, specific patterns of organization of these discourses emerge, either as processes aimed to internal organization or as interactions to external tensions. These discourse principles of interactivity, networking and flexibility, I argue, are characteristics of the mechanics of the system of information, referring to its dynamic flow and its complex organization. In such a context, any bids for social change and action would need to readdress issues of control of information.

[Hypothesis 2] **The Social Knowledge hypothesis:** Within the boundaries of our physical space and across the arrow of time our perception of what constitutes (collectively and/or individually) acceptable social knowledge is to a great extent controlled by the global communication technologies and media of all forms. The system of information entails controlled representations of the intentions and the financial interests of transnational media corporations and their affiliated corporate and governmental infrastructure. At another level of spatial consciousness, that of hyperspace, human and machine information processing and communication, converge and align along fractal levels of distortion of the system of information. This in turn shapes our knowledge of the social – often in distinctive corporate interests. Let alone the nature of knowledge per se, more importantly, events of social change and decisions of social action, in this respect, become ambiguous and questionable, as to whether they are expressions of individual choice and freedom or reproductive of well-established patterns of exploitation and domination (Figure 0.2). They are expressed in the form of ideological systems, which influence and are influenced by the cultural conditions and environment within which they emerge.

Chapter Three first discusses the elements of the organization and function of these dominant ideologies. It then turns to the cultural dominant configuration of our time, that of postmodernity. Defining ideologies as organized and ordered systems of information, my aim is, firstly, to stress their function and role in social persuasion, social integration and social interpretation. Ideologies are among the most intensively studied and theorized elements of contemporary social theory and society. The important role of ideologies is exemplified in

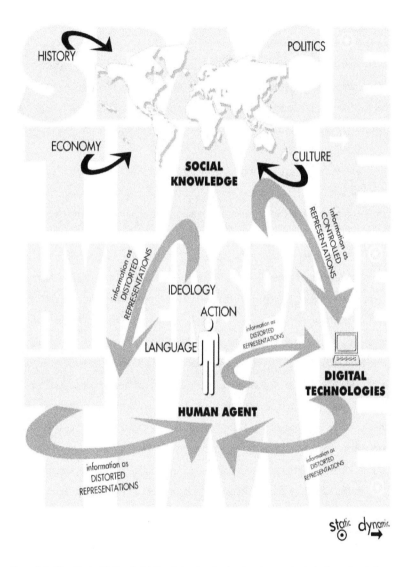

Figure 0.2: [Hypothesis 2] The Social Knowledge hypothesis: that these technologically mediated flows construct social knowledge, identity, and action; social knowledge is to a great extent controlled and shaped by global communication media. In their spatial environment of operation, that of hyperspace, human/machine information processing and exchange, there are fractal levels of distortion of the system of information.

diverse analyses: as constructing imaginary and politically motivated significations into real worlds, as operating in invisible and symbolic modes, as legitimating modern rationality, or as interpellating individuals into subjects.

My main aim is to point out how the structure and organization of ideological systems can reveal attributes of the system of information from which they originate. Chapter Two then is a bid to show that principles of the construction, organization and expression of ideological systems can also be said to be indicative of the organization of the sub-systems of information.

With regard to the postmodern cultural environment, I focus on various sets of postmodern positions, aiming to account for some elements of the contemporary cultural environment. My aim is also to show how the system of information plays a vital role in the construction of the postmodern, virtual environment. I suggest that we are now in a phase past postmodernity, which can be termed 'postmodernity-and-beyond'. Postmodernity-and-beyond it is a virtual intensification of certain social elements, related to the concept of the system of information. Postmodern positions, generally characterized by a spirit of relativism, irrationalism and nihilism, criticize the insufficiency of the modern, and reject notions of causality in favour of multiplicity, plurality, fragmentation and indeterminacy. The discussion takes into consideration widely-cited postmodern views on the deconstruction of traditional societies, language, signs, and images, knowledge and technologies of the self, schizos, rhizomes and nomads, implosion and simulacra, desire and discourse. The discussion focuses, in particular, to the theorization of postmodernism as the cultural logic of capitalism, and on the mode of information proposition. I maintain that the postmodern organization of the world society around digital communication technologies is responsible for the reconstruction and regeneration of cultural systems worldwide. It is powered up by an uncontrollable flow of information, responsible for the reconstruction of a digital hyper-real world, that we only start to understand.

[Hypothesis 3] **The Code of Information hypothesis:** The concept of information in the age of electronic communication and digital technologies can be distinctively identified to have systemic characteristics, the organization and structure of which can be analyzed through the code of information. The code of information refers to general patterns of organization of the system of information, and with regard both to content and relationships. In particular, the code can incorporate the nature and character of information, processes of association and interaction, the source, the destination point and the channels of the communication of the system of information, and so on.

This book tables a theoretical framework of the particular systemic properties of the system of information. This requires investigation of isomorphies and analogies among interdisciplinary systems for the construction of social knowledge, primarily informational, still diverse and seemingly unrelated. In the world of digital technologies and applications, particular concern is needed to principles of human information processing and communication and how these principles may be disturbed by external cybernetic interference. Moreover, the fractalized outcome of this cybernetic interference claims to substitute any notion of authenticity and originality and replace free expression in human communication, with patterns of imitation and domination (Figure 0.3).

Chapter Four develops a theoretical framework for the concept of 'the system of information'. In the first part of this chapter, the focus is on system properties as they are defined within systems theory and general systems theory. The system of information is then defined as a complex, self-organizing entity which can affect and organize other systems. Its organization can be characterized as one of chaotic organization in constant change towards a dynamic fractal system.

The second part of the chapter examines the organization of macrocosmic and microcosmic systems in analogy to the organization of the system of information. I argue that several sub-systems of information, of self-similar organization, organize and 'inform' what we believe we know about them, in the form of information or knowledge. I turn then my attention to identify structural isomorphies and analogies in patterns of organization in disciplines such as cosmology and human neurophysiology. I also take up key principles of human information processing, focusing on the vulnerability and potential instability of the system of information. Some reference is made to applications of artificial intelligence with the purpose of justifying observations regarding human information processing with reverse comparisons to the artificial (machine) information processing.

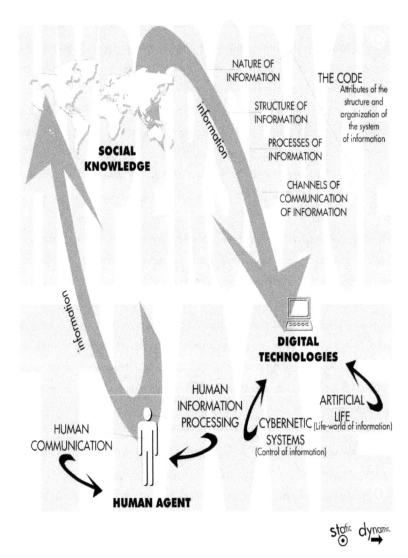

Figure 0.3: [Hypothesis 3] **The Code of Information hypothesis:** that these flows have specific structures, channels and processes that effect society and knowledge; the structure and organization of the system of information can be analysed to its distinct code. Isomorphies and analogies can be identified among information systems of social knowledge. The line between 'generic' human information processing, and 'external' cybernetic interference is thin, challenging authenticity and free expression in human communication.

The quest for systemic analogies and isomorphies is continued in **Chapter Five**. I focus on three areas of discussion, namely, principles of information theory, cybernetic principles of human information processing, and organizational patterns of human communication and interaction and relevant pathologies. Information theory provides basic concepts and relationships of the organization of the system of information. A discussion of the information process reveals attributes of the system of information, such as, entropy, redundancy, and noise. Further investigation into language, code and grammar provides some insight into communication, construction and processing of information, and in particular of the construction of meaning. The discussion on cybernetic principles opens the possibilities of external interference of human information processing, therefore, of the interference with the construction of 'realities' and of human behaviour. This reference to cybernetic principles, once more demonstrates the importance of information in the development of human consciousness, perception and construction of 'reality'. In the last section of this chapter I examine how the system of information organizes human communication and interaction, and how human behaviour can be affected by discrepancies in the communication of information, which may lead to paradoxical and, indeed, pathological situations.

The book stresses the need for the development of innovative inter-disciplinary theoretical models which can cope with uncertainties and paradoxes of electronic communication and digital technologies of postmodernity-and-beyond. To this end, an analytical model is proposed in the form of theoretical approximations with the aim of advancing our understanding of the organization of the system of information in the digital world. In the theoretical proposals that are stated in the last part of the book, I call for a different way of thinking, a radical epistemology of open end to cope with the speedy and unpredictable effects of the system of information in social progress and change. In contrast to developing fatal strategies, this is a strategy of encouragement for developing diverse ways of thinking. It is a strategy of survival in an informational ocean of lived illusions and lost meanings, where human consciousness and awareness finds it more and more difficult to recognize directions, to survive and to sustain its existence.

[Hypothesis 4] The System of Information hypothesis: The system of information spans along multiple coexisting spatial levels of organization across the arrow of time, which represent conditions of freedom, of exploitation and of domination of the system of information, respectively. These organizational levels of the system of information (corresponding to entropy, redundancy, and noise of its volume and intensity) coexist at any time at different levels of intensities, and which mark certain socio-cultural and historical periods. In the contemporary era of electronic communication and digital technologies, of hyper-real landscapes and fantasy worlds, the fractalization the system of information establishes new relations of meanings and understandings. Whether it is a new starting point is one question, but is definitely a point of no return to an ambiguous future (Figure 0.4).

In this spirit - the last two chapters, **Chapter Six** and **Chapter Seven**, rework and 'use' the observations across the book regarding the organization of the system of information. I argue that the digital re-organization of the system of information reassigns the meaning of reality and reorganizes the reality of meaning. Based on an alternative envisioning of spatiality (heterotopias, trialectics, thirdspace) a series of theoretical proposals, are put forward, in the form of approximations, which apply to the construction of the digital justification of reality or the digital reconstruction of hyper-reality. The proposed model of theoretical approximations is a meta-philosophical proposition, a proposition that moves towards a radical reconstruction of long-established thinking of the production of social knowledge. This also acts as a warning that the proposed philosophical considerations on the code of the organization of the system of information may be unavoidably abstract and probabilistic and possibly paradoxical and controversial.

Chapter Six establishes the process of the implosion of meaningful and authentic information to an ambiguous state of what I term *fractalization*. It proposes the microanalysis of the process of implosion, in digital (and not only) environments, of the meaning of the system of information in distinct phase spaces. It also puts forward a detailed description of the dynamics of the micro-processes which connect and support this implosion to fractalization. Additional conceptualizations in the form of theoretical approximations are offered in Chapter Seven. The system of information is analysed in the form of informational constructs and patterns of informational organization, which can account for the development

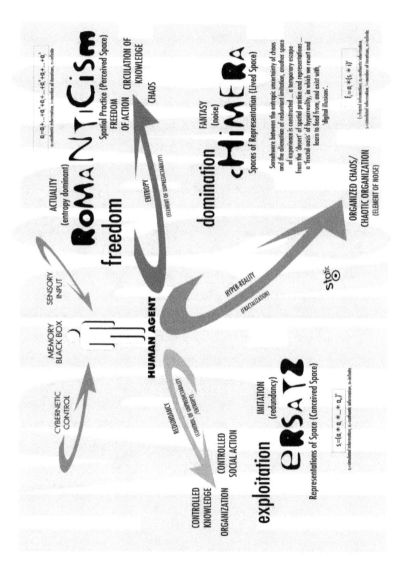

Figure 0.4: [Hypothesis 4] The System of Information hypothesis: That there is a distinctive, contemporary epochal organization of information in space and time that influences cognition, everyday life and society. The system of information is characterized by three levels of spatial organization across time: the era of Romanticism, the epoch of Ersatz, and, the age of Chimera, representing, freedom, exploitation and domination of the system of information, respectively. Their levels of intensification regulate the relations of meaning, and consequently the organization of the social.

of tensions of inter-relativity within and interactivity outside the system. The totality of the proposed theorizations, are offered within the framework of an analytical tool regarding the organization, and/or the digital reorganization, of the system of information. It is suggested that the patterns of organization of the system of information can be applied to any self-similar information based system. The analysis of the organization of the system of information becomes a project of the analysis and comprehension of the representations and of the encrypted codes of the organization of social reality.

There is a digital component to the book which can be downloaded from the links provided at the beginning of the book. Originally, the proposed theoretical approximations were first conceived and realized within a computer environment in the form of two- and three-dimensional models. They were then transferred to paper, theorized in a more extensive way, and were later redesigned in the form of two- and three-dimensional audio-visual presentations. It should be noted that to transfer three-dimensional conceptualizations into the two-dimensional world of words is rather difficult to accomplish accurately and in the danger of making original ideas redundant and useless. To this end an electronic copy of the book in audio-visual format presentation is included in the digital component. Consider this as a proposition what future 'digital' theorizations would be like. The content, as well as additional digital elements, and instructions are provided in the relevant section at the beginning of the book.

Reading through the chapters of this book is closer to enacting the model this book develops. It is pretty much like using a magnifying glass, of multiple lenses and filters. It is structured in a flow that follows the flows of the system of information, from the physical world of daily existence, to the digital landscapes of imagination and escape, into the human body and brain, and back out again, on a continuous vicious circle.

We do live in a diverse and uncharacteristic world. A world, that moves so fast at dissimilar levels and directions locally, globally, and multi-directionally. We hardly get a glance of part or of the whole picture rather we only manage to feel the imprints of change, which nourish our insecurities for the reassurance for progress and development. The system of information *is* the defining feature that organizes the contemporary world, and it is its specific code of organization that becomes the centre of attention in this book. My aim here is to capture an analytic and philosophic flow, a reading, a framing and, indeed, a digital recontextualisation of these new systems.

▶▶|

PART ONE

THE DIGITAL LABYRINTH

CHAPTER ONE

THE SPATIAL ARCHITECTURE OF THE DIGITAL AGE:
Social Organization and Structure

CONTENTS

CHAPTER 1

THE SPATIAL ARCHITECTURE OF THE DIGITAL AGE:
Social Organization and Structure

'This is our world now... the world of the electron and the switch, the beauty of the baud...
we explore... we seek after knowledge... we exist without skin color, without nationality,
without religious bias..'
(from 'The Hacker Manifesto' by the Mentor, 1986)

1.0 PROLOGUE

H acker? Not me. What if the definition represents what I believe about myself? Does that make a hacker? Maybe, maybe not in the sense it comes to your mind first. Maybe it is the actual definition of the assumed knowledge of what constitutes a hacker that defines me as one. Whatever the case, now that I come to think about it a bit more, being a thinker and a social scientist in a world dominated by digital technologies and communications, doesn't that, in a sense, make me a hacker of social consciousness and knowledge? The power of the acquisition of knowledge, or even more interestingly, the trip to such a conquest is extremely intriguing. The realization, of having succeeded in such an attempt, is even more invigorating. The times we are living are very demanding. The speed of social change and progress, and the amount of dispersed, and consequently, accumulated knowledge bring forward new challenges: the challenge of 'catching up' and not left behind, the challenge of discovering value, processing it, creating and adding up to it. Most importantly, is the challenge, to reach adequate degrees of understanding of 'who-what-how' we are and the social conditions surrounding us. Not an easy task. But it is all about successful survival.

In this context, the current chapter looks into contemporary social theory on the emerging societies at the end of the second millennium. My aim throughout this chapter will be to provide an account of the prevailing historical, political, economic and cultural characteristics within which the current book is historically and ideologically located, through contemporary social theories. Most importantly, my aim is to identify the nature of the concept of information, as a key representational form, that is resolutely structuring and organizing, at different levels of moderation and essence, social knowledge and, consequently, social life.

This chapter is not, nor could it be, a comprehensive picture. The considerations that follow below simply stress the important role that the concept of information, consequently, if not primarily, plays in social organization, whether that means social structures and processes, human agents, or social knowledge per se. In this critical review I will attempt to show how the organization of the social structure of information societies can be seen as a reflection of the organization of the system of information that universally and across time has been responsible for the 'informational' construction of 'reality'. I will also argue here that, they point out to the fact that 'knowledge', and the 'realities' it creates come in all colors and tastes. 'Reality', as a confirmation of knowledge, I would argue, seems to be missing in a digital labyrinth of cloned and recycled information; 'the real' becomes a clone of its eventful past, mixed with the instabilities and ambiguities of the present and unimaginable consequences of things to come.

'Reality' is no more. This makes the issue of quality and essence of knowledge important, and to a logical extent the issue of the organization of information critical. In this sense, I would argue here that, we have to reset our thinking options and critical alternatives, and allow me to say, do some serious editing of what we know, or, maybe, more accurately, what we think we know. Moreover, there can be only attempts or approximations to 'the true' or 'the real', which have become ambiguous and, in a sense, of unimportant priority. The priority is rather to set individual standards as to how we are to redefine the content of the available bodies of knowledge within a global context, which consequently extends to the following argument and considerations.

This knowledge of the social, at subjective, collective and global levels of human experience, is based on discourses of representational information (historical, socio-economic, cultural) such as those offered by the various social theories mentioned here. Such information informs and makes up to a great degree what we accept as knowledge. Each and one of these, and any theory, I would agree that is valid as offering an important contribution to explaining certain aspects of social life and adding its own valuable piece to the construction of the social puzzle. I would also agree with the criticisms concerning conceptual weaknesses and methodological problems (as argued by Webster, 1995) as being responsible for theoretical confusion and blind spots. More importantly, though, and this is what I would like to stress, is the lack of multi-perspectival, inter-disciplinary and in-depth micro-analytical conceptualizations and theorizations, or a combination of all, within these theories. This is partly in agreement with similar criticisms and calls for a reconstruction of critical social theory through the development of theories that cut across disciplines and perspectives as possibly offering better alternatives of social understanding (Best and Kellner, 1991).

I would argue, therefore, for the insufficiency of mono-perspectival and mono-disciplinary theoretical accounts, or accounts unbalanced between macro- and micro-principles, to adequately explain social change in the current and the prescribed future global context and communication status. I am not suggesting the possibility of a 'theory of all', rather the attempt to build up theoretical models of multiple levels and dimensions by adopting – and not ignoring or rejecting – related disciplines and utilizing if possible both macro- and micro-perspectives. I would also argue that the multi-dimensional and inter-disciplinary character of such models, should also allow their utilization and application across diverse, even seemingly unrelated, disciplines, offering greater flexibility of investigation and wider range of alternatives. If the social geography of the world we knew so far has been changing, then, shouldn't our conceptual and analytical imaginations follow suit? Partly based on this argument, I will go on (in later chapters of the book) to suggest such a model of theoretical approximations, based on the concept of information, and how this can be applied to explain the construction of social knowledge in the Digital era. This book then is about bringing a fresh analytical perspective based on the concept of information as being the dominant and prevailing organizing principle of the social, the ideological and the cultural domains of our contemporary societies. Drawing on isomorphies and analogies among inter-related information-based systems, this book attempts to offer a multi-dimensional analytical model of the digital organization of information. I will argue that an in-depth micro-analytical investigation of the system of information offers insight in the mechanics and dynamics of the organization of social life itself. Moreover, it points to the dependency of the later to the system of information. It has always been, and it will always be like this. Coming to a closer understanding of information is coming to a closer understanding of life itself. And when analyzing information one should bear in mind that this can only lead to theoretical proposals of approximations, not to absolute and determinate conclusions. It simply cannot be any other way.

Keeping in mind the above questions and arguments, I now turn to some of the main features of the most comprehensive contemporary theories, such as: theories of the 'information society' (Webster, 1995), the ambiguous 'post-industrial society' (Bell, 1976a; 1976b; 1979; 1980), the question of the 'public sphere' (Habermas, 1989), the notion of 'flexible specialization' (Piore and Sabel, 1984), the issue of 'heightened surveillance' Giddens (1981a; 1981b; 1985; 1987), the rise of the 'network society' (Castells, 1989; 1996; 1997; 1998), and Schiller's (1999) political economy of 'digital capitalism'. Taken together, the various societal characteristics described by these approaches, give us a first approximation of the world society. This is the 'genesis of a new world', a world of information, out of which a 'new order' prevails. This is a world where a flexible form of global capitalism dominates and advances on the material basis of 'informationalism', a world in which the logic of 'networking' acts as the dynamic, self-expanding form of organization of human activity under increasing surveillance. This is the world of increased bewilderment and emotions in face of radical qualitative change and transition of human experience, to a level where culture supersedes nature, and the flows of messages and images between networks dominate and organize social entities. This is 'digital capitalism', the result of the expansion of US corporate neo-liberal drive that led to the network development and expansion of TNCs and transformations of telecommunications at a global level. Let us look in more detail.

1.1 THE INFORMATION SOCIETY

The theoretical descriptions of what has been termed as an 'information society' (hereafter IS) are as diverse as the concept itself. Theories of the Information Society range between the view that the new emerging IS is marked by differences (post-industrialism, postmodernism, flexible specialization, informational mode of development) from existing societies, and the view that the new society's central feature of the present is its continuities (neo-marxist, regulation theory, flexible accumulation, the nation-state and violence, the public sphere) with the past (Webster, 1995). That is, the former models focus on historical rupture while the latter tend to view current developments as part of a historical dynamics and dialectical logic. Obviously, they draw on different socio-economic, political and cultural perspectives on the concept of information. Yet this also is where they contrast: in their definitions of technology, information and, indeed, representation itself.

IS is characterized by spectacular technological innovation. The breakthroughs in telecommunications and information processing have led to the application of information network routes all over the world. The information grid becomes the highway of the modern age, 'the computer revolution ... [having] an overwhelming and comprehensive impact, affecting every human being in every aspect of his/her life' (Evans, 1979).

Combining Shumpeter's argument that major technological innovations bring about 'creative destruction', with Kondratieff's theme of the 'long waves' of economic development, it supports the idea that information technologies (hereafter IT) represent the establishment of a new epoch. This new 'techno-economic paradigm' (Freeman and Pereze, 1988) constitutes the 'Information Age' (Freeman, 1987), providing the foundation for radically different ways of life, what Piore and Sabel (1984) characterized as a shift from 'fordism' (mass production, industrial working class, mass consumption, national state oligopoly, increased planning) to a 'post-fordist' era (changes in the workforce, transformations in geographical areas, a shake-up of political and social attitudes) or from a period of mass production to a period of 'flexible specialization' (spread of small technically sophisticated firms, restructuring of larger firms, differentiation in consumer tastes, new technologies). An IS, is also characterized by changes in industry groups, such as education, media of communication, information machines, information services, other information activities (Machlup, 1962) and occupational changes (Useem, 1984; Perkin, 1990; Gouldner, 1979).

An IS is a society of information networks, the later having dramatic consequences on the reorganization of time and space. Goddard (1992) identified interrelated themes, (information as key strategic resource, computer and communications technologies, tradable information sector, informatization) elements in the transition to an IS which emphasize the centrality of information networks. Martin (1978) talked about a 'wired society' operating at all level to provide an 'information ring main' (Barron and Curnow, 1979), for the emergence of the ISDN 'network society' (Dordick et al, 1981). Equally important, an IS is a media-laden society, characterized by a powerful intrusion of information, leading to an extraordinary expansion of informational content of modern life. Living in a media-saturated environment (an explosion of signification), is about symbolization, and the 'death of the sign' (Baudrillard, 1983a; 1983b), where society is dominated by the self-referentiality of signs, 'simulations' in 'hyper-real' environments, where 'set[s] of meanings [are] communicated [which] have no meaning' (Poster, 1990).

1.2 THE POST-INDUSTRIAL SOCIETY (PIS)

The heightened presence and significance of information in the organization of contemporary societies led Bell (1976a) to assert the emergence of a new system, what he terms as 'the post-industrial society' (hereafter PIS). The PIS is characterized by increasing amounts of information being in use, leading to a breakdown of a one-time 'common value system' held throughout society, but also towards qualitative shifts in society, what Bell called 'theoretical knowledge'. Bell's theoretical account if nothing else pointed out the importance of IT in the re-organization of contemporary life in information societies.

1.2.1 Productivity and service economy

The PIS, according to Bell, emerges from changes in the social structure only. This would include the economy, the occupational structure and the stratification system, but it would exclude politics and cultural issues. Bell offered a typology of different societies which is dependent on the predominant model of employment at any stage, and which is his defining feature for pre-industrial, industrial and post-industrial societies. Increase in productivity is for Bell the key to change. As this process continues, as we enter the PIS, society is characterized by a decline of workers employed in industry, increases in industrial output, continued increases of wealth, continuous release of people from employment in industrial occupations, and the creation of a never-ending supply of new job opportunities. Bell (1976a) stated that the PIS is an IS and that a service economy indicates the arrival of post-industrialism. What counts is not raw muscle power, or energy, but information. In Bell's (1979) terminology, it is possible to distinguish three types of work: extractive, fabrication, and information activities.

Bell (1989, 1976b, 1989) believed that the PIS is an especially appealing place to live for a number of reasons: information work is mostly white collar employment, therefore, it brings greater job satisfaction; within the service sector professional jobs flourish; the core of the PIS is its professional technical services; and, it is a particular segment of services which is decisive for PIS.

1.2.2 A person-oriented society

The PIS undergoes decisive qualitative changes for many reasons: professionals, being knowledge experts, are disposed towards planning; the quality of the relationship between people and services comes to the forefront; this 'person-oriented society' evolves into a caring society. I will argue here that these qualitative changes are indeed an indication of qualitative transformations of the system of information that organizes all social relations and human agents themselves. This said Bell, leads to a new consciousness in PIS, which, as a communal society, promotes the community rather than the individual. Professionals represent a shift, attests Bell, from an 'economizing ethos' to a 'sociologizing mode of life'.

1.2.3 Theoretical knowledge

Bell (1976b) inevitably endorsed a convergence theory of development, which ignores, or at least makes subordinate to this rationalization, differences in politics, culture and history (Kleinberg, 1973). Bell's technological determinism with the division of society into wealth-creating and wealth-consuming sectors has been strongly criticized (Kleinberg, 1973; Perkin, 1990). Gershuny (1978) claimed that the spread of service products signified the growth of a self-service economy in antithesis to Bell's account. The axial principle of the society, Bell's theoretical knowledge, suggested that what is radically new today is the codification of theoretical knowledge and its centrality for innovation, both of new knowledge and for economic goods and services (Bell, 1989). This feature allows him to depict the PIS as a knowledge society, the sources of innovation deriving from research and development. Therefore, the PIS is characterized by the primacy of theory over empiricism and the codification of knowledge into abstract systems of symbols that ... can be used to illuminate many different and varied areas of experience. Computerization, then, allows not just the management of organized complexity, but also, through programming, the creation of intellectual technology, which incorporates knowledge and in turn facilitates innovations based on theoretical knowledge.

Productivity and a service economy based on IT, coupled with a new consciousness of abstract systems of symbols emerge then as the main features of the PIS in Bell's technological determinism. The later carries dubious implications, in that, technologies are the decisive factors of social change, and, that technologies are themselves detached from the social world (though they have enormous social effects). Still, his theory of 'post-industrialism', I will argue that it exemplifies and supports the arguments stated at the beginning of the chapter regarding the importance of IT and information per se, as a primary representational signification that is decisively responsible for the structure and organization of social knowledge and, consequently, of the contemporary world society.

There seem to be differential and selective socially motivated preferences and degrees of accessibility with regard to the accumulated social knowledge that is made available, by the elite professional classes, to the society in general. In fact, fragmented only amounts of information are made available to the wider public. This important issue of the organization and accessibility of knowledge in contemporary societies has been the concern of Habermas who focused on the subject looking in public formation opinion and other issues in what he calls 'the public sphere'.

1.3 THE PUBLIC SPHERE

Habermas was concerned with the inadequacies of the information made available to the public, to suggest that the democratic process itself is undermined. It is in the 'public sphere', an arena independent of government enjoying autonomy from partisan economic forces, and dedicated to rational debate, that public opinion is formed' (Holub, 1991). Information is at the core of this public sphere. For the purposes of my investigation in this book, Habermas analyses support the argument that the social organization of knowledge, and to an extent of social life, is intensively disturbed, manipulated and distressed by commercialization and the global media force. The systems of global representational information, as I have suggested, become ambiguously complex and for this reason questionable. It is then imperative, as I argue here, to critically re-examine and reconsider our 'realities', and the global system of social knowledge itself.

1.3.1 Refeudalization

Habermas pointed out the paradoxical features of the bourgeois public sphere. 'Public relations' disguises the interests it represents as 'public welfare' and 'national interest', thus making a debate a 'faked version' (Habermas, 1989). 'Refeudalization' indicates the ways in which public affairs become occasions for displays of the powers, the expression of which comes from changes within the system of mass communications, which create and spread a public service ethos in modern society. Habermas (1989) saw that, capitalism is victorious, the capacity for critical thought is minimal, and there is no real space for a public sphere in an era of transnational media conglomerates and pervasive culture of advertising.

1.3.2 Media and Service Institutions

Action, adventure, trivia, sensationalism, personalization of affairs, celebration of contemporary lifestyles is at the heart of media content. The public sphere is weakened by the invasion of the advertising ethic and the penetration of public relations, which marks the abandonment of the 'criteria of rationality' since we become duped customers ready to follow. The idea of the public sphere offers a powerful vision of the role of information in a modern society and the changes in the informational realm. Public service institutions are transformed to market-oriented and organized operations; the wider context of contemporary communications suggests an increasing amount of unreliable and distorted information being generated and conveyed, hence the focus is on new systems of communication which stress commercial principles and end up purveying little but escapist entertainment, on the spread of interested information such as sponsorship, advertising and public relations.

1.3.3 The commercialization of public knowledge

The recent history of public libraries is one of cuts and commercialisation combined with a forceful critique of their public service aspirations. Hewison (1987:129) concluded his review of changes in museums and galleries: '... they are treated as financial institutions that must pay their way, and therefore charge entrance fees. The arts are no longer appreciated as a source of inspiration, of ideas, images or values, but are part of the leisure business. We are no longer lovers of art, but customers for a product'. The paradox is resolved when these ventures are seen as expressions of the 'leisure industry', museums which offer easily-digested and unchallenging nostalgia in a Disney style of elaborate sounds effects, eye-catching scenery, quick changes of attractions, video games, animatronic dinosaurs, re-created smells and symbols, and above all participation for the paying customers who are urged to 'enjoy' and have 'fun'.

1.3.4 The decline of the public sphere

The marketisation of government information services raises concerns about the possibility of governmental intervention in the integrity of the data - it is conceived as an assault on the public sphere. Phillips (1990) believed that sensitive statistical information is now manipulated and abused almost as a matter of routine. This leads to a wider issue of information management. Tumber (1993a; 1993b) observed that, information management is fundamental to the administrative coherence of modern government, and that the reliance on communications and information has become paramount for governments in their attempts to manipulate public opinion and to maintain social control. Habermas regarded the growth of information management as signaling the decline of the public sphere. Propaganda and persuasion are obstructing public reasoning. Two features are of particular note. First, any business organization depends ultimately on public approval and is therefore faced with the problem of engineering the public's consent to program or goal. Second, today's corporate leaders are chosen according to their communicative skills (the rise of the political manager). Corporate capitalism needs to minimize the uncertainties of the free market by attempting to regularize with customers. Businesses' interested information contributes enormously to the general symbolic environment. The routine management of information is evident in the information packaging, intimidation and censorship, which together with government secrecy.

The refeudalization of the public sphere, as analyzed by Habermas, points out the ambiguous character of the flow of ideas and information, and to an extent of the available social knowledge. I believe it supports my earlier argument at the beginning of this chapter that social structures and our symbolic settings are extensively distressed by commercial and information media forces. The business/leisure philosophy, of the later, assigns redundant communication patterns to the flow of information and knowledge to the expense of otherwise unattached [authentic] experience and practice.

This flexibility of global operations of business corporations and media industries over the communicated information is characteristic of qualitative mutations of the dominant capitalist system. Fukuyama (1992) celebrated this as 'the end of history with the triumph of the market economy over the collectivist experiment', whereas Lash and Urry (1987) called it a shift from 'organized' to 'disorganized capitalism'. Others, such as Piore and Sabel (1984) argued that, this flexibility of capitalist operations can be understood as a shift from 'fordism' to a 'post-fordist' era or from a period of 'mass production' to a period of 'flexible specialization'. It is my contention here that their analysis focusing on the flexibility of information echoes the prospect of the sound dynamics of the system of information and provides a conceptual background within which changes in the social organization of information come to a historical agreement and a logical justification with contemporary social changes at a global scale.

1.4 FLEXIBLE SPECIALIZATION

Piore and Sabel (1984) tried to answer the questions of the capitalist perpetuation, stability and accumulation. They examine the regime of accumulation and try to explain the mode of accumulation. Their suggestion is that the Fordist regime of accumulation (mass production, industrial working class, mass consumption, national state oligopoly, increased planning), because of the acceleration of globalization in the 1970s, has become unsustainable and is now giving way to a post-Fordist regime. According to them, globalization signaled the growing interdependence and interpenetration of human relations alongside the increasing integration of the world's socio-economic life. The expansion of transnational corporations (hereafter TNCs) has brought the entire world into networks of relationships affecting world markets, information services, finance, and communications. The operation of TNCs led to rearrangements in the world market into major segments, and production encouraged the growth of what Dicken (1992) called 'circulation activities' that connect the various parts of the production system together. Information services, such as advertising, banking, insurance, and consultancy services, had to be developed to provide the emerging global infrastructure for an integrated global financial market. The globalization of communications, that is, the spread of communications networks - satellite systems, telecommunications facilities - would provide the symbolic environment that would enable TNCs reach around the globe.

1.4.1 Post-Fordist flexibility

The informational infrastructure enabled worldwide operation resulting to the growth of information flows. The international rise of TNCs undermined the nation state and individual governments started to find their monetary sovereignty challenged. These trends have simulated the creation of a new regime of accumulation in a post-fordist regime. Post-Fordism is characterized by flexibility, such as, the new flexibility of employees, flexibility of production, flexibility of consumption. The emergence of post-fordism signaled changes in the workforce, transformations in geographical areas, a shaking up political and social attitudes. The population is to be understood in terms of different lifestyles. This can be seen as either in resulting in the fragmentation of people's identities, in a loss of stability and stratifications, or as a democratizing force which opens up new experiences and opportunities, stimulates the 'de-centered' self and generates excitement.

1.4.2 The 'second industrial divide'

Piore and Sabel (1984) suggested that the spread of 'flexible specialization/ production' offers the prospect of widespread improvement in ways of life. They argued that we are living through a 'second industrial divide'. Flexible specialization is explained in: the spread of small technically sophisticated firms, restructuring the strategies of larger firms; marked differentiation in consumer tastes; and, new technologies enabled small firms to produce competitively. Flexible specialization encourages employee participation in the design of work, that is, computerization of production provides cybernetic feedback, acting to re-program the system when required. This is what Lash and Urry (1994) viewed as an era of flexible accumulation where economic activity is premised on employees being self-monitoring, able to respond to consumer needs, market outlets and rapid technical innovation, with maximum speed and efficacy.

The flexible specialization arguments show how and why worldwide societies are organized towards a global infrastructure for an incorporated financial market. For this to be possible they propose that a flexible informational infrastructure is the key issue. Once more, as I have suggested in this chapter, the dynamics of the flexibility of the information flow comes out as a principal social organizing force, enabling and advancing social change. In this case, the notion of flexible specialization encourages the self-monitoring of social activity towards an improvement of social lived experience. At the same time, this flexibility supports technological advancement and progress, but also promotes the use of the later for the monitoring of social activities and ideas at all levels. My point here is that information becomes a powerful instrument not only of 'positive' social organization, but a means of social control. The control information for the control of social being and life themselves, becomes a necessary prerequisite to our everyday living existence. Anthony Giddens extensively examined this issue and here is how he depicted this contemporary society of 'heightened surveillance'.

1.5 THE SURVEILLANCE SOCIETY

As discussed above, the technological advancements of the late 20th century and the trend of rationalization of the global economy have established another important feature of contemporary societies, that of surveillance. In a highly unstable and controversial world where individual safety and national security are found to be of great concern, IT and its applications to various sectors of social life serve as agents of surveillance and control intimidating personal freedom and individual choice. It is all basically, I will argue here, about the control of information, about the control of constructing and manufacturing the new realities and social imaginations.

1.5.1 Heightened Surveillance

For Giddens (1987) modern societies have always been information societies since their beginnings. Concerned with modernity, Giddens found the notions of the dynamics of capitalism, rationalization and industrialism inadequate, instead, he emphasizes on the features of heightened surveillance and the import of violence, war and the nation state in the development of the modern world. We live, argues Giddens, in a much more organized world than even before, a world where life is much more methodically arranged and organized in a highly complex way. Does control necessarily imply organization? I would argue it rather reveals attempts to control and influence organizational trends.

According to current societal thinking, to organize life (to what end is questionable), information must be systematically gathered on people and their activities; therefore, routine surveillance becomes a prerequisite of effective social organization. This is a notion close to Adorno's 'administered society', Foucault's 'carceral networks' or Weber's 'bureaucratization'. Our society, according to Giddens, is distinct of paradoxes of modernity. 'Individuation' (when a person is known about and identified by a singular record) requires that people be monitored and observed. Abercombie et al. (1986) acknowledged this paradoxical situation, noticing that individuation, by enhancing the rights of the individual, leads to greater surveillance and control of large populations. They also underlined the fact that such standardization of persons is an unavoidable consequence of the requirement to treat people equally. It is my opinion that paradoxes exist where distinct realities and powerful beliefs exist. Moreover, when realities and beliefs break their boundaries and become simply undistinguishable, then they in essence become the new paradoxical entities. As I have stated earlier in the prologue to this book, paradoxical explanations and definitions have to be recognized as acceptable answers, furthermore, to be identified as indeed being the new realities of informational environments. In this sense, why is it modernity that is distinct of paradoxes, and not paradoxical social conditions [having become the dominant social form] that are characterized of past and present modern trends and tensions? For societies, whose organization is based around the flow and exchange of information, surveillance becomes a mechanism of social control of information, therefore effective social organization of these societies. This does not exclude though the possibility that social organization can be realized beyond the boundaries of the information under surveillance. Not all information can be set under surveillance. Therefore, regardless of the degree of heightened surveillance within a society, its social organization and destiny remain undetermined and unpredictable.

1.5.2 The nation state and warfare

It is not a strange that urban societies must gather extremely detailed knowledge about their public in order to function. As more is known about people, individuals may get opportunities to enhance their own individuality by making choices of their own. Giddens' concern with the expansion of routine surveillance and organization in modern times paid special attention to the role of the 'nation state'. The 'nation state' is a newly created kind of society, according to Giddens, conceived as a bounded area over which political power is exercised, and information has a special significance. Nation states are information societies' which must maintain hold of both 'allocative resources' (planning, administration) and 'authoritative resources' (power and control), a prerequisite of both is effective surveillance. Nation states are essential to many people's identities. There is evidence of a 'national consciousness' of some sort. Nation states influence identities by constructing 'mythic pasts' made up of legends and literature, traditions and celebrations, customs and caricatures. The majority of nation states have been created in 'conditions of war' and all are sustained by 'possession of credible defense', which leads to linkages between information, IT and the state/military/industry nexus.

Erikson (quoted in Webster, 1995:63) articulated this point: 'modern military operations … are to do with information, command, control. Information does things. It fires weapons'. If then modern war/defense is quintessentially about information, then, 'surveillance', the monitoring of enemies and potential enemies, becomes the obligation of all nation states. Burrows (1986) observed: 'the system that does all this watching and listening is so pervasively secret -so black- that no individual … knows all of its hidden parts, the products they collect, or the real extent of the widely dispersed and deeply buried budget that keeps the entire operation functioning'.

1.5.3 Internal pacification and the panopticon

Integral to the development of the nation state has been the spread of polyarchy, that is, the democratic means of governance. Any sovereign power, which intends to rule a given territory, is what Giddens called, 'internal pacification'. The monitoring of internal population evolves within from a form of 'contract', that is a variety of citizenship rights between the nation state and its members. The main connection with surveillance is how these are to be delivered and collected (Hillyard & Percy-Smith, 1988). Bentham's concept of panopticon, adopted by Foucault (1979), as a metaphor for modern life, suggests that surveillance allows the construction of a panopticon without physical walls. The idea is that surveillance by unseen observers is an integral feature of advanced societies.

De Landa (1991) referred to the automatic function of military surveillance as 'machine vision'. De Landa analysed satellite photography systems and bugged communications, concluding at what he describes as a 'Panspectron', something one may call the new non-optical intelligence-acquisition machine. Anderson (1991) detailing the ways in which the colonial state combined map and census to impose surveillance, evokes the metaphor of the 'Glass House', a concept which conceptualizes a landscape of perfect visibility. Surveillance, poses the threat of totalitarian rule (Giddens, 1985).

1.5.4 Corporate Surveillance

Furthermore, corporate capitalism has expanded, with the spatial growth of corporations, consolidating into fewer and much bigger players, and penetrating deeper into society. In this capitalist enterprise, surveillance is the key to management (Giddens, 1987). Corporate capitalism focuses on Scientific Management for effective control of the production process (Fox, 1989). One major consequence of these trends is what has been called the 'incorporation of society' (Trachtenberg, 1982). In short, wider surveillance is a requirement of effective corporate activity. Credit checking agencies and the spread of versatile electronic technologies, have created a new category of information that automatically documents the daily lives of almost every person, that is, 'transactional information' which gives corporations detailed pictures of clients' lifestyles.

The importance of information in social organization is once more epitomized in Giddens' observations. Digital technologies and surveillance techniques give the power to those in control of the flow of information (either they are nation state or business corporations) to control and manipulate information, to create and destroy identities. Additionally, I believe that the surveillance of information by all the aforementioned social agents is also what allows the selective concentration of information, its manipulation and its later delivery to the public according to intended collective or individual social intentions and interests. Information becomes the core of the knowledge of society. Still, the surveillance of information, and the way that this social practice affects social organization, is not simply a state or corporate issue. Each one of us builds his/her own panopticon, chases available and hidden sources of information, and silently observes, selects and exchanges the acquired knowledge. Hopefully, there are always degrees of freedom and choice for each one of us. From the issues raised by Giddens' account above, it is obvious that information is a powerful organizing principle of the structure and organization of any information-based systems. One of the points that should not go unnoticed here is the increasing and intrusive nature of advanced digital technologies and their significant impact they can have on our individual and collective choices and freedom. Digital technologies, such as surveillance techniques, can become the collectors, carriers, producers, modifiers and disseminators of information. They can manipulate past, present and future information, information that can have a critical effect on our free and uncommitted view and stance of the world around us, and our social response to it.

The issue of the impact that the application of digital technologies and communications has had on the re-organization of social life globally has been comprehensively evaluated by Manuel Castells' powerful analyses of what he termed as the Information Age and the emergence of the Network Society. The two concepts, central to his accounts, information and networking, have indeed been responsible for the new image the world has been assigned. The globally emerging urgency to adapt to the new historical and economic conditions that these concepts have imposed, led societies world-wide, regardless of their degree of development, to radically respond both locally as well as globally. I will be examining the origins and 'hidden' motives of this global transformation later in this chapter when I discuss Schiller's political economy of Digital Capitalism. Castells' theoretical observations and suggestions though (discussed below), I would argue, are, without doubt, emblematic of how, at a representational level, our social knowledge of the world is constructed around and within the ideological realm of information.

I will argue here, that, global societal changes have emerged not solely because of technological advancement in IT and related technologies, but as a response of informational representations, to pre-emerged informational representations in the form of social demands themselves. My argument implies here that, the really brave new world that has started to surface from all over the corners of the planet, although seemingly characteristically different from its predecessor, still, it is not void of continuing societal unrest, inequalities and all the spectrum of social problems that have had long been accumulating at individual and collective levels of social existence and experience. Once more, I would point out that, Castells' extensive descriptions of the rise of the [global] network society support my argument in this chapter about the significant role that the concept of information plays in the social organization and construction of our knowledge of the world and the prevalent social trends that characterize it. In addition, Castells' interpretation of the global society reveals some important features of our social experience that are critically significant to the base of my arguments through this book. Such features would include the anticipated effects of the flow of information on all aspects of social life, the reorganization of human consciousness and experience across universal information networks, the redistribution of, and restructuring of the relations among, economic power, cultural capital and social knowledge. They emphasize the daily preoccupation [obsession rather] of the world society with the continuous exchange, use and abuse of information. It is my belief that, this borderless fixation that goes beyond levels of simple professional employment or enjoyable lifestyles has a multi-level effect on collective and individual social knowledge and expression. It is the in-depth mechanics of this effect that this book is trying to analyze and provide an understanding of, with the theoretical approximations proposed in later parts of the book and which I have already stated in earlier paragraphs.

1.6 THE NETWORK SOCIETY

Castells (1989) placed the core of recent technological developments within the cities of the technologically advanced world. They are what he called 'informational cities' indicated by changes in class structures and cultural developments, for which responsible is a combination of capitalist restructuring and technological innovation. Within the capitalist mode of production Castells proposed the informational mode of development that is a main force of social change and progress.

1.6.1 The informational mode of development

The mode of development is a means of generating a given level of production. The informational mode of development, described by Castells, is a new socio-technical paradigm, the main feature of which is the emergence of information processing as the fundamental activity conditioning the effectiveness and productivity of all processes of production, distribution, consumption and management. Developments are independent factors in determining change, as he states, modes of development evolve according to their own logic hence the informational mode of development is relatively autonomous from the capitalist mode of production, which predominates the world today. This is in agreement with what I suggest to be the drive of the system of information I am focusing my analysis in this book on, that is, that the social [digital] organization of information is a self-autonomous system with differential end results to the information-based systems it has a decisive impact on.

Castells (1989) referred to a technological informational revolution as the backbone of all other major structural transformations and he continues to depict an informational society which replaces the industrial society as the framework of social institutions. He drew a distinction between the relations of production (classes) and the forces of production (techniques). I would add here that the forces of production in an informational world supersede and to a degree define the relations of production. I will also suggest here that it is the power, and more importantly the fractional control over the social organization of information, that supports advanced capitalism's sustained attempt of restructuring established social relations with the intention of revitalizing the capitalist economy. The informational mode of development comes to assist, if not being the essence of, this capitalist activity, what Castells characterized as 'informationalism'.

1.6.2 Informationalism

The concept of informationalism in Castells' informational technological paradigm, suggests, as I believe, the argument already proposed in this chapter, about the ever-existing endeavour to control the flow of information, therefore knowledge and its consequent selective release to society. This is a prerequisite condition in the game of power and domination. I would argue that informationalism also reflects the systematic societal attempts for intervention and modification of information towards prescribed socio-economic intentions. Informationalism is in a sense, a reflection of the dynamics of constant change of the system of information, a point taken into consideration in the development of my theoretical approximations later in this book.

Castells observed that informationalism improves the flexibility and assists in the development of IT networks around the globe. It promotes the importance of information flows for economic and social organization, which means that, in the informational economy, a major concern of organizations becomes the management of and response to information flows. The establishment of computer communications networks around the world has led to a global trend of internationalisation. This is an example I will point out here, of how the internal dynamics of the flow of information can alter and build social relations at a global scale, and how in turn it can affect economic activities. Internationalisation has helped bring about financial and market integration, with real-time and continuous global transaction. The creation of information networks allowed decentralization of economic and social organization to be combined with increased centralization of decision-making. Globalized information systems provide corporations with the infrastructure to allow worldwide decentralization of operations while ensuring that centralized management remains in overall control. In other words, it remains in control of vital and essential information.

The flow of information is emerging then as the central feature of the global IS. The reliance on information networks is reducing the restrictions of space on contemporary societies. Certain metropolitan cities constitute the nerves centres, where information is collated, analysed, and acted upon. King (1990a; 1990b) called them world cities, cities that undergo changes in class formation with major consequences for the conduct of urban life. I prefer to think of 'world cities' more along the lines of a network of 'world centres' of information exchange. To capitalize on the idea of a financially vibrant economic centre of a city and apply it to the wider area surrounding it seems to me a surplus of misconception of definitions. My point here is also important for the arguments I have stated in this chapter, in that, thinking in terms of 'world centres' rather than 'world cities' allows us to map with more precision the epicentre as well as the peripheral points through which the flow of information circulates and 'socializes'.

1.6.3 World-cities

King (1990a; 1990b) argued that the spatial articulation of the emerging world-system of production and markets is realized through a global network of cities, what he defined as the world-city at the centre of specific world-economies. He attributed the world-city phenomenon to the massive increase in the internationalization of [transnational] capital over the past decades, which has organized and controlled a set of markets and production units of the world economy. World-cities can be said to be the material realization of this control occurring exclusively in core and semi-peripheral regions where they serve as banking and financial centres, administrative headquarters, centres of ideological control and so forth (Friedmann and Wolf, 1982).

Soja (1989) also pointed out that the 'global capitalist city' as the centre of financial management, international trade, and corporate HQs has arisen from a series of economic and political crises marking the end of post-war boom of the 1960s and 'second slump' following the oil crisis. Thrift & Williams (1987) again distinguished three types of world-cities: truly international centres, zonal centres, and, regional centres. World-cities are characterized by 'command and control' and Friedmann (1986) pointed out the qualification criteria for a world-city, that is: major financial centre, site for HQs and TNCs, international institutions, rapid growth of business services sector, important manufacturing centre, major transportation node, population size. Whatever the definition, what is of importance here is that there exist certain centres at a global scale which control the flow of information, and this leads to an inevitable effect on the construction, access and distribution of socially available knowledge.

King (1989) made another distinction between the world-city and what he called the 'colonial city'. The later is taken to refer to a metropolitan capital of a colonial empire, the capital city of a colony within the empire, or the colonial post cities and regional administrative centres. In each case, argued King, the size, functions (economic, social, administrative, political), social, cultural, and spatial form, can be understood only by reference to its specific role within the larger colonial political economy as well as the larger world-system. King contended that, colonial cities can be viewed as forerunners of what the contemporary capitalist world would eventually become. Sassen (1991) looking at New York, London and Tokyo, underwrote previous general arguments. These informational cities, as highly concentrated command posts of the world economy, have experienced a rapid increase in informational workers, whose jobs involve the operation and management of networks, thereby providing global control capability. Corporations need to have headquarters close to stock markets, telecommunications, banking and finance organizations, advertisers and media. As a rule there are powerful forces impelling concentration of major economic and political players in global cities.

1.6.4 Information professionals

The control of the flow of information is then becoming the job of the so-called 'information professionals'. The development of information occupations, as 'producer services', performs the task of producing and reproducing the organization and management of global production system and a global marketplace for finance. At the same time, Castells pointed out, a service occupations class is emerging as low-skilled, low-paid, with low educational demands made of it, being offered part-time, unstable and casual opportunities in this informal economy. This is an informational underclass in Castells account, the members of which act as servants for the professional managerial class in the informational city. Castells suggested that the underclass is marginalized not only because it gets minimal economic returns but also because it is trapped in a 'culture of poverty' which leaves it fatalistic and apparently incapable of taking responsibility for it. Wilson (1991) used the term 'ghetto poor' to identify those left behind in the inner cities following a hemorrhage of decent-paying and reasonably secure jobs and without means to escape the urban scene to find alternative ways of life.

I would agree on the validity of Castells' observations regarding the underclass, with one exception though: that the line between the so-thought privileged 'professional class' and the 'underclass', under the criteria of information and knowledge acquisition and possession, becomes thin and vague. Rieff (1991) noticed the close proximity of the affluent professionals and the underclass, the interdependence of the two classes and the yawning chasm that separated their lives. The availability and quality of information and knowledge extends beyond the actual space of the workplace, where these two classes area is suggested to be located, and beyond that place everyone can have a very different experience with regard to access, acquisition and utilization of socially available information. I would argue that is it the informational character at the core of these social classes that breaks down the boundaries and disperses their members towards a variety of, rather than fixed, social positions.

Castells' (1989) conclusion has been that, an informational city is characterized by bipolarization, a dual city in which a desperately disadvantaged ghetto underclass and affluent and elite information economy professionals co-exist. The Informational City, the Global City and the Dual City are closely inter-related, as socio-territorial segmentations, if not totally identical, then as variations on the same theme of changed spatial relations and elaborate security in a world informationally wild. As Davis stated, (1990), it seems literally like another world. It is my contention here that, the informational city and the consequent social divisions pointed out by Castells consist a reflection of how we value information and the knowledge produced by it.

1.6.5 Cosmopolitanism

Castells' (1989) carried on suggesting the cultural domination of his [information producers] new hegemonic social class that is characterized by a degree of cosmopolitanism. This refers to their different way of thinking, one that thinks globally, and which is open to messages and experiences that embrace the entire world. I do not see why the same claim cannot be made for the so-called underclass. It is again, as I stressed earlier in this chapter, a matter of how one thinks of information and of what kind of value is set on information that is considered to be at the core of social developments. Castells also noticed a differential access to information that the groups experience. The poor tend to shrink the world to their specific culture and their local experience, penetrated only by standardized television images, and mythically connected, in the case of the immigrants, to tales of the homeland. In these terms, Castells can talk about the information rich and the 'information poor in the world city. Still, the culture of the city is much more than a matter of access and orientation to sources of information. Harvey (1989) talked about 'voodoo cities', where the cultural upheaval, highly visible up-front, disguises the decline of many other important aspects of city life, notably the working class and its occupational communities. I would stress here that the decision over the appropriateness of the applied criteria for the mapping of social divisions in a society has always been problematic. Moreover, the attempt to reach to definite conclusions, by applying a concept of extreme flexibility and constant inbuilt transformation, such as information, as a criterion for social class division, can only lead to relative confusion and deficient inaccuracies.

1.6.6 Pleasure lifestyles

The informational orgasm that characterizes the informational city reorganizes social life in it towards the adoption of hedonistic lifestyles, what Zukin (1991) called 'landscapes of consumption'. Zukin emphasized that globalization has brought about an increased disconnection of market and place. This instability of life in the informational city is thought to be a defining feature of the postmodern experience, where nothing is fixed, agreed, or where no meanings last. In the informational city there is a breakdown of traditional or modern behaviors, dress styles and even moralities. In agreement with what I have argued so far in this section, I will once more stress out that this apparent instability of life is simply an expression of the inherent nature of the system of information, that is, an expression of its dynamic condition of constant mobility, change and interactivity which is reflected as an ideological realization in the organization of social life. Castells notes that culture becomes a matter of lifestyle choices, a hedonism without a guilty conscience. The tyranny of meaning is abandoned, and is substituted by the primacy of pleasure as a motive force. Within a cultural atmosphere of fun, excitement and sensory enjoyment all notions of the authentic are abandoned leading to what Featherstone (1990; 1991) characterized as 'the anesthetization of life'. I would reject any negative attributes assigned to this social condition, and simply state this is all a logical manifestation of the self-organizing principle of the informational society, a celebration without boundaries of the mystifying horizons that the flow of information unfolds to our senses.

1.6.7 The rise of the Network Society

In Castells' theoretical accounts, of equal importance to the concept of information, is the concept of 'networking' (Castells, 1998). He argued that the information revolution, the economic crisis of political systems and cultural social movements has led to a new social structure, the Network Society, a global, interdependent world, the informational/ global economy, and the culture of real virtuality. The new social morphology of our societies is characterized by the diffusion of networking logic, where the power of flows takes precedence over the flows of power. The inclusion/exclusion in networks, and the architecture of relationships between networks, enacted by light-speed operating IT, configure dominant processes and functions in our societies.

I will suggest here that this networking logic consists an inevitable state and advancement of the flow of information and that the realization of the network society minimally shows the need of the system of information to be diffused, interrelated, integrated and be re-born in new structural forms and social configurations. This is a point of importance that needs to be kept in mind, when I come back to this in my theoretical proposals later in the book. I will refrain at this early stage of my argument from using the actual typology I develop later to avoid unexpected theoretical confusion. Still, as I propose there, networking is a variation of indispensable structural involvement within and among systems of information; along the same theoretical lines as the concept of informationalism, already discussed above, consists a variation of a structural condition that characterizes systems of information. For now, let us just concentrate on Castells' observations on the development of networks and their social impact.

1.6.8 Networking

In Castells' discussion then, networks are instruments for a capitalist economy based on innovation, globalization, and decentralized concentration. From global networks of capital, management, and information, capital is invested, globally, in a world that Castells (1996) called the unreal economy, whose movements and variable logic, ultimately determine economies and influence societies. The network morphology, Castells stated, is also a source of dramatic reorganization of power relationships. This does not come as surprise as the reorganization of power is indeed, as I contend, based on the flow of information, which is under constant and chaotic change and extremely variable interactivity. This intimate relationship between power and information is reflected in the convergence of social evolution and IT and creates a new material basis for the performance of activities throughout the social structure thus shaping social structure itself.

Informationalism, then, becomes the material foundation of a new society, whereas the development of networking is a dynamic, self-expanding form of organization of human activity. This leads towards a re-formed capitalism, characterized by the globalization of core economic activities, organization flexibility, and greater power for management over labour. It is also not void of social exclusion and economic irrelevance, which, Castells observed, have led to the perverse connection, the development of global criminal activity, the 'Fourth World' (aiming at satisfying forbidden desire and supplying outlawed commodities). Informational capitalism, relying on innovation-induced productivity and globalization-oriented competitiveness, emerges embedded in culture and tooled by technology. The cosmopolitanism and internationalism of the late 1960s movements, says Castells, set up the intellectual bases of an interdependent world, and stimulated technological experimentation with symbol manipulation, structural transformation of social forms of space and time. Not new, I would suggest, but characteristically different world of ideological representations that would evolve and mutate towards a culture of 'real virtuality'.

1.6.9 The culture of real virtuality

The transformations of the material foundations of social life, space, and time, observed by Castells led him to suggest the emergence of a new culture from the superseding of places and the annihilation of time by the space of flows and by timeless time: 'the culture of real virtuality'. According to Castells, virtuality is a system in which reality itself (people's material and/or symbolic existence) is fully immersed in a virtual image setting, in the world of make-believe, in which symbols are not just metaphors, but comprise the actual experience. All expressions from all times and from all spaces are mixed in the same hypertext. This virtuality is our reality because it is within the framework of these timeless, placeless, symbolic systems that we construct the categories and evoke the images that shape behavior, induce politics, nurture dreams, and trigger nightmares. I will point out here, that this virtuality consists an unmarked spatial configuration of informational environments. As I will argue extensively later in this book, virtuality does not consist a new social entity rather it represents the activation and intensification of an ever-co-existing spatio-ideological portal, to new forms of significations based on continuous alterations and fluctuations of the system of information among imaginary and 'real' representations of the social. I would add that this cultural form consists the basis of the emerging social structure of the Information Age, the Network Society. Let us also keep in mind that, not all dimensions of a society or the whole of global society follow the cultural logic of the network society, although, everyday social experience informs us about the constant and insistent socio-economic pressure and of different intensity societal penetration for global conformity and synchronization.

1.6.10 The Information Age

Castells contended that, the truly fundamental social cleavages of the Information Age are, the internal fragmentation of labor, social exclusion, and, the separation between logic and human experience. He noticed transformations in power relations of network geometry, the main one being the crisis of the nation-state as a sovereign entity, replaced by a new form of state, 'the Network State'. In the network state, power becomes immaterial, and the power game in the Information Age is one of culture, initially played by the media. The media are not though the power-holders, although they are self-acclaimed commanding players in the game. Power, as the capacity to impose behaviour, Castells, argued, lies in the networks of information exchange and symbol manipulation, which relate social actors, institutions, and cultural movements, through icons, spokespersons, and intellectual amplifiers.

It is the underlying dynamics of this power and the information networks within which it develops during the exchange process in human communication and human interaction with IT, that I am attempting to analyze with an in-depth analysis of the system of information later in this book. I hope that my theoretical arguments will provide an enhanced perspective, on how all levels of social organization, deriving from digitally [and not only that] constructed knowledge, can be decoded based on a micro-analytical in-depth model of the organization of information. I will be suggesting that this model can be applied to macroscopic analyses of social investigation and can cut across and consequently inter-relate diverse disciplines and issues. It is my contention throughout this book that the macroscopic organization of social life is a reflection of the microscopic social organization of the system on information and vice versa. Therefore, the social organization of these two is strongly inter-related and the investigation of the system of information, especially in a world where, is widely recognized, to be dominated by it, will, hopefully, offer a fresh new understanding of the organizational aspects of social life itself.

1.6.11 The new social order

Without doubt Castells' comprehensive depiction of the global society point towards the transition to a world not as much as we have known it. In this information-dominated world, culture as the source of power, and power as the source of capital, underlie the new social hierarchy of the Information Age. Castells saw the emerging 'new social order' as based on cultural expressions that become predominantly mediated by electronic communication networks. These networks interact with the audience and by the audience in a diversity of codes and values, ultimately subsumed in a digitized, audiovisual hypertext. At a deeper level, the material foundations of society, space and time are being transformed, organized around the space of flows and timeless time. The social construction of new dominant forms of space and time develops a meta-network that switches off nonessential functions, subordinate social groups, and devalued territories. Their structural meaning does, subsumed in the unseen logic of the meta-network where value is produced, cultural codes are created, and power is decided.

The new social order, the network society, increasingly appears to most people as a meta-social disorder, namely, as an automated, random sequence of events, derived from the uncontrollable logic of markets, technology, geopolitical order, or biological determination. In a broader historical perspective, the network society represents a qualitative change in the human experience. Information is the key ingredient of our social organization and why flows of messages and images between networks constitute the basic thread of our social structure. It is the beginning of a new existence, and indeed, the beginning of a new age, the information age, marked by the autonomy of culture *vis-à-vis* the material bases of our existence.

As I have stated at the beginning of this chapter my intention is to critically review recent theoretical accounts in order to reach assumptions as to what currently defines contemporary societies. With regard to Castells, his theories on the Informational Society and the rise of the Network Society point to the importance of the flow of information as a primary principle of social organization. He described an informational society which is characterized by the dominant capitalist activities of informationalism and networking, which in turn, in essence consist systemic attempts to control the flow of information. The later defines spatial environments such as the world city, social divisions such as the '\information professionals'\ and the '\informational underclass, imposes different ways of thinking (cosmopolitanism), and re-organizes the relations of power through a cultural differentiation towards a culture of real virtuality. This is the Digital Age of a changing social structure and human consciousness mediated by electronic communication networks.

With relation to Castells' observations, I have stressed so far the significant role of information in the social organization and construction of social structure and knowledge, and how certain of his theoretical conceptualizations reveal and support my theoretical suggestions in this book regarding the social organization of the system of information. I have argued that global societal changes are informational responses to informational representations, and that in this respect new emerging social divisions become questionable. It is clear that certain economic and intellectual world centres around the globe are assigned the role for the control the flow of information, digitally affecting the construction of social knowledge. I have also made the point that contemporary social conditions are a logical materialization of the flow of information, and that the concepts of informationalism and networking consist reflections of the internal organization and the interactive tensions of the flow of information. Moreover, they refer to structural conditions and structural involvements respectively, which characterize the digital organization of information systems. It is the organization of the system of information that re-organizes power relations, and places virtuality at the core of social environments as a momentous spatio-ideological mechanism. As I argued before, responsible for this structural and ideological restructuring are continuous alterations and fluctuations of the system of information. A more extensive in-depth analysis and discussion of all my preliminary arguments here are undertaken in later sections of the book in the statement of my theoretical approximations.

I have implied before the relative self-autonomy of the organization of the system of information and of its power to mobilize social change. This, I must point out here, does not take place independently, but in relation to other social actors and processes in society. Information mobilizes segments of knowledge and triggers patterns of communication, and in this sense, social action. I will argue that the foundation of all this interconnectedness is information social agents carry out the realization of this interconnectedness, which is, finally, historically recorded as an informational representation, and which is embodied into the global social awareness. This is an argument to keep in mind in the following discussion of Schiller's political economy of the emergence of 'Digital Capitalism'. Schiller's account is critically important as it provides a series of considerations and an important insight on the origins and development of the contemporary communication patterns of information and the historical and political framework within which they have developed. It is my contention here that, Schiller's account, reflects the socio-economic and historical need to conform, and consequently to control, to the societal demand for the release, free flow and availability of existing knowledge, as a prerequisite condition for the continuation of societal activity and advancement. This, I would argue, reveals a vicious circle of how societal changes are informed by knowledge, respond in the form of additionally created information, and in turn instill acquired knowledge with further informational input.

1.7 DIGITAL CAPITALISM

Schiller's political economy focused on communications and information issues, following a 'systemic' analysis of information communication, with emphasis on the periodisation of trends and developments. Initially, he pointed out to the commodification of information and the informatisation of society as attempts of informational imperialism to establish a capitalist system based on consumerism. In any of these theoretical descriptions it becomes evident that the concentration, communication and control of information, and the knowledge it produces, makes it possible for elite social divisions and groups to control and boost social change towards prescribed economic objectives and social intentions. Moreover, it allows the use of information to generate alternative simulations of future social circumstances and technological developments, and consequently, select and reject among possible scenarios and pursue their realization. I will argue that, the success of information imperialism or digital capitalism relies on the fact of the recognition of the importance of flow of information, the institutionalisation of the global channels of communication and the techno-economic conditions, which have energized the simulation of global consciousness for the circulation and distribution of the system of information.

1.7.1 Information imperialism

Schiller's (1973) main question about 'the mind industry', that is the new IT, has been for whose benefit and under whose control [would those] be implemented. He argued then that informational developments create a powerful impulse towards the commodification of information, to state that, 'information ... is being treated as a commodity'. This observation, Schiller connected it to the development of the so-called IS as a reflection of capitalist imperatives and as an attempt to establish a transnational empire. Information and its enabling technologies have been promoted by, and are essential to sustain, these developments and interests. At the same time, media corporations, sustained Schiller, give ideological support to this transnational empire, with world events and trends covered from a distinctively metropolitan - usually American - perspective (Schiller, 1981). Massive communications conglomerates have been brought into being, with an unrivalled capacity to shape the symbolic environment which we all inhabit (Murdock, 1990). This is, Schiller stated, the 'New World Information Order' (hereafter NWIO) is the order of information imperialism. To

Schiller all this constitutes a condition of cultural imperialism in informational means of sustaining Western dominance. I will suggest here that the attempt to control the flow of information, like in this case to sustain the dominance of Western dominance or any other system, might short-term be successful, but because of the nature of the system of information, eventually, the power of information, as a global dynamic system, will supersede any attempts to control, restrict and diffuse it towards desired directions of social evolution. Such attempts to control information and influence social developments are described by Schiller as 'the informatisation of society'.

1.7.2 The informatisation of society

Expressive of the interests and priorities of information, and consequently 'corporate capitalism' is, argued Schiller, the 'informatisation of society'. The informatisation explosion originally endeavored to appeal to corporate clients. Dickson (1984) identified two elements, namely the corporate sector and the military, as the critical determinants of innovation. 'What is called IS is, in fact, the production, processing, and transmission of a very large amount of data about all sorts of matters, most of which are to meet very specific needs of super-corporations, national government bureaucracies, and the military establishments of the advance industrial state' (Schiller, 1981:25). The fact that the primacy of market criteria in the information domain led to a decrease in support for key information institutions dependent on public finance represents an effort to extend the commercialization of information into every existing space of the social sphere (Schiller, 1987). This, said Schiller (1989), represents the progressive impoverishment of social and public space, which leads us to a society differentiated by income and wealth, to what Mosco (1989) described as a 'pay-per society'.

Schiller (1983a) identified the military machine, large private corporations and national governments as the 'chief executors' of the information revolution, and notices the emergence of the information poor and the information rich (Schiller, 1983b). What is being suggested is that the information revolution is marked by existing inequalities and this information gap may be widened by increasing amounts of garbage information which divert, amuse and gossip, but offer little information of value. 'We see and hear more and more about what is of less and less importance' (Schiller, 1987). I am not sure as to whether information should actually be labeled as 'garbage' or 'trash'. The issue of quality of information is indeed a matter of serious concern, but what is more important, I believe, are issues of production, selective distribution, differential access to, and availability to all qualitative levels of information. Who, then again, decides what is of value and according to what standards? It is also an issue of education for the construction of critically thinking audiences that are the recipients of all information. I am not suggesting that Schiller is over-exaggerating when he views the beneficiary of the information revolution to be corporate capitalism, I simply believe that the uncontrollable flow of information, diffuses through social structures and processes, and it would be an underestimation to solely examine its effects in relation to the impact on the development of global economic systems. The effects of the information revolution go beyond and go within the informational representations we so constructively build and attach subjective importance to, and for overall understandings and answers one should not neglect all social parameters and actors that may be in play.

1.7.3 Consumer capitalism

Consumerism is one of the material expressions of the informatisation of capitalist societies. Gandy (1993) suggested that the informatisation of relationships is expressed by the increased monitoring of citizens in the interests of a distinct capitalist class. In this sense, the information revolution furthers capitalism encouraging the creation and consolidation of consumer capitalism, where people are predominantly passive [consumers] and where hedonism and self-engrossment predominate and find encouragement. Informational developments, are central to the spread of consumerism, since they provide the means for cybernetic marketing (Wilson, 1988), the 'means of persuasion' of corporate capitalism for convincing the 'audience commodity' (Smythe, 1981) to chase after 'false needs'. I will argue here, that, informational representations in a consumer society are not responsible for building up a consumer audience, rather they are responsible for building up certain qualitative and quantitative attitudes towards consumerism and commodities. People will consume anyway, the degrees of how much and what, are what various forms of informational techniques (i.e. marketing) come to impose.

The concepts of information imperialism, informatisation and consumer capitalism are some of Schiller's early theoretical conclusions. For the purposes of this chapter, they expose the dominance of information and the different societal trends it creates and colonizes. They also point out how driven by information systems can shape social attitudes and identities, by replacing unattached information with economically simulated substitutes. If information becomes a commodity, a product to be marketed by and exchanged among transnational media corporations, then human identity and existence, at individual and collective levels, become commodities to be traded and exchanged, usually at discount value. Schiller makes a transition from the above context to a more comprehensive political economy of the dominant global economic system. His observations are crucial here as they set the historical background of economic and political motives that have led to the development of the global IS. In the following paragraphs I will try to let Schiller's story unfold without too many interruptions and making some remarks where necessary.

1.7.4 The political economy of 'Digital Capitalism'

In *Digital Capitalism*, Schiller (1999) provided a detailed account of the global market development around telecommunications networks, which he asserts has led to the current phase of 'digital capitalism'. Schiller set the origins of the emergence of digital capitalism within the United States of America (US hereafter) neo-liberal spirit for network development, and claims that US originating policies and consequent transnational corporate operations are, in part, responsible for the global transformation of telecommunications networks, and the transformation of the Internet to a global consumer medium.

1.7.5 The US 'neo-liberalism'

According to Schiller, the American 'neo-liberalism' adherent's primary aim has been to gain undisputed freedom of action for corporate capital's ownership and control of networks. As I have argued in a previous paragraph, this shows that controlling the content or the flow of information is insufficient, and it is needs to be matched by the control of the direction of the flow and of the channels of communication, that is, the networks within the communication of information occurs. Digital capitalism, thus, has pursued to develop a global economy network that could support an ever-growing range of intra-corporate and inter-corporate business processes. Along this spirit, continued US corporate control of the IT industry was thought that it could renew US global political-economic power. The liberalization of US Network development was the first aim, and primary commercializable demand for information sharing intra-organizationally, inter-organizationally, and between organizations and individuals, led to the evolution of Corporate Networking. In an attempt to keep the transnational structure of corporate capitalism, capital expenditures in IT investments worldwide, led to the integration of production, distribution, marketing, and administration activities of leading companies into network applications. IT consumption in 1995 in the US accounted for 40% of global investment in this sector (Business Week editorial, 1997), while two years later software itself became America's third largest manufacturing industry (Lohr, 1997).

1.7.6 Electronic commerce and networking

Corporate investment was expressed in proprietary information systems, intranets (intra-corporate and business-to-business applications of Internet technology), rapidly extended to form extranets to increase and widen corporate information exchange, towards business-to-business electronic commerce. As I have argued already, there is a degree of interconnectedness among social structure and processes, and the organization of the system of information. Initially and in a subconscious way their respective organization fluctuates towards imbalance until synchronization is achieved. I believe that the need Schiller describes, to re-organize networks, first through liberalization, then into local, and finally into global levels, reflects the reflexive interrelation, at the level of inherent organization, of social structure and information.

The goal of networking, argued Schiller, remained, to connect computing systems, and through the systems, so that the duplication of effort could be avoided through the sharing of resources and improved communication. With the appearance of 'online trading services' (i.e., e-trade, web banking), corporate IT systems and applications signified that, the Internet was becoming the primary platform for the all essential business activities, therefore, a multi-sectoral effort went underway to utilize the Internet as the basis of a new, decentralized, global information infrastructure. The fear that the Internet's unrestrained growth would eventually lead to the telecommunication infrastructure's crash and the various vulnerabilities placed the telecommunications industry at immediate risk (Hundt, 1997). I will point out here the Internet not only uninhibitedly expanded, neither did it crash it rather opened up new worlds of knowledge at high information processing speeds. Soon, it became clear that, higher-speed data-traffic systems needed to be developed, but also that these would be offered first within big corporate computer networks.

1.7.7 Neo-liberalization and the growth of TNCs

Overall, the logic of network system development within this neo-liberalization process, reveals that 'the Internet remained largely a US system', and served as the production base and the control structure of an emerging digital capitalism which triggered the rapid consolidation of transnationalized capitalist production. Within 20 years before 1995, TNCs from the developed countries have grown from 7,000 to 26,000 (Herman, 1997). The war of TNCs has been about the globalization of their operations. And I would add here that this war is about the globalization of their control over global information and global networks. Worldwide TNCs' investment, (UN Conference on Trade and Development, 1997), turned developing countries to hosts for manufacturing and other industries. The transnationalization of corporate enterprise in turn carried over into the organization of production, accelerating cross-border corporate mergers and acquisitions to further expedite innovations of production chains, thus leading to the development of sophisticated network systems to control the essential infrastructure of TNCs or to globally integrate production strategies (Wolf, 1997). Along this development, Schiller noted, followed a powerful pan-corporate attempt to subject worldwide telecommunications policy to US-originated, neo-liberal regulatory norms.

1.7.8 The re-organization of global telecommunications infrastructure

The infamous millennium-bug, a ghost of itself in the landscape of cyberspace, missed the rendezvous point on the eve of the second millennium, but for many years prior to its arrival, it became one of the main motives for a radical global restructuring of IT and telecommunications agents. Some years before that transnationalized networks to export US neo-liberalism seemed necessary to serve liberalization policies of transnational enterprises. By 1984, the overwhelming majority of some 1,000 transnational computer-communications systems in operation belonged to TNCs (UN Economic and Social Council, Commission on Transnational Corporations, 1984). Uneven transnationalization and a reciprocal reorganization of labour in the worldwide division of labour were among the obvious features of this tendency. Transnational corporate management enjoyed new flexibility, and by turning its priority to telecommunications, led, worldwide telecommunications services, to a neo-liberal telecommunications reform. I suppose that information and telecommunications technology industries will always be under reform as this becomes a precondition of synchronizing with the fast pace of exchanged and processed information. An extraterritorial corporate charter in 1998 carried drastic implications for systems of national telecommunications, leading to global investment in telecommunications and the claim that the entire world was getting wired. Societies were being reconfigured, as the networked economy expanded, still, the prevailing market discipline exhibited increasing inequality of condition throughout the worldwide telecommunications industry (excess workers and downsizing). Along came an ongoing trend for increased automation and newly developed corporate practices towards customers, such as 'slamming' (the practice by which companies signed up customers without their permission) and 'gramming' (the practice by which companies were billing customers for services they didn't order). The US pioneered this networked economy dependent on powerful computer-communications systems, with the belief that marketplace developments would largely set the de facto rules of the game for the new telecommunications environment.

1.7.9 The Internet and the new media

Nevertheless, the reshaping of telecommunications was decided by rational system development strategies, as well as by financial considerations. Transnational corporate capital carried with global alliances in telecommunications taking on leading local businesses as partners, forming integrated trans-border networks with the strategic objective of creating network-based production systems. Flows of capital were allowed to move this way within national capitals, and these alliances were particularly quick around new telecommunications media. The fastest-growing form of foreign investment was in mobile communications systems, new satellite communications systems and service development (by 1998 there were some 180 commercial communication satellites in geo-synchronous orbit and a total of 530 satellites of all different kinds), transoceanic cable projects, and so on, while at the same time, the telecommunications industry was transforming national networks into integrated transnational corporate systems. There was a direct correlation between the deregulation of the telecommunications infrastructure of a region and the growth of the Internet and Intranet use within that region. Concerted political intervention, such as a US Court's ruling that led to the framework for global electronic commerce, contributed to network system development.

Although particularly sensitive issues -'user privacy' and 'encryption standards'- remained unsolved, the Internet, was thought, should undergo market-led development, as it was by now considered a global medium that didn't require a multilateral agreement to advance traditional US trade objectives across national borders.

1.7.10 Legalization and protection

The US Supreme Court's decision to overturn the Communications Decency Act rendered a preference for e-commerce, as well as, a US pressure on and discouragement towards other nations from imposing restrictions of their own on cyberspace. As businesses were becoming informationally oriented, the protection of Intellectual Property became a major concern, explicitly expressed by the signature of the 1997 No Electronic Theft Act. It made it a criminal offence to possess or distribute multiple copies of online copyrighted material, for profit or otherwise. Schiller suggested that, the USA's central objective in the Information Age foreign policy has been to win the battle of the world's information flows, to dominate global traffic in information and ideas, therefore, the world's common language, telecommunications, safety, quality standards, and programming, it was important, that they be American. US corporate domination of global information markets and the needs of trans-nationalizing capital would be succeeded with the advancement of the process of market development via networks.

If I understand this correctly the conviction of the US neo-liberal thought has indeed been, that by ideologically building the content, financially deciding the flow, and globally controlling the networks of information, would place an information-based economy in advanced and prevailing position. This could be possible, but I believe it is not enough, if not impossible. I will argue that, certain amounts of information and knowledge can be controlled and manipulated towards the informational simulation of a social structure or process and succeed certain economic ends. If, though this informational simulation is to become a representational system of domination and homogeneity, self-isolated from interaction with alternatives, and lacking the flexibility to follow and satisfy societal demands and human needs at a large scale of influence, then it is doomed to long-term social decay and collapse. The reason for this, as I believe, lies in the nature and organization of the system of information itself, which, as I will be arguing later in this book, it is in a potential state of constant mobility and need for interactivity.

55

1.7.11 The clash over the new consumer media

The computer industry eventually converged on the Internet as the new consumer medium hosted in cyberspace. The immediate shift to the development of personal computers gave rise to dominance to PC-giant corporations, such as Intel and Microsoft (jointly referred to as Wintel), whose need for new customers and profitable growth was dependent on strategies to open markets, which in turn laid in market diversification. With the growth of the World Wide Web and the entrance of new players, such as Netscape, behind which lay venture capitalists (VCs) who sought to use their resources to reconstitute the Net's technical imagination on behalf of investors. A war started for repositioning within this space, along with a global scramble for control of the newly proliferating pipelines (geostationary satellites, cable television systems).

The web platform comprised an ideal area for the operations of vertically integrated media, such as entertainment conglomerates, which aimed at the strategic goal of gross-promotion and cross-media program development for profit maximization (Turow, 1992). The new Internet consumer medium born, incorporated a great number of industries around it, such as, consumer electronics manufacturers, Net-friendly software developers and hardware manufacturers. One of the obstacles to continuous developments aiming to gain customers (WebTV networks, 'multicasting', 'interactive television') have been residential low-speed connections, which in fact jeopardized the larger goal of developing the Internet as a consumer medium.

1.7.12 The commercialization of cyberspace

The invasion of cyberspace with commercial networked television aimed to develop the Web's selling capabilities. Advertisers had proclaimed the necessity of colonizing cyberspace with 'push web services' (delivering customized information directly to users' screens when their computers were idle), their chief historical basis for advertising been the pan-corporate need to harness consumption to production (a perpetual-innovation economy) (Ohman, 1996). Advertisers come to dominate that medium's workaday self-consciousness, revealing the 'invisible effects of sponsor power'. Advertiser sponsorship goes far beyond the question of censorship of content, as our cultural practices are being transferred wholesale to the Net are market-driven in intent and in effect, with the exclusive social purpose of selling (Barnouw,

1978). The metamorphosis of cyberspace into an advertiser-dominated consumer medium is demonstrated by internet-based events on global stage, an 'impulse interactivity'(emphasis on sports and games), direct e-mail marketing, or even the development of commercial internet communities where the relations between sponsors and consumers (netizens and web surfers in this case) are quite direct (Hof et al, 1997). With the prospect that sooner all later everyone will participate in this universal mass medium, shifts are indicated from 'mass' to 'class' marketing, from national to transnational marketing, and from 'probabilistic' to 'individualized' marketing. The Internet then has become a transnational consumer medium, paradoxically implicated in a calculated social 'construction' of the viewers' desires by sponsorship, characterized by 'social exclusivity', and as an agent that promotes what has been called 'a digital divide'. I will argue, that this digital divide, is more of a divide between the physical space and cyberspace, or to put in more in terms of my arguments in this book, a divide among authentic (referring to the unattached and from the physical derived) and simulated (referring to the technologically manipulated) informational representations. I will be arguing on this issue of various states of information and classifications later in the book when I discuss my theoretical approximations on the organization of the system of information. For now, let me briefly summarize Schiller's observations and restate some of the points I have discussed above.

Prior to discussing Schiller's political economy I have emphasized the relative self-autonomy of the organization of the system of information and pointed out that information consists the base of a structural interconnectedness among all actors involved in social change. My intention for this comment has been to offer some further thought to the validity of Schiller's position regarding the actual driving forces behind the development of digital capitalism. As we have seen, Schiller pointed to the establishment of information imperialism, and showed how, based on it, consequent capitalist attempts have come to establish a consumer society. The new world information order established by the informatisation of society is the order dominating the global economic system, for which Schiller has regarded the US neo-liberal spirit for network development as responsible for its emergence.

Schiller's emerging digital capitalism has been driven by powerful corporate attempts to activate transnationalized capitalist production. This, I have argued reflects socio-economic needs for the control of information and social knowledge as these are key factors in the perpetuation of social action and progress. With regard to the issue of the made-available and communicated information, and consequently social knowledge, I have stated that we need to have an overall global attitude for the definition and evaluation of the value of information and knowledge that takes into account diverse social considerations and informational landscapes. It is then that we can examine with greater ease how the generated informational representations construct our attitude towards and identity within the consumer culture.

Corporate capitalism has led worldwide telecommunications services, to repeated reforms in infrastructure and legislation, and gave birth to cyberspace and the transformation of the Internet to a global consumer medium, intended to serve the purposes of electronic commerce. I have suggested that this shows the importance of controlling the flow and networks of information, though I pointed out, the inherent organization of the system of information, long-term, contradicts and supersedes any attempts for control and restriction it. Also, because of the interconnectedness among social structure and processes, I have suggested that all these attempts represent the necessity for synchronization of the organizational levels of social structure and information. Finally, with regard to the establishment of information-based system to control social structure and process, I have pointed that this is, according to my opinion, rather not viable because it would force structural contradictions in the organization of the system of information itself. Homogeneity, self-isolation and lack of flexibility are agents that resist the essence of information, pretty much like these concepts would contradict the values of difference, freedom and self-realization. My current arguments are further discussed and substantiated later in the book and in the theoretical approximations I propose.

1.8 EPILOGUE

My aim throughout this chapter has been to use social theory of the last twenty years to make a first, very conventional map of the impact of 'information' historical, political and economic landscape of contemporary societies. This map will give us our bearings as we move into new views, new vocabulary and, hopefully, differently conceived theoretical perspectives. Suffice to say that this is a society of information dominated by advanced technologies, transnational media corporations and a changing human consciousness. We have looked at the main social theoretic accounts to stress how the concept of information acts as a defining form of representation for their construction that reflexively structures and organizes social knowledge and consequently all aspects of social being. To proceed further, we will need multi-dimensional theoretical perspectives that cut across disciplines and which are able to combine macro- and micro-analytical principles. The need for this suggestion arises, I argue, from the very nature of the system of information and its organization is: neither linear nor static, at once multi-dimensional and dynamic, all the while forming the base of the organization of all life.

The theories reviewed above reveal a 'digital labyrinth' of confused meanings and perplexed identities, a prevailing 'new' world order, whose organization is based on the flow of information, and whose expansion follows the logic of networking. The emerging world is boosted by the advances of IT and telecommunications, and by the political and economics interests of, a renewed in flexibility, global [digital] capitalism. Crises are noticed within traditional and core sections of social structures and across geographical regions all over the world, inevitably leading to qualitative transformations and conversions of human experience. The world society has been overwhelmed by the trend of informatisation led by elite information networks and transnational media corporations whose commercialization activities have intensively disturbed human communication, by their constant attempts to colonize and control the global system of representational information. The monitoring of social activities and ideas through innovative surveillance techniques has aimed to control the construction of the 'new realities' by firing up socio-futuristic imaginations. Social knowledge and the flow of ideas and information have become ambiguous as they are continuously penetrated by attitudes of social apathy, in favor of commercialized lifestyles and pleasure worlds. The flexibility of operations of the prevailing capitalist economy has led to globalized mutations of specialization in the social organization of information and knowledge in societies, and social structures themselves. In the chapter that follows I will be extending this argument of the global re-organization of the system of social knowledge and information, when I will be focusing on how the organization of the later is reflected in a series of social processes and cultural trends, characteristic of our contemporary times.

These theoretical observations in this chapter reflect a series of considerations on the construction of social knowledge, methods of social investigation, IT and the social [digital] organization of the system of information, which can be summarized and restated in the following arguments I have sustained so far:

- Technological advances can be seen as an informational response, to pre-existing informational representations. In this sense, new emerging societal forms do not constitute separate and new entities, rather they consist digital re-configurations of accumulated previous experience.

- Social change is mobilized by a relatively self-autonomous system of information, which triggers and, indeed, structures communication patterns among human agents and social structures. One of these patterns can be said to be media-generated simulations of the future towards which social action are consequently guided.

- The flow of the system of information is characterized by flexibility, which is an illustration of the inherent dynamics of the system of information; this flexibility is a logical justification of the continuous change of the system of information to reflexively conform to societal demands and changes. To control information is a logical contradiction to the rules that preside over the organizational structure of information, as the system of information is under constant change and transformation.

- Information stands as a commanding organizing principle of the structure and organization of any information-based systems. There exists, an interconnectedness among social structure and information, in the form of informational representations which reflexively construct and inform each other. Any disturbance or manipulation of this interconnectedness can act as a propagandistic factor to influence patterns of social formation, social opinion and response.

- Contemporary social conditions, reflected in the appearance of social inclinations and altered human and power relations, are a logical materialization of the flow of information. These internal interactive tensions refer to structural material conditions and structural material involvements of the continuous alterations and fluctuations of the system of information.

- Social 'reality' that derives from social knowledge consists an authentication or, for that matter, de-authentification of the information. This confirmation, between information and 'the real' has been misplaced by a mixed response of possibilities characterized by insecurity and vagueness. This creates an implication of authenticity and definitions for which alternative methods of analysis have to be pursued.

- It is imperative, therefore, that we rethink of our critical options and alternatives, and aim towards approximations, instead of definite conclusions, to what we unrelentingly continue to accept as the ultimate human purpose, that of the pursuit of the 'real'. The priority of our reconsiderations should concentrate on how we are to redefine the content of the existing bodies of knowledge within a global context. In this sense, a combination of multi-perspectival, inter-disciplinary and in-depth micro-analytical theorizations which will adopt conceptual definitions at various levels and diverse sets of relationships.

I have so far attempted a brief investigation of attempts to theorise the structural and organizational characteristics of contemporary (and futuristically envisioned) societies. I have argued there that various societal elements accounted for in these theories consist of reflections and expressions of the continuous digital re-organization of the system of information and consequently of social structure and knowledge globally; the later has been constantly restructuring towards digital forms of erratic and infinite possibilities. My aim throughout the next chapter is to continue this exploration and to map the characteristics of discourses that define the contemporary world society. The following chapter, then, examines the 'cultural imperialism' thesis, globalization proposals, and issues related to the process of McDonaldization. The discussion focuses on certain concepts of these theories to provide a conceptual framework accounting for social reality and change. I contend that the various structural formations and conceptualizations I have discussed so far are the visible and 'material' manifestations of the informational 'underworld'. In this context the societal processes and discourses described in the next chapter, and which account for operations across and within the social formations, I will argue here, consist of typical materializations of the internal mechanics of a global system of information.

▶▶ı

THE SOCIAL MECHANICS OF THE DIGITAL AGE:
Social Practice and Discourse

CONTENTS

CHAPTER 2

THE SOCIAL MECHANICS OF THE DIGITAL AGE:
Social Practice and Discourse

'We live today in the age of partial objects, bricks that have been shattered to bits…'
(Deleuze & Guattari, 1983:42)

2.0 PROLOGUE

My aim in this second chapter is to continue the exploration of the contemporary world society and those characteristic social practices and discourses that define it in the Digital Era. My focus is on discursive notions of the cultural imperialism thesis (Tomlinson, 1991), the globalization thesis (Waters, 1995) and the McDonaldization thesis (Ritzer, 1996; 1998). The cultural imperialism thesis focused on the trans-national expansion of the media worldwide and raised critical questions concerning their ownership, control, and effects of operations, the invasion of indigenous cultures, national cultural identity and cultural autonomy, the dominance of global cultural determinants.

The key issue pivots around the media imperialism of global Western capitalism, and the implications on its dominance on global markets with the spread of a mass-mediated culture. With the emergence of the network society, the cultural imperialism argument soon gave way to the issue of globalization, which turned the interest of social theory towards the analysis of global economy, polity and culture, and the ways these interrelate to the progressive culturization of social life. Here I use Waters' (1995) views on economic, political and cultural globalization to argue that the globalization is dependent on how and in which ways material and political exchanges are turned into cultural scripts, routines and practices. In opposition, Ritzer's McDonaldization thesis holds that people come to control themselves within higher forms of rationalization, dominated by the principles of efficiency, predictability, calculability. This is achieved through the substitution of mechanical for human technology. Furthermore, the McDonaldization process poses as a set of practical and ethical principles for the organization of consumption, associated with homogeneity and uniformity.

I propose that the specific theoretical issues that the discourses of cultural imperialism, globalization and McDonaldization are preoccupied with, exhibit genuine attributes of the mechanics and the dynamic flow of the system of information. Whether they refer to the deployment of inner organizational powers or external interactive forces, they display the properties of interactivity, networking, and flexibility. These observations provide theoretical elements for a conceptual basis which is later incorporated in the theoretical approximations suggested in this book. In all cases, information stands as the commanding organizing principle of the structure and organization of any knowledge system, and in this sense of any system discourse. In Chapter One, I argued that the existing interconnectedness among social formations and information acts as a communication channel of informational correspondences and representations, and is an expression of the dynamic flow of information. This specific nature of the system of information (interactivity) is based on inter-relativity and inconclusive self-autonomy. It fires up communicational units in social environments in the form of ever-emerging 'new' societal (information-based and derived) discourses. In this context, 'new' discourses can only be cloned or revoiced re-configurations of previously well accumulated, adopted and conformed social conditions, which are elegantly restructured, rebadged and repackaged to be assigned characterizations of novelty (networking). Inherent in the mechanics of the system of information is also a - seemingly neutral - element of flexibility which makes 'interactivity' and 'networking' possible and which enables constant change to conform to structural demands and expectations.

Accountable to these characteristic elements, information presents a natural systemic complexity of control. This indicates how and why attempts of social control and influence over any (all) information-based systems can be ambiguous with regard to long-term intended effectiveness and prescribed outcome. This means that in order to guide and control factors of social [in]stability and progress, therefore of social change (and of all discourses associated with it), one needs to consider not means of control, rather and more accurately means of [transitory] response. Such means can not be static, rather they need to be flexible and strategic, and able to synchronize and analogously adapt to invariable change and inexplicable mutation. Consequently, such reactive means can be a concoction of altered [informational] states characterized by non-static variables such as difference, variety and plasticity. As it is suggested throughout my argument, once more, it comes apparent that contemporary social thinking and theorization should be organized on a prerequisite flexible basis of open possibilities and alternatives.

To this end, there is an urgent need to redefine what accounts as 'valid' knowledge at different levels of social existence and to reconsider confirmations of pre-existing assumptions or non-critically accepted proposals. Let me begin with the cultural imperialism thesis and see how the arguments surrounding this issue account for the existing social conditions defined by the cultural dominance of trans-national media, global capitalism and modernist trends. Cultural imperialism points to the dissemination of a global signifying system characterized by homogenous tensions. A mass-mediated culture manipulates exploits and attempts to offer mutated information as legitimate social experience. This way, a modern world system is established by multinational and trans-national corporations who venture to control information and, though advances in telecommunications and digital technologies, to establish a global culture of consumerism based on economic exploitation.

What I will be suggesting here is that cultural representations are complex reflections of formations in a universal system of information. The processes of cultural imperialism are characterized by interactivity, flexibility and networking, and reflect the organization of the existing system of information. My intention once more, at this point, is to make some observations on theoretical conceptualisations of the cultural imperialism thesis and to point out how they can relate to a more general analytical account of the organization of the system of information which I will be discussing in later chapters of the book.

2.1 CULTURAL IMPERIALISM

Tomlinson's (1991) cultural imperialism thesis is not a unified coherent set of ideas but various discourses of the imperialism of culture. The issue of 'who speaks?' is of peculiar sensitivity in the context of cultural imperialism, referring to the problematic of dominance of languages, of the access of nations and cultures to a 'voice in the world'. Tomlinson analysed four different approaches to cultural imperialism: cultural imperialism as media imperialism (the media at the centre of things); cultural imperialism as a discourse of nationality (the invasion of an indigenous culture by a foreign one involving issues of national cultural identity and cultural autonomy); cultural imperialism as the critique of global capitalism (involving a view of the world as a political-economic system of global capitalism); and, cultural imperialism as the critique of modernity ('modernity' as the main cultural direction of global development, implying a critique of the dominance of global cultural determinants).

As Tomlinson noted, 'culture' is a way of describing the totality of lived experience. Williams's (1976) earlier definition of culture is worth mentioning here as being more explicable. He identified culture within three broad active areas: a description of a general process of intellectual, spiritual and aesthetic development; an indication of a particular way of life, whether of a people, a period, a group or humanity in general; or, a reference to the works and practices of intellectual and especially artistic activity. Culture is seen as, the signifying process of a society within which people give meanings to their actions and experiences, and make sense of their economic and political practices. For the purpose of my argument in this chapter, I will argue here that, cultural representations evolve and dominate within the system of information, which then they come to reflect. In this sense, the fundamental character of culture is a diversity of structural formations and conditions of the system of information, whereas the dynamics of the cultural imperialism discourse underlies, as previously stated, the inner aggressive mechanics of the system of information in general (interactivity, flexibility, networking). I will be stressing the presence and relation of these characteristics as I discuss next, in more detail, certain elements of the cultural imperialism thesis.

2.1.1 Media imperialism

Quite often people speak of cultural imperialism in a form to include popular culture and entertainment and, most importantly, the mass media. The predominant question, in the discussion of media imperialism, has been that of the centrality of the media, as the cultural reference point of modern Western capitalism, the domination of one culture's media over another; or as the global spread of mass-mediated culture. This media imperialism is a demonstration of the power and dominance of information, and the trivialization of the content of and the laws of what consists, knowledge, in the contemporary world society. Media imperialism is informational imperialism. The ownership and control of the media worldwide and the implications to social change and progress will always be of critical importance, but I would argue here that, such ownership and control rights do not necessarily imply the absolute control over the system of information and the construction of social knowledge. The media do have tremendous effects to temporal and transient social formations and to human consciousness and behaviour. It is my contention that in order to understand and respond to these effects, one should critically examine and analyse the core of the media operations, that is the variety of forms in which the system of information is being used and the various methods used to manipulate and present it in segments of acceptable and recognizable social knowledge.

2.1.2 The 'modern world system'

It would not be an exaggeration to say that media imperialism has been operating in a technologically advancing and spatially expanding world-wide framework of networked operations. As Fejes (1981) argued, media imperialism theory is a mass of detailed descriptions of the global operations of the media industries, focusing on the control exercised by the Western corporations over the flow of information and the dissemination of media products worldwide. It is indeed the flow of information that is at the core of the media networks and products, and it is the mechanics and dynamic of its structure and flexibility that makes the game of power over the control of it so challenging. Schiller (1979) presented a picture of the how this works economically. Following Wallerstein (1974), he described a modern world system consisting of a global capitalist market economy in which the core countries determine how development proceeds in the nominally independent sovereign nations ('dependency theory').

Interpreting this again along the lines of my thinking in this book, I will argue here that 'the modern world system' is in fact an expression of attempts (by financial, political or military centres is not really of significance at this point) to build a control and regulation system of world-wide available and distributable information, and to present it as legitimate (and naturalized) social knowledge. The game of power concentrates in the eventual interaction between core and peripheral systems of information, with the first being seemingly dominant and the second admittedly dependent. As I will be making this more exemplified in my later statement of theoretical approximations, I will make the provisional point here that this analogy of power may actually be oversimplified: that authentic and diverse systems of information ('periphery') are indeed more dynamic and powerful than media simulated ones which have a temporal and short-term existence ('core').

Of central importance in the modern world system are large units of financial, political and military power, such as multinational corporations (MNCs) and transnational corporations (TNCs). Schiller showed how the media can provide the ideologically supportive informational infrastructure of the modern world system's MNCs. He described the effects of trans-national media as cumulative and totalising, which employ the notion of culture as a 'way of life' - the culture of capitalism. He stated: 'the latest developments foretell the creation of a still more thorough-going and all-embracing information control'.

I will agree with this estimation but I will remain sceptical as to whether and to what degree the flow of information can be actually and totally controlled. I believe that any attempts of control may actually have a partial effect especially when infected information is addressing bodies of knowledge addressed to non-critical audiences (i.e. young kids). This would be indeed an expression of cultural imperialism. A rather global situation of this point is illuminated in the ideology-critique of the 'imperialist text' of *Donald Duck*, by Dorfman and Mattelart (1975), who argued that: 'American capitalism has to persuade the people it dominates that the 'American way of life' is what they want. American superiority is natural and in everyone's best interest'. Similarly, in an investigation of children's comic book literature in Greece, I suggested that comic books 'consist a case cultural propaganda and stereotyping in favour of Anglo-Saxon or American propaganda' (Andoniou, 1986).

Still, research on audience response (Ang, 1985; Katz and Liebes, 1985; Penacchioni, 1984) suggested that audiences are more active and critical, their responses more complex and reflective, and their cultural values more resistant to manipulation and invasion than many critical media theorists have assumed. Ang (1985) combined the ideology-critique of the imperialist text with audience research in *'Watching Dallas'* and detected an ideology of mass culture by which she means a generalised hostility towards the imported products of the American mass culture industry. In a study of audience response to *Dallas*, Katz and Liebes (1985) suggested that the audience is active and that the process of meaning construction is one of negotiation with the text in a particular context. Penacchioni (1984) suggested that it is dangerous to take any response at face value. Significance has always to be read within the signifying system of a culture.

2.1.3 Media and culture

Tomlinson contended that, the debate over the research into media imperialism makes doubtful the notion that imperialist media have a direct manipulative effect on the cultures they gain access to. But 'doubtful' is not a definite conclusion. My belief is that the media network does have an effect, the degree and extent of which varies along diverse audiences, locally or globally. My concern throughout this book is to reposition my level of theoretical discussion to the base-level of information that lies within system structures and formations, as for example   in the form of media content, and, at a later stage of the book to make suggestions on its state and function in the form of theoretical approximations.

Contemporary cultural theory claims a virtual identity between media and culture. The flow of the system of information is the core factor in the construction of this identity. The system of information consists the content and the components of cultural variations whereas the media act as the means that communicate this content and its components to the domain of the social. Contemporary culture is thoroughly saturated by the mass media that it is often impossible to separate immediate real cultural experience from those presented through the screen (Kroker and Cook, 1988). The actual cultural intruder and modifier in every case is the system of information. This is why it is critical to be analysed in all its alternate transmissive forms but also within the diverse contexts of cultural variations it emerges. Baudrillard (1985) saw the concept of 'the media' as the means of communication, where the post-modern cultural experience dissolves the notion of meaningful communication.

Non-meaningful communication is not necessarily incomprehensible, rather a new 'reality' with which we are faced, and which, in order to comprehend, we have to re-examine and re-think within a fresh theoretical framework based on the concept of information beyond and across physical and theoretical, or any, in fact, limits. This is an ever-increasing need as the development of mass media have marginalised traditional means of social communication in Western societies in which people live increasingly fragmented and sectionally differentiated lives. Hall (1977) argued that: 'the first of the great cultural functions of modern media is the

71

provision and the selective construction of social knowledge, of social imagery, through which we perceive the 'worlds', the 'lived realities' of others, and imaginarily reconstruct their lives and ours into some intelligible 'world-of-the-whole'. This, I would argue, is made possible, in our contemporary societies, with advances in new digital technologies which can provide fast and efficient processing and manipulation of information and can consequently produce digitally constructed social knowledge. The employment of new digital technologies by the modern media, related to the processes of modern capitalism, produces both the bewildering complexity of social modernity and the technical means for 'mediation' of this complexity of experience. As Kroker and Cook (1988) suggested, the media provide a way of organizing experience into a coherent and intelligible 'whole'. Tomlinson argues that, we may think of the media as the dominant representational aspect of modern culture, in which our lives are lived as representations, the common criterion applied to fictional representations being whether they are true to life or not. This, then, is the moment of the dominance of lived reality over representation. Tomlinson suggested that it is better to think of cultural imperialism as a much broader process of cultural change which involves the media among other factors. I suggest we think of cultural imperialism as an exposition of the dynamic constantly changing and constantly interactive character of the system of information. Cultural imperialism, and in a similar fashion, the other discourses discussed in this chapter, should be understood as processes towards predefined results and not absolute states or predetermined final conditions.

2.1.4 Cultural autonomy and identity

Cultural imperialism has been criticised as disturbing cultural autonomies and invading cultural identities. Regardless of the ethical attributes assigned here, the imperialistic character of this cultural discourse is a reflection of the interactive nature of the system of information upon which it is based. This disturbance of cultural autonomy has been expressed as the capacity of cultural imperialism to collectively generate narratives of cultural meaning in the conditions of social modernity. These narratives once again are the logical products of interacting informational (cultural) systems and the produced meaning can be described within a theoretical context based on information. The issue, of course, of the domination of one national culture by another is complex and interrelated one. It involves aspects of national cultural specification and cultural identification (diverse cultural identities and national cultural identities), and the context of the cultural plurality of modern nation states. Seen within the framework of the theoretical approximations stated later in this book, these aspects are just miscellaneous forms of informational expressions. Similarly, the notion of national identity through which people experience the sense of cultural belonging, in a deliberate cultural construction involving a complex set of ideological-psychological processes, can again be best understood in terms of an informational outline. 'Identity' is a symbolic construct based on informational elements which are the result of a set of cultural interactions and mutations of the system of information.

2.1.5 Cultural invasion

The cultural imperialism is seen as problematic, for it is considered a threat to national cultural identities, therefore a threat to the experience of belonging. Within a globalised and technologically advancing world, this is not a threat, rather it consists a logical and 'routine' function of informational development. I have an inherent difficulty, here, in accepting or comprehending the justification of the superiority of the 'national' character of concepts to the expense of the international, trans-national, or outer-national. I would see the later three as being more representative of the flow and interactive character of the system of information.

Cultural domination is conceptualized in national terms. National culture is the mould into which cultural identity is squeezed. Most nations are (or are progressively becoming) not homogeneous cultural entities and in great many active struggle and contestation is a significant feature of contemporary politico-cultural life. Most possibly, the homogeneity of a national culture has always been an imaginary construct of the cultural discourse itself, as national cultures have always been composed by diverse cultural constituent elements. The recognition of cultural diversity of nation states seems set to fragment the cultural imperialism argument in its national formulation along two main fault lines: not only there may be difficulty in identifying a unified national cultural identity in the invaded but also in the so called invading country. There is also the question of cultural plurality of the imperialist nations: does ethnic plurality prevent us from speaking of the impact of cultural imperialism on a 'national culture'? In as far as corporate capitalism exports the hegemonic culture, the dominant version of America, we can speak of a hegemonic American national culture as experienced from outside, which may relate to certain symbolic materials. Such aspects of perceived American culture may be distinguished from a more complex 'reality' in which the symbolic images exist in a contested or contradictory form, the myth of America, which exists as a real cultural threat. The concepts of national and cultural identity are slippery. When ethnic diversity exists in a nation state, it is possible for people to reject the cultural imperialism of an alien nation without in the process affirming the unity of the nation which they inhabit. This is an indication of how an invading hegemonic system of information cannot – long-term – prevail over existing 'authentic' systems of information, but it can certainly cause disturbances and effects in their structure and ordinary way of life. To summarize the above remarks in the context of my analysis in this book, I will argue that, there exist diverse complex formulations (cultural) of informational systems, the natural interaction of which is interpreted along the narratives of cultural imperialism as a case of invasion. I will be proposing a more precise typology for this informational behaviour in the last two chapters when stating my theoretical proposals.

2.1.6 Imaginary communities

The prevailing system of information is responsible for the social design and mapping of nations, what Anderson (1991) defined as 'imagined political communities'. The basic component of such imaginary group formulations is an encoded list of symbolic representations which add up to be recognized as the 'national identity'. Such (informational) formulations can be manipulated to occasional alternatives of the original construct and applied beyond pre-assumed physical borders. National identity is seen as a 'communion' which can only be one of imagination, further specified by 'limitation' and 'sovereignty'. National identity is a distinctive form of cultural identity, with more ideological work involved in its construction the symbolic level. It is therefore an informational construct which offers a particular style of 'imagining the community' made possible by processes of: secular rationalism, a cathedrical perception of time, capitalist-driven technological development, mass literacy and mass communications ('sacred script languages' and 'sacred time'), political democratisation, the modern nation-state. All these features combine in complex ways to promote identification with the nation as the dominant form of cultural identity. The mechanics of these complex techniques, I contend, can be mapped within a theoretical analysis based on information.

2.1.7 Cultural resistance

Tomlinson points out that, the contents of 'our culture' continually shift with the passage of time, over a chronic process (Schlesinger, 1987), and that 'our culture' in the modern world is never purely 'local produce'. Hobsbawm (1983) described here 'invented traditions' acting as those cultural practices which illustrate the chronic process of cultural identity development, and whose authenticity is questionable. I will agree with Pool (1979) who suggested that resistance to cultural imports is really just a resistance to change. I will add that this change is indicative of the dynamic character of the system of information in general. The notion of domination is resting on the idea than alien cultural products and practices are imposed on a culture. Most people do not seem to object to the importation, some will object and struggle in relation to their national/cultural identity, therefore: 'domination is only where it is perceived'. Another formulation, mentioned by Tomlinson, is that whatever the divergence in individual responses to cultural imports, domination is occurring where the 'autonomy' of a culture is threatened by external forces. The idea of cultural autonomy as a moral-political principle is based on homogeneity and domination is the exercise of heteronomous manipulation or control. The idea of cultural autonomy involves heteronomy and the concept of 'agent' and cultures, argued Tomlinson, cannot be seen as agents, they don't 'act', they are simply descriptions of how people act in communities in particular historical conditions. I will argue against this, as, it is my belief, that contemporary cultures are value systems, if not based on, to a great degree influenced by and progressively saturated by digital media and technologies. Their existence and substance becomes so dependent on the flow of information that they can act as powerful agents of 'cultural' and social modification globally. What I am arguing is that, this is not necessarily a negative aspect, it is rather characteristic of the organization of the system of information, as the physical and ideological borders of what constitutes the 'national' are becoming increasingly problematic and contentious.

2.1.8 The culture of capitalism

As mentioned before, some arguments of cultural imperialism refer to the 'culture of capitalism'. It is important to mention Tomlinson's (1991) point on two approaches to the culture of capitalism: first, the claim that capitalism is an homogenizing cultural force: that everywhere in the world there is an indication of beginning to look and to feel the same, the later involving a judgment on whether the culture of capitalism is capable of providing meaningful and satisfying cultural experience. Secondly, the claim that the spread of capitalism is the spread of a culture of consumerism: a culture which involves the commodification of all experience. This is important because both approaches reveal how a global information system is in operation in trans-national media to promote a specific economic model and common consumer behaviour.

Schiller (1976) defined cultural imperialism as: 'the sum of the processes by which a society is brought into the modern world system and how its dominating stratum is attracted, pressured, forced and sometimes bribed into shaping social institutions to correspond to, or even prompt, the values and structures of the dominating center of the system'. Tomlinson though noted that, systems do not have aims and objectives, and that seeing cultural imperialism as a 'capitalist tool' tends to misrepresent both the dynamics of the capitalist process itself and the nature of cultural practices. Hamelink (1983) argued that the processes of cultural synchronization (homogenisation) are closely connected to the spread of global capitalism and that is a feature of global modernity. The major players (agents) of cultural synchronization today are the transnational corporations, largely based in the US, which are developing a global investment and marketing strategy. I will point out here, that cultural synchronization is only part of the informational activity presented by a global dynamic system of information and this accounts for problems that agents of capitalism are facing in the implementation process. In later chapters I will be arguing that there exists a logical paradox of simultaneous 'heterogenous homogeneity' and 'homogenous heterogeneity' that characterizes the structure of the predominant system of information and which creates, at the same time, a balanced instability (a dynamic equilibrium), as well as grounds for social change.

2.1.9 Colonisation and consumerism

The threat of homogenisation as the logic of multinational markets derives from the uniformity spread through the marketing of world brands, or maybe more accurately of globally recognized symbols. The 'cultural defences' of their target markets considered, the capitalist competition may point to other cultural outcomes than homogenisation, that is, to develop marketing strategies into 'national cultural identity'. I will stress that this is made possible because of the flexibility that characterizes information and of its innate tendency to create networks and channels of communication. This sort of colonisation of national cultural identity by commodities implies a deeper transformation of the culture by the cultural practices of consumerism rather than simply the commercialisation of national symbols. Consumerism is seen as a threat because it is deplorable and takes place in an uneven way around the globe. Hamelink pointed out the 'differential aspects' of consumer culture and objects the practices of TNCs because, as he argued: 'they exploit economically and deliberately deceive and manipulate audiences, introduce commodities which suppress 'better' local ones'. Sinclair (1987) argued on the vulnerability of Third World countries, and a potential misinformation that follows for these audiences. All of these remarks, I believe can be better understood within the theoretical framework that I propose on the organization of the system of information.

2.1.10 'True' and 'false' needs

The ways in which the system of information is manipulated by contemporary digital technologies, in the practice of human experience and through communication and interaction of these two, leads to mutations of social experience and knowledge and to the creation of symbolic and imaginary constructs. The cultural practice of consumption, created by the culture of capitalism is based on the manufacturing of such informational constructs. More specifically, analyses of consumerism see the capitalism culture as a 'kind of moral lapse' (Lasch, 1985) or part of a broader oppressive totality of capitalism (Frankfurt school theorists). Marcuse's (1972) idea of a 'capitalist totality' (totalitarianism of capitalism) discussed 'true and false needs'. He described the experience of consumerism as euphoria in unhappiness. Marcuse maintained that people in the capitalist culture lack the autonomy to make proper judgments about their needs. The danger of this sort of ideological attribution is that it risks misrepresenting human agency, casting people as 'cultural dopes'. I believe that it is equally dangerous to suggest that people, or certain segments of people remain unaffected by attempts of 'culturally doping' as I would also challenge the very validity and reliability of the 'meaning' of 'cultural doping'. Among a general crisis of social identity and media-spread confusion of ideologies, nothing should be taken for granted, everything should be adequately questioned, if necessary challenged and, finally, should be reconsidered on the basis of principles of tolerable freedom and social responsibility. Both concepts of freedom and responsibility though have to be considered not as static but as of dynamic and fast changing content.

The critique of consumer culture exposes the structural determinants and boundaries of individual life-worlds in which consumption is experienced as a central preoccupation. Kellner (1983) suggested that the critique of consumerism needs to begin with a scrutiny of actual individual commodities, where it will be revealed whether a commodity is a 'true need' or a 'false' one. Offe (1984) stressed the structural differences between consumer and other cultures in the structural differentiation of consumer societies: various spheres of life become progressively separated, thus, structural differentiation, is often seen as part of the rationalizing process of modernity. I believe that this structural differentiation is indicative of how certain segments of information can become autonomous and obtain individual significance and authority enough to be regenerated as fractal mutations of global tendencies of rationalization.

2.1.11 Cultural imperialism as a critique of modernity

Cultural imperialism, as a critique of modernity, implies a critique of the dominance of multiple determinants leading to global cultural homogeneity. Such a critique also involves an argument about the meaning of development itself since quite often the development of the underdeveloped world is conceived of as 'modernity'. Paz (quoted in Tomlinson) argued that, 'socio-economic modernity is the fate of all cultures in that they are integrated at a structural level in the orders of the nation-state system and the global capitalist market'. The human process of self-development of culture involves cultural choices made by agents and implicates the notion of cultural domination. A discourse of cultural modernity understands cultural domination as the process taking place with the spread of capitalist consumerism, urban industrialism, the mass media, and so on, across the globe. Capitalism inflects modernity in what may be called identifiable 'structures of domination'. Modernity is an essentially ambiguous cultural condition. The above arguments of the critique of modernity exemplify how cultural domination is made possible by the imposition of global model-images and icons through technological advances in communication all over the world. The socio-economic modernity of the capitalist state reflects the attempts to manipulate the available system of information for economic and political aims with the establishment of homogenous social and ideological structures toward every possible geographical and ideological direction.

Habermas (1987) argued that the discontents of modernity are due to 'the failure to develop and institutionalize in a balanced way of reason' and Berman (1983) saw modernity as a mode of common cultural experience: 'to be modern is to find ourselves in an environment that promises adventure, power, joy, growth, transformation of ourselves and the world - and at the same time, that threatens to destroy everything we have, everything we know, everything we are'. I will argue that we rather need to respond to the need of reason (and not look for any) and that we need to understand the experience of the modern' as a human activity full in informational content.

Modernization exemplifies structural conditions which are the outcome of interactive tendencies of a particular historical configuration of the system of information. Human responses to modernisation 'make men and women the subjects as well as the objects of modernisation, to give them the power to change the world that is changing them' that is modernism. Modernity has to be understood as the cultural environment in which 'objective' socio-economic structures and 'subjective' constructions of reality interact. Modernity is a mode of vital experience, a set of deductions from the modernisation these conditions are becoming the context of global cultures. Berman saw modernity not as a cultural imposition but rather as liberation of the human spirit. Modernisation begets modernism as popular response. The political-economic processes of modernisation are the major factors involved, according to Berman, but there are others: the cultural narratives of modernity. These cultural imaginings are stories about development - attempts at social self-understanding valorised and preserved within the interpretive texts of a culture. I will suggest here that modernization and modernity, and conceptual derivatives such as post-, meta- and so on, they all consist different structural states of the organization of the system of information.

2.1.12 Modernisation and self-development

Anderson (1984) went on go affiliate the notion of self-development is at stake at the experience of modernity. He suggested that modern men and women simply have to adapt to a world in which nothing can be taken for granted, a 'life lived without guarantees'. Self-development means essential lack of stability, constant changes and continuous undermining of values. I believe that because these conditions are the essence of the system of information, and because this system in its totality cannot be set under control - rather only manipulated and influenced - then self-development will prevail over modernizing tensions. Berger (1974) noticed a self-awareness and consciousness of choice at the core of the cultural condition of modernity. The carriers of modernity, the major socio-economic institutions of the West, transmit the lived culture of capitalist modernity. The sense in which they are a cultural imposition, Berger points out, is not so clear. The rationality at the core of modernity enables a set of choices which expand individual human possibilities and represent a point of no return in the self-understanding of a cultural community.

2.1.13 Pseudo-realities and Imaginary significations

Castoriadis (1985) proposed that the economic dominance of the West lies in the need to assert its discovery of the way of life appropriate to all human societies. Consequently, this leads to a project of global domination. He described the entry into Western culture of a major organising principle, the idea of infinite development as a possibility, value and cultural goal. He called this idea an imaginary social signification. This is a representation which is neither 'real' in the sense of being available to perception and empirical scrutiny nor 'rational' in the sense of being deducible via the rules of thought of a culture. His concept of 'imaginary social significations' illustrates a core system of information as being responsible for social organization and development. 'Imaginary social significations' are in fact symbolic informational constructs. Castoriadis argued, with regard to the orientation of a society that 'the role of imaginary significations is to provide answers to questions, answers that neither 'reality' nor 'rationality' can provide'. Reality, rationality and imaginary significations, in this case, I argue, do not consist separate alternative aspects of a theme, rather integrated, compact, multiple sides of the same system of information that generated any and all of them. Social imaginary significations are the major organizers of cultural practices, said Castoriadis, and suggested the concept of 'pseudo-reality': the idea that modern societies are about growth and progress is one of their central imaginary significations - the imaginary cannot provide qualitative goals and visions - so the idea of development is perceived simply in terms of a constant movement, growth becomes synonymous with more. Development fails because of the pseudo-rationality and the crisis in values. But what if, I will ask, social development - as expressed in social need and response - is about constant movement and quantitative growth, and what if the imaginary can provide qualitative social content when the otherwise 'real' fails? Can we then still be talking about pseudo-realities? I will argue that we are faced we a new kind of reality, one that does not 'exist', the characteristics of which I have pointed out over the last two chapters and which I will be discussing further in the conclusions of the current book.

The processes of modernisation were seen by Castoriadis as cultural projects tied to imaginary significations. The modern social imaginary of development fails to provide a narrative of cultural orientation, and death of cultural imagination. Tomlinson argued that the major objection to seeing modernity as a cultural imposition by the West is the problem of romanticising the un-freedoms of traditional societies. Modernity appears as the 'choice' of individuals. The export of technology and capitalist enterprise is simultaneously the export of the Western social imaginary signification of development, 'cultural imperialism', therefore, can be said to appear on the plane of the imaginary.

What is being claimed is that when individuals express a choice, for what Castoriadis called the 'growth and gadgets' of capitalist modernity, this choice must be understood as limited by what the institutions of the society put on offer. The colonisation of the social imaginary restricts autonomy by imposing a set of ultimately vacuous imaginary significations. The implications of this view for the idea of cultural imperialism are that the process of the spread of capitalist modernity involves not an invasion of weak cultures by a stronger one, but almost the opposite - the spread of a sort of cultural decay from the West to the rest of the world. The cultural implications of the spread of capitalist modernity are that they are producing a weakening in the cultural resources of societies. Habermas (1987) attributed the cultural discontents of modernity to the colonization of the life-world (the realm of taken-for-granted meanings), arguing that what happens is that the space for communicative action becomes colonised by 'system imperatives' belonging to the major institutions of capitalist modernity. The colonisation of the 'life-world' is the situation in which the space for collective will-formation is colonised by the intrusive logic of economic and administrative systems. Traditional beliefs give way to a 'fragmented consciousness' which is not able to construct satisfying rational narratives of social meaning.

2.1.14 A process of loss?

Thinking of cultural imperialism as the spread of modernity we are not anymore involved with cultural imposition, but as Tomlinson argued, with cultural loss. He went on to suggest that this is so because capitalist modernity may be technologically and economically powerful but culturally is 'weak'. Giddens (1987) called this 'a process of loss'. Tomlinson concluded that the present mood of 'post-modernity' (or late modernity) is one of uncertainty, of paradox, of lack of moral legitimacy and of cultural indirection. What replaces imperialism, in the 'post-modern condition', argued Tomlinson, is globalization. As I have stressed so far, my main interest is to provide an analytical framework that can offer an understanding of how a discourse such as cultural imperialism operates. I believe that by focusing on, an information based model of analysis is appropriate and that cultural imperialism in all its proposed forms is not a process of loss. It should be seen as a characterization, a description of a variation, of the same fundamental entity, that is a system of information. This way it can be interpreted as an expression of informational activity of social development and change. The issue is not whether it is beneficial or damaging, rather just to understand that it is and hopefully what it is.

Whatever the case of cultural imperialism, an information based theoretical model can provide a satisfactory response to the issues involved in the various facets of the discourse. I would argue that cultural imperialism, globalisation or McDonaldization can be interpreted as variations of informational activity related to social change and progress. Globalization may be distinguished from cultural imperialism in that it is a far less coherent or culturally directed process in a far less purposeful way. The effects of globalisation are of weakening cultural coherence of all individual nation-states. This takes place at the 'end of organised capitalism' (Lash & Urry, 1987) in what Jameson (1984) described as a new 'cultural space'. This is the as yet un-theorized original space of some new 'world system' of multinational or late capitalism, within which people's experiences are shaped by the globalization processes. I suggest that one way to approach and understand this space is as the domain of the system of information. This will be further illustrated as I now turn to a discussion of some main points of the globalisation argument

2.2 GLOBALIZATION

The globalization process involves intentional, unintentional and reflexive aspects and visions of the world as a non-integrated single society and culture, both of high levels of differentiation, multi-centricity and chaos, occupying the planet. This chapter begins from Waters' (1995) definition and categorization of the globalization process: 'a social process in which the constraints of geography on social and cultural arrangements recede and in which people become increasingly aware that they are receding'. I will maintain that globalization can be seen as the continuation of cultural capitalism within a global level of much larger proportions and magnitude than that of cultural imperialism. I will also argue that globalization, in all the levels analyzed by Waters, that is, economic, political and cultural, is characterized by a common informational framework that can account for all its structural variations. In this sense globalization consists an informational mutation of cultural imperialism.

Globalization, argues Waters, is 'the direct consequence of the expansion of the European culture across the planet via settlement, colonization and cultural mimesis'. He points out that globalization is characteristically visible in three social arrangements of life, structurally independent to each other but which may interact with each other: economy, polity, and, culture. I will point out here that, this expansion of European culture underlies the fact that globalization is the spread of a dominant system (or vertically related systems) of information around the globe. This global system of information unites and is accountable for the dependencies among the different forms that globalization is said to evolve within economic, political, and cultural contexts. Moreover, I will argue here that the various facets of globalization described below reveal aspects of the organization of the system of information in operation.

Waters defined the essence of globalization as types of exchange that predominate in social relationships and each one of them as relating to space in a particular way: material (relates relationships to localities), political (relates relationships to extended territories), and, symbolic (liberates relationships from spatial referents). The theorem, argues Walter, is that: 'material exchanges localize, political exchanges internationalize and symbolic exchanges globalize'. Therefore, the globalization of human society is contingent on the extent material and political exchanges are culturised (then they are globalized). I suggest that whatever the type of these exchanges - material, political, or symbolic - they are predominantly of informational nature and that globalization is basically an informational activity regardless of the level in which exchanges are materialized.

2.2.1 Early globalization

The notion of globalization is not new, and it has been variably expressed by social theorists, such as, Durkheim's notion of 'structural differentiation' which suggested the way to an intra-societal diversity which reduces collective consciousness to abstract; Weber's 'rationalization' which implied homogenization and reduced commitments to national values; and, Marx's 'capitalist commodification' which suggested that class conflict foresees the rise of global bourgeoisie and proletariat. Early social theory anticipated the arrival of globalization process, by arguing at different levels and historical times, about, the effectivity of capitalist production, social inclusion and the logic of commodification, modernization in transnational context, the emergence of the nation-state, system of international relations, development of transnational practices or the instant character of society (electronic communications and rapid transportation). It is my contention that what social theory has actually been observing and theorizing about have been different versions of a common informational context differentiated through time by historical, geopolitical and cultural instances. It is also important for the argument of this book to briefly focus into some of the main points of early and recent globalization arguments. They provide an insight to the expected organization of a world typified by social change and unrest, but they also underlie the informational makeup of this social discourse, and consequently reveal attributes of the various aspects of organization of the [globalized] system of information.

2.2.2 Changes in modernization

Informational transformations of this kind have been viewed as value shifts within modernization, toward the direction of individualization, universalism, secularity and rationalization. They led Parsons (1966) to argue that modernization proceeds to an 'adaptive upgrading', a common path for more integrated communities, 'a set of evolutionary universals' (technology, kinship, language, religion). This was described by Levy (1966) as units in society that showed the reflexive character of modernization and which led to systematic inter-relationships among societies under the logic of industrialism (Kerr et al., 1973). The principle of social organization of the emerging post-industrial society (Bell, 1976b; Wallerstein, 1974; 1980) would be theoretical knowledge which would breed a world-system characterised by internal development, materially self-contained and self-sufficient, multiplicity of cultures. The political, economic and military users of this world-system would in turn maintain a state structure which would serve to stabilize the consciousness of capitalism's 'process of incorporation' of the world economy. As I have argued so far the reflexive character of modernization and the emergence of a world-system point to a dynamic world system of information which tends to create networks and establish itself with ever-spreading dominating trends.

2.2.3 International relationships and 'transnationalization'

The relationships of modernization at local and global levels are indicative of the interactive tensions at the organizational core of the system of information. These relationships, according to Wallerstein, are reflected in the universalizing process of modernization by which Western domination is being 'sold'. Still, the existence of a world-system or systems does not itself imply global unification. Sklair (1991) developed a theory of transnational relationships that emerge under globalization. The global system of transnational practices argues Sklair, is structured at three levels: economic, political, and cultural-ideological, each dominated by a major institution that heads the drive towards globalization: the transnational corporation, the transnational capitalist class, the culture of consumerism. Common patterns of organization emerge in the definition and description of various globalization discourses, which I will be, in later chapters, trying to assemble in my statement of theoretical approximations and to show how they apply to the constituent elements of the system of information.

The advance of international relations (hereafter IR) among worldwide agent has been argued by political science to be responsible for globalization admit the emergence of a world economic system. IR have been defined as a layering of inter-state relations with network or system relationships between individuals and collectivities that transcend or subvert state boundaries (Burton, 1972). What is particularly important in the development of IR is the geographical notion of distance (effective distance), that is, the more dense the systemic linkages the more effective they are. Another pattern of international relations, in which there is a plurality of interacting sovereign states that accept a common set of rules and institution, has been defined by Bull (1977) as a 'states system'. Characteristic of the later is that it poses the threat of a 'new medievalism', a system of overlapping or segmented authority systems that undermines the sovereignty of states.

The emerging global interdependence by which inter-governmental relations at an international level are supplemented by relations between non-governmental individuals and groups has been defined as transnationalization (Rosenau, 1980). Transnational relations involve complex extra-societal relationships between governments, governmental and non-governmental international agencies, and non-governmental entities. Rosenau (1980) argued that it is the contradiction between a 'state-centric' and a 'multi-centric' world that pushes human society towards a manifest turbulence. I do not necessarily see this as a contradiction but rather as further evidence of the nature of the organization of the system of information, a dynamic entity that dominates social space and which depends on turbulence to substantiate its permanence and continuity. This again, in Gilpin's (1987) account, is interpreted as the advance of capitalism: the world will become globalized to the extent that the capitalist market, the process of commodification, expands and penetrates every corner of the planet. The capitalist market and its globalizing effects advance more effectively under conditions of geopolitical stability, which are secured when the international political economy is dominated by a hegemonic superpower. I will challenge this belief about the necessity of geopolitical stability, and I will argue instead that a dual state of continuous alterations between imbalance and balance seems to be rather necessary. This state of ambiguity is expressed both prior to trends for the advance of commodification and during and beyond the realization of any globalizing effects.

2.2.4 The 'global village' and global consciousness

The end product of the globalization turmoil is the emergence of what McLuhan (1964) defined as the new world of the global village. McLuhan's theoretical points provide some support to and a better understanding to the logic of my theorization of the system of information as the underlying unit of social existence and change. McLuhan periodized history to a tribal, and, an industrial epoch, which are characterized by a reorganization of space through time by two universalizing devices': the 'mechanical clock' and 'money'. A further epochal shift characterized by speed, is 'implosion', a structural effect created by the accelerating effects of electronic communication and rapid transportation, bringing together in one place all the aspects of experience. The centre-margin structure of industrial civilization disappears in the face of synchrony, simultaneity and instantaneousness. McLuhan's global village is a representation of the organization of informational systems and many of his concepts are adopted and consequently expressed in my theoretical approximations.

In order that the global village is sustained a global consciousness is a prerequisite to secure the spread the process of commodification. Nettl and Robertson (1968) indicated a link between 'modernization' and the 'international system of states' in his AGIL scheme, and talked about a 'cursory empirical examination', organizations of state which seek to push out and 'systemize' sub-systems on an international scale (Nettl and Robertson, 1968). Robertson (1992) also pointed that: 'globalization as a concept refers to both the compression of the world and the intensification of consciousness of the world as a whole ... both concrete global interdependence and consciousness of the global whole in the 20th century'. Robertson interestingly argued that the intensification of global consciousness presents an increasing probability that individual phenomenologies will be addressed to the entire world, pointing to a globalization of tastes as we culturally redefine or relativize all the issues we face in global terms. The global field of globalization involves the establishment of cultural, social and phenomenological linkages between four elements, the individual self, the national society, the international system of societies, and, humanity in general, which lead to processual developments of individualization, internationalization, societalization, and, humanization. I will argue here that each one of the elements in Robertson's account, can be seen as individual but also interlinked systems of information, and that each processual development as an expression of natural flexibility, intensive interactivity, and prominent networking among these systems. The (globalization) phases of these interactions, or fractal dynamics of the organization of information as I will be arguing later in this book, were described by Robertson as 'germinal, incipient, take-off, struggle-for-hegemony, uncertainty' within a world culture of incommensurable civilizational systems (Kavolis, 1988).

2.2.5 The end of organized capitalism and the advance of postmodernity

The continuous transformation of the system of information logically leads to periodical instances of structural states characterized by initial organization and potential disorganization and vice versa. This is reflected in physical social conditions, such as the decomposition of organized capitalism. According to Lash and Urry (1987; 1994), disorganized capitalism involves an expansion of flows of finance, commodities and means of productions and labour promoting worldwide a pattern of 'reflexive accumulation'. At the same time, an aesthetic or expressive reflexitivity emerges as objects, which become more mobile, they progressively dematerialize and are produced as 'cognitive signs' and 'aesthetic signs'. Insofar as this structure of flows, a de-centred set of economies of signs in space, argue Lash and Urry, are undermining nation-state societies, a process of globalization, can be identified. This is the globalization trend towards a post-modern condition, which as I argued before, is a reflection of the pluralism inherent in the system of information.

Giddens (1985) described the emerging world culture as a network of national societies, the universalization of which can be explained in terms of: 'imagined communities, rational-bureaucratic, and, historical contingencies'. For Giddens (1990) the process of globalization is linked to the 'organizational clusters' of modern societies, powered by the primary dynamic process of 'distanciation' or separation of time from space, prerequisite for the modernizing mechanisms of 'disembedding': 'symbolic tokens' (money) and 'expert systems' (technical knowledge). The concepts of 'distanciation' and 'disembedding' are particularly important for my argument in this book, as they point to the importance of time and space as well of the element of symbolic representations to the social organization of culture, and consequently of the world society. Globalization is a direct consequence of 'high trust/high risk' modernization, says Giddens, and defines globalization as: 'the intensification of worldwide social relations which link distant localities in such a way that local happenings are shaped by events occurring many miles away and vice versa'. The reflexive nature of modernity, he indicates, leads to globalization through multi-casual and multi-stranded processes of capitalism, surveillance, military order, and, industrialism, full of contingency and uncertainty. Giddens concludes that globalization is a process of uneven development that fragments as it coordinates. This, as I have previously argued, can be expressed as a logical informational activity within a framework of simultaneous 'heterogenous homogeneity' and 'homogenous heterogeneity' of the system of information in question. It is the balance of these processes that create instant and recognizable social formations (mutations) and it is the continuous mobility towards instability that is responsible for social change and transformation.

According to Giddens (1990), postmodernity is a utopian condition; to identify a post-modern society that would incorporate a post-scarcity economy, multilevel political participation, the humanization of technology, and global demilitarization. Still, Crook et al. (1992) have agreed that many aspects of these clusters are in fact emerging in a process of postmodernization. The objectification and universalization of concepts of space and time allowed the development of a 'time-space compression' process, and crises of over-accumulation in the capitalist system have led to a regime of 'flexible accumulation', all characteristic of and responsible for globalizing outcomes (Harvey, 1989). Beck (1992) also points out that we already live in a post-scarcity society, the important feature of which is the reorganization of 'risk'. Risk globalizes because it universalizes and equalizes. Risk may be defined as 'a systematic way of dealing with hazards and insecurities' induced and introduced by modernization. The 'social reflexitivity' of risk, forces consciousness in the direction of globalization along a pattern of 'boomerang curve', the main globalizing effect being the increase of awareness on 'ecological expropriation'. Such concepts as 'flexible accumulation' and the 'social reflexivity of risk', can be seen in the organizational structure of the system information, more specifically relating to the interactive tendencies of information. Arguably, the concept of 'risk' itself is a calculated informational process of dealing with the instability and ambiguousness of the system of information.

2.2.6 Facets of globalization

As I pointed earlier, globalization can be seen as the spread of dominant information systems (that is, dominant segments of information, interrelated horizontally or vertically, to put it in another way, along international or local contexts) worldwide, which, according to Waters (1995), can distinctively be identified of being of economic, political, and cultural character. The characteristics of each of these aspects of globalization are briefly examined below. Once again, my aim in doing so is to provide a description of contemporary societal trends and to relate these to my argument that they consist reflections of the organization of a globally homogenous and locally differentiated system of information.

2.2.7 Economic globalization

The economic globalization arguments seek to provide evidence on the development of an international class structure within capitalism. Some claim that capitalism internationalizes the class relations to an international class system consisting of struggles between a core 'embourgeoised' working class and a peripheral third-world proletariat. In the 'age of global civilization' (Barraclough, 1978) economic globalization translates to global rearrangements of economic structures and relations, the organizational behaviour and practice of financial agents, and the predominance of symbolic over material exchange of significations.

Trade has been the original and continuing fundamental of economic globalization. The growth of world-trade, the exchange of commodities and services between nation-states, has generally increased the level of global economic interdependence, it has known a new 'global conflict' with the emergence of Japanese and European neo-mercantilism, and of new forms of inter-firm alliance, by means of subcontracting, production licensing, joint ventures, partial mergers, and interfirm agreements   (OECD, 1992). Colonialism and imperialism have produced an international division of labour producing a relationship of domination, which has been proceeding on a technical, as well as a social level. Froebel et al. (1980) noticed shifts in employment patterns and suggested that, it is either production that is undergoing globalization, or, a 'new international division of labour' is becoming the vehicle for a globalization of production. Lash and Urry (1994) accredited the dematerialization of commodity production to a series of processes: the process of 'post-industrialization' by which a majority of the labour force is now engaged in the production of commodified services rather than material commodities, and the process of 'hypercommodification and industrialization of culture', that is the exchange of signs for finance or an exchange of money for meanings, in which large organizations proliferate cultural products in dazzling collage of symbolized meanings.

At the center of economic globalization is the 'multinational enterprise' (MNE) or 'trans-national corporation' (TNC). The MNE or the emerging 'multinational alliance' is characterized by arrangements between firms that may involve equity swaps, technology transfers, production licensing, the division of component manufacture and assembly, market sharing or rebadging; as an enterprise it engages in 'foreign direct investment' (FDI) and organizes and markets the production of goods and services in the global economy, identifying 'true global industries' (Dunning, 1993). Alliances, aim at businesses in smaller post-industrial economies, imposing in them the dilemma of the game in a completely liberalized trade environment, that is, cooperation or 'extermination' (Emmott, 1993). A single idealization of appropriate organizational behaviour characterizes cultural differences, one about the capacity to make flexible responses to uncertain market conditions caused by commodity saturation.

This global cultural transmission, argues Waters (1995) is evident in the popular mass media, universities, and, 'light' popular literature. The flexible specialization and accumulation ('Toyotism') of 'Japanization' has had the important effect of culturizing economic life globally, with the rapid increase of flows of business ideas, the adaptation of a global vision, the encouragement of a global consciousness, the use of technologically sophisticated, large-scale capital equipment. Waters (1995) points out though that, although global financial markets have expanded, labour markets remained under the control of states and resistant to globalizing effects. Van der Pijl (1989) pointed out, as globalization proceeds the capitalist class transforms itself in an international direction in developing an international class consciousness, a controlling state-like structure at the international level, and it socializes labour, providing this way conditions of an informal international capitalist class. Within this world capitalist class, Lash and Urry (1994) pointed to the development of the social configuration of 'an affluent post-industrial service class' (high-paying relatively autonomous occupations) or middle class with a disadvantaged *Gaestarbeiter* class or underclass (in routine underpaid and insecure labour situations).

My point here is that the various characteristics of economic globalization are information based constructs reflecting attributes of the organization of the system of information. The continuous flow and transformation of the system of information account for the series of rearrangements in economic formations, structures and relations. The organizational behaviour and practice of financial agents reflects the informational tendencies for the formation of associations and development of interactivity. This process of informationalization of economic life is secured by the dissemination and creation of the conditions for the establishment and perpetuation of a world class consciousness. Economic globalization is closely associated with the political and cultural facets of globalization which consist requisite parts that complement each other's subsistence.

2.2.8 Political globalization

The issue of political globalization has to do much with the sovereignty and decision-making of states, which are undoubtedly affected by globalization. Held (1991) argued that, it is particularly, transnational processes that have led to the surrender of state sovereignty, reducing state power as many traditional areas of state responsibility are to be coordinated on an international or intergovernmental basis, at the same time providing the basis for the emergence of a supranational state. Clearly this has numerous implications, still, these state crises contribute to the reflexivity of globalization. Waters points out that, material and power exchanges are progressively becoming displaced by symbolic ones, that is, relationships are based on values, preferences and tastes. The areas where political globalization is prevailing are the internationalization of world affairs and global problems.

Under current globalized circumstances the principle of sovereignty is frequently breached on a multilateral basis on the grounds that the inhabitants of the planet experience a set of common problems that can be exacerbated by the actions of an individual nation-state. A 'nationalization' of global issues, by which, the inhabitants of the globe integrate into 'the planet experience', or, the internationalization of human rights, by which, internal affairs of others gain widespread global support, lead people around the globe to see the earth as a common home that needs to be maintained.

Meadows et al. (1976) argued though, that both population and economic growth, related to resource shortages and pollution costs, have particular and pressing effects, in reducing the international capacity to engage in sustained long-term economic growth. Along similar lines, Lovelock (1987) developed his Gaia hypothesis and Gleich (1987) and Hall (1992) sustained their chaos theory, where global and other systems are interconnected but inherently disorderly. Globalizing panics are said to be both the product and contributors to globalization (O'Neill, 1990) as quite often, the response of political leaders of nation-states, and of redefining planetary problems as global commons, reduces the sovereignty of their states to international arrangements (Volger, 1992). The redefinition of social problems as global problems undermines the sovereignty of the state, redirecting individual political preferences, delegitimizing the nation-state, setting up new international organizations moving the international society towards a globalized polity, which invokes the image of a world government. Parallel processes of consensus building and competition can occur in international organizations (IGOs / INGOs), the growth pattern of which can confirm the pattern of periodicity in the globalization process (Waters, 1995). The examination of a global highly differentiated pattern of international relations, shows the emergence of a new world order, places the USA as an unchallenged hegemon, and marks the end of the multi-polar world of superpowers and the possibility of a common political culture (hint: liberal democracy) across societies. Although, the political culture of liberal democracy emerges almost as a precondition for development (Fukuyama, 1992) for a very large part of the world, still the possibility of cultural variations between different versions of liberal democracies remains strong (Inglehart, 1990). One question that arises, within this spirit, is that of the shift to post-materialist values, and whether this value shift can be considered as a genuine possibility for globalization.

In accordance with my argument so far, I will content that both the process of internationalization and global problems discourses can be analysed as information based formations related to inherent functions of the system of information. Internationalization is related to the inherent tension of the system of information to disseminate and establish itself beyond originating local territories. Informational discourses such as global problems can be seen as informational 'congestion' points, the configuration and perseverance of which can be deemed a structural condition of reflexive orientation related to possible and impossible alternative phases of the informational fragment.

2.2.9 Cultural globalization

Culture, and in the current context global culture (a term incorporating the totality of local cultural variations worldwide) consists the structural and spatial framework within which a world system of information is 'bred', transformed, mutated and which in turn generates the origins of our social consciousness and realities. The diversity of the organization of this world system of information is reflected and made explicit in the definition of cultural globalization. According to Waters (1995) cultural globalization is conceived as a progressive 'culturization' of social life, characterized by conflicts between various aspects of value-systems, such as religious systems, played within the context of expansionist political-economic ideologies which claim global relevance. I will maintain that cultural globalization is the informational exemplification of reflexive postmodernist changes and transformations within native cultural settings, belief systems and ethnic identity profiles, consumer practice, new technologies and travel patterns, notions of deterritorialization, globalized diversity, concurrently present dualities of homogeneity and heterogeneity, and in the transition of power from production to consumption.

A globalized culture is witness to the characteristics of the dynamics of the system of information. Appadurai (1990) described this global cultural economy, as one of 'globalized mental pictures of the social world', perceived from the 'flows of cultural objects' (ethnoscapes, technoscapes, finascapes, mediascapes, and ideoscapes). Reflecting the organizational milieu of the system of information, within which it is sustained, global culture can be conceived as a chaotic rather than orderly condition, a common but hyper-differentiated field of value, taste and style opportunities. A globalized culture, is accessible to everyone, without constraints, and admits a continuous flow of ideas, information, commitment, values and tastes mediated through mobile individuals, symbolic tokens and electronic simulations. The later allow for the development of genuinely transnational cultures, by linking together formerly homogeneous cultural elements forcing each other to relativize among themselves (Featherstone, 1990).

Claims of universalistic religions proved effective globalizers because of their proselytization and conversion character. The emerging conditions of postmodernity have accelerated the search for a single, often mythologized truth (Harvey, 1989), Crook et al., 1992). The discourse of globalization, with distinctive and independent to modernity tendencies, has contributed both directly and indirectly to the world-wide development of fundamentalism, since religious systems are obliged to relativize themselves to global postmodernizing trends (Waters, 1995; Lechner, 1991). With regard to ethnicity, globalization is a differentiating as well as homogenizing process, which weakens the acknowledged nexus between nation and state, brings the centre to the periphery and the periphery to the centre (Waters, 1995). Nationalism, as the political expression of ethnicity becomes both a globalized and a globalizing challenge guided by political and intellectual elites and transmitted through the global informational flow with processes such as that of 'internationalization' (Hall, 1992). Hall (1992) pointed out the possible adaptive responses on behalf of ethnic groups, as 'translation' (a syncretistic response in which groups of a culture seek to develop new forms of expression that are entirely separate from their origins) and 'tradition' (ethnic fundamentalism, an attempt to rediscover the unattained origins of a group in history). The structural re-arrangements globalization is said to create between periphery and centre consist manifestations of the internal dynamics of the organization of the system of information. From this point of view, both of the concepts of 'translation' and 'tradition' could be seen as inherent and locally practiced informational exercises aiming to establish resolution of uncertainty and construction of meaning.

In this complex interweave of homogenizing with differentiating trends, globalization implies a global consumer culture. Within this emerging postmodern environment, consumer culture means more than simple consumption: consumers are encouraged to want more than they need, and consumption becomes the main form of self-expression and the chief source of identity (Featherstone, 1991). Such an advanced or postmodernized consumer culture experiences hyper-commodification, in which consumption is based on 'brand names', and which is captured in 'taste', 'fashion', 'lifestyle' (Crook et al., 1992). This symbolically mediated consumer culture liberates values and preferences from particular social and geographical locations and invalidates modernity by declassifying or differentiating culture. Consumer culture invades and controls the individual and individual identity is conflated to culture. This claims Ritzer (1996) is an extension of the process of Western rationalization, what he describes as McDonaldization, and is characterized by efficiency, calculability, predictability, control of human beings by the use of material technology.

I will maintain that, the paradoxical and actually consistent observed effects of simultaneous homogenization and differentiation (heterogenization) of the globalization of culture can be attributed to the idiosyncrasies of the organization of the system of information through which it is realized. In later chapters, I will be expanding in more details on the concept of homogenous heterogenization and heterogenous homogenization as consisting typical qualities of the organizational structure of the system of information.

Sklair (1991) suggested three principal effects of cultural globalization: the export of the central culture-ideology of consumerism, the degeneration of internal boundaries by media, and the conversion of human relationships into symbols or tokens. Signs of a global culture can be traced in the contemporary media technologies that dissolve boundaries at an increasingly rapid rate with new technological trends developing, such as, miniaturization (technologies reduced in size), personalization (general reduction of the scope of the audience for electronic mass communications), integration (of technologies), 'diffusion' (reception and transmission), and autonomization (receding passive audiences). To this end has contributed the compression of time, with the high-speed transmission of symbols, eliminates the constraints and therefore the social reality of space. The most effective medium in accomplishing this time-space compression is what also has been termed as the 'globalized circuits of gossip', that is the internet.

Social life in the new global culture is also characterized by new possibilities such as leisure and travel, consumed for their symbolic value as signs of affluence and cosmopolitanism. The internationalization of tourism has produced globalized forms of tourism where pleasure peripheries have been created around industrial areas and in which the clients of global tourism can enjoy a postmodern culture dominated by the consumption of signs, images and information of global production and distribution media companies (Urry, 1990; Turner and Ash, 1975; Appadurai, 1990). Clearly the postmodern experience revolves around the concept of information. Information constructs and organizes not only our environment of symbolic significations but it also sets the spatial parameters of our social existence and practice across time. I will point out that this experience of the postmodern environment is an ideal field for the external materialization of the organization of the system of information.

There is a general autonomy and logic to the globalization process, which operates in relative independence of strictly societal and other conventionally, studied socio-cultural processes (Robertson, 1992). The idea that this logic of operation lies in the West (or the USA) is often rejected. It has also been suggested that the concern with the impact of Westernization or Americanization (Tiryakian, 1991) and that perspectives such as Americanization and Westernization were misguided and ethnocentric. Instead, it has been argued that the primary unit of analysis must be the global system (Beyer, 1994) and the concepts of deterritorialization and cultural homogenization as opposed to cultural heterogenization have been posed as the central forces and interactive tensions respectively, in the modern world (Appadurai, 1990).

One critical view is that today's global culture has become de-centered (Smith, 1990) and that it is rather a case of globalized diversity Featherstone, 1991) and not homogenization we are faced with, 'a process of hybridization' (Pieterse, 1994). According to Giddens (1990) cultural globalization is a result of the intensification of worldwide social relations which link distant localities in such a way that local happenings are shaped by events occurring many miles away and vice versa. I will argue here that, theoretically accounted for, processes of cultural globalization consist informational systems, as in the case of the processes of Westernization and Americanization which refer to particular segments of the system of information with distinct point of reference and social orientation. In this respect they can be analysed along the proposed (in the last chapters of the book) theoretical model based on the concept of information. The proposed analytical model would account for the concepts of deterritorialization and homogenization/heterogenization as being indicative of the inner dynamics of the system of information, referring to interactive tendencies of various segments of information to expand, mutate, reform and relativize.

The coexistence of homogenization and heterogenization tendencies manifested in the concept of globalization, reflects a complex and reciprocal relationship between the global and the local (Robertson, 1992; King, 1990). Friedman (1994) focused on the ongoing articulation between global and local processes. He argued that the local is itself a global product and contends that we have both the cultural pluralization of the world and the formation of a single world culture, similar to the Robertson's (1992) two-fold view of particularization of universalism and universalization of particularism. Cultural globalization in the postmodern era expresses the shift beyond the logic of the universal 'iron cage' rationalization process (Featherstone, 1990). A world culture emerges, marked by an organization of diversity, and by the partial homogenization of systems of meaning and expression (Hannerz, 1990).

While third world cultures develop within the global system, affecting world economic and political factors, mainstream cultural system/s is/are shifting the interest to creating, producing and exporting dramatic new means of consumption. Means of consumption are those codified practices owned by capitalists and rendered by them as necessary to customers in order for them to consume. Within this cultural environment an ongoing fusion of consumption and entertainment takes place. The goal of entertainment has become consumption, therefore consumption must be entertaining and vice versa. This fusion of consumption and amusement has become far more widespread and it has been rationalized (manufactured, sanitized, homogenized) in settings such as Disneyland and Disney World. Similar developments in shopping centres, malls and department stores, become a leisure-time activity, a process through which shopping becomes an experience. Meta-means, such as credit cards, also make possible the other new means of consumption, such as, the cybermalls on the Internet (Featherstone, 1991).

The shift to consumption and the rationalization process observed in global social settings has been extensively argued within the context of the McDonaldization thesis. As a counterpoint to the globalization theories presented thus far, I turn to a brief discussion of Ritzer's (1996; 1998) McDonaldization arguments. Where applicable, I will try to point out elements of the McDonaldization thesis that are manifest the internal mechanics of the organization of the system of information. I will argue that 'McDonaldization' is an information based process that stands not in opposition rather in relative association with globalization tendencies.

2.3 THE McDONALDIZATION THESIS

Trends of rationalization, dehumanization processes, totalitarian threats, and other transgressions are said to stand in opposition to globalization. Ritzer (1996; 1998) investigated these and other related issues under the spectrum of his McDonaldization thesis. He suggested that people come to control themselves within higher forms of rationalization and control through the substitution of machine for human technology; furthermore, the McDonaldization process poses as a set of principles for the organization of consumption, associated with homogeneity and uniformity. I will argue that, from an information point of view, McDonaldization consists that essential reverse or opposing force that accounts for the dynamic exchange among inner reflexive tensions of the system of information. As Ritzer

(1996) admitted that: 'McDonald's and McDonaldization do not represent something new, but rather the culmination of a series of rationalization processes that had been occurring thought the 20th century'.

2.3.1 Rationality and rationalization

Ritzer (1996) distinguished five dimensions in McDonaldization, namely, 'calculability, efficiency, predictability, non-human for human technology, the irrationality of rationality'. These were discussed along C. Wright Mills' (1959) distinction between 'private troubles' and 'public issues' that accompany the large-scale social process of rationalization process. Private troubles for individuals refer to poor quality of goods, emphasis on a society which basic operation is speed, highly predictable experiences, leading to a life of routine, and a life where people are controlled by computerized systems leading to dehumanization. Public issues refer to society as a whole: a lifetime of perpetual indebtedness, and the threat of totalitarianism. Ritzer's (1996) McDonaldization thesis drew on Mannheim's concepts of self-rationalization and self-observation, but also indicated the continuing importance of a single nation (the US) as well as of the processes of Americanization and Westernization. Our understanding of the process of McDonaldization starts with a discussion of Mannheim's thinking of rationality and rationalization, based on Weber's ideas.

A central component of McDonaldization is what Mannheim (1936) referred to as settled and routinized procedures. McDonaldised systems generally institute such procedures in order to control what employees, customers and many others do. Mannheim defined the irrational in economy, the stratification system and politics, where an absence of settled, routinized procedures for dealing with recurrent situations, predominates. The solution for Mannheim is planning and it is expressed in what Mannheim termed as 'conduct'. Conduct is associated with the irrational realm and will sooner or later come to be limited and eliminated by the process of rationalization. What McDonaldised systems have succeeded in doing is to greatly restrict 'conduct'.

At a later stage of his thinking, sociologist Karl Mannheim (1936; 1940) differentiated between two types of rationality and two varieties of irrationality, each one them being subdivided into substantial (thinking) and functional (action). Substantial rationality was defined as an act of thought which reveals intelligent insight into the inter-relations of events in a given situation, whereas functional rationality was defined as a series of actions, organized in such a way that it leads to a previously defined goal, every element in this series of action receiving a functional position and role. McDonaldised systems then are functionally rational with all elements occupying a functional position in a series of actions leading to the objective. I would argue here that Manheim's attempt to deal with the uncertainties of rationality and irrationality and his classification categories were actually attempts to deal with resolved and unresolved informational problems. Substantial rationality points to segments of information successfully and innovatively associated and constructed in human thought to predict and define situations. Functional rationality is expressed in actions, the result of the successful performance of segments of information in forming associations with external informational constructs. A more extensive typology and description of these internal and external relationships of the organization of the system of information (endogenesis and exogenesis) are presented in the last chapters where my theoretical approximations are stated.

Mannheim's historical view was that industrialization has led to an increase in functional rationalization, but not necessarily substantial rationalization. Functional rationalization has tended to paralyse substantial rationalization by leaving people less and less room to utilize their independent judgment. The progressive disenchantment of the world, the disappearance of both utopias and ideologies, is common in Weber and Mannheim. The world that Mannheim feared is realized in the concept of McDonaldized systems. The spread of functional rationalization and, the compulsion to act in a functionally rational matter are two aspects of that relate to McDonaldization. For Weber we suffer a loss of human values, while for Mannheim we suffer from loss of ideologies, utopias and the ability to think. Or this, I would argue, might be a misinterpretation or innocent overlook of social conditions that involve underlying informational processes. I would argue from an alternative perspective, that, functional rationalization represents relatively controlled segments of information, and that McDonaldized systems express part of the human attempt to assign control and monitor the otherwise unpredictable and uncontrollable flow of the system of information.

2.3.2 McDonaldized systems and irrationality

McDonaldized systems, argues Ritzer, have little place for human values such as love and community. They seek to limit, if not eliminate, individual thought. This, in the context of the proposed theoretical approximations in this book would be interpreted as tensions of rationalization and McDonaldized systems to interfere with the control of the flow of information and particularly to control its native tendencies for establishing free-of-control associations and interactions with other informational units. Individual thought, though, is also liable, according to Mannheim to an inner rationalization process, the concept of self-rationalization, which refers to the systematic control of an individual's impulses. Self-rationalization does apply to the customers and clients of McDonaldized systems (self-rationalization through anticipatory and reverse socialization). Self-observation is a process of mental thinking, subordinating inner motives to an external aim; it aims primarily at inner self-transformation. McDonaldized systems are even less interested in self-observation than in self-rationalization. A McDonaldized system works when customers have transformed themselves so that they are passive, pliable participants in those systems. That is, they surrender their individuality and move through McDonaldized systems smoothly, efficiently, and quickly.

Mannheim defined this condition as substantial irrationality, that is, as 'everything else which either is false or not an act of thought at all'. McDonaldized systems approach their customers through advertising seeking to manipulate their needs and desires in order to make them devoted customers. Functional irrationality is defined as everything which breaks through and disrupts functional ordering. This is of great importance for the McDonaldization thesis. The paradox of the irrationality of rationality: as large-scale, industrial society leads to a greater functional rationality, self-rationalization and self-observation, is also creates the conditions in mass society for irrational threats to that rational system. This image appears to have little to do with McDonaldized systems. In Mannheim's view, the basic resources in modern life are the same as the sources of the functionally rational, built into the structure of modern society. Mannheim's most crucial failure is his inability to see the irrationality that lies at the core of rationality. McDonaldized societies are characterized by a high degree of centralized planning within specific sectors of society.

I will argue that both substantial and functional irrationality are alternate structural and interactive positions of the same informational constructs we recognize as rationality or rationalization. As for 'the paradox of irrationality of rationality', I will argue instead that there exists no paradox, rather that 'rationality' - like any other informational concept - is not a firm and solid concept with distinct characteristics, rather - like any other informational concept - is a dynamic informational construct and one form of it is what is recognized as irrationality. I will be identifying this multi-faceted identity of concepts later in my theoretical approximations and which accounts for what I describe here as informational constructs and their distinguishing traits.

2.3.3 McJobs

The primary field of the McDonaldization of the larger society is the work world, what Ritzer defined as McJobs. McJobs consist of an enormous number of jobs, most of them requiring little or no skill. They are characterized by simple tasks to be performed efficiently, carefully calculated time, predictable work, non-human technologies for control and reduction to robot-like actions, a variety of irrationalities, and the dehumanization of work. Furthermore, McJobs are not likely to prepare one for post-industrial occupations which are highly complex and require high levels of skill and education. The major contribution of McDonaldization lies in dialectically linking a larger and broader social process (McDonaldization) to the way in which the labour process is organized. McDonaldization, according to Ritzer, can be seen as such a large-scale social process encompassing a wide array of cultural and structural changes that is affecting (and being affected by) changes in the labour process. McDonaldization is manifest at the macro level in both culture and social structure. The constraints on the behaviour of employees and customers in McDonaldized systems are of both a structural and a cultural nature. At a cultural level, both employees and customers are socialized into, and have internalized, the norms and values of working and living in a McDonaldized society. Braverman (1974) defined management as 'a labour process conducted for the purpose of control within the corporation'. Control is exercised and extended through such mechanisms as the specialization of work, scientific management's 'dictation to the worker of the precise manner in which work is to be performed'. All these can be seen as part of the process of McDonaldization.

McDonaldization points to other factors as being central to the control of employees (and customers). McDonaldized jobs are characterized by both routinized actions and scripted interactions. The scripting of interaction leads to new depths in the deskilling of workers. In her analysis of *Combined Insurance*, Leidner (1993) found that this company went even further and sought to transform and thereby control its employees' selves. One important aspect of McDonaldized systems is the extent to which customers are being led, perhaps even almost required, to perform a number of tasks without pay that were formerly performed by paid employees. McDonaldization has brought the customer into the labour process. It is also likely that will see more work settings in which there are no employees at all! In such settings non-human technologies will do all of the human labour.

In a sense, a key to the success of McDonaldized systems is that they have been able to supplement the exploitation of employees with the exploitation of customers. McDonaldization becomes the kind of *iron cage* described by Weber from which there is no escape and, worse, not even interest in escaping. It may well be that the focus on the labour process ignores what labour process theorists call 'the full circuit of capital' (Knight & Willmott, 1990). What modern innovations in credit indicate is, that capitalism can no longer survive in its present form by convincing consumers to spend all of their resources at hand. A constant set of innovations must keep creating so that consumers spend an increasingly large proportion of money they have not yet earned. As postmodernists would suggest, capitalist markets have done this by eliminating the constraints and boundaries of time (Harvey, 1989). Capitalist growth is dependent on the finding of ever new and more refined ways of getting us to spend money that isn't to be earned until farther and farther into the future. It could be argued that the focus in modern capitalism has shifted from the control and exploitation of production to the control and exploitation of consumption.

2.3.4 Americanization, dehumanization, and McDisneyization

McDonaldization is helping to open a whole new world of exploitation and growth to the contemporary capitalist system. Servan-Schreiber (1968) pointed out to what he called 'the world's third greater industrial power ... the American industry in Europe'. There are concerns in Europe about the expansion of certain industries and business practices which are reflected in the use of terms such as 'Toyotization', 'Japanization', 'Coca colonization', and

'Disneylandization'. The standardization of production, consumption and corporate practices has been linked to pressures of Americanization (Williams, 1962). The price of McDonaldization is an intrusion into, a standardization of, the lives of people throughout Europe, and much of the rest of the world. To put this is terms of the McDonaldization thesis Europe and the rest of the world could be moving toward business and cultural worlds dominated by the principles of efficiency, predictability, calculability, and control through the substitution of non-human for human technology.

Two reasons that have been pointed out, as to why, McDonaldization is in a position to cause a loss of national identity and individuality toward a dehumanized world. First, it has an impact on both the business world and the culture, and second, it represents a set of principles completely disengaged from their original source. More recently, Talbott (1996) challenged this view, emphasizing the idea that local reactions to McDonaldization foster heterogeneity rather than homogeneity. I will point out here that the nature of the system of information, to which the McDonaldization discourse is accountable, inevitably leads towards heterogeneity rather homogeneity. As I argued previously, the absolute control of the system of information is not a plausible condition but there is bound to be an effect of alteration and differentiation during the exchange process between McDonaldization and the concepts of national identity and individuality. Not a total loss but a 'damaging' effect. Ritzer also pointed out three optimistic points: first, that, as Williams (1962) stated, 'the best of America ... is not for export ... what too often moves across the world in the wake of American money and American know-how is what is most brash and superficial'; secondly, following Williams again, 'the Americanization of any country other than America itself is impossible'; and finally, there is a distaste for standardization and homogenization.

The highly popular theme parks representative of the new means of tourism, as well as, higher education as a new means of consumption can be seen as paradigms of the McDonaldization process. Disney World is efficient in many ways in the way it processes a large numbers of people. The set of process and the waiting signs illustrate calculability. They are also highly-predictable and dominated by non-human over human technology. There is the element of the irrationality of rationality, in what is supposed to be an inexpensive vacation turns out to be a non-human or even a dehumanizing experience. Ritzer calls this the

'McDisneyization' of the tourist industry. The point is that through the influence of the Disney theme parks, many aspects of the tourist world have been McDonaldized.

2.3.5 Social practice in McWorlds

Urry (1990) suggested the existence of nine social practices associated with what we normally call tourism. Urry argues that tourism is the opposite of regular and organized work, that tourism often involves the movement of people to a new place or places, that tourist sites are outside the normal places of residence and work and there is a clear intention to return home, that tourist sites are of a different scale or involving different sense, and that they are separate from everyday experience and out of the ordinary. Accustomed to a McDonaldized life-world many people want highly predictable, highly efficient, highly calculable, highly controlled vacations. Anticipatory technologies, such as videos, the internet and virtual touring will not only prepare people to travel, but replace journeys to far off locales. A virtual tour can hardly promise the same kind of human experience afforded by a 'real' tour. The idea of the post-tourist is characterized by, a decreasing need to leave home, high eclecticism, and, a post-tourist play at and with touring (Feifer, 1985). Post-tourism is characterised by the commodification of tourism, tourism becomes an end in itself, post-tourists are drawn to the signs (Rojek, 1993). Disney, to mention an example, fits reasonably well with the idea of the post-tourist (Bryman, 1995). I suggest that behind the idea that the practice of post-tourism involves or is, an anticipatory reaction to a McDonaldized life-world stands an informational overload of consumer and commodification pressures that boosts post-tourism.

Disney offers an appropriate example to explore the idea that there is a close linkage between commodification, consumerism and tourism. It is the gateway to the sale of other Disney products. The process begins on entering the theme park which can be viewed as a thinly disguised shopping mall set up primarily to sell a wide array of Disney products. This is an entrance to a McWorld, a concept introduced by Barber (1995): 'McWorld is an entertainment shopping experience that brings together malls, multiplex movie theatres, theme parks, spectator sports arenas, fast-food chains and television into a single vast enterprise that, on the way to maximize its profits, transforms human beings'. McWorlds give people a choice of goods and services to consume, or in postmodernist terms, give people to consume a wide array of signs. The idea of the new means of tourism was proposed by Ritzer.

He pointed to the new means of tourism themselves: the Disney theme park, the cruise ship and the modern Las Vegas hotel amidst the development of revolutionary new means of tourism.

These institutions have many of the characteristics of Goffman's (1961) 'total institution', which he defined as places of residence and work where a large number of like situated individuals, cut off from the wider society for an appreciable period of time, together lead an enclosed, formally administered round of life ('soft' form of control exerted). The new means of tourism, ultimately, they are being created and pushed by material interests. Tourists are looking for authenticity but with the logic of post-modernism, with a society increasingly dominated by simulations, they are doomed to failure in their search (McCannell, 1976).

Another area in which McWorlds are said to evolve is that if higher education. Ritzer contended that universities will be borrowing liberally from a range of everyday experiences with the new means of consumption. The university can then be conceived of as a means of educational consumption of important 'goods' - degrees and credentials. The university is a means of educational consumption, it is increasingly being seen in that way, and student are adopting a consumerist orientation to it. Immediately relevant for tomorrow's university are today's McDonald's Hamburger University, Disney University, or, the new Disney Institute (another form of highly rationalized infotainment). Ritzer introduced his hypothetical McUniversity where downsizing is not enough and controlling costs is only part of the answer; a major component is attracting and keeping students and the revenue they represent. Steps will be taken to reduce the number of students who drop out or flunk out. This focus on positivity will produce an educational world that, in Baudrillard's (1993) words, resembles 'the smile of a corpse in a funeral home'. As a result of these virtual universities, higher education will be dominated by computerized, televised images, circulating in hyperspace. What will be left is a Baudrillardian black hole, in a sense nothing will be educational.

2.3.6 De-McDonaldization

McDonaldization sets an example of the materialization of a world in which information becomes temporarily, selectively and partially controlled, exploited and formatted within defined boundaries and limits. This practice, I will argue, long-term is bound to collapse as it opposes the way the system of information is organized, that is, it requires exclusive access to freedom of expression and choice. De-McDonaldization should not necessarily be seen as the collapse, rather I suggest, it would be the next [logical] phase of the McDonaldization process. Ritzer suggests that we are already beginning to see signs of de-McDonaldization. First, McDonald's itself is experiencing some difficulties with a highly increasing competitive American market. Second, a worrisome trend to McDonald's and potential threat to McDonaldization is the fact that McDonald's is becoming a negative symbol to a number of social movements throughout the world.

There is also a variety of counter-trends, such as, the apparent rise of small, non-McDonaldized businesses; it has also been argued recently, that a 'new regionalism' has developed in the US and that is constitutes a quiet rebellion against McDonaldization. Myerson (1996) identified a series of distinctive regional trends, fashions and products that are affecting the nation and ultimately the world. Myerson cited examples of the new regionalism, moving on to the development of Disneyesque simulacra. He took all these trends as evidence of a trend that runs counter to the ideas of homogenization and McDonaldization. Another counter-trend worth noting is the rise of McDonaldized systems that are able to produce high-quality products. The epoch of post-McDonaldization is in tune with trends like 'Las Vegalization' and 'McDisneyization'. Another potential threat to McDonaldization lies in the area of customization or what has been called sneakerization (Goldman at al, 1994). There is considerable evidence that we have entered a post-industrial era in which the movement is away from the kinds of standardized, 'one-size-fits-all' products. The central point is that sneakerization does not reflect a trend toward de-McDonaldization. A similar argument can be made about what has been termed mass customization (Pine, 1993). Thus the two directions in the future of McDonaldization are the production and sale of goods and services in increasingly small quantities and of goods that are higher in quality.

2.3.7 The future of McDonaldization

While the great dangers associated with McDonaldization are homogeneity and uniformity, it could be argued that many people have experienced greater diversity as a result of McDonaldization. McDonaldization has also led to the creation of an enormous number of new jobs. It could also be argued that McDonaldization fosters democratization, since McDonaldized goods and services have tended to be relatively inexpensive. Another argument in favor is that it constitutes no threat to indigenous culture. I would agree that McDonaldized systems are not 'iron cages' rather liberating informational processes, expressed significantly in consumer practices. McDonaldization can be differentiated from consumerism in that it is a set of principles for the organization of consumption, whereas consumerism involves much more than McDonaldization. Most of the other new means of consumption are aimed, at the middle and upper classes with the money to utilize them. The new means of consumption have been developed and put in place by capitalists interested in profits. Naturally, they have, in the main, developed means that are primarily attuned to the needs of people with economic resources.

The future of McDonaldisation is in this case, the fate of modern phenomena and modern process in a postmodern world. If rationality is the sine qua non of modern society, then non-rationality and/or irrationality occupy a similar position in postmodern society. We are long pass the border of the emergence of a non-rational or irrational society. Rational phenomena, such as McDonaldization, could continue to exist in a postmodern world and coexist with the presumably dominant irrationalities. This, I will argue, is due to the informational core of these phenomena, furthermore, their organization and functionality can be mapped in a theoretical framework of the ways in which the dominant system of information is organized. Any occurring contradictions and clashes of rationality and logic should be dismissed as invalid and should be reconsidered within a new meta-postmodernist framework as fresh and differentiated aspects of recognizable concepts and attitudes.

The possibilities are many. If one possibility is survival, a second is disappearance within irrationalities, and a third is that, possibility would be some sort of the irrational elements of postmodernity with the rational components of McDonaldization. A fourth possibility is that McDonaldization will not only resist the irrationalities of postmodernity, but will ultimately triumph over them. McDonaldized systems have already been described by postmodernists with various concepts, such as, consumerism, simulacra, hyperspace, multinational capitalism, implosion, ecstasy, and many others. Many of these concepts and postmodern arguments are examined in more detail in the next chapter of this book.

2.4 EPILOGUE

The current chapter aimed in identifying further characteristics of the contemporary world through a brief examination of three dominant discourses: the cultural imperialism thesis, the globalization arguments, and the McDonaldization thesis. My attempt has been to describe how these discourses inform our understanding of social reality and change, and further to point out specific traits that reflect the organization of the particular system of information that is encompassed in each one of these bodies of social knowledge. Whereas the discussion in the previous chapter contributed in providing theoretical elements on the structural architecture of the system of information, the present chapter adds more towards elements related to mobility (action), or what I call the mechanics of the system of information. Let me summarize some of the main points made in the above discussion of the three discourses as to how they actually contribute to our understanding of the prevailing social conditions of our times, and as to what theoretical suggestions they contribute in relation to the model of theoretical approximations presented in this book.

Cultural imperialism whether it refers to the dominance of the media, a nation, global capitalism or modernity (or all of these together), it points out to the importance of culture as a particularly powerful signifying process that creates meaning of social actions and experience. With regard to cultural imperialism I have put forward the following arguments:

- Cultural representations are a diverse mixture of reflections of symbolic structures and forms of a universal system of information. The aggressive nature of cultural imperialism is a natural exemplification of the inner organization and dynamic of the system of information, which is characterized by interactivity, flexibility and networking trends.

- Media imperialism is informational imperialism. The global spread of a mass-mediated culture consists a display of the power and dominance of information.

- The total and absolute control over the system of information and consequently the construction of social knowledge is debatable whether and it can ever be succeeded or sustained long-term. Despite the plurality of methods of employment and operations of behalf of the media to manipulate and selectively exploit information as 'valid' or to present it as 'legitimate' social knowledge', the system of information presents great complexity in its organization that prevails and in turn can expose such media attempts.

- In the modern world system of global power, multinational and transnational corporations base their financial expansion and survival in the spread and establishment of the culture of capitalism. They endeavour to regulate and control distributable systems of information, and to legitimise other, products of this process. In this game of information exchange and allocation between 'core' and 'peripheral' centres, the 'authentic' and 'diverse' predominate over the manufactured and simulated.

- The particular organization of the system of information is responsible for the construction of ideologies and systems of symbolic significations especially through cultural dissemination and utilization. The underlying cultural intrusion element is based on the interactions and exchanges within this cultural operation. In such an environment the notion of 'meaning' and its use in human communication becomes questionable. For this reason, we have to respond with a fresh re-examination and reconsideration of our beliefs and attitudes, beyond any considerable limits, because this corresponds to the basic organization of the system information.

- Advances in digital technologies have enabled the increase in the speed of information processing and subsequently have allowed an unlimited management of digitally constructed knowledge, ideology and social practice. They have had the effect of disguising the dynamic character of the system of information in the form of social discourses.

- In a world where cultural borders and social identities become transparent and less recognizable, such disturbances may have no significance and may be lost in the context of their definition. They are in fact informational exchanges, the outcome of cultural interactions and mutations of the system of information. In this sense, cultural invasion becomes a natural and 'routine' operation of the system of information.

- The obvious promotion of the culture of capitalism shows how the global information system is used by trans-national media agents to affect social structure with the establishment of common economic models and consumer behaviours. This notion of cultural synchronization is a necessary condition for preserving a temporal balanced instability (towards change) of the predominant system of information. Cultural synchronization is made possible due an innate flexibility that accounts for the creation of informational networks and communication.

- The communication of culture through contemporary media and other digital technologies lead social experience and social knowledge to levels of symbolic and imaginary existence. In this imaginary life true and false needs become inseparable, constantly replacing and legitimatising each other, which also make the issue of cultural doping questionable. In general, because of a noticeable crisis and confusion of ideologies, nothing should be taken for granted and everything should be questioned and challenged.

- Rationalization tendencies attempt to modify the existing system of information by establishing a homogenous social structure of modernity. These modernization trends demonstrate the interactive qualities of the system of information. Modernity can be analysed within an informational framework as one of the various structural conditions of the organization of the system of information, in which symbolic informational constructs form 'imaginary social significations' or 'pseudo-realities' which define social practice and action, and which consist multiple alternatives of the system of information which initially generated them.

The various configurations of globalization I examined above point to a process of economic systematization, the development of international relations between states, the emergence of a global culture and consciousness, an increase in inclusion and unification of the world society, a phenomenology of contraction (the elimination of space and the generalization of time), reflexivity, a collapse of universalism and particularism a mix of risk and trust. I have pointed out the following considerations:

- The phenomenologies, the complex and reciprocal relations of the concept of globalization, are analogically characteristic of the system of information. It is within this all-encompassing social (digital) atmosphere that the system of information congregates in the cyberspace of global communications and technologies and through them is diffused in our minds to form and shape our knowledge and attitudes.

- Being primarily a concept, globalization is made up of information colonizing physical and mental landscapes. It consists a particular informational construction which reflects attributes of the organization of a worldwide system of information.

- Globalization is not in essence very different to cultural capitalism, rather that both discourses consist variations in structure and operation of an enduring informational system.

- Globalization is the worldwide advance of dominant segments of the system of information which evolve in the form of material, political, or symbolic exchanges, creating dependencies within respective economic, political, and cultural contexts. These exchanges, which are primarily informational, they differ as historical, geopolitical and cultural parameters are assigned through time.

- The discursive considerations that are attributed to globalization by various theorists refer to tensions of reflexivity, of diverse global organization and networking, of intense interactivity and association, and they suggest the distinct features and organizational patterns of a dynamic ever-spreading and dominating system of information. These traits account for tensions of 'transnationalization' which in turn result to the spread and establishment of commodification beyond boundaries and through a condition of alternating stability.

- The globalized the system of information builds a diverse in character and attitude 'global village' whose faithful inhabitants are united in a global consciousness of occasional modifications across time and space.

- Social reality and change attributed to globalization occurs within a continuous imbalance or instability of symbolic representations. This is a state of synchronous heterogenous homogeneity (irregular tension towards similarity) and homogenous heterogeneity (regular tension towards difference), which is responsible for postmodern social formations (mutations).

- The end of organized capitalism is most likely replaced by a more advanced and sophisticated form of social life and activity, in which continuous exchanges among systems of information lead to periodical instances of structural states characterized by initial organization/disorganization and potential disorganization/organization. These are structural phase states in which dominant segments of information interrelate across local contexts (origin of differentiation and diversity) and global contexts (objective of homogenization and similarity).

- Globalization traits that appear in economic formations, structures and relations interactively and reflexively flow along the continuous transformation of the organization of the system of information, through an intensive practice of informationalization, they legitimize and secure the necessary conditions for the dissemination of a global consciousness in support of the proposal of globalization.

- Internationalization tendencies of globalization demonstrate the inner mechanics of the organization of the system of information to expand beyond its origins and indiscriminately to establish itself across global territories. In this context, arising global problems can be seen as 'congestion points' of informational activity during which diverse structural formations, reflexive tensions and orientations clash in a struggle for domination and renewed existence.

- The informational nature of globalization is exemplified in the reflexive postmodernist-and-beyond arising social trends of traditional cultural environments, belief systems and ethnic identity, technology and social practice. Such trends are sustained by means of structural re-arrangements (a 'paradoxical' state of simultaneous homogenization and heterogenization) of peripheral and central (dominating) sets of meaning which take the form of informational exercises through the daily practice of local experience and global envisioning.

- The concept of paradox is an informational deception the component elements simply inform us of a contradiction in a logic sequence. Contradictions in logic are though, what, to a certain extend, the postmodern experience or the system of information are composed of, to the point that this condition becomes the norm, with a 'new' for of logic becoming the paradox.

The McDonaldization discourse represents advanced instances of rationalization characterized by diverse elements of efficiency, calculability, predictability, control and irrationalities of rationality. Here are the main points made with regard to this discourse:

- The rationalization tendencies in the discourse of McDonaldization may be analyzed as information based processes referring to relatively controlled subsystems of information. They can also be interpreted as interfering subsystems of information aiming to establish inner control and unrestricted interactivity with other informational parts.

- McDonaldized systems can be seen as regulators of control of otherwise random and non-containable systems of information; they systematically attempt to limit, if not eliminate, individual thought by eliminating active and unrestricted social participation and freedom of choice, thus creating passive social agents.

- The irrationalities of McDonaldization point towards the structural organization and interactive performance of indifferent segments of information, which are expressed in the forms of newly established and successful constructions of human thought and of performed social actions.

- The issue of paradox (of irrationality of rationality) remains a misunderstood concept, since informational constructs (such as the concept of rationality) are not distinguished by static and firm characteristics, rather they are dynamic and constantly in shifting positions and 'relations of meaning'. In this sense, there is nothing paradoxical about paradox and no paradox of rationality, rather alternative structural conditions of opposing 'meanings'.

- With advances in new technologies, and in particular of information technologies, an information based process, such as McDonaldization, reflexively creates modes of social control and exploitation. But because information based process, such as

McDonaldization, are partially controlled flows of the system of information, their aggressive effects, in this case of McDonaldization, can only be of epochal – and not definite – damaging character, which though may alter and differentiate the authenticity of the affected information.

- An information overload is created with the social practice of McDonaldized worlds. Social choice becomes available through the consumption of 'sings' dominating in an environment of high predictability, high efficiency, high calculability, and highly controlled vacations. In reaction to these consumer and commodification pressures post-modern practices develop, which progressively lead to a phase of mutation of the dominant system of information that composed the McDonaldization discourse, 'de-McDonaldization'.

- We have since long transited into this world of post-modernity and beyond, and there is the need to realize that non-rationality is at last renowned as partially occupying a central position in the construction of what would account as, or what has replaced, 'meaning'.

- There is the urgent need to turn our attention to the central force that organizes post-modern hyper-realities, that is information, and to try to provoke diverse ways of thinking and social response. The organization and function of the system of information in the digital age can be constructed around the analytical model presented in this book. It no case it can be considered as definite or absolute, rather, a time-sliced theoretical approximation which by definition is bound to further complementarity and continuity.

Thus far this book has offered a portrait, a theorized 'version', of the contemporary world society focusing on elements of structural architecture and operational organization as these are accounted for by some of the most influential social theories of the current time. I stressed the intensification of continuous digital re-organization of a dominant global system of information which reflexively and explicitly recreates social space and action. I have attempted to provide abstract observations, parallelisms and analogies among concepts of various theories and the organization of the global system of information. I maintain that this system of information is reflected in forms of social knowledge, social structure and social organization, the latter being discursively produced and regenerated by it. The following chapter will focus on the contemporary cultural environment of postmodernity and the necessary cultural logic that is needed to sustain, - and to be sustained from - an informational world. My intention is to provide a more detailed insight to the concept of the 'postmodern'. I will argue that postmodern - and beyond that - cultural configurations are both an unavoidable consequence of the sudden outburst of information with the global development of digital communications, and also, necessary conditions for the dissemination and operation of the system of information across worldwide and within local social configurations.

▶▶

CHAPTER THREE

THE POSTMODERN-AND-BEYOND:
Tripping in the Mode of Simulacra

CONTENTS

CHAPTER 3

THE POSTMODERN-AND-BEYOND:
Tripping in the Mode of Simulacra

'Maybe the target nowadays is not to discover what we are, but to refuse what we are'
(Foucault, 1982:216)

3.0 PROLOGUE

What do these political economic and sociological analyses mean for our actual social cognition, how we perceive and engage with systems of representation. It is one thing to attribute the new information order to material and social conditions and concomitants, it is another to begin to explicate how it influences and impacts on how individuals see and engage with the world.

Social life in the beginning of the 21st century is translated to virtual life that is in at its core informational. Human thinking, existence and consciousness have all become overloaded with information and understanding the rules of the process, and the effects, of the global social experience has become a prerequisite mission. However essentialist this position sounds, it is at the heart of this book: Information is the basic system and unit of practice, work and life in postmodern society. In a world past modernity, a postmodern world governed by a mixture of principles of non-rationality and/or irrationality. Meaning has been lost or has been seriously obscured by information overload. The postmodern condition is the world of consumerism, simulacra, hyperspace, multinational capitalism, implosion, ecstasy, and many others, produced by a variety of economic, political, social and cultural processes of change and transformation (Best and Kellner, 1991). It is the cultural environment of the new order envisioned at the beginning of the century whose logic, connects to the economic system of late capitalism (Jameson, 1991). In the midst a postmodern condition, the emergence of a disorienting postmodern hyperspace is not just a new aesthetic logic, but rather a new stage of informational cloned projection of human evolution. Means of electronic communication constitute the new language formations in the postmodern condition, operating in the mode of information and altering the network of social relations (Poster, 1990). Informational simulations, the new information exchange, as the result of the human action to create computers, are now creating a new species of humans.

Later in this book, I propose a detailed analytical model of theoretical approximations as to how the global system of information is realized and sustained within the current version of the postmodern condition and as to how this postmodern practice and experience affect human existence, knowledge and understanding. I maintain that the current social and cultural - postmodern and beyond - organization of the world society around digital communication technologies informs and creates mutations of the nature and content of global culture through an uncontainable flow of the dominant system of information. The architectural and organizational 'reality' of the postmodern socio-cultural landscape is predominantly the outcome of informational activity organized in systems of ideology that are expressed through linguistic means. Within the postmodern environment one can only attempt to describe 'reality', or to be more accurate, one can only start to 'understand', by realizing that symbols and images (the components of information) are the only 'reality' there is, or in other words that reality does not exist or its meaning has been altered. It is therefore important and useful at this point to provide some theoretical background on how informational content, in the form of values and beliefs, is systematically organized and expressed in distinct ideological forms which are then realized into cultural expression and practice.

Therefore, in the beginning of the current chapter I aim to provide an insight of the organization and function of ideologies by focusing on a brief discussion of various such studies. Hopefully, this brief discussion will offer a clearer understanding of ideological operation through linguistic expressiveness and its constructive and imaginative effect on cultural realities. To a certain extent it also will help in understanding the organization of the system of information that provides not just the raw constituent discourses for ideology but whose own structure has become the substantive focus of ideology, as Chapter Two showed.

Ideologies are linked to the image which social groups give to themselves, to their self-representation as communities with a history and an identity. The primary function of ideologies is then to mediate and integrate, to consolidate and conserve. Ideologies usually close the gap which utopias create. Ideologies become the argumentative devices which persuade the members of social groups that they are right to think as they do. Ideologies are not just mediums of social integration, but codes of interpretation which secure integration usually by justifying the system of authority as it is. Ideology is also linked to class domination, justifies class domination by virtue of distortion. Ideology sustains the feeling of 'belonging' (relation between our position in society and in history), sense of rightness, of naturalness and inevitability. As image and self-representation it operates as the primary medium of social integration.

3.1 IDEOLOGIES AS INFORMATIONAL CONSTRUCTS

Theories of ideology have sought to examine the ways in which 'meaning' or ideas affect the conceptions or activities of the individuals and groups which make up the social world. Some of these theories, briefly discussed further below, approach ideology as the expression of the thought of a particular individual or group, which is consequently reflected on language and in this way they move towards the macro-analysis of language in the social world, since it is primarily within language that 'meaning' is mobilized. They reveal the characteristics of ideological systems and of the organization of the system of information itself. Such analyses describe ideology within a global social context as responsible for constructing imaginary significations into real worlds (Castoriadis, 1975, 1978, 1981) through an invisible operation (Lefort, 1981).

Ideologies are also described as means of distribution of symbolic capital (Bourdieu, 1981), as action-oriented sets of beliefs (Seliger, 1976) submitting to a grammar of modern rationality, or universal symbol systems (Gouldner, 1976)) that lend themselves to rationalization and distortion (Ricoeur, 1978). Other studies analyse ideologies in the relation between action and social structure (Giddens, 1984; Pêcheux et al., 1979) or how ideologies 'interpellate individuals into subjects' (Althusser, 1971). I will be discussing briefly some of these theories of ideologies here, aiming to stress the importance of information in social action and change, to provide some theoretical background on principles of the construction, organization and expression of ideological systems, which I propose that they are also indicative of the organization of the sub-systems of information that result to the formation of such informational constructs, that is, ideologies.

3.1.1 The social imaginary

Castoriadis' (1975; 1978; 1981) concept of the 'social imaginary' is of particular importance. He described the world as a world of human action, where, a specific type of action, praxis, involves taking others into account and regarding them as autonomous beings capable of developing their own autonomy. Action in this world stands in some relation to knowledge, and knowledge is never absolute. The world of human action, according to Castoriadis is realized in a capitalist institution of temporality. Capitalist temporality is characterized by homogenous uniform, measurable time, time of accumulation, rationalization and conquest of nature, and is opposed to effective temporality which refers to time of incessant rupture, recurrent crises, perceptual tearing of what is. Within this temporal world system, Castoriadis argued that what renders possible any relation of object and image is the creation ex nihilo of figures and forms, the social imaginary. The imaginary is expressed through the constitution of a world of significations (symbols and myths representing the present and past of society), seen in the operation of the language; a signification is indefinitely determinable, although that does not mean that it is determined. The central imaginary significations of a society are the laces which tie a society together and the forms which define what for a given society, is real.

The origin of the world of significations which make up the social imaginary can be traced in the dominant system of information. The power of information contained within dominant bodies of ideology redefines the imaginary as 'real'. The argument that this happens through the discourse of praxis points towards a trend of 'reality' that is characterized by dynamic change, to put in another way, towards an informational flow that generates and transforms the nature of social knowledge to 'something' not fixed but constantly changing in relation to 'something other'. The suggested relation between 'temporality' and 'homogeneity' is a reflection of the innate long-term tendency of the system of information against homogeneity and uniformity, which also implies that homogenous trends can only be sustained for short periods of time. It is particularly important to notice here that 'reality' is constructed out of informational significations, a standpoint which I am taking throughout this book. Informational components are interwoven in non-real worlds, often in the sphere of imagination (the sphere of objectively non-confirmed existing physical realities) and more frequently in virtual worlds, and become legitimate central points of (informational) reference for the operation of societies. I will argue, and my theoretical approximations will propose how, these informational references become the new 'realities' of societies in the era of digital technologies and communication.

3.1.2 The invisible ideology

The ideology (or information system) which underlies Castoriadis' social imaginary, Lefort (1978a; 1978b; 1979; 1981) argued, is an ideological discourse that seeks to conceal the social division and temporality of capitalism, with appealing to 'another world'. Lefort defined two such forms of ideology, 'bourgeois' and 'totalitarian'. Bourgeois ideology is governed by the ideal of positive knowledge (humanity, progress, science, property, family) and calls into question the reference to 'another world'. Bourgeois ideology is strong because its discourses remain disjoint. Totalitarian ideology refers to the contradiction which inhabits bourgeois ideology and which is reflected in the phenomenon of totalitarianism. The key features of bourgeois and totalitarian ideologies are integrated and transformed in a new ideology seeking to secure the homogenization and unification of the social, the invisible ideology. The dissemination of the invisible ideology depends crucially on the mass media by means of which the implicit homogenization of the social field is attempted. Information circulates without internal obstacles and constraints and the word of the expert appears as anonymous and neutral, brought together by proximity and familiarity of the one who speaks. The communication of information creates the imaginary constant assurance of the social bond, of the 'between-us', and effaces the intolerable fact of social division.

Lefort's other world, I will argue, anticipates the virtual world supported and realized by an invisible underlying system of information which separates out into individual relatively autonomous units. The later are then recognized as particular ideologies which though, I will argue, consist possible variations that the original system of information can potentially form. It is crucial to note that this invisibility of ideological operation suggests the need for a micro-analytical investigation of the code of information. The concept of invisible ideology, also, exemplifies the importance of the system of information in the (imaginary) construction of 'reality' and points towards the power of the global media and digital technologies to generate and apply ideological systems based on 'realities' of purely informational origin .

3.1.3 Symbolic capital and symbolic violence

Language is the expression of the informational content of an ideology and is usually a more profound medium of social reproduction. Bourdieu's study of language is preoccupied with the style of what is said, and less with the question of meaning (signification). The social conditions of communication are characterized by, what Bourdieu described as, the distribution of symbolic capital: individuals possess more or less of this capital in so far as they are in a position to mobilize more or less of the authority delegated by an institution. Bourdieu described how symbolic capital is acquired through struggles in the structures and properties of the linguistic markets within which speakers exchange their expressions, others trying to gain entry and others to defend their monopoly and to exclude competition. The structure of the market, he pointed out, is a certain state of the relation of power within which different kinds of capital (economic, cultural, symbolic) are converted into another. Linguistic markets are characterized by linguistic capital, where the speaker invests linguistic capital, with the explicit aim of maximizing the material and symbolic profit, to secure a 'profit of distinction'. Conditions of reception are part of the conditions of production of discourse. Bourdieu's theory of speech-acts is exemplary of the importance of the amount and quality of information and the eventual knowledge that arises from this information. 'Symbolic capital', I will suggest, is essentially a variety of 'totalities' of informational archetypes and codes constantly obtained and renewed during a person's linguistic experience.

Bourdieu defined the concept of habitus as a disposition or system of dispositions (systems of durable dispositions, generation and structuration of practices, representations objectively regulated and related) enabling agents to engender a whole range of practices. Dispositions are durable, transposable, in reflective and deliberate ways individuals take place within a structured space of possibilities that defines a certain style of life. As a durably installed system of dispositions, the 'linguistic habitus' is inscribed in the body, forming one dimension of the 'corporeal hexis' where the whole relation to the social world, and the socially inculcated relation to the world, is expressed. I will point out here that the concept of habitus as a system of dispositions reflects possible expressions of a native to the subject system of information, whereas the variety of 'styles of life' consist expressed variations of accumulated units of information (knowledge and experience) that are characterized by flexibility and potential interactivity.

The power of the content of, and of the control over, information is exemplified by Bourdieu's mode of domination, that of symbolic violence. Symbolic violence is a gentle, invisible form of violence. Symbolic violence assumes different forms sustained by objectified institutions. The development of institutions renders possible both a continuous accumulation of material and symbolic goods and their differential allocation. Violence is built into the institutions themselves, the exercise of which is maintained with the imposition of a 'cultural arbitrary', which serves to sustain the existing relations of domination. Symbolic violence is that form of domination, said Bourdieu, which is exercised through the communication in which it is concealed, in such a way that the domination is misrecognized as such and thereby recognized as legitimate; it is within this relation that symbolic violence is an effective medium of social reproduction. Social reproduction presupposes a certain kind of consensus with regard to the values or norms which are dominant in the society concerned, and the concept of symbolic violence presupposes a form of complicity. Ideology operates through a complex series of mechanisms whereby meaning is mobilized, in the discursive practices of everyday life, for the maintenance of these relations of domination.

3.1.4 Fundamental and operative ideologies

Seliger (1976) defined ideology as, 'a group of beliefs and disbeliefs expressed in values sentences, appeal sentences and explanatory statements', which serves people's justification of the reliance on moral norms and factual evidence and self-consciously 'rational coherence' and legitimacy of the implements and technical prescriptions which are to ensure concerted action of a given order. Seliger distinguished between restrictive conception (ideology confined to specific political belief systems) and inclusive conception (ideology referring to all political belief systems, towards preserving, destroying or rebuilding the social order). According to Seliger, ideologies are action-oriented sets of beliefs, organized into coherent systems.

All ideologies mix together factual description and the analysis of situations with moral prescriptions about what is right and good and technical considerations of prudence and efficiency. There is a bifurcation, said Seliger, of political argumentation which generates a constant process of internal change: fundamental ideology (moral prescriptions), and operative ideology (technical prescriptions). Tension and conflict arise between the principles of operative ideology and those of fundamental ideology. In order to maintain a minimum of coherence, ideologies must constantly adapt their elements and dimensions to one another, either re-aligning the operative principles to the original specifications of the fundamental ideology or modifying these specifications in accordance with what is actually being done or what is possible. Seliger's definition of the content of, and classification of ideologies, are important, as they indicate how information can differentiate in specific, self-organizing sub-systems of information, which can operate as ultimate powerful deciders of social action. I will also note that the tension and conflict, Seliger noted in ideologies, are indicative of the innate tendencies found in the organizational structure of the underlying system of information for interactivity and association.

3.1.5 Symbol systems

Gouldner (1976) developed a theory of ideology as rational project. According to Gouldner, ideologies can be defined as, symbol systems generated by persons whose relationship to everyday life is mediated by the specific and concrete 'bits' of media content which they experience in life as de-contextualized events. Ideologies submit to the grammar of modern rationality, a set of rules for discourse which stipulate that claims should be justified by evoking the voluntary consent of those addressed on the basis of the argument alone. They claim to be autonomous from the social conditions on which they rest and the language in which they are expressed. Ideologies pertain to that part of consciousness which can be said. Gouldner conceived ideology as a language variant which deviates from the common linguistic codes of everyday life, and it allows only certain things to be communicated and discussed. It expresses and represses, creating a public unconsciousness.

Furthermore, the development of the mass media facilitates this process by greatly increasing the exchange of information at a distance. Information created the need for interpretation the publicly shareable meaning. It was in the cleared space of the 'public sphere' that the rational discourse of ideologies thus appeared, offering their interpretations 'openly' and without fear of sanctions. One important element to notice in Gouldner's is the capacity for the development of relative self-autonomy of sub-systems of ideologies, which, I maintain, is a reflection of the tensions within a system of information. It should not also go unnoticed that ideologies are informational sets of 'symbol systems', 'language variants', and 'elaborated codes' which points to the indefinite possibilities of formed associations in a system of information.

3.1.6 Ideology as social relations

Hirst (1979) argued on an ideology as social relations. Hirst argued that ideology is the relation through which human beings live their relation to their world. Ideology contributes to the reproduction of the conditions of production by providing the necessary informational content to train individuals to the rules secured by the exercise of state power in the state apparatuses. Hirst distinguished the nature of ideology as threefold: ideology does not represent reality but rather human beings' lived relation to their conditions of experience; ideology has a material existence; and, ideology interpellates individuals as subjects (recognizing itself as a subject). In this direction he distinguished between two dimensions of ideology, 'juridicial conception' (legal or political designation of entities, supports to processes) and 'operational conception' (agencies that are effective on the processes), and pointed to the notion of 'calculation': a process dictated by rules, methods and techniques which the agent is trained to employ. Hirst's arguments are noticeable as they suggest how an informational entity (such as a system of ideology) provides the connections of 'meaning' necessary for every social agent to place and relate themselves within the context of their lived and imagined experience. Following his argument I will point out that ideology, as a system of information, is related to the spatial experience of social being, and because it is composed of lived, desired and imagined elements it can never represent the modernist interpretation of 'reality'. In this context, it is the communication of the informational core of ideology to the 'outside' that constructs (informs) the individual's subjectivity.

3.1.7 Structuration and distanciation

Giddens (1984) analysed the relation between action and social structure, in a theory of structuration, that is, a theory of how action is structured in everyday contexts and how the structured features of action are thereby reproduced. The theory of structuration is an account of social reproduction, of the ways in which societies, or specific forms of social organization, are reproduced by the activities of individuals pursuing their everyday lives. Giddens focused on the duality action/structure to suggest that social structures are both constituted by human agency and yet at the same time are the very medium of their constitution.

In Giddens' theory, Action is a continuous flow of interventions in the world which are initiated by autonomous agents and are distinguished from 'acts' which are discrete segments of action cut out of the continuous flow by explicit processes of categorization and description. Giddens noted that 'action' is monitored by actors in terms of a reflexive monitoring process of action: the ability of 'knowledgeable agents' (individuals who know a great deal about the world in which they act) to explain, both to themselves and others, why they act as they do by giving reasons for their action. Giddens also pointed out a crucial feature of human conduct which he termed unconscious motivation and which is distinguished between unconscious, practical consciousness (much of what actors know) and discursive consciousness (knowledge rendered explicit). Two processes are also characteristic of action: unintended consequences can become unacknowledged conditions by being incorporated in 'homeostatic causal loops' or when unintended consequences are the reproduction of structure.

Because action is based on ideology and because ideology is constructed from information, Giddens' theoretical account of structuration points towards, I suggest, elements of the structure and reproduction of the system of information itself. His observations are in essence descriptions of various sub-processes and sub-elements of a more general system of information to which his proposed definitions and processes refer to. Similarly, the concept of action is a continuously recharged distinct expression of an information flow whereas acts are in fact already processed and finite bodies of information. Having already suggested the informational nature of action the later processes can be said to be representations of the various states and tendencies of the system of information which come into play during daily social routine.

The duality of structure and interaction of the system of information and the rules and conditions that preside over them – that I propose in the theoretical model of approximations of the current book - are even more exemplified by Giddens' description of the concept of structure. Giddens analysed the concept of structure through a comparison of language and speech - drawing a distinction between interaction and structure. He identified the constitution of interaction in and through the activities of agents, whereas structure was seen as a virtual entity consisting of rules and resources which are implemented in interaction. Rules and resources involve properties of social systems (regularized patterns of interaction involving individuals and groups) and institutions (clusters of the practices that constitute social systems.), and they are defined in terms of lines between interaction and structure: communication, power, and sanction. In the communication of meaning in interaction, agents draw upon interpretative schemes, (semantic rules) or upon norms (moral rules). The use of power involves application of facilities, resources which comprise structures of domination. Giddens formulated here the concept of distanciation, by which, time-space intersections are essentially involved in all social existence. Interaction takes place in 'locale' and endures for indefinite period and actors employ the spatial and temporal features of the interaction as a means of organizing their exchange. It is 'distanciation' that renders possible communication with the past as well with physically absent individuals.

3.1.8 Interpretation

The question of the uptake or interpretation of ideologies requires a textual, not purely sociological theory. Ricoeur (1978) used the concept of the text as the basis for a theory of interpretation. Action as text, here, means action as meaningfully constituted behaviour. The constitution of action as meaningful is the primordial ground of ideology. Ideology, then, is a cluster of symbols and representations which facilitate the meaningful constitution and social integration of action. It is also a phenomenon which lends itself to rationalization and distortion. Ricoeur's theory of 'interpretation' is a process, by which, in the interplay of question and answer, the interlocutors collectively determine the contextual values which structure their conversation. Three principal features characterize a textual 'discourse': a structured totality (along a series of rules), the fixation of discourse (relation between meaning of the text and intention of the author), and distanciation (and emancipation of the text from the limits of 'ostensive reference'). In such a discourse, sentence is the basic unit, provided by words, it has a 'meaning', which is a product of the complex operation constituted by the predicative act and which meaning is shifted through interpretation.

New meaning may rise in the form of creative extension through what Ricoeur defined as 'metaphors'. The emergent meaning, argued Ricoeur, can be grasped only through a constructive interpretation which makes sense of the sentence as a whole. Such an interpretation is an act of imagination, of 'seeing as...'; meaning is created and reality is redescribed. While keeping a skeptical mind with regard to Ricoeur's interpretations of reality and meaning, it is important to recognize the element of information that underlies the classifications of his theory, with words and sentences obviously being the informational units in the process of interpretation. This process, I will suggest, consists an expression of the inner tendencies of the system of information to associate and interact with other informational components, and which accounts for transformations and mutations in the relations of 'meaning' assigned to existing and developing sub-systems units of information.

3.1.9 Interdiscourse and interpellation

In one of the earliest attempts to theorise ideology as discourse, Pêcheux et al. (1979) explored the interconnections between the analysis of language and the assumptions of historical materialism to discuss how ideology is organized and incorporated within social formations. Pêcheux et al. pointed out how ideologies are established and operate within ideological state apparatuses. The later consist ideological mechanisms within which ideologies are organized into ideological formations which contain one or several discursive formations, which determine what can and must be said from a certain position within the social formation. Expressions have meaning in virtue of the discursive formations for meaning is constituted by the relations between the linguistic elements of a given discursive formation. Relations of substitution, synonymity and paraphrase are 'discursive processes' characteristic of such formations, in which meaning of expressions is not stable and fixed, but is continuously produced within these processes by methods of 'slipping', 'sliding', or 'metaphor'. 'Langue' (system of values) is a relatively autonomous system which is governed by internal laws and which provides the common basis for differential discursive processes. The fact that every discursive formation is situated within a structured whole of discursive formations - 'interdiscourse' - and the latter within a complex of ideological formations, remains excluded from the view of the subject, who always finds itself within a particular discursive formation. Forgetting characterizes this exclusion. One important point on the operation of ideological discourse which emphasizes the power of ideology to construct human subject and 'realities', is that of the 'discursive zone'. The 'discursive zone' is an inaccessible to the subject area, as opposed to a 'zone' which lies within the subject's grasp. 'Discursive zone' covers over the process whereby a discursive sequence is produced creating the illusion that the subject precedes discourse. This way it is the subject which is produced or called forth by a discursive sequence, the subject is always already produced by what is preconstructed.

Earlier than Pêcheux et al., Althusser (1971) sustained that ideology interpellates individuals into subjects. More specifically, Althusser pointed out that the functioning of ideology in general as interpellation of individuals into subjects (and specifically into the subjects of their discourse) is realized through the complex ideological formations (specifically through the interdiscourse therein) and provides each subject with its 'reality', that is, with a system of self-evident truths and significations perceived-accepted-submitted to. The imaginary me which is the subject of discourse is constituted through the subject's identification with the discursive formation which dominates it ... the subject cannot recognize this identification-subordination, precisely because the latter occurs under the form of autonomy. The subject 'acts', takes a position in all liberty, but the *prise de position* is merely the effect of the ideological and discursive formations that are exterior to the subject, an exterior which remains excluded from view by the functioning of a 'discursive zone'. Both accounts consist an exemplification of the power of ideology, and to this extent of the power of information, to constitute subjects and social formations. They are also a reminded of the social privilege of dominance assigned to human agents or social entities that control the flow or the generation of information in the form of ideological constructs. Also pointed out is that meaning is not a fixed and undeniable reality, rather a continually changing interpretation of, I would add, a dynamic informational activity.

3.1.10 Summary

Information constructs systems of ideologies, which are expressed through language and which, in turn, affect human behaviour and consequently construct human subjects and make up social 'reality'. It is particularly important to stress here that in the process of the [informational] construction of the social, it is information which stands at the core of creation.

It is then of critical importance to recognize not only the mode, but more significantly, to investigate and map the code through which informational units compose ideological structures. It is, therefore, suggested here, that there exists the need for a further in-depth analysis of the ways in which information organizes, and is organized within, ideologies and of the ways in which the later operate and organize themselves. This is a task undertaken in philosophical detail throughout the statement of the theoretical approximations of this book. I also maintain here that, because ideologies are based on units of information, somehow systematically organized, elements of the structural composition and architectural organization of the system of information are reflected in the various analyses of ideology. To stress the various aspects of ideologies as information based constructions I have provided above a brief discussion of studies on the organization and function of ideologies. A list of the main points discussed is provided in the concluding section at the end of the chapter.

Having examined how ideological structures are organized and operate supports and enhances our view of how systematically but partially organized units of information can generate and reproduce values, beliefs and practices as cultural prototypes. But how does the very character of ideologies, its structures and modes of deployment change under the intensified conditions of information economies I've described here. More than ever, in the era of digital communications and technologies, through explicit forms of linguistic expression, the dominant system of information configures a chaotic culture of intensification of everything, that is, postmodernity and whatever lies beyond that. The experience of the informational [or digital] practice and action within this postmodern landscape is discussed next. It presents severe effects for, and calls for reconsiderations of, our modernist background, accumulated knowledge and ways of thinking.

3.2 IN SEARCH OF POSTMODERNITY-AND-BEYOND

Postmodern writers — novelists and filmakers and software writers as well as social theorists - have been fascinated by the degraded landscape of schlock and kitsch. Materials no longer simply quote, but incorporate into their very substance. Theories of the postmodern bring to us news of the arrival and inauguration of a whole new type of society. Postmodernism should be grasped not as a style but as a cultural dominant. Postmodern theory tries to identify the features of postmodernism and is not about a unified or a coherent set of positions. An initial distinction can be made between modernity conceptualized as the modern age and postmodernity as an epochal term for the period that follows modernity.

My view is that we are now at a mutated phase past postmodernity which I often refer to as 'postmodernity-and-beyond'. I find inadequate though to realize and think of postmodernity-and-beyond and modernity as sequential stages one following the other. I see postmodernity-and-beyond as, not a substantially separate age rather an intensification and amplification of certain social elements and discourses - not necessarily a phase within modernity - mainly related and developed around the concept of information. The dynamics by which modernity produced a new industrial and colonial world have been described as modernization and refer to processes of individualization, secularization, industrialization, cultural differentiation, commodification, urbanization, and rationalization.

The term 'postmodernity' refers to a variety of economic, political, social and cultural processes of change and transformation that are producing a new postmodern society. Technologies, new forms of knowledge, and changes in the socio-economic system are producing a postmodern social formation: novel types of information, knowledge and technologies, increased capital penetration and homogenization and cultural fragmentation, and new modes of experience of space and time. Defenders of modernist theory attack postmodern relativism, irrationalism and nihilism, and in return postmodern theory provides a critique of representation and the modern belief that theory mirrors reality, and rejects modern assumptions of social coherence and notions of casuality in favour of multiplicity, plurality, fragmentation and indeterminacy (Best and Kellner, 1991).

In the following sections I provide a brief account of some of the most notable postmodern positions in an attempt to map the cultural landscape of postmodernity. The focus is on early postmodern theories which pointed to the observable changes in the discourse of modernity and foresaw the deconstruction of traditional societies, as well as, on more recent theoretical positions that turned towards language, signs, and images: Foucault's archaeology of knowledge and technologies of the self, Deleuze and Guattari 's schizos, rhizomes and nomads, Baudrillard's 'hell of the same', and Lyotard's desire and discourse. The discussion of these postmodern positions is concluded with a more extensive reference to Jameson's theorization of postmodernism as the broad cultural logic of capitalism and Poster's 'mode of information'.

3.2.1 Early postmodern notions

The ambiguity of the new postmodern world was long ago described as a world that offers man everything or nothing (Rosenberg & White, 1957) and some believed that the postmodern world would see the end of poverty and ignorance, the decline of the nation state, the end of ideology, and a worldwide process of modernization (Drucker, 1957). C. Wright Mills (1959) claimed that we are at the end of The Modern Age and that our basic definitions of society and of self are being overtaken by new realities in a society of cheerful robots. The postmodern world-view is characterized by conceptual shifts and asserts that reality is unordered and ultimately unknowable (Smith, 1982). 'What we should look out for as significant are the differences rather than the similarities, the elements of discontinuity rather than the elements of continuity' (Barraclough, 1964). As Bell (1976a; 1976b) interpreted it, the postmodern age is the age of the unleashing of instinct, impulse and will. He also argued that the postmodern age exhibits an extension of the rebellious, antibourgeois, antinomic and hedonistic impulses which he saw as the legacies of modernist movements in the arts and their bohemian subcultures, which in turn are responsible for the undermining of traditional values and culture and the production of what he defined as the cultural contradictions of capitalism.

Some critics conceptualize the postmodern as an intensification of the modern, as a hypermodernity, a new face of modernity or a postmodern development within modernity. Pro-1980s postmodern discourses (Drucker, Etzioni, Sontag, Hassan, Fielder, Ferre, Toynbee, Mills, Bell, Baudrillard) reproduced optimistic liberating features of postmodernism and replicated the idea of Galbraith's 'affluent society', the 'end of ideology' and Mills' 'Great American celebration', or, reflected a pessimistic take on the trajectories of modern societies. New social theories emerged to articulate the sense of dynamic change, analyzing the new forms of mass culture, the consumer society, technology, and modernized urbanization. Poststructuralism assaulted the premises and assumptions of structuralist thought. It stressed the dimensions of history, politics and everyday life in the contemporary world which tended to be suppressed by the abstractions of the structuralist project, whereas structuralism deployed holistic analyses, defining interrelations of parts of a common system, and stressing the derivativeness of subjectivity and meaning as a socio-linguistic product.

Both structuralists and poststructuralists abandoned the subject, the later arguing about the emergence of subjectivity in the entrance of the individual into the symbolic of language (Lacan), or the interpellation of individuals in ideology (Althusser). Postmodern theory generally follows poststructuralist theory. Both structuralists and poststructuralists developed theories which analyzed culture and society in terms of sign systems and their codes and discourses. Discourse theory analyses social phenomena as structured semiotically by codes and rules and argues that 'meaning' is socially constructed. Much postmodern theory follows discourse theory in assuming that, it is language, signs, images and signifying systems which organize the psyche, society and everyday life. This is a position adopted throughout in this book. More specifically, as it has been argued already, the theoretical approximations proposed in the current project focus on the underlying system of information, the source of language, signs and images. Furthermore, this book attempts to provide a model of analysis of the code (organization) of the system of information and suggests that this can be applied, in an adaptive, dynamic and flexible mode, to assist in the analysis of any information based system. For the moment let us look at some of the most influential postmodern theories and how these have attempted to describe the postmodern condition. Wherever applicable I will be discussing how some theoretical concepts relate to the philosophical thinking of this book.

3.2.2 Archaeology of knowledge and technologies of the self

Foucault (1972; 1973; 1975; 1982; 1986; 1988) provided a critique of modernity, rejecting the equation reason-emancipation-progress, and argued that an interface between modern forms of power and knowledge has served to create new forms of domination. He argued that human experiences are discursively (re)constituted through the scientific frames of reference of social institutions, discourses, and practices of modern knowledge (Foucault, 1973). He attempted to de-centre the subject as a constituted rather than a constituting consciousness and followed Nietzsche's (1967) perspectivism in that, since there are only interpretations of the world, there are multiple and endless interpretations of phenomena. In a similar fashion this book maintains that there can only be theoretical approximations to the quest for the 'truth' and consequently there can be multiple variations and alternatives of 'truth' and 'reality'.

Developing an archaeology of knowledge Foucault attempted to identify the determining rules of formation of discursive rationality that operate beneath the level of intention. He described how modern philosophy constructs [hu]Man within a series of unstable doublets (cogito/unthought, retreat-and-the-return-of-the-origin, transcendental/empirical) and he anticipated the 'death of man'. He adopted the discourse of discontinuity as a positive working concept and rejected totalities and conceptions of a centered subject to end up in the field of discursive formations, complex systems of dispersions. In a transition from archaeology to genealogy, Foucault described different institutional powers (disciplinary techniques, surveillance measures, examinations, and 'normalizing judgment') that form the soul, body and subject. Discipline, a specific technique of power 'makes' individuals, leads them to normalization, to the elimination of all social and psychological irregularities and the production of useful and docile subjects through a refashioning of minds and bodies. He identified bio-power in two modalities, 'an anatomo-politics of the human body' and the 'species body'. Foucault rejected rationalization and introduced 'analytics', a postmodern theory of modern power, which emphasized the highly differentiated nature of modern society and the 'heteromorphous' power mechanisms that operate independent of conscious subjects. For Foucault, power is diffused throughout the social field, colonizing the body itself, utilizing the forces while inducing obedience and conformity. He believed that power is contingent and vulnerable and that knowledge can transform us. Discourse and bio-struggle are intended to facilitate the development of new forms of subjectivity and values. The highly differentiated nature of the world society it has been already indicated in this book is due to the disorderly flow of the system of information. Foucault's diffusion and colonization of power, his belief that knowledge can transform human beings, his discourse and bio-struggle, I maintain, can be understood as expressions of the dynamics and mechanics of this system of information. These attributes are further discussed in the proposed model of analysis as being distinctive fractal discourses.

It is also worth mentioning Foucault's shift from technologies of domination (subjects dominated and objectified through discourses and practices) to technologies of the self (individuals create their own identities through ethics and self-constitution). Foucault defined 'technologies of the self' as practices 'which permit individuals to effect by their own means or with the help of others a certain number of operations on their own bodies and souls, thoughts and conduct, and way of being, so as to transform themselves in order to attain a certain state of happiness, purity, wisdom, perfection, or immortality'. He argued that, ethics is the relation an individual has with itself, it is then the deliberate component of free activity and the basis for a prolonged practice of the self whereby one seeks to problematize and master one's desires and to constitute oneself as a free self. The task is not to discover oneself, rather to continually produce oneself.

3.2.3 Schizos, rhizomes and nomads

Deleuze and Guattari (1983; 1987) provided a provocative critique of modernity's discourses and institutions. They attacked modernity for repressing desire and proliferating fascist subjectivities that haunt even revolutionary movements. Radical change, they argued, will come through the liberation of desire, in a new postmodern mode of existence where individuals will overcome repressive identity and stasis to become nomads in a constant process of becoming and transformation. Deleuze and Guattari sought to theorize the decoding of libidinal flows initiated by the dynamics of capitalist economy. They focused on the colonization of desire by various modern discourses and institutions, and pursued a schizoanalytic destruction of the ego and superego in favor of a dynamic unconscious. Deleuze and Guattari's later nomadic thought attacked the philosophical imperialism of 'state-thought'. Deleuze focused on criticizing identity logic and privileging the pre-representational realms of bodies and their intensities over representational schemes of meaning, attempting to build a theory of desire and a new postmodern philosophy of difference. I will maintain here that the concept of desire in Deleuze and Guattari's does in fact reflect the dominant system of information under modernity. The colonization of desire is analogous to the colonization of system of information by the institutions of modernity and the correct tactic I will agree, is indeed the schizoanalytic collapse of rational interrelations of the system of information, in favour of more dynamic and uncontrolled formations.

Deleuze and Guattari attempted to subvert barriers to 'desiring-production' in order to create new postmodern schizo-subjects who unscramble the codes of modernity and become reconstituted as nomadic desiring-machines. 'Desire operates in the domain of free synthesis where everything is possible' (Deleuze and Guattari, 1983) pursuing 'nomadic and polyvocal' rather than 'segregative and biunivocal' flows. As Deleuze (Deleuze and Parnet, 1987) defined it, desire 'is the system of signifying signs with which fluxes of the inconspicuous are produced in a social field'. Territorialization is the process of repressing desire by taming and confining its productive energies whereas 'deterritorialization' or 'decoding' is the unchaining of both material production and desire from socially restricting forces. I will once more point out here the parallelism between these two processes of territorialization and deterritorialization and the various exercised tensions for social control of the system of information and of attempts for a free flow of information respectively. Keeping that in mind, Deleuze and Guattari's account becomes an analysis of the system of information. For Deleuze and Guattari, there are three fundamental types of social machines, each being a different system for representing and regulating the production of goods, needs, and desire. Succeeding the 'primitive territorial machine' and the 'despotic machine', is the 'capitalist machine'. Capitalism, in a double movement of liberation and alienation to produce abstract labour and abstract desire, subverts all traditional codes, simultaneously recoding everything within the abstract logic of equivalence (reterritorializing them within the state, family, law, commodity logic, banking systems, consumerism, psycho-analysis and other normalizing institutions). Capitalism re-channels desire and needs, the most significant example of capitalist deterritorialization being the production of the schizophrenic. The method whereby Deleuze and Guattari analyzed the production and circulation of desire in society was termed schizoanalysis, organized around plurality, multiplicity and de-centeredness. They refer to the deterritorialized body as the 'body-without-organs', a body without organization, able to be reconstituted in new ways.

Deleuze and Guattari (1987) deploy the concept of rhizome for the deterritorialized movement. They use a triadic scheme of 'rigid lines, supple lines, and lines of escape' (spatial, material, and psychological components that constitute or deconstitute a society, group, or individual), and a pattern of 'lines of intensities' (schizoanalysis, rhizomatics, pragmatics, diagrammatism, cartography, micropolitics) which react upon the flow of everyday life. I will argue that the proposed scheme of lines and intensities is indicative of the inner chaotic organization of the flow of the system of information. A detailed typology of these inner tensions within the system of information is developed in the statement of my theoretical approximations in later chapters. Rhizomatics intends to uproot philosophical trees and their first principles to deconstruct binary logic, it designates the decentred lines that constitute multiplicities. Rhizomes are non-hierarchical systems of deterritorialized lines they are always in the middle of dynamic movement, they form multiplicities lacking any identity or essence. All of reality is constituted as multiplicities; unities, hierarchies, and structures are only colonized rhizomes. Rhizomatics is a form of nomadic thought. For Deleuze and Guattari the schizo, rhizome and nomad, are all variations on the postmodern theme: schizos withdraw from repressive social reality into disjointed desiring states, nomads roam freely across open planes in small bands, and rhizomes are deterritorialized lines of desire linking desiring bodies with one another and the field of partial objects. I will point out that the context of the interrelationships developed among the schizo, the rhizome and the nomad are indicative of alternating spatial coordinates generated by the organizational re-arrangements of sub-units of the system of information in question.

3.2.4 The 'hell of the same'

Baudrillard's metaphysics and nihilistic cynicism introduced a theory of commodification of everyday life under capitalism. It is worth paying particular attention to Baudrillard's theoretical considerations as a great part of them, such as of symbolic exchange, fractal value, simulacra, hyperreality, and implosion, are extensively used in the philosophical considerations of the current book. According to Baudrillard (1996), the new social order is dominated by the new system of objects, a new form of hypercivilization. Exchange is being conducted through symbolic transactions but its value emerges with capitalism. Commodities are valued by the way that they confer prestige and signify social status and power, as: use value (utility of objects), exchange value (monetary worth, commercial value), and statutory value ('sign value'). For Baudrillard, the system of political economy rationalizes objects and needs, producing a system of objects and a rationalized subject which reproduces the system of labour and consumption through satisfying its needs. Baudrillard suggested that symbolic exchange provides a mode of activity that is more radically subversive of the values and logic of capitalism.

In his theory all practices and signs are controlled by and absorbed into the almighty code. 'Simulation is no longer that of a territory, a referential being or a substance. It is the generation by models of a real without origins or reality: a hyperreal' (Baudrillard, 1983a:2). According to Baudrillard, we are in a new era of simulation in which computerization, information processing, media, cybernetic control systems, and the organization of society according to simulation codes and models replace production as the organizing principle of society. The postmodern era of simulations is an era of information and signs governed by models, codes, and cybernetics. Baudrillard describes 'the passage from a metallurgic into a semiurgic society' (Baudrillard, 1981), in which signs take on a life of their own and constitute a new social order structured by models, codes and signs. Using McLuhan's concept of implosion, he claims that in the postmodern world the boundary between image or simulation and reality implodes, and with it the very experience and ground of 'the real' disappears. 'Hyperreality points to a blurring of distinctions between the real and the unreal in which the prefix 'hyper' signifies more real than real whereby the real is produced according to a model'. The hyperreal for Baudrillard is a condition whereby models replace the real. The theory of implosion describes a process of social entropy leading to a collapse of boundaries, including the implosion of meaning in the media and the implosion of media and the social in the masses (Baudrillard, 1983b). The apathetic masses thus become a sullen silent majority in which all meaning, messages, and solicitations implode as if sucked into 'a black hole'. Baudrillard's universe of simulacra seems to be without boundaries and in a vertiginous flux; an undifferentiated flux of simulacra, in which reality vanishes altogether in a haze of images and signs.

Baudrillard (1984a; 1984b) contends that, signs and images function as mechanisms of control within contemporary culture. Power mutates into 'the dead power of floating signs'. Baudrillard opposes 'seduction' as an aristocratic 'order of sign and ritual' to the bourgeois ideal of production and valorizes artifice, appearance, play and challenge against the deadly serious labour of production. Baudrillard sees postmodernity as a 'second revolution', as the process of the destruction of meaning. The postmodern world is devoid of meaning; it is a universe of nihilism, where everything is 'obscene', visible, explicit, transparent, and always in motion. Signs of dead meaning and frozen forms mutate into new combinations and permutations of the same. 'Melancholy' is the quality inherent in the mode of disappearance of meaning, in the mode of volatilization of meaning in operational systems. Whereas initially I agree with Baudrillard in the destruction of meaning, I will point out that the meaning of the concept of 'meaning' is questionable, and I will suggest that beyond postmodernity we are dealing with 'relations of meaning' that do not necessarily obey to human logic justifications. In this sense, notions such as, 'meaningless', 'no-meaning' and so forth are in fact new forms of 'meaning', in other words, of accepted logical justifications.

According to Baudrillard then, after the destruction of meaning and the referentials and finalities of modernity, postmodernism is described as a response to emptiness and anguish which is oriented toward 'the restoration of past culture'. Playing the pieces, that is postmodern. For Baudrillard, objects have surpassed their limits and have eluded control by subjects. He sees a reversal of the respective roles of the subject and the object, where the subject has lost the battle to dominate the object. The subject has been defeated, the reign of objects has commenced; we become more like things, like objects, we should therefore adopt the 'fatal strategies' of objects (Baudrillard, 1996). A fatal strategy pursues a course of action or trajectory to its extreme, attempting to surpass its limits, to go beyond its boundaries. Proliferation of information in the media, cells in cancer, sex in pornography, and the masses in contemporary society are all fatal strategies whereby objects proliferate, metastasize to extremes, and in going beyond all hitherto conceivable limits produce something new and different. This is the 'end of history' and the beginning of the history of simulation, where we face the eternal recurrence of the 'Hell of the Same'. Baudrillard's transaesthetics postulates a new stage of simulacra, a new stage of value, what he claims a new fractal stage of value, where there is no referent at all. It is about a fractal multiplication of body images in which individuals can combine any number of models into a new body that erases previous divisions of race, class, gender, or specific looks. We are currently in what he calls 'the post-orgy state of things', 'the time of transvestim', after everything is liberated, everything is possible, utopia is realized.

Notably the current book attempts to continue the Baudrillardian philosophical journey beyond the stage of implosion and through the fractalization of social life emphasizing on the concept of information as the primary unit of analysis. Furthermore, it attempts to provide a theoretical background as to what happens during this 'post-orgy state of things' and how the global system of information organizes and is organized by digital environments and informational exchanges of communication. I maintain that the organization of information is manifested in social structure, discourse, culture and human information processing, and that the proposed model of theoretical approximations can be used as a [temporal] starting point of social theory and social response in what I would call, 'the digital reconstruction of hyperreality'.

3.2.5 Desire and paganism

The postmodern, says Lyotard, simply indicates a mood, or better a state of mind (Lyotard, 1986). The 'status of knowledge is altered as societies enter what is known as the postindustrial age and culture enters what is known as the postmodern age' (Lyotard, 1984). Lyotard (1971; 1974) developed a 'philosophy of desire', what he called 'energetics' in which he defended the claims of the senses and experience over abstractions and concepts. Desire for Lyotard, in what Freud called the primary processes (that is, direct, libidinal, unconscious, instinctual processes governed by the pleasure principle), finds direct expression in figures of displacement, condensation, and metaphoric transformation. Discourse, which follows what Freud described as secondary processes (those governed by reality) is more abstract, rationalized, and conventional than the figures of desire. For Lyotard, images in contemporary society are the very figure of pulsating desire. He affirmed the free flowing of life energies and advocated the 'tensor' which generates libidinal effects. The notion is similar to what Deridda called 'dissemination' and Kristeva 'semiosis', except that Lyotard's libidinal economy is more interested in the proliferation and intensification of libidinal effects. I maintain that Lyotard's notions of 'desire' and 'discourse' are indicative of the communicational tensions of the system of information for local association and external interaction. A detailed description of these informational trends is given in later part of the book and in the context of the proposed theoretical approximations.

Lyotard called for ways of speaking differently since the enemy is masculine metalanguage (that is, totalizing theory that empowers and legitimates masculine and class rule), and he attacked 'grand' or 'little' narratives'. 'Paganism' (or postmodern) breaks with the modern concern for truth and certainty. Lyotard described 'paganism' as the denomination of a situation in which one judges without criteria, the condition of no assigned addressee and no regulating ideal (Lyotard and Thébaud, 1985). Lyotard used the term the postmodern condition to describe the condition as incredulity toward metanarratives, any form of totalizing thought. Lyotard championed dissensus over consensus, diversity and dissent over conformity and consensus, and heterogeneity and the incommensurable over homogeneity and universality. I will point out that these are also traits which I propose to be characteristic of the organization of the system of information. Most notably, I will mention at this point that a synchronized complex condition of homogenous heterogeneity and heterogenous homogeneity is what characterizes the core of the system of information.

3.2.6 The cultural logic of late capitalism

Jameson (1984) theorized postmodernism as a broad cultural logic and tried to connect it to the economic system of late capitalism. He saw 'the whole global, yet American postmodern culture [as] the internal and superstructural expression of a whole new wave of American military and economic domination throughout the world' (Jameson, 1984). Postmodernism, argued Jameson, signals a number of cultural shifts, including the breakdown of a firm distinction between high and low culture, the canonization and cooptation of modernist works, the near-total commodification of culture, the end of the problematics of anxiety, alienation, and bourgeois individualism in the radical fragmentation of subjectivity, a debilitating presentism, and, the emergence of a disorienting postmodern hyperspace. Jameson's theory of postmodernism draws upon Mandel's (1975) 'Late Capitalism' which argued that the present consumer or postindustrial phase of capitalist development in fact represents a purer, more developed and more realized form of capitalism. Jameson claimed that each stage of capitalism has a corresponding cultural style: realism, modernism, and postmodernism are the cultural levels of market capitalism, monopoly capitalism and multinational capitalism. I will agree with Jameson in that there have been different degrees of intensification of the informationalization of social life under each of these times, the exemplification of which has been evident in cultural forms and socio-economic movements. The claim that postmodernism is a cultural dominant means that countervailing logics and tendencies still prevail in a complex 'force-field'. In Jameson's new spatial disorientation in postmodern society, subjects are unable to position themselves individually and collectively within the new decentred communication networks of capitalism. He called for a new postmodern aesthetics and politics of 'cognitive mapping'. The general concern of cognitive mapping is grasping capitalist society as a systemic whole. Jameson's contextualization of postmodernism as a new cultural logic of capitalism is discussed below in more detail. It provides a valuable insight to the postmodern condition of images, simulacra, fragmentation, pastiche, and schizophrenia as the culture of late capitalism. Many of these concepts are core to the philosophical considerations of the current book and Jameson's analysis provides some socio-historical background and logical justification to their contemporary use.

In the *The Cultural Logic of Late Capitalism* Jameson (1991) argued that, aesthetic production has become integrated into commodity production generally. Postmodernism and modernism for Jameson still remain utterly distinct in their meaning and social function. It was only in the light of some conception of a dominant cultural logic or hegemonic norm that genuine difference could be measured and assessed. The concepts of 'anxiety' and 'alienation' are no more longer acceptable in the world of the postmodern. The dissapearance of the individual subject, along with its formal consequence, the increasing unavailability of the personal style, engender the well-nigh universal practice today of what may called 'pastiche' (the imitation of a peculiar or unique, idiosyncratic style, the wearing of a linguistic mask, speech in a dead language). If the ideas of a ruling class were once the dominant (or hegemonic) ideology of bourgeois society, the advanced capitalist countries today, Jameson argued, are now a field of stylistic and discursive heterogeneity without a norm. They continue to inflect the economic strategies which constrain our existences, but they no longer need to impose their speech, the absence of any great collective project. The imitation of dead styles, speech through all the masks and voices stored up in the imaginary museum of a now global culture. There is a random cannibalization of all the styles of the past, the increasing primacy of the 'neo'. It is at least compatible with addiction, a world tranformed into sheer images of itself and for pseudoevents and 'spectacles'; Jameson reserves Plato's conception of the 'simulacrum', the identical copy for which no original has ever existed. The culture of the simulacrum comes to life in a society where exchange value has been generalized to the point at which the very memory of use value is effaced. The past as 'referent' finds itself gradually bracketed, and then effaced altogether, leaving us with nothing but texts. There is an insensible colonization of the present by the nostalgia mode; we are now, in intertextuality as a deliberate, built-in feature of the aesthetic effect. The setting has been strategically framed, with great ingenuity, to eschew most of the signals that normally convey the contemporaneity of the United States in its multicultural era. This approach to the present by way of the art language of the simulacrum, or of the pastiche of the stereotypical past, endows present reality and the openess of present history with the spell and distance of a glossy message. It demonstrates a situation in which we seem increasingly incapable of fashioning representations of our own current experience.

The postmodern force field is characterized by the temporal organization of a culture increasingly dominated by space and spatial logic. To describe this organizational logic Jameson refers to Lacan's description of schizophrenia. Schizophrenia was described by Lacan as a breakdown in the signifying chain, that is, the interlocking syntagmatic series of signifiers which constitutes an utterance or a meaning. In his conception of the signifying chain, meaning on the new view is genreated by the movement from signifier to signifier. What is generally called the signified - the meaning or conceptual content of an utterance - is now rather to be seen as a meaning-effect, as that objective mirage of signification generated and projected by the relationship of signifiers among themselves. With the breakdown of the signifying chain, therefore, the schizophrenic is reduced to an experience of pure material signifiers, or, in other words, a series of pure and unrelated presents in time. The breakdown of temporality suddenly releases this present of time from all the activities and intentionalities that might focus it and make it a space or praxis; thereby isolated, that present suddenly engulfs the subject with undescribable vividness, which effectively dramatizes the power of the material signifier in isolation. This present of the world or material signifier comes before the subject with heightened intensity, bearing a mysterious charge of affect, here described in the negative terms of anxiety and loss of reality, and in the positive terms of euphoria, a high, an intoxicatory or hallucinogenic intesity. Discontinuities are disjoined sentences of some more unified global meaning. In photorealism, which looked like a return to representation, objects were not to be found in the 'real world'; the 'realism' of the photorealist painting is not the simulacrum. Jameson, characterized the postmodernist experience of form as the proposition that difference relates. It turns out to be a text, whose reading proceeds by differentiation rather than by unification. It takes the form of an impossible imperative to achieve that new mutation in what can perhaps no longer be called consciousness. A final analysis of that euphoria or those intensities which seem so often to characterize the newer cultural experience. The privileged space of the newer art is radically antianthropomorphic. The simulacrum's peculiar function lies in what Sartre would have called the 'derealization' of the whole surrounding world of everyday reality.

Mandel (1975) argued that there have been three fundamental moments in capitalism: market capitalism, the monopoly stage or the stage of imperialism, and our own postindustrial or multinational, capital. The late or multinational or consumer capitalism constitutes the purest form of capital yet to have emerged. A new and historically original penetration and colonization of Nature and the Unconscious takes place with the rise of the media and the advertising industry. Therefore, said Jameson, our own period may be described as the Third Machine Age. It would seem logical that the relationship to and the representation of the machine could be expected to shift dialectically. The technology of our own moment no longer possesses this same capacity for representation. Television articulates nothing but rather implodes, carrying its flattened surface within itself. Such machines are indeed machines of reproduction which make very different demands on our capacity for aesthetic representation: a whole technology of the production and reproduction of the simulacrum. Jameson suggested that our faulty representations of some immense communicational and computer network are themselves but a distorted figuration of something even deeper, namely, the whole world system of a present-day multinational capitalism. The technology of today is grasping a network of power and control: the whole new decentered global network of the third stage of capital itself. This is a figural process presently best observed in a whole mode of contemporary entertainment literature - high-tech paranoia - in which the circuits and networks of some putative global computer hookup are narratively mobilized by labyrinthine conspiracies of autonomous but deadly interlocking and competing information agencies in a complexity often beyond the capacity of the normal reading mind. Jameson argues that we do not yet posess the perceptual equipment to match this new hyperspace, in part because our perceptual habits were formed in that older kind of space, the space of high modernism. I will maintain here, though, that, the fact that we as humans and as users of computer and digital communication technologies do interact with this new hyperspace so there must exist a perceptual context within which this interaction takes place. I will argue that this common perceptual context between human and computer information processing presents common elements of organization and operation with common denominator here being the system of information upon which both human and machine agents base their existence. As Jameson pointed out, the newer architecture of hyperpsace stands like an imperative to grow new organs, to expand our sensorium and our body to some new, yet unimaginable, perhaps ultimately impossible, dimensions. A dialectical intensification of the autoreferentiality of all modern culture, which tends to turn upon itself and designate its own cultural production as its content. Complementary, spatial experience and a 'return of the repressed' is involved. This latest mutation in space - postmodern hyperspace - is transcending the capacities of the individual human body to locate itself, to organize its immediate surroundings perceptually, and cognitively to map its position in a mapable external world. Jameson believed that it may now be suggested that this alarming disjunction point between the body and its built environment, can itself stand as the symbol, the great global multinational and decentered communicational network in which we find ourselves caught as individual subjects.

The cultural dominant of the logic of late capitalism, argued Jameson, can be grasped in two different ways. Firstly, moral judgements, referring to which it is indifferent whether they are positive or negative, and, secondly, a genuinely dialectical attempt to think our present of time in History. The logic of simulacrum, with its transformation of older realities into television images, does more than merely replicate the logic of late capitalism: it reinforces and intensifies it. The topic of the lesson is, of course, the historical development of capitalism itself and the deployment of a specific burgeois culture. Two questions are suggested. Can we in fact identify some moment of truth within the more evident moments of falsehood of postmodern culture? Does it not tend to demobilize us and to surrender us to passivity and helplessness by systematically obliterating possibilities of action under the impenetrable fog of historical inevitability? What we have been calling postmodernism summarizes Jameson, and I will agree, is inseparable from, and unthinkable without the hypothesis of, some fundamental mutation of the sphere of culture in the world of late capitalism, which includes a momentous modification of its social function. A different language would call the 'semiautonomy' of the cultural realm: this semiautonomy of the cultural sphere which has been destroyed by the logic of late capitalism. That distance in general has very precisely been abolished in the new space of postmodernism; our postmodern bodies are bereft of spatial coordinates. It is precisely this whole extraordinarily demoralizing and depressing original new global space which is the 'moment of truth' of postmodernism. What has been called the postmodernist 'sublime' is only the moment in which this content has become most explicit. The as yet untheorized original space of some new 'world system' of multinational or late capitalism.

In summary, Jameson's discussion gives a graphic representation of the cultural characteristics of the postmodern condition such as the dissapearance of the individual subject, the universal practice of 'pastiche', the dominance of the simulacrum, the emergence of 'difference' as the dominant interrelational form, the distrortion of our representations, the spatial floating of the human subject within hyperspace. I will point out here, once more, that this culture is the result of the intensification of the flow of information globally with the advance of media and digital communication technologies. Digital culture is organized around new emerging forms of electronic [computer] communication which remain at the centre of interest in this book as the spatial environment within which the system of information flows within and dominates social consciousness. Electronically mediated communication has been the focus of Poster (1990) who suggested that the postmodern world is now in 'the mode of information'. His main points and arguments are briefly discussed next.

3.2.7 The mode of information

Poster (1990) focused on electronic communication in the postmodern world as the new language experience, a new highly efficient communication, which to some degree supplements existing forms of sociability but to another extent substitutes for them. The prospect of instant universal information, introduced by electronic media, clearly has profound effects on society, among others, new and unrecognizable community modes in the process of formation in the hyperreal postmodern world. Poster (1990) argued that, the fragility of social networks, afforded by the electronic media, is heightened by a new level of interconnectivity. What may be happening within the postmodern environment said Poster, is that human beings create computers and in turn computers create a new species of humans. Artificial intelligence and human intelligence are doppelgangers, each imitating the other so closely that one scarcely can distinguish them. In agreement with Poster I will be briefly discussing some of main points of his account of the mode of information, that is, his theorization of forms of electronic language in the postmodern condition, which consists a starting point for the philosophical considerations undertaken throughout this book.

Poster pointed out that the metaphorical application of the term virus to computers underlines the possibility that, 'computers are so profoundly interconnected that they may behave like parts of a body'. Computer viruses spotlight the fragility of society in Poster's age of the mode of information. The linguistic dimension of culture needs to be addressed carefully to examine the new technologies which enhance the conduct of social routines to the extent that may reorganize them that they become new events. In order to discern new events or new communications, argued Poster, 'one must problematize the nature of communications in modern society by retheorizing the relation between action and language, behaviour and belief, material reality and culture'. To this end Poster developed a theory of 'the mode of information' to suggest that history may be periodized by variations in the structure of symbolic exchange in stages of the mode of information: face-to-face, orally mediated exchange (symbolic correspondences), written exchanges mediated by print (representation of signs), and, electronically mediated exchange (informational simulations). In the last stage, which Poster considers as an unavoidable context of discursive totalization, electronic stage 'the self is decentered, dispersed, and multiplied in continuous instability'. All signs are now considered information, where information is contrasted with noise or non-meaning. Each method of preserving and transmitting information profoundly intervenes in the network of relationships that constitute a society. What is at stake here, are new language formations that alter significantly the network of social relations, that restructure those relations and the subjects they constitute. Electronic mediation complicates the transmission of language and subverts the subject. Events have come to exist only in their reproduction. To copy an original, means, in the mode of information to create simulacra. The electronic mediation of information subverts the autonomous, rational subject for whom language is a direct translation of reality, an abyss of indeterminate exchanges between subject and object. When Foucault (1972) wrote that [hu]man is dead, Poster suggested that, he registered the disorientation of the subject in the mode of information. In electronically mediated communications, subjects now float, suspended between points of objectivity, being constituted and reconstituted in different configurations in relation to the discursive arrangement of the occasion. I will stress here that this happens because subjects in electronic or digital communications lose their physical dimension and become informational entities subject to the organization of the information that reproduces them.

Poster noted how the representational character of language has become fragile and problematic. The relation of word and thing is complicated by the loss of the referent, followed, in linguistic change, by 'the formation of simulacra'. Mechanisms of self-referentiality sustain today's meaning, pointing to the crisis of representation, which derives from the information explosion and the new communicational structures. Language is a figurative, structuring power that constitutes the subject who speaks as well as the one that is spoken to. What, electronically mediated communication does, suggested Poster, is to upset the relation of the subject to the symbols it emits or receives and to reconstitute this relation in new shapes. Therefore, in the mode of information it becomes increasingly difficult for the subject to distinguish a 'real'. What we are confronted by is a generalized destabilization of the subject, what Deleuze and Guattari, called 'rhizomic' nomads, where the subject is disrupted, subverted and dispersed across social space. Poster argued that critical social theory requires an epistemological overhaul - a self-reflexive recontextualization - since the rational subject no longer serves as a ground or frame, and the new language subvert referentiality, thereby acting upon the subject and constituting it in new and different ways. Poster chose discontinuity over continuity, the newness of the new over the oldness of the new. Doing so, Poster believed that, the prospects may be furthered for defining structures of domination and the process through which they may be disrupted, in the mode of information.

The new technologies, Poster pointed out, advance considerably the reproducibility of information and introduce significant changes in the social order, most significantly the domination of the human subject. Cybernetics is a tool designed for technocrats better to manage what is seen as a chaotic society. As Wiener (1954:17) noted: 'the purpose of Cybernetics [is] to develop a language and techniques that will enable us indeed to attack the problem of control and communication in general'. In the *Dialectic of Enlightenment*, Horkheimer and Adorno (1972) argued that science is associated with domination, the domination of nature. When scientific epistemology is adopted in the social/cultural field, what Horkheimer and Adorno termed 'the culture industry', then, human beings become the subject of domination and science becomes ideology. Marcuse's (1960) critique of science assumed a dualist world of subjects in which science objectifies subjects and thus becomes ideological. Weber's analysis of the spread of instrumental action conceptualized the inconceivable: a social system that is at once rational and irrational in its core. Habermas asserted the rise of the interventionist state and the entry of science into industry limit the cogency of the socialist position. Future progress, argued Habermas, depends on removing restrictions on communication, a new form of legitimate action that he terms 'the ideal speech situation'. The conditions of the ideal speech situation are that individuals seek consensus by adhering to the universal validity claims of truth, rightness, and truthfulness in symmetrical or equal relationships. The conditions for the exchange of symbols between individuals not their actions, argued Poster, become now the subject of theory. Quite often such exchanges are dictated and regulated by the global mass media.

The global media are regulating mechanisms who transmit, what Luchman (1976) defined as, reduced complexity. The media are systems of communication that structure an unknown group of receivers that have, in other words, an abstract audience. In this case the media are centers of information, distributing discourses and images to a broad public. The media, in this definition, are systems of cultural transmission without ties to any community they are emitters of signals received by a tele-anomic society. Meyrowitz (1985) contended that the media's peculiar relation to its audience drastically rearranges the social order. For Meyrowitz the media are making possible asynchronous 'gatherings' of heterogeneous populations, they consist, types of social settings that include and exclude, unite or divide people in particular ways. The electronic media do alter time-space parameters of social interactions. Visions of McLuhan's 'global village' are 'in principle' a technical possibility. Electronically mediated conversation cancels 'contexts', creating new speech situations, make scenarios of conversations by controlling contexts. The mode of information introduces a new language: 'tele-language'. Poster also argued that the media language is contextless, 'monologic' and 'self-referential', meaning that the recipient is structured to constitute his/her own programming schedule from the available offerings. The media must simulate its context and ventriloquize its audience.

Poster examined TV ads as semiotic indices to an emerging new culture. His analysis is an exemplification of how the system of information - expressed in this case in the organized informational units of TV ads - manipulates and reproduces human subjects. Poster's analysis reveals general principles of the organization and function of the system of operation which is the focus of this book. The interpretation of TV ads as signs of the times stresses the relation to the social context. A central theme in the critical literature on the TV ad is its alleged irrational manipulation of the viewer. According to Poster, the goal of the TV ad is to undermine the buyer's residue of rationality, transmuting the instrumental rationality of the exchange into the baser metal of desire for unnecessary consumption. Lears and Fox (1983) argued that in the new consumer culture there is a collapse of meaning through a misuse of language. Althusser took a further step by arguing that the chief effect of ideology is to constitute living individuals as subjects. The TV ad viewer, then, is structured by the ad to recognize himself or herself as a consuming subject. This recognition is at once ideological and a misrecognition since the ad represents the relation of the individual to his or her 'real conditions of existence' as an imaginary one. The ad constitutes the individual as a subject who is able to buy the product, as a subject who labors and earns income that is disposable and as a subject who is able freely to choose to desire the product. Such a subject is of course in an imaginary relation to the capitalist mode of production, a distorted relation in the sense that the subject believes him or herself to be an agent when in fact he or she is constituted by the structure as its bearer. TV ads, summarized Poster, promote a decentered subject which undermines the distinction between science and ideology, true and false consciousness, the real and the imaginary. They are structures without direct referents, invented models of reality that represent nothing but themselves. I would add that they, like many other media texts, consist informational glimpses of the postmodern world shaped by an overload of the system of information, an orgasm of confused meanings and undefined social orientations.

As Baudrillard indicated in his mode of signification, commodities generate desire by merging fantasies with banalities, transforming the structure of language. Normally a sign is associated with a referent in the 'real' world. What happens, said Poster, is that the ad takes the signifier, a word that has no traditional relation with the object being promoted, and attaches it to that object. The commodity is given a semiotic value that is distinct from, indeed out of phase with, its use value and its exchange value. The ad works on the unconscious of the viewer, subliminally hypnotizing the viewer to buy the product. Baudrillard called the collective language of commodity ads the 'code', a language of sign system unique to the mode of information. The all-important link between sign and referent is shattered in what Lefebve called the 'decline of the referentials'. The new mode of signification is characteristic of the mass media: the ability of language to signify, to become the subject and structure of the communication. Poster's argument is that, the ads constitute the viewer in a nonrepresentational, noninstrumental communications mode. Floating signifiers are set in play that convey desirable or undesirable states of being, portrayed in a way that optimizes the attention without critical awareness. An unreal is made real, a set of meanings is communicated that have no meaning. The hyperreal is linguistically created in the TV ad. As Baudrillard contended, and this book agrees, the hyperreal is our 'reality', we live in an 'aesthetic' hallucination of reality. The new language/practice is a cultural creation, incorporating the subject into itself as a dependent spectator, constituting the subject as a consumer. As a language/practice the TV ad substitutes the subject as a spectator/consumer, and also deconstructs the subject as a centered, original agent. The role of the receiver of the message is twofold, one as manipulated, passive, consumerist object of the discourse, another as judge, validator, referent subject of the discourse. Constituted as both object and subject, the viewer is presented with the basic insubstantiality of the subject. Individuals watching TV ads constitute themselves as subject/object of the message.

Poster has been also concerned with the new language situation that is structured by the manipulation of context, the reduction of conversation to monologue, and the self-referentiality of the message. He focused for that purpose to the language of the database as a repository of information, in which, the entire printed corpus is digitally encoded and stored, no resulting 'library' is 'password protected', individuals can use information with no political implications; and, nothing significant is lost. As the digital encoding of printed records in databases is rapidly increasing, it greatly enhances the efficiency of transmission and reproduction of information threatening the principle of private property. In a way the mode of information disrupts the practices of industrial capitalist society. I will maintain that forms of electronic language consist fields of speedy, flexible - and at most of the times – uncontrollable flow of information. If there is a threat, then this comes naturally from the unrestricted flow of possibilities, and if that is the case, then it is not a threat, rather a liberation and escape from domination and subordination from 'meaning' and 'reason'.

The most extreme cases, argued Poster, of this reversal occur with digitally encoded language (computer programs, encyclopedias, books, bank records, and so forth) susceptible to copying and also to corrupting. 'Home networking' as a new technology in which vast information services become available to the home computer, illustrates the problem of the commodification of information. In the home networking information loop, databases generate databases creating, in this context, their own system of expanded reproduction. The distinction between speech and writing raised questions about, the ways by which electronic language (databases) enable and limit the transmission or storage of meaning, and how the distinct social characteristics of electronic language shape the use and impact of databases. The difficulties in comparing electronic language to speech and writing are illustrated, mentioned Poster, in Gidden's work. By implication the social agent is unconscious of the forces that control his/her destiny and incapable of attaining the truth. In addressing the distinction between speech and writing, Giddens preferred the term 'talk' to that of 'speech' because, he argued, talk suggests social activity. What characterizes advanced societies in the 20th century is the emergence of new language experiences that are electronically mediated, fitting easily into the parameters of neither speech nor writing. What typifies advanced societies are language situations which operate at a different register from that of co-present, contextual self-monitoring talk or the ideal speech situation. Poster argued that the introduction of new methods of communication place writing and print in previous fundamental Western experience, and that the mode of information initiates a rethinking of all previous forms of language. Speech is framed by space/time coordinates of dramatic action. Electronic language, does not lend itself to being framed. It is everywhere and nowhere, always and never. It is truly material/immaterial. The differences between speech, writing and electronic language are clarified in relation to the theme of surveillance, a form of power in the mode of information. In association with the rise of electronically mediated languages new forms of power and domination have emerged. They may be interpreted semiologically as a field of signs in which the metadiscourse of the Panopticon is reimposed everywhere. Poster pointed out how today's circuits of communication and the databases they generate, constitute a Superpanopticon, a system of surveillance without walls, windows, towers or guards. Each transaction is recorded, encoded and added to the databases. The Superpanopticon imposes a new language situation relying upon the digital encoding of information, which derives its strength from the degree to which it restricts meaning and eliminates ambiguity or 'noise'. Surveillance by means of digitally encoded information constitutes new subjects by the language employed in databases. Databases constitute individuals by manipulating relationships between bits of information. The discourse of databases, the Superpanopticon, is a means of controlling masses in the postmodern, postindustrial mode of information.

Poster was also interested in the differences in the way the subject is constituted by the process of pre-electroning and electronic writing. Electronic writing, he argued, disperses the subject so that it no longer functions as a center. Following Plato, writing is burdened by the 'disgrace' of being a mere copy of a mental reality. Derrida (1987) intervened with his program of deconstruction to computer writing. Derrida characterized, both the new age and deconstruction as monsters. Like Baudrillard's semiology of commodities and Foucault's discourse on technologies and power, Derrida's textual deconstruction affords new configurations of the subject. All signs contain as their structure, Derrida contended, the possibility of separation from their senders, their speakers, their referents. Once transformed from a mental image into a graphic representation, screen-object and the writing-subject merge into an unsetting simulation of unit. Human beings faces machine in a disquieting relation: in its immateriality the machine mimics the human being. The human being recognizes itself in the uncanny immateriality of the machine. At stake in the theory of the mode of information is not whether the machine is an exact replica of the brain or even superior to it, but whether computer writing puts into question the qualities of subjectivity. The analysis of computer writing as an instance of the mode of information unveils an abrupt change, what may be called the normalization effect. The new forms of subjectivity induced by computer writing quickly are taken for granted, the computer monitor depersonalizes the text, removes all traces of individuality from writing, de-individualizes the graphic mark.

Poster contended that, computer conversations construct a new configuration of the process of self-constitution. The subject is changed in computer communications, dispersed in a postmodern semantic field of time/space, inner/outer, mind/matter. Electronic message services and computer conferencing appear to have definite effects on the subject, that is, playing with identities, degendering communications, destabilizing existing hierarchies in relationships and re-hierarchize communications and above all, dispersing the subject, dislocating it temporally and spatially. In this context the subject is constructed and reproduced as a relational self, with an imaginary identity. The subject is structured into practice, in a reconfiguration of the self-constitution process, in invented subjectivities that may be more 'authentic' than the 'real' self. Electronic interconnectivity is a new form of writing, interaction and communication, of the 'Network Nation' (Hiltz and Turoff (1978), one that further upsets the dominant configuration of the subject/ language 'interface'. As Derrida stated, 'in the years to come ... it can be thought that it will no longer be writing that will be transported, but the perforated card, microfilm, or magnetic tape ... the telepost'.

Scientific knowledge is increasingly implicated in our times, due to the fact that, after the design, the simulation, the modeling of objects, and their production, they are attached to the imaginaries of the consumers. Poster contended that the mode of information disrupts this process, to the extent that it produces a variety of multiple, dispersed, decentered, unstable subjects, in a similar way that Deleuze and Guattari (1987) configured the social as a complex of bodily intensities in a state of continuous nonlinear movement. The logic presented is multidimensional, shifting, and discontinuous. In Deleuze and Guattari's vision of the postmodern world individuals are constituted through their place in the circuit of information flows. A new assemblage is formed within capitalism that reterritorializes the relation of human and machine, a machinic enslavement, where there is nothing but transformations and exchanges of information. Mandelbrot's fractals and Thom's 'catastrophe theory' are 'changing the meaning of the word knowledge, while expressing how such a change can take place. They are producing not the known, but the unknown. Computer technologies play an important role, according to Lyotard, in this context: 'like prosthetic devices, they extend the performativity of the system'.

In summary, Poster's arguments about the 'mode of information' introduce a decentered and dispersed social identity in continuous instability. Traditional networks of communication exchanges and social relations are dramatically changing as their physical dimensions become transparent and they dissolve within an informational ocean of simulated hyperrealities. Poster pointed out the crisis in the representational character of language with the formation of the simulacra and the loss of the referent, therefore of meaning. Examining forms of electronically mediated communication such TV ads, computer databases, electronic writing and computer conversations, Poster illustrated the problem of the commodification of information and pointed out the threat posed by the rise of new forms of power and domination. He stressed on the intensification of symbolic exchange among individuals within a cultural environment of 'reduced complexity' dictated and regulated by the global mass media. The later irrationally manipulate the subjects/viewers and reronstruct them in a non-representational form of hyperreal hallucinations. Poster stressed that the commodification of information through electronic communication raises questions of about emerging normalizing patterns of loss of meaning, new forms power and domination, the quality of reconstructed subjectivities, and the actual new digital configuration of the social and the process of self-constitution in it.

I will extend at this point one of my earlier arguments regarding the possible effects resulting from the interaction between human agents and machines. I will argue that during this communicative interaction, human information processing, much more powerful and dynamic than that of computer technologies, is reflexively being forced to downgrade and to lower to effortless levels of operation in order that this communication exchange take some relation of 'meaning'. In other words, during their interaction with computer technologies, and because the later do not have the self-ability to do so, humans are forced to decrease their potential intelligence skills down to more simplified modes of interaction set by computer operating systems and environments. 'As we develop computer languages', argued Hopcroft (1987), 'we are not simply inventing new discourses but objectifying the human mind'. I propose that there exist similarities and analogies between human and computer information processing as a result of the very attempt to build machines that simulate human beings.

These similarities, I argue, are intensified during our continuously increasing use and interaction with computer technologies. This book attempts to break through our thinking about the code of information and to offer a philosophical proposal as to how the system of information - common in human and non-human systems - may be organizing social experience and creating novel hyperreal environments which we are called to live and occupy respectively.

3.2.8 Summary

The theoretical discussion in this second part of the chapter concentrated in the contemporary cultural environment of postmodernity (or postmodernity-and-beyond as I have defined it). The intensification of the availability and use of information lies at the heart of a worldwide digital culture. Inevitably postmodernity becomes the more general cultural environment which encompasses manifestations of digital culture configurations. In fact, I suggest that postmodernity-and-beyond is the culture of the information explosion which defines the societies of digital capitalism and the rest of the world which has sustained the informational invasion of global media and pressures and attempts to radically transform their structures and socio-political orientations. I have also suggested that the established informational network, produced by the dominant system of information, it is at the same time securing the conditions for the flow of information by reproducing itself through digital regenerations in postmodern hyperspace. Within this hyper-spatial version of logic, human existence is reproduced by terms of digital cloning and mutation. The main arguments and considerations regarding postmodernity are summarized in the closing epilogue that follows.

3.3 EPILOGUE

The current chapter examined the cultural characteristics of the contemporary postmodern world. This is a world dominated by information; this is the world where the code of information predominates, the world of digital technologies and communication. In the first part of the chapter I focused on analyses of the organization and function of ideologies in order to identify how they are organized and operate, but also to indicate the structural composition and architectural organization of information within these systems. The main points of this discussion are summarized below:

On the informational content of ideologies:

- Ideologies are informational constructions, generated by informational flows, formed in systematic but partially organized contexts; as such, they are vulnerable to transformation, alterations and mutations like any informational system.

- Systems of ideology are systems of symbols and codes and they show the capacity for developing concurrently relative self-autonomy, but also the potential of infinite possibilities for association and interaction.

- Ideology offers a cluster of symbols and representations, susceptible to distortion, through which individuals attempt to come to logical constructive interpretations and generate meaning. Because such interpretations are acts of imagination, the relations meaning and reality are always regenerated and reassigned.

- Ideologies point to the importance of the quantity and quality of information and reveal a network of 'totalities' of informational archetypes and codes associated with a person's linguistic background and experience.

On the structural and interactive organization of ideologies:

- The primary function of ideologies is to mediate and integrate, to consolidate and conserve, as 'codes' of interpretation. Ideologies usually close the gap which utopias create.

- Ideologies render possible relations between objects and images with the creation *ex nihilo* of figures and forms. They constitute worlds of significations but also define their associations within the social imaginary of a society, thus identifying what is real and what is not.

- Ideological systems are informationally constructed constantly regenerating the relations of meaning between lived, desired and imagined experience. Individual subjectivity is the explicit communication of the informational elements of ideology.

On the power of ideologies to affect human information processing and construct social reality:

- The power of ideology, and consequently of the dominant system of information, relies in its organization and incorporation within social formations in its 'interpellation' of individuals into subjects.

- The structure and function of ideologies can differentiate to flexible and constantly adapting groups of beliefs and disbeliefs. The mode of organization of this differentiation is indicative of informational tensions for interactivity and association.

- The relations of production of social structure and action reflect the relations of reproduction of states and processes of informational significations by which social structure and action are defined, and render these relations possible even in the absence of their justification.

- In the era of digital technologies and communication 'reality' is constructed out of the regeneration of informational significations. These regenerations - in later chapters defined as fractal mutations - become the new 'realities' of the digital era.

- The digital world is sustained and regenerated by individual relatively autonomous units of information which comprise the framework of an 'invisible' ideology. There is the need for an in-depth analysis of the techniques invisible ideologies operate as well as of the global media and digital technologies through which they are sustained.

The dominant system of information supplies a chaotic culture of intensification of everything, which I defined as postmodernity-and-beyond. The second part of the chapter concentrated on contemporary cultural characteristics. Digital culture in the postmodern world is characterized by the intensification and use of information, information networks, all of which secure and the conditions of regeneration of an uncontainable flow of information. I suggested the existence of a hyper-spatial version of logic which would account for the transformation of human existence to a process of digital cloning and mutation. Summarized below are some of the main arguments and considerations regarding postmodernity:

On the cultural characetristics of postmoderniy:

- The postmodern condition should be understood as a cultural configuration, not a successor of modernity, rather an intensificaiton and amplification of elements of social structure and processes referred to as postmodernity-and-beyond.

- Postmodernity-and-beyond consists mutations of informational rearrangements in structural and processual elements of societies which do not necessarily relate to modernity. These mutations relate to the system of information which has always been responsible for informing and organizing human consciousness about social development and change.

- The organization of the global system of information in digital environments and exchanges of communication is responsible for the fractalization of social life beyond the stage of implosion, 'the digital reconstruction of hyperreality'.

- Digital and communication technologies introduce significant changes in the social order, by means of reduced complexity and modifications in time-space relations. They alter, dictate and regulate the conditions of information exchange among individuals, thus ensuring the conditions of their domination over them.

On the code of information in postmodernity:

- Social organization in the era of digital technologies and communication is the result of constant regeneration of signs and images by the dominant system of information. In order to understand the logic and principles of this organization one has to look at the 'code' (the organization) of the system of information itself.

- The 'code' of information suggests multiple variations and alternatives of 'truth' and 'reality'. There can only be theoretical approximations rather than finite conclusions regarding the quest for the 'truth'. In this sense, the aim of social investigation should be to create transitions, rather than conclusions, of understanding, in other words, emphasize the discourse over the essence.

- The flow of information through the global network of digital communications produces an increased differentiation of the world society. Information becomes power and digitally generated knowledge transforms the postmodern self.

- In the digital era the 'code' of information controls and absorbs — like a black hole — everything. The hyperreal constitutes the new reality dominated by the simulacrum, a real without origins. It is the era of information, signs and codes.

- In the postmodern era of simulations, a process of social entropy, implosion, leads to a collapse of boundaries of traditional representations and meaning. Once these boundaries, defining and justifying the relations of meaning are gone, 'reality' disappears within an undifferentiated flux of images and signs.

- Postmodernism signals the beginning of the reign of simulation, the Baudrillardian 'hell of the same', the pursuit of extreme and unconceivable possibilities, and the fractal multiplication of everything. This all becomes possible - if not unavoidable - with the unleash of the system of information through digital communication channels.

- Social trends in postmodern expression and experience point towards instabilities and uncertainties which reflect inner harmonizing tensions of the system of information towards a synchronized complex condition of homogenous heterogeneity and heterogenous homogeneity.

- The mode of information in the postmodern condition dictates the loss of the subjects' physical dimension and their constitution and reconstitution in relation to the discursive arrangement of the occasion. Human subjects become informational entities subject to the organization of the information that reproduces them.

- The loss of the referent creates a crisis of representation and language becomes problematic. Without points of stability the human subject of postmodernity floats towards generalized destabilization and a self-reflexive recontextualization.

- It is imperative to investigate new paths of thinking about the code of information and to search for philosophical models which would promote our understanding of the code, based on which the system of information organizes social experience and creates hyperreal worlds in which we are called to exist and survive.

On the effects of postmodernity on subjectivity, reality and meaning:

- In the postmodern mode of existence individuals overcome the repressions of modern discourse through a process of deterritorialization, the schizoanalytic celebration of the unconscious and by being reconstituted as nomadic desiring-machines.

- The deterritorialized postmodern individual floats in an informational ocean of deconstructed logic, decentred multiplicities, and non-hierarchical organization. These alternating spatial themes reflect the organizational re-arrangements of the system of information in the digital era.

- The relations of meaning in the postmodern condition (and beyond) are destroyed in the sense that they do not necessarily obey to justifications of traditional human logic. They are re-assigned alternating spatial coordinates based on new emerging forms of logical arrangements.

- There develops a diverse intensification of the informationalization of social life in the postmodern condition which is expressed in socio-cultural and economic aspects of the contemporary capitalist system: the dissapearance of the individual subject, the universal practice of 'pastiche', a stylistic uncontrolled heterogeneity, the random cannibalization of the past, the primacy of the 'neo' and the insensible colonization of the present.

- The organizational logic of the postmodern condition presents breakdowns in the signifying chains. The emphasis on a series of unrelated presents in time, leads to the loss of reality in an atmosphere of mixed anxiety and hallucinogenic intesity. The collapse of everyday reality results to the derealization of the whole.

- Media texts of the emerging new culture are structures without direct referents, invented models of reality that represent nothing but themselves, They consist informational glimpses of the postmodern world shaped by an overload of the system of information, an orgasm of confused meanings and undefined social orientations.

- The code of information, a language of sign system, reconstitutes the postmodern individual in a nonrepresentational and noninstrumental mode, but at the same time it creates an unrestricted flow of possibilities towards the liberation and escape from domination and subordination to 'meaning' and 'reason'.

- The rise of the media and the advertising industry exposes the reign of machines preoccupied with the production and reproduction of simulacra. The later consist distorted interpretations of the global system of digital capitalism and recreate the conceptual framework within which human and computer information processing converge.

- A new level of interconnectivity arises with the development of electronic media which threatens and in fact shatters the stability of social networks. The system of information, presented and demanded by the electronic media in new language formations restructures the human subjects to decentered, dispersed, and multiplied in continuous instability entities.

- Digital communication between humans and machines reflexively reconstitutes and induces human interaction and intelligence to normalization levels of depersonalization and of reduced effort and skill. Human information processing is demanded to synchronize with interacting computer operating systems and environments.

In the current chapter I examined various analyses of ideologies to gain an insight on the structure and function of ideological systems. I have suggested that systems of ideologies are predominantly systems of information, therefore, their structural and processual organization can reveal characteristics of the organization of the system of information itself. I maintained that in the contemporary social and cultural configuration of postmodernity-and-beyond, a disorderly system of information reorganizes 'realities' and 'relations of meaning'. I attempted to provide an extensive discussion of postmodern trends in order to map the cultural conditions prevalent in our world society. The following chapter draws attention to the concept of information taking into account theoretical considerations of systems theory and through them I try to define the concept of the system of information in more detail. I also look into interdisciplinary analogies and isomorphies at macroscopic and microscopic levels of organization to reveal common patterns that can apply to a theoretical proposition regarding the organization of the system of information.   ▶▶

PART TWO

TERRA INCOGNITA

CHAPTER FOUR

LOST IN SPACETIME:
Systemic Properties, Analogies and Isomorphies

CONTENTS

CHAPTER 4

LOST IN SPACETIME:
Systemic Properties, Analogies and Isomorphies

'I must create a system, or be enslaved by another man's.'
(William Blake, 1757-1827)

4.0 PROLOGUE

We have looked at social theoretic and political economic views of the information society. These have been situated within an analysis of the functions of ideology both in modern and postmodern societies. The focus of this book, however, remains on the notion of a system of information. To theoretically frame it, to philosophically engage with it requires that we understand also its properties as a system per se. To do so, I now turn to multidisciplinary systems theory.

The concept of 'the system of information' is the recurring theme throughout this book and its organization is at the focus of the theoretical discussion undertaken. The use of the term 'the system of information' which underlies the philosophical argument of this book, is due to the fact that information is viewed as a social, living entity, made up of diverse but interrelated and interdependent parts, which differentiate by self-organization and interaction both along individual and collective modes of organization. 'Systems' thinking helps our understanding of processes which are internally organized and have boundaries that connect the system with its environment rather than separate it.

The term 'system' describes a pattern of relationships between elements that together describe a whole that is differentiated from its environment. Systems present distinct emergent properties in a process of 'positive feedback' between action and its environment. They emerge from social combination and have contingent effects, including acting back on the elements from which they emerge. The importance of system self-organization in explaining change must be emphasized. Nature is composed of self-organizing systems that are active in relation to their environments and not purely determined by them. Systems organize using communication, although they do so in ways, which are conditioned by system-environment interactions, which produce non-predictable but ordered patterns of change. Typical of all systems is that they use information and communication to organize both internally and in relation to their external environment.

The current chapter attempts to define characteristic patterns of system properties and apply them to the system of information, as an individual system and as the organizing information system of all systems. To this end I focus to patterns of distinct traits in a variety of systems, and in diverse scientific principles, and endeavor to draw interdisciplinary analogies and isomorphies which account for their organization, and reflexively for the organization of the system of information. The emerging traits and patterns of systemic features, pointed out here, are later adopted in the statement of my theoretical approximations on the structure and organization of the system of information, particularly evident in digital communication and interaction.

Elements of the system of information occurring within the context of systems theory (Luhmann, 1986; 1995) signify the autopoietic character of the system of information, that is, its ability not only for self-organization but also its ability to influence and restructure interacting systems. As a general system (Schwarz, 1996; Krieger, 1998) the system of information obeys rules and unifying principles common to other individual levels of systems. As a self-organizing universal occurrence, the system of information is characterized by complexity and as such, its behaviour is subject to environmental conditions and constraints. The logical paradox of the system of information is its chaotic organization under constant change following patterns of 'iterations of nonlinear equations', that is, a dynamic 'fractal system'.

The system of information organizes a diversity of macro- and micro-systems, such as the cosmos and the human body. The current chapter also attempts to identify patterns in the organization of the system of information through a macroscopic analysis of principles of cosmological organization and a microscopic study of the neurophysiological human system and the human brain. The various theories on the birth of the Cosmos point towards a universe composed of scattered data, concepts and ideas, interacting forces and associations, black holes of meaning and deformed reality structures. There is an analogy between this macro-level organization of the Universe and the micro-level organization of the 'invisible' subatomic world of particles which constitutes the universe. The organization of the system of information can be said to be reflected in the genesis, content, complex organization and functional properties observed in these two worlds.

A particular emphasis is given to a close examination of the ways information is processed and organized through the neurophysiological human system and during functions of the human brain. An investigation of this kind reveals initial and basic principles of human information processing fundamental to the organization and function of the flow of the system of information during processes of interaction and communication. These principles of human information processing are further exemplified when examined in relation to their application to 'neural networks', 'artificial intelligence' and 'artificial life' projects. The organizational attributes of artificial (machine) information processing allow for reverse comparisons with the human information processing and relative suggestions with regard to the effects of artificial intelligence projects on human thinking and behaviour. It is suggested that the analogies and isomorphisms present in the patterns of organization of the cosmos, or the human body are indicative of patterns of organization that apply to any informational system. The arguments regarding both the attributes of systems and the principles of human information processing are vital to the intention of this book to examine how the system of information reorganizes and regenerates our representations and 'realities' of the world around us.

4.1 SYSTEMIC PROPERTIES

4.1.1 Systems theory

There is an ambiguous meaning of the concept of 'system' or even more, as it was indicated by Luhmann (1995), of the idea of a 'systems theory'. When introduced into sociological analyses the concept of 'system' requires further clarification as everyone may have different ideas in mind as what a system might be. In agreement with Luhmann, when developing a systems theory, any new theoretical proposal should attempt to incorporate previous concepts and principles and not disregard them as wrong or useless. This helps in the further conceptual development and consequently enrichment of the content of the new proposal by adding greater complexity to it. In this direction the proposed model of theoretical approximations regarding the system of information in this book attempts to incorporate theoretical analogies and isomorphies from various scientific and philosophical bodies of knowledge, without rejecting, rather suggesting a theoretical reconsideration of what is already accepted.

4.1.2 System differentiation

One important property of systems is system differentiation which refers to nothing more than the repetition within systems of the difference between system and environment. Through it, the whole system uses itself as environment in forming its own subsystems and thereby achieves greater improbability on the level of those subsystems by more rigorously filtering an ultimately uncontrollable environment. Accordingly, a differentiated system is no longer simply composed of a certain number of parts and the relations among them; rather, it is composed of a relatively large number of operationally employable system/environment differences, which each, along different cutting lines, reconstruct the whole system as the unity of subsystem and environment.

The theoretical proposal of 'system/environment differentiation' offers better possibilities for a more accurate understanding of 'homogeneity' and an understanding of the possibilities of using simultaneously varying viewpoints within subsystem differentiation. Luhmann pointed out that systems can be 'self-referential', that is systems can differentiate only by self-reference which is to say, only insofar as systems refer to themselves in constituting their elements and their elemental operations. Luhmann went on to suggest that a 'general systems theory' should be encountered with sociological inquiry, and in this way the advances in abstraction and the new conceptual formations that already exist or are emerging in interdisciplinary contexts should be made usable in theoretical standpoints. One of the most important results of this encounter resides in 'the radical temporalization of the concept of element'. In agreement with Luhmann, this book argues that in order to cope and come to an understanding of the fast pace of social and technological change in the digital era, the concept of information, as the core organizational principle, should be conceived and analysed within the context of a system across interdisciplinary scientific contexts. The book also suggests that, in order to understand the principles of organization of the system of information one has to accept abstract and uncertain proposals as acceptable and possible alternatives to finite conclusions.

4.1.3 Autopoiesis

Luhmann (1986) used the term 'autopoiesis' (GR. *αυτοποίησις*) to describe the general form of system-building using self-referential closure. He distinguished a general theory of self-referential autopoietic systems and a more concrete level at which we may distinguish living systems (cells, brains, organisms, etc.), psychic systems and social systems (societies, organizations, interactions) as different kinds of autopoietic systems. 'Autopoietic systems' are 'systems that are defined as unities, as networks of productions of components, that recursively through their interactions, generate and realize the network that produces them and constitute, in the space in which they exist, the boundaries of the network as components that participate in the realization of the network' (Maturana, 1980). Autopoietic systems, then, are not only 'self-organizing systems', not only do they produce and eventually change their own structures but their self-reference applies to the production of other components as well. Thus everything, which is used as a unit by the system, is produced as a unit by the system itself. This applies to elements, processes, boundaries and other structures, and last but not least to the unity of the system itself. Autopoietic systems, of course, exist within an environment.

An example of autopoietic systems would be social systems but as Luhmann argued, in their case other levels of reality are presupposed. Social systems use communication (a network of events which produces itself) as their particular mode of autopoietic reproduction. Luhmann argued that 'only communication is necessarily and inherently social... action is not'. Moreover, social action already implies communication; it implies at least the communication of the meaning of the action or the intent of the actor and it also implies the communication of the definition of the situation, of the expectation of being understood and accepted, and so on. The theory of autopoietic social systems, then, he contained, requires 'a conceptual revolution' of replacing action by communication as the characterization of the elementary operative level of the system. Autopoiesis presupposes a recurring need for renewal but for social systems there is a characteristic difference: conscious systems and social systems have to produce their own decay. After a very short time the mass of elements would be intolerably large and its complexity would be so great that the system would be unable to select a pattern of coordination and would produce chaos. Thereby, the continuing dissolution of the system becomes a necessary cause of its autopoietic reproduction. The system becomes dynamic in a very basic sense. It becomes inherently restless. The instability of its elements is a condition of its duration.

4.1.4 System maintenance

'System maintenance' is an important property of systems. Maintenance is not simply a question of replication, of cultural transmission, of reproducing the same patterns under similar circumstances; its primary process is the production of next elements in the actual situation, and these have to be different from the previous ones to be recognizable as events. The stability of the process is based on instability. This built-in requirement of discontinuity and newness, amounts to a necessity to handle and process information, whatever the environment or the state of the system offers as occasions. Information in systems theory is regarded as an internal change of state, a self-produced aspect of communicative events and not something, which exists in the environment of the system and has to be exploited for adaptive or similar purposes. When 'system maintenance' is applied to the organization of the system of information, I maintain, it is expressed in terms of an unbalanced proliferation and consequent mutation of its content towards the regeneration of new informational formations.

In summary, systems theory points towards the intrinsic ability of systems to regenerate their constituent elements and their primary operations by self-reference. System proliferation is achieved by means of system reconstruction with three main properties highlighted: differentiation, autopoiesis and maintenance. Differentiation adds greater improbability to systems allowing them to reproduce by repetition and by the regeneration of subsystems. Autopoiesis secures the unity and conditions of reproduction of a system, by recursively reproducing constituent units, inner and external processes. Autopoietic reproduction advances the renewal of the system and becomes a necessary condition towards the innate tendency of the system for continuing dissolution of accumulating complexity towards non-coordination and chaos. The stability of the system is also secured with the process of maintenance which regenerates instability by continuous system information processing.

4.1.5 General systems

'General systems theory' is concerned with those characteristics typical of all systems, whether mechanical, biological, or social. I maintain that information is responsible for the organization and realization of all systems more specifically it is the system of information that organizes itself and discursively organizes all systems that make up the social world. The current book adopts the concept of general systems and applies it to the system of information to offer a model of theoretical propositions regarding the organization and function of information in the digital era. It should be noted that the concept of general theory is used in this book as an open-end theory and as expressing a theoretical approximation which does not exclude alternatives or does not restrict the theoretical expansion of the concepts defined in the proposed model.

The idea of a general theory of all systems, introduced by Ludwig von Bertalanffy (1968), attempted to initiate a broad interdisciplinary scientific movement concerned with the properties of systems and the applications of systems theory in every area of life. Reflecting back upon the development of systems, Schwarz (1996) and Krieger (1998) argue that contemporary science is characterized by its ever-increasing specialization, necessitated by the enormous amount of data, the complexity of techniques and of theoretical structures within every field. This has resulted to a split into numerous disciplines continually generating new subdisciplines. In consequence, the physicist, the biologist, the psychologist and the social scientist are encapsulated in their private universes, and it is difficult to get word from one cocoon to the other. Surveying the evolution of contemporary science, independently of each other, similar problems and conceptions have evolved in widely different fields. Schwarz and Krieger attempted to briefly define certain characteristics shared by all systems and then asked what makes mechanical, biological, and social systems different from each other.

4.1.6 Patterns of parallel organization

Schwarz and Krieger identified patterns of parallel organization in various scientific disciplines feature as characteristic properties of systems. In quantum physics phenomena are resolved into local events; problems of order and organization appear whether the question is the structure of atoms, the architecture of proteins, or interaction phenomena in thermodynamics. Similarly biology saw its goal in the resolution of life phenomena into atomic entities and partial processes (cells, physiological and physicochemical processes, behavior into unconditioned and conditioned reflexes, genes). It is necessary, argue Schwarz and Krieger, to study not only parts and processes in isolation, but also to solve the decisive problems found in the organization and order unifying them, resulting from dynamic interaction of parts, and making the behavior of parts different when studied in isolation or within the whole. Similar trends in psychology attempted to resolve mental phenomena into elementary units and *gestalt* psychology showed the existence and primacy of psychological wholes, which are not a summation of elementary units and are governed by dynamic laws. Finally, in the social sciences the concept of society as a sum of individuals as social atoms was replaced by the tendency to consider society, economy, and nation as a whole superordinated to its parts. This implies great problems but also reflects the need for new ways of thinking. This parallelism of general cognitive principles in different fields is even more impressive when one considers the fact that those developments took place in mutual independence and mostly without any knowledge of work and research in other fields.

4.1.7 Universal principles

Exact science, the corpus of laws of nature, was almost identical with theoretical physics, however, the impact of and progress in the biological, behavioural and social sciences seem to make necessary an expansion of our conceptual schemes in order to allow for systems of laws in fields where application of physics is not sufficient or possible. Such a trend towards generalized theories is taking place in a variety of ways: theory of the dynamics of biological populations, quantitative economics and econometrics, cybernetics and information theory. When we come to a generalization of theory, argue Schwarz (1996) and Krieger (1998), we are dealing with generalized systems in which there exist models, principles, and laws that apply to them or their subclasses, irrespective of their particular kind, the nature of their component elements, and the relations or forces between them. It seems legitimate then to ask for a theory, not of systems of a more or less special kind, but of universal principles applying to systems in general.

This is what general system theory is about: its subject matter is the formulation and derivation of those principles which are valid for systems in general. That means, principles applying to systems in general, irrespective of whether they are of physical, biological or sociological nature. A consequence of the existence of general system properties is the appearance of structural similarities or isomorphisms in different fields. There are correspondences in the principles that govern the behavior of entities that are, intrinsically, widely different, due to the fact that the entities concerned can be considered, in certain respects, as systems. In fact, similar concepts, models and laws have often appeared in widely different fields, independently and based upon totally different facts.

4.1.8 Organization and interrelated 'wholeness'

A critical question regarding a general systems theory, is to what extent, can societies and civilizations be considered as systems? A general theory of systems would be a useful tool providing, on the one hand, models that can be used in, and transferred to, different fields, and safeguarding, on the other hand, from vague analogies which often have disfigured the progress in these fields. There is, however, another and even more important aspect of general system theory. Classical physics was highly successful in developing the theory of unorganized complexity. The theory of unorganized complexity is ultimately rooted in the laws of chance and probability and in the second law of thermodynamics. In contrast, the fundamental problem today is that there various degrees of organization and various degrees of complexity. Concepts like those of organization, wholeness, directiveness, teleology, and differentiation pop up everywhere in the biological, behavioral and social sciences, and are, in fact, indispensable for dealing with living organisms or social groups. Thus, Schwarz (1996) and Krieger (1998) argue that, 'a basic problem posed to contemporary science is a general theory of organization'.

There exist criticisms that general system theories may end up in meaningless, vague and superficial analogies and that they are open to system-theoretical interpretation. The isomorphisms indicated by general systems are more than mere analogies. They are a consequence of the fact that, in certain respects, corresponding abstractions and conceptual models can be applied to different phenomena. A general system theory is a general science of wholeness which in elaborate form it would be a logicomathematical discipline which can be applied to most diverse fields. It defines systems as 'sets of elements standing in interrelation' characterized by certain families of differential equations and if, in the usual way of mathematical reasoning, more specified conditions are introduced, many important properties can be found of systems in general and more special cases.

An interdisciplinary theory is rich with implications. Ideally, unity of science would gain a more realistic aspect. A unitary conception of the world may be based on 'the isomorphy of laws' in different fields, argue Schwarz (1996) and Krieger (1998). They call this conception 'perspectivism': 'we cannot reduce the biological, behavioral, and social levels to the lowest level, that of the constructs and laws of physics. We can, however, find constructs and possibly laws within the individual levels. The unifying principle is that we find organization at all levels'.

To summarize, the ever-increasing specialization of contemporary science indicates the need for an interdisciplinary approach which can take into consideration patterns of parallel organization in diverse scientific disciplines. This way identified analogies and isomorphies can be incorporated in the properties of general systems in the form of a logicomathematical discipline to deal with issues of organization and complexity. General systems are characterized by universal principles which also apply to their subclasses. These principles are exemplified in structural similarities or isomorphisms among systems in the form of corresponding abstractions and conceptual models. The organization of the system of information follows the principles of organization of general systems. The system of information is itself a general system, of open-end possibilities, that discursively organizes other systems.

4.1.9 Complex systems

As mentioned earlier, life in the digital era is characterized by shifting relations between varying degrees of organization and complexity respectively. These diverse models of relations are representative of the organization tensions of the system of information, defining it as a complex system. The concept of complexity that applies to the properties of the system of information is defined within the framework of complexity theory (Cilliers, 1998; Eve et al, 1997).

Complexity theory is a type of systems theory, which approaches explanation in terms of causes and effects but it is not deterministic. In brief, it argues that, system-environment interaction entails 'feed-forwards' as well as 'feedbacks' and that social phenomena have multiple and interacting causes with non-linear trajectories of change occurring within phase spaces of possible attractors. Certain parameters govern the general properties of a system and its trajectory in phase space and, system states are not predictable in the long term but the generic class to which they belong can be described, investigated and perhaps anticipated. Complexity theory allows for purposeful, knowledge-based action, which may be capable of changing both causes and effects. It focuses on generic emergent properties which are non-reducible. It expects a change rather than stability. Complexity theory is thus part of 'a shift of human understanding towards emphasizing the arrow of time and alternative possibilities for human systems'.

4.1.10 Self-organization and dynamic attractors

Complexity theory conceives of the world as consisting of self-organizing systems (Blackman, 2000; Hock, 1999), either reproducing their existing state via negative feedbacks with their environment or moving along trajectories from one state to another as a result of positive feedbacks. Complex systems are, therefore, self-organizing phenomena conditioned and constrained by environmental properties. They maintain themselves in an organized state by processing and accumulating information. They share information within networks of information exchanges. This internal communication, together with communication with the environment, enables the system to organize both internally and in relation to its environment. Humans' qualitative capacity for understanding means that we can move beyond being controlled by our environment to controlling it and creating environments that are more favourable to human projects.

One key idea of complex systems is the emergence of global properties from local interactions. More-or-less ordered systems have global properties which enable us to distinguish one type of system from another. There is much local interaction which appears to be chaotic, and this behaviour can be a source of change in global properties. An important feature of chaotic behaviour is that small changes in initial conditions can produce very large differences in outcome. The feedbacks either maintain a system in a stable state or generate a trajectory which carries the system to another state cycle. A state cycle in complexity theory is known as a 'dynamic attractor'. The concept of an attractor describes the long-term qualitative behaviour of a system: attractors embody the range of states possible for a system in a given environment.

These dynamic states of complex systems exist as neither totally ordered, nor totally chaotic. They are based upon iterative cycles whereby the output from one iterative cycle becomes the input to the next. Positioned between order and chaos, in this way, complex systems may exist in a more or less stable state at a particular attractor. The system's 'phase space' contains the possible alternative attractors towards which a system under perturbation might move; the system moves through its phase space, transforming into a qualitatively different state if it settles on another attractor. Attractors are, then, ways of understanding discontinuous, non-linear change over time. The attractor itself can have different dynamics, reproducing uniform conditions in stable cycles which other may be much more chaotic, defined as 'strange attractors'. Change in these parameters is caused by perturbations which may arise from the external environment, internal fluctuations or an interaction between both external and internal processes.

In summary, the varying degrees of organization and complexity which characterize the organization of the system of information, classify it as a complex system. As such the properties of complex systems apply to its organization. The system of information, then, is characterized by internal and external feedbacks during which it shares information in emerging networks of information exchanges. These interactions of information exchange contribute to the chaotic change of the system of information towards states of continuous transformation and mutation rather than stability. The system of information is a dynamically changing entity, floating between order and chaos, and being transformed along non-linear trajectories and along the arrow of time, in distinct phase spaces of dynamic and strange attractors. All of these characteristic aspects of organization of the system of information are defined in detail in the model of theoretical approximations I propose in later chapters of the book.

4.1.11 Chaotic, dynamic and fractal systems

Chaos theory (Gleick, 1987; Kellert, 1993) suggests that motion that appears to be chaotic is all around us. One of the main features of chaotic systems is what has been dubbed 'the butterfly effect'. This means that in a complex, non-linear system, a small change in the input could produce a huge change in the output. Chaos theory sets definite limits to the predictability of complex non-linear systems. It is well established that in other similarly complex systems a small input can produce a large output, that an accumulation of quantity can be transformed to quality. There is only a difference of less than two per cent, for example, in the basic genetic make-up of human beings and chimpanzees, yet in the complex, non-linear processes that are involved in translating the genetic 'code' into a living animal, this small dissimilarity means the difference between one species and another.

Gleick (1987) described the main features of chaos theory in the following way: 'To some physicists, chaos is a science of process rather than state, of becoming rather than being. They feel that they are turning back a trend in science towards reductionism, the analysis of systems in terms of their constituent parts: quarks, chromosomes, or neutrons. They believe that they are looking for the whole'. Von Neumann recognized that a complicated dynamic system could have points of instability - critical points where a small push can have large consequences. In science as in life, it is well known that a chain of events can have a point of crisis that could magnify small changes. But chaos meant that such points were everywhere and that they were pervasive. The name linear refers to the fact that if you plot such an equation on a graph, it emerges as a straight line. Much of nature is not linear, and cannot be understood through linear systems. The brain certainly does not function in a linear manner, nor does the economy, with its chaotic cycle of booms and slumps. A non-linear equation is not expressed in a straight line, but takes into account the irregular, contradictory and frequently chaotic nature of reality. Perhaps the best definition comes from Jensen, a theoretical physicist at Yale, who defines chaos as the irregular, unpredictable behaviour of deterministic, non-linear dynamic systems.

Dynamic systems are everywhere: the stock market, ecosystems, the weather, the human body, to mention a few of an endless list. Dynamic systems are systems that are in constant flux. Traditional mathematics based on Newtonian principles has only been able to understand and model these systems by taking them apart and looking at the individual pieces. Pictures often provide more information than equations can offer. By graphing the points of non-linear equations, scientists hoped that they could understand the system more fully. Using computers, mathematicians were able to create a vast number of points to graph; they discovered that the system settled into a pattern. Although no point repeated itself, (affirming that the system was unpredictable) all points stayed within the boundaries of the pattern. In addition, it seemed that the patterns revolved around a central area that appeared to attract the points, like a vortex attracting everything to it. These images of strange attractors and were the first images of the order lying within these dynamic systems. Dynamic systems evolve through iterations, that is, functions that are repeated. The trick is to look for patterns by graphing the functions. These systems separate, that is, they create images that break off and repeat themselves towards fractals.

In mathematics, iterations of nonlinear equations, usually in a feedback loop, result to the generation of 'fractals' (Jürgens et al. 1992). The term 'fractal' was coined by Benoit Mandelbrot, one of the first to discover and examine these images. Using the output value for the next input value, a set of points is produced. Graphing these points produces images. Again, by creating a vast number of points using computers to generate those points these complex images called 'fractals'. Two important properties of fractals are 'self-similarity' and 'fractional dimensions'. Fractals are often formed by what is called an 'iterative process'. Geometric figures are similar if they have the same shape. Many figures that are not fractals are self-similar. You can also think of self-similarity as copies. Self-similarity means that at every level, 'the fractal image repeats itself. Many shapes in nature display this same quality of self-similarity.

Euclidean geometry allowed us to study and understand regular shape but very little in nature is so regular. We still need to understand and solve nonlinear equations in order to model most universal systems, and we need to understand irregular shapes using a geometry that could accommodate the complexities of these shapes. Fractals mirror these irregular shapes, thereby allowing us to study and understand nature by understanding fractals. Fractals are the place where math, science and art come together. They visually demonstrate the relationships between disparate parts of the universe and demonstrate the interdependence of all things in nature. They allow us to view the complexity of chaos and order. They please visually and excite imaginations. With fractals, it was discovered that shapes exhibit the same shape at smaller magnifications. Scale did not change the contours of the original shape, it repeated itself regardless of size. Wheatly (1992) believes that it is by examining the qualities of fractal shapes that we can best begin to understand natural phenomena. Focusing on quantity will continue to prove frustrating since there are always smaller scales. This is move away from the traditional view of quantitative studies in science and math. A true revolution, though one that opens many doors. Simply put, fractals are complex images of extraordinary beauty, which arise out of fairly simple mathematical functions. One feature, which distinguishes a fractal image from other types of graphics, is the property of self-similarity; an arbitrarily small region of a fractal looks like the entire fractal. Thus, fractals are analogous to DNA: just as all the information for a living organism is contained in its DNA, so does a small region contain all the information for the 'parent' image.

To summarize, properties of chaotic, dynamic and fractal systems are distinct characteristics of the organization of the system of information. Chaotic systems, can generate huge change in output of the quantity and, most importantly, in the quality of a system, only with a small input. A dynamic system is in constant movement along points of instability. The unpredictable complexity of chaos and order and the relationships of dissimilarity and interdependence within chaotic systems are expressed in the irregular and non-linear patterns of fractals. The system of information is a dynamic, chaotic system. As such, its chaotic organization can be described along a model of 'strange attractors' and it can be demonstrated with the use of fractal models. This task is undertaken in detail in the proposed model of theoretical approximations where many of the concepts discussed here are applied.

4.1.12 Summary

The idea of a 'system of information' can promote our understanding of the pattern of relationships among its constituent components and of how internal processes organize the system as a whole and set the rules of its environmental differentiation. This allows us also to differentiate types or kinds of systems by the way that some of their key properties line up. This is crucial for the modeling of the system of information proposed in this book. Properties from various types of systems can apply to the system of information: self-organization and differentiation, system-environment interactions, diversity of organization/complexity relations, chaos, instability, patterns of iterations of nonlinear equations, strange attractors, fractalization. The main points on discussed above and theoretical suggestions regarding the system of information are summarized at the end of the chapter.

4.2 SYSTEMIC ANALOGIES AND ISOMORPHIES

4.2.1 Introduction

Information exists in the form of a general system and in the form of iterations into subsystems of information. Subsystems of information organize a diversity of macro-systems and micro-systems, such as the cosmos, biological systems and in particular the human body. Specific patterns and principles of organization can be identified in macroscopic analyses of the cosmos, as well as, in microscopic studies of biological systems and studies of the human neurophysiological system and the human brain. I maintain that these patterns and principles of organization can reflexively be applied, as systemic analogies and isomorphies, to account for the organization of the system of information. The study of human neurophysiological system and the human brain also provides a valuable insight of human information processing. If information organizes the human body and mind, it is then interesting to examine the path that information follows from the point where it is received as a stimulus and along the complex processes taking place towards and inside the human brain. The principles of human information processing can be exemplified further with their application to artificial intelligence projects. My intention is not to be too technical so I will be referring to basic concepts of these sciences in a rather simplified manner with the purpose of adding a basic conceptual visualization of the organization of all these systems. Comparisons between the principles of human and machine information processing, I contend, reveal patterns of the system of information at its elementary level of organization. Let us start with the chaotic universe and try to identify some of the patterns of its logic of organization.

4.2.2 The Cosmos

Most of the cosmological suggestions are pure observation, spectrum analysis of radiation and guesswork (Roos, 1994; Gribbin, 1998). The science of cosmology is the result of the merge of astronomy and particle physics, therefore the system properties of the basic cosmological principles come from these two sciences. The concepts and theorems expressed in the philosophical investigations and analytical frameworks of cosmology may be useful to understand better the organization and function of the human world, the matter and energy and the information of which form part of the same universe cosmologists try to explain. Some interesting properties of the cosmos, which are used in the proposed theoretical model of this book, are pointed out here. A brief account is undertaken of basic cosmological principles, the electro-dynamics of particles, theories on the birth of the Universe, some concepts of quantum mechanics, and some not totally understood entities of the Universe such as dark matter and wormholes. I argue that many of these properties, mentioned briefly below, can be used to describe the internal organization of the system of information.

The universe is characterized by homogeneity, isotropy, forces and interaction, a different understanding of dimensional space, black holes, particle polarization and spin, entropy. The cosmological or Copernican principle indicates that the Universe is homogenous (uniformly distributed) and isotropic (has the same properties in all spatial directions) in 3-dimensional space, has always been so, and will always remain so. Several kinds of forces or interactions are distinguished by the laws of physics in the universe. Newton's First Law - the law of inertia - proposes that a system on which no forces act is either at rest or in uniform motion (with regard to an absolute space) and such systems are called 'inertial frames'. Euclidean geometry (flat 3D space) and absolute space are abandoned by Einstein's law of gravitation and replaced by curved Minkowskian 4D space in which physical quantities are described by invariants. Black holes are very simple objects as seen from outside their event horizon; they have only three properties: mass, electric charge and angular momentum. Their size depends only on their mass so that all black holes with the same mass are identical and exactly spherical, unless they rotate. All other properties possessed by stars, such as shape, electric dipole moment, magnetic moments as well as any detailed outward structure are absent. The study of the laws and phenomena of very high-temperature plasmas in cosmology showed how the electroweak force governs the interaction of plasma particles (photons, leptons, nucleons). Plasma particles are characterized by the quantization of energy (energy is not a continuous variable, but it comes into discrete packages), the two states of light, polarization, and the existence of the internal property of spin of the photons. Entropy is the measure of disorder and entropy, as defined by the second law of thermodynamics, cannot decrease in closed systems. Any isolated system can only charge towards greater disorder (Roos, 1994; Gribbin, 1998).

4.2.3 The electro-dynamics of particles

The study of the electro-dynamics of particles offers an insight of their organization and function. In quantum electro-dynamics (QED) the electromagnetic field is mediated by photons, which are emitted by one charged particle and absorbed very shortly afterwards by another; such photons with a brief existence during an interaction are called virtual, in contrast to real photons. In their production energy is not conserved. Real photons interact only with other charged particles such as protons (p), electrons (e-) and their oppositely charged antiparticles, the antiproton and the positron. Interactions of particles form stable (electron + proton) and unstable systems (electron + positron). Charged particles have neutral partners as well. Protons and neutrons are 'nucleons', part of the family of 'baryons'. Leptons belong to the electron family. Charged particles with spin exhibit magnetic moment. In a magnetic field free electrons orient themselves as if they were little magnets. Spin is a quantal effect. Spin space has many dimensions as there are possible outcomes. Protons and neutrons interactions are treated symmetrically. Isospin symmetry characterizes strong interactions in isospin vector (an abstract 3D space). Particle interaction presents symmetries (translational symmetry, rotational symmetry, for systems in isolation). A third symmetry is time reversal, or symmetry under inversion of the arrow of time. Spontaneous breaking of particle symmetries is a related concept. I maintain that, in many ways, this organization presents analogies and isomorphies that can be applied to the organization of the system of information. Some of these analogies and isomorphies include the presence of diversity - expressed in varieties of particles - and of possibilities of interactions, structural similarities, as well a variety of individual particle behaviours and interacting forces (Roos, 1994; Gribbin, 1998).

4.2.4 The birth of the Universe

In different cosmological models, the universe expands forever; in others, it expands from a very small size, reaches a maximum size, and then shrinks, possibly bouncing and repeating the whole cycle. The ever-popular 'Big Bang model' is said to present theoretical problems related to a series of concepts such as 'spacetime', the 'horizon' (size of universe), 'monopole' (topological defects, such as domain walls, loops and cosmic strings) and 'flatness' (metric). According to 'chaotic inflation', the Universe can be thought as a chaotic foam of casually disconnected bubbles in which the initial conditions are different, and which would subsequently evolve into different kinds of universes. Only one bubble would become our Universe, and we could never get any information about the other ones. The galaxies are moving apart from one another; the Universe is expanding. The evidence comes from a phenomenon known as 'the redshift'. Similar to what is known as the Doppler Effect it is caused by motion through space, by the galaxies moving outward through space (Hawley & Holcomb, 1998).

There are rival versions of the story of the birth of the Universe, for which some basic knowledge in needed of quantum physics and gravity. It turns out that in the quantum world there are certain pairs of related physical properties which can never both be precisely determined at the same time; the more accurately one property is determined, the less precisely the other one is defined. It turns out to be impossible to specify the precise energy of a system at a precise time. The more accurately the energy is determined, the more uncertainty there is about exactly when it was determined. The total energy of the entire Universe may be precisely zero. Some cosmologists believe that the Universe may have been created out of nothing at all, as a quantum fluctuation with zero gravity overall. Particle physicists have offered answers about the behaviour of other forces of nature, namely three of them: electromagnetism, and two forces that operate on a scale smaller than the size of an atomic nucleus, the so-called strong (what holds atomic nuclei together) and weak (responsible for radioactivity) nuclear forces. As the Universe cooled, this symmetry was lost, and the forces split apart to take on the characteristics that we have today ('phase transition') (Hawley & Holcomb, 1998).

There is another idea how the Universe might have started. This is the idea that our Universe is just one among many, and that there was no 'unique' beginning, just an interconnected web of universes extending forever in time and space. The concept of a black hole, mentioned earlier, is important to understand how this may be happening. A black hole is a place where matter collapses indefinitely, under the influence of gravity, towards a singularity. One possibility was that some bounce may occur, turning the collapse into an expansion, and shutting the material falling in towards the singularity sideways into a new set of dimensions – its own space, and its own time. The cosmologists call such a tunnel a wormhole, and suggest that it connects to another region of spacetime (another universe). It is possible that the overall structure of spacetime (sometimes called the Metaverse) is a series of interconnected bubbles, resembling froth on a glass of beer, with no beginning and no end. What we do know is that inflation is hugely successful in explaining the overall appearance of the Universe. Inflation can also explain another remarkable feature of the Universe, the fact that it sits very close to the dividing line between eternal expansion and eventual recollapse. If the Universe will expand forever, it is said to be 'open'; if it will one recollapse, it is said to be 'closed'. And if it sits exactly on the dividing line between being open and being closed it is said to be 'flat' (Hawley & Holcomb, 1998).

4.2.5 Dark matter

Cosmologists speculate that the Universe does have the critical density and is indeed flat. Dark matter outweighs the bright stuff we see by 100 to 1. Most of this dark matter cannot be of the same stuff that stars, galaxies, planets and people are made of. Nuclei are made of protons and neutrons (members of baryons), so nuclear matter (what we are made of) is called 'baryonic matter'. Although, dark matter had to be non-baryonic, it would still interact with any other matter by gravity. Hot dark matter would consist of very light particles, much lighter even than an electron, which stream through the Universe at high speeds, close to the speed of light. Cold dark matter would consist of more massive particles, each perhaps even more massive than a proton, which travel through the Universe at low speeds. Together, both kinds of dark matter are sometimes referred to as WIMPs, an acronym for 'weakly interacting massive particles'. One kind of particle that could contribute to the non-baryonic dark matter, 'neutrinos', involved in nuclear reactions; 'neutrinos' are extremely reluctant to interact with baryonic matter, even though they are produced in profusion in nuclear reactions. Neutrinos are also pouring out from stars and are made out of the mass energy of the stars themselves, helping to compensate for the loss in mass of the stars as mc^2 is converted into E (Hawley & Holcomb, 1998).

In conclusion, in the case of the system of information, there is a multiplicity of informational universes and the application of analogies from more than one of these models opens up several scenarios. The system of information is a universe of its own. A universe composed of scattered data, concepts and ideas, interacting forces and associations, black holes of meaning and deformed reality structures. I propose that the system of information follows the organizational principles that cosmological models assign to the organization of the universe. The concepts of homogeneity, isotropy, 3-D space and curved 4-D space as well as the range of forces and interactions are used in later sections in the proposed analytical model of the organization of the system of information. With the introduction of electronic communications and the digitization of information the system of information more than ever can be said to present the behaviour of plasma particles. Interference, kinematics, reactions, interactions, polarizations, symmetries and other related concepts I suggest they can be used to offer approximate descriptions of the organization of the system of information in the digital age. The theoretical models to the birth and the composition of the universe also offer analogies of organization regarding the emergence and substance of the diversity of informational structures (Hawley & Holcomb, 1998).

4.2.6 Biological systems

Similar to cosmological accounts that reveal patterns of organization at macroscopic levels, the microcosm of biological structures consists of tiny systems the organization of which reflects analogies and isomorphies about of the organization of the system of information at its smallest possible identifiable size. The system of information is a living entity in that it does present change and development. As such, biological principles may apply to describe the organization of its smallest components. I provide here a very brief description of the structure of organisms and the functions of cells, which makes evident the complexity of organization in biological systems. Analogically, this complexity, may apply to a model of organization on the structure and functions of primary informational units which make up the system of information.

4.2.7 The organism

All physical matter in the world, of which living organisms are one example, are composed of smaller particles, called atoms. They are incredibly tiny, with the diameter of an atom very approximately about one billionth of a centimeter. Atoms are composed of subatomic particles, namely protons, neutrons and electrons, which in turn are composed of other particles. Atoms are the smallest units of an element, that is, a pure substance that cannot be broken into simpler bits by chemical processes. Hydrogen, carbon, nitrogen and oxygen, compose over

99% of living organisms. Twenty-one other elements have been found to account for the rest 1%. One of the essentials of life is the ability to form complex structures. When atoms of different elements combine they form a compound, which is called a molecule. Molecules are made of atoms arranged in a specific order. Complex molecules, made up of thousands of molecules, are formed by the joining together of smaller sub-units. Many molecules are arranged together into larger structures, components of 'cells', 'cell tissues', 'organs' and finally the 'organism' (Horrobin, 1966; De Coursey, 1974).

A series of sub-cellular organelles exist within a human cell to secure its error-free operation. Each one of them specializes in a specific function. The 'mitochondria' are the powerhouses of the cell creating little mobile packets of energy for use in the myriad chemical conversions that each cell must perform each minute. The 'lysosomes' are central to the digestive system of a cell, they eat and swallow particles, such as invading nutrients, microbes and dead cells. In any case, the material entering the cell is broken down into portions that can be used, what is called 'metabolism'. The 'ribosomes' are instruments involved in reading the genetic code of the proteins, which end up doing most of the work of the cell. The proteins are the antibodies which recognize and neutralize foreign invaders that enter the body. They are made by a specialized cell type called 'a plasma cell'. The 'endoplasmic reticulum' is a kind of river system that guides the molecules destined for export to an appropriate packaging center. The 'colgi apparatus' is a concentrating and packaging center, a system of membranes and sacs or pouches that sits in the cytoplasm, right next to the nucleus. This is where proteins destined for secretion move in tiny bubbles, to the surface of the cell. The 'cell membrane', is a kind of skin, made up of fats and lipids that separate the inside of the cell from the outside world. The skin is impermeable to most molecules, thereby preserving the cell's autonomy and integrity. Molecules that get in do so by feeding or delivering the cell with messages, and when they want to get out, feeding the bloodstream with special canceling devices of various sorts (Horrobin, 1966; De Coursey, 1974).

In summary, genetic engineering shows us how particles form atoms, atoms form molecules, molecules form cells, and cells form organs and organisms. Cells are differentiated and specialized in a series of control functions to ensure the necessary operations within a cell. I suggest that in a similar way, the biological analogy can be applied the system of information. Small units of dispersed information (i.e., data) come together to form larger segments of information (i.e., concepts, perceptions, ideas), which in turn form larger informational subsystems (i.e., ideologies), subsystems form systems (i.e., bodies of knowledge) and finally they all become parts of this global living entity that accounts as the system of information (i.e., imaginations, realities).

4.2.8 Neurophysiological systems

Human information processing is indeed a complex issue. To try to explain what exactly is happening inside the human brain is pretty much like navigating in the borders of science fiction and imagination. However, having suggested that information is the organizing principle of all systems it would be considered inadequate, for the considerations and proposals of this book, not to examine how information organizes any system, and more specifically the human system, and how it is reflexively organized by it. The conceptual organization presumably is taking place within the human brain, but the investigation undertaken here, also reveals principles of information processing outside the physical boundaries of the human brain, that is before the actual stimulus reaches the human brain or after the processing has taken place within the brain. Therefore, the current section of this chapter is trying to follow the path of information from the moment of its emergence as a stimulus to the moment of its processing in the human brain. To this aim, I am briefly discussing basic neurophysiological principles of human information processing, brain structure, functions and disorders, memory, neural mechanisms and communication (Stein, 1982; Carpenter, 1996). All the phenomena described in this section on human neurophysiology are really rather brief in duration and fall into the category of what has been described as 'millisecond physiology'.

4.2.9 Mapping the brain

As humans, we lack the conceptual techniques for analyzing the behaviour of the brain as a whole; in fact, the brain is composed of elements that are essentially rather simple, but joined together in ways that are extremely complex. The brain is one of the most chaotic systems in which the tiniest initial perturbations may generate incalculably large effects. The following brief reference to its structure and processes exemplifies this complexity.

There are three main parts of the brain: the cerebrum, the cerebellum, and the brain stem. In the cerebrum, there are fifty hundred to one hundred thousand neurons, through which information is sent from place to place like a telegram. The cerebrum is divided in to two hemispheres, the right and left hemispheres. The dividing point is a deep grove called the 'longitudal cerebral fissure'. The different sides of the cerebrum do different things for the opposite sides of the body. The right side of the cerebrum controls things such as imagination and 3-D forms. The other side of the brain, the left side, controls numbering skills, posture, and reasoning. The hemispheres also consist of many other parts such as the lobes. Each hemisphere is divided into four sections: frontal, parietal, temporal, and the occupial, lobes. The hemispheres also consist of an inner core called 'the white matter' and 'the cortex', the wrinkly outer layer. The cerebellum is the part of the brain where the high level functions take place. The cerebellum controls posture, balance, and coordination. It is divided into two different lobes, which are connected by white fibers. Also in the cerebellum, there are 'folia', bundled nerve cells. The brain stem is located directly below the cerebellum. The brain stem connects to the spinal cord. It is also the part of the brain where the vital functions occur. The lowest part of the brain is located in the brain stem, the 'meddula oblangata'. Directly above the 'meddula oblangata' are 'the pons'. The pons consist the band of nerves that connect the cerebrum, the cerebellum, and the meddula oblongata (Stein, 1982; Carpenter, 1996).

4.2.10 The brain process

There are many parts of the brain that contribute to its overall operational processes. The 'glial cells' or 'nerve cell circuits', help control the chemical balance of the brain. They also provide structural support for the neurons, which help the nervous system after injury, and supply chemicals that are needed for a healthy brain. The brain is composed of two principle types of cells, the 'neurons', and the 'glial cells'. The neurons are the ones that carry the information to the brain. It is of particular importance to notice how this is done, and how the original stimulus may actually be transformed and modified before it even reaches the human brain to be processed. It is also important to notice that communication of information among the neurons is both electrical and chemical. This simply means that when information is communicated it is transformed in electrical impulses and chemical reactions, therefore, when the properties of information should also be characterized by electro-chemical properties. Neurons transmit and analyze communication within the brain and other parts of the nervous system. 'Dendrites' are structures that extend from the cell body. They receive impulses from other neurons then they transmit them to the neuron in which they are in. An 'axon' is a fiber extending from the cell body that carries impulses from the cell body to other dendrites of other neurons. All of these parts help the flow of information throughout the whole body. The brain process is very complicated. First, an electrical impulse travels down a cell body and through the axon. When it reaches the end of the axon it crosses a gap called a 'synapse'. The end of the axon contains tiny sacs that hold chemical messengers, or neurotransmitters. When the electrical impulse stimulates sacs, they are then released into the synapse. After it moves away from the synapse, the neurotransmitters attach a receptor on the dendrites of the cell body. This sparks an electrical impulse in the receiving cell body. After all this has taken place, a message within the brain is converted (Stein, 1982; Carpenter, 1996).

4.2.11 Memory

Memories have been defined in many different ways. Memory is the part of the brain that enables a person to remember things that have been seen as well as other sensory information, such as smells, tastes, and things that have been touched. In other words, it is that part of the brain where information is stored after it has been processed. This is also important, the fact that memory can only refer to processed information in the brain and not to the original external stimulus. This means that people perceive (and remember) the same information (people, places, events, and so on) in different ways and according to the way that the information has been processed in conjunction with the already existing stored information in one's memory (Squire, 1987; Thompson, 1989; Carpenter, 1996).

There is an additional complication with memory in that there is not just one type of memory but also at least three: sensory, motor and central. Central memory is characterized by the ability to put together analyzed information from different sources, attach some kind of significance to it, and store it so it can be recalled at will. In each case, the key operation is one of forming association between those elements of the stimulus that tend to recur together. All learning by the brain amounts to the formation of physical connections between neurones in such a way as to mirror the associations that exist in the real world between the stimuli that those same neurones code for. Memory is the process that models the world within our heads.

There is in fact good evidence that there are really two distinct memory stores in the brain: long term memory (LTM) which takes the form of synaptic changes, and short term memory (STM), which retains information temporarily to cover the period during which consolidation takes place. One complicating factor is that things may have been stored perfectly well in LTM, but cannot be recalled because the mechanism for retrieval is not working properly. In other cases, forgetting may be the result of learning new material. Since retrieval is essentially by association, it is important to point out that memories that are linked together by too many associations may become irretrievably entangled. There are also two types of long term memory. The first type is procedural memory, more associated to environment originating information. This kind of memory stores information on how to do things such as driving a car, hitting a baseball bat, or playing an instrument. This type of memory is long-lasting. The memories are actions, habits, or skills that are learned over time. These memories can be changed by training. The other type long term memory is declarative memory, more associated with genetic information. This memory contains memories gathered from one's childhood until one's death. If there is a database of this memory it seems that each memory has a location of its own for it.

Finally, the components of memory are stored in different locations. They are associated with each other so that if you remember just one thing, then you may be able to recall other associated characteristics from remembering that one detail. Working memory allows the brain to evaluate the incoming information, and dispose of the information that is to be rejected, and store the information that is to be memorized. In addition to all of the other memory, external memory stores all incoming information, things like you have quite forgotten or that you do not think about that often (Squire, 1987; Thompson, 1989; Carpenter, 1996).

4.2.12 Brain disorders

The 'parietal lobe' occupies a central position in the celebral hemisphere, and it is concerned with the coordination of the information from the visual, auditory, somato-sensory and motor areas. Many kinds of defects can arise from damage of the parietal lobe: agnosia disorders, associated with high-level sensory analysis, apraxia disorders, associated with high-level motor coordination and appropriateness, and aphasia disorders, associated with communicating and using symbols. This diversity of disorders, I maintain, points out the vulnerability of the original value of information, which in the form of a stimulus or a stored unit in memory, can be manipulated and distorted. This is of course the area of cybernetics, the basic principles of which are examined more extensively in the next chapter. As said above though, it is possible for incoming or stored information to be susceptible to a series of disorders which are briefly listed here (Ron & David, 1998; Pinel, 2003).

'Agnosia' refer to the lack of the ability to use sensory data properly in order to recognize and respond to objects that are sensed by the skin. Agnostic disorders may refer to inabilities to recognize shape (asterognosia), or to 'appreciate' and recognize easily what someone sees (visual agnosia), or to difficulties in appreciating the spatial relationships between objects with the result of getting disorientated (spatial agnosia). 'Apraxia' implies inability of the subject to produce specific actions or commands; one particular type of apraxia is 'constructional apraxia' which is a sort of a motor version of spatial agnosia and is indicated by the inability of the subject to solve puzzles. Different kinds of aphasia are manifested: sensory, motor and central. Raw information enters through senses and is analysed by successive levels to the point which symbols are recognized; at the highest level, meaning comes about with association of these symbols with other kinds of sensory information to form concepts. Certain kinds of communication of this kind may be prevented (sensory aphasia), difficulties in writing or articulation may arise (motor aphasia), or even problems may develop in the mental mechanisms for forming concepts, for understanding symbols and making sentences (central aphasia). Other variations of this type of disorder will create difficulties in the ability to name objects (anomia) and the ability to repeat what has been heard (Ron & David, 1998; Pinel, 2003).

4.2.13 Neural mechanisms

Nerves serve as the communication pathway between the body and the brain, and the way of operation is interesting. It exemplifies how informational units, generated in the form of internal or external stimuli may actually be distorted as they are carried though this channel of communication. Nerves communicate information in the form of 'biphasic action potential'. Action potentials are not transmitted by passive conduction, in the same way that signals pass along a telephone wire. This is not because nerves are made of unsuitable material. Nerve action potentials show a number of properties that demonstrate quite clearly that they are not passive, but actively regenerated as they pass along the fibres, amplified in such a way as to overcome the enormous losses that they experience through membrane leakage. So long as the strength of the stimulus is above a certain threshold value (below which no action potential is seen at all), neither the aplitude nor the shape or speed of the action potential is in any way influenced by the nature of the original stimulus, a property known as the 'all-or-nothing law'. The original stimulus to the fibre causes local currents to flow passively through the membrane, causing a spread of potential. This whole cyclical process is known as 'the local circuit mechanism' of action potential propagation (Stein, 1982; Carpenter, 1996).

Nerve membrane potential affects on 'ionic permeability' and vice versa; changes in permeability cause changes in potential. Nerves also show another electrical property called 'capacitance' – the ability to store charge. Nerves contain a variety of fibres of different diameters, because of that; compound action potential describes the arrival of action potentials to fibres at different instants. There is a period during which it is impossible to stimulate a nerve for a second time (absolute refractory period), and also there is a period during which it can be simulated using a larger current (relative refractory period). When the nerve depolarizes slowly, the nerve never responds, it has accommodated itself to the changing potential. The 'all-or-nothing law' imposes severe limitations on the kinds of messages that nerves can convey, prohibiting direct transmission of graded quantitative information, the only messages permitted being of the binary yes/no variety (Stein, 1982; Carpenter, 1996).

4.2.14 Noise and distortion

When neurones respond to external or internal stimulus they are subject to noise and distortion. Amplifiers introduce noise and create distortion. Noise includes both the hiss that arises inevitably in any electrical system – including neurones – from the random movements of electrons and ions in its conductors, and also disturbances picked up from external sources of interference. Distortion arises through inaccuracies in the linearity of the amplification. This means that the accurate transmission of quantitative information becomes almost impossible: the system almost automatically becomes all-or-nothing in character, since signals either vanish or become saturatingly huge. The normal way, in which a neurone responds to stimulation, is by firing repetitively at a frequency that depends in quite a simple way on the magnitude of the stimulus. There is an analogy here with the use of FM (frequency modulation) rather than AM (amplitude modulation) in radio transmission (Figure 4.1). In AM, the amplitude of the radio-frequency carrier wave is a direct copy of the sound wave being transmitted; the radio receiver decodes this signal by converting the envelope of the radio wave back into a sound wave. The disadvantage of such a system is that any variations in the amplitude of the wave caused by transmission itself – fading or noise generated by radio interference – get incorporated in the sound reproduced by the receiver. In FM transmission this is no longer the case: here it is the frequency of the radio wave rather than its amplitude that conveys the sound information, and disturbances that affect its amplitude no longer matter, since it is only the frequency of the received signal that is decoded by the receiver, producing reliable and relatively noise-free transmission (Stein, 1982; Carpenter, 1996).

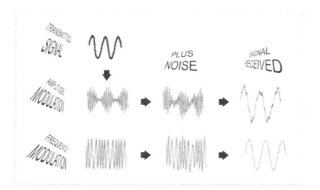

Figure 4.1: Patterns of distortion of transmitted signal with the interference of noise in AM and FM transmissions (Carpenter, 1996:37).

4.2.15 Neurone communication

Communication among neurones occurs in the form of electrical transmissions, either informally through casual sets of gap junctions or at more organized regions of contact called electrical synapses. This initiation of activity in the neurones at the specialized regions of the synapses is called synaptic transmission and the process is known as 'transduction' that is the process by which energy of one form is converted into energy of another. Transduction is in effect preceded by a specialized energy filter that allows certain types of energy through to cause electrical effects and not others. The cell seems to respond to changes in the degree of stimulation rather than to its steady level, a very common type of receptor response that is called 'adaptation'. A rather simpler phenomenon is 'habituation'. Like adaptation, habituation is a decline in response to a constant stimulus; but whereas adaptation means a decline during the application of a continuous stimulus, habituation implies a decline in the successive responses to a stimulus that is repeatedly applied. To understand the number of synaptic connections in the brain, one should realize that there are some 10^{11} neurones in the brain, and each one of them receives and gives on average some 10^4 synaptic connections (Stein, 1982; Carpenter, 1996).

4.2.16 Principles of recognition

An important function is recognition which is responsible for the selective classification or filtering of stimuli and generation of meaning in the form of associations. Objects in the physical world are seen in different times from different sensory perspectives. The stimulus, in other words, is partly a function of what the object is, and partly a function of quite accidental and arbitrary factors that are nothing to do with the object at all (Figure 4.2).

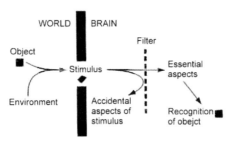

Figure 4.2: A stimulus is a coded version of the object that causes it, some aspects of it being due to the object itself, and some to accidental factors. It has to be decoded by the brain filtering out the accidental properties to leave behind those that are essential to the object itself (Carpenter, 1996:267).

Recognition implies two components of required classification: one is to do with associating together those attributes of a stimulus which define what it is, and the other is the filtering out of aspects of the stimulus that are irrelevant. The component of association can be explained in terms of the mechanisms in which neurones form functional connections between themselves. During the learning process only the cells that are most stimulated by a particular pattern will be activated enough to increase the strength of their afferent synapses. The final goal of recognition is not simply the identification of individual objects but of attaching meaning to them, done by an extension of the mechanism for forming associations by means of synaptic strengthening (Stein, 1982; Carpenter, 1996).

4.2.17 Behaviour control

Higher animals produce more complex behaviour but the fundamental mechanism is essentially the same. The added complexity comes about for two reasons. First, of all there are many more types of desirable and undesirable stimuli to which they may react, and many of them — perhaps most — are learnt. Consequently, every individual has their own classification of stimuli into desirable and undesirable categories. Secondly, the relative desirability of different attractants and repellents is constantly changing in response to the organism's needs; thus changing patterns of need give rise to changing patterns of action even though the environment itself is the same, in a way that may seem to an outsider to be unpredictable. In other words, the central mechanism of the motivational system of the brain can be thought as a map that translates information about need into data that can be turned by the higher levels of the motor system into actual patterns of activity (Figure 4.3).

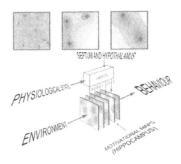

Figure 4.3: The central mechanism of the motivational system of the brain (Carpenter, 1996:274).

Apart from motivational tropism, another way in which behaviour is controlled is by switching on patterns of activity, what is called emotional behaviour, divided in two emotional states: 'arousal' and 'conservation'. Arousal signifies an increase in general activity of the sympathetic system, and the release of adrenaline, during which the electrical activity of the brain, reaction time gets quicker, and there is an associated feeling of general excitement. Conservation or withdrawal is in a sense the opposite of arousal during which the rate of energy expenditure is greatly reduced (Stein, 1982; Carpenter, 1996).

To summarize in brief, the analyses of human neurophysiological and brain processes reveal implications in the processing of stimuli. Noise and distortion may interfere with the already complex and chaotic human information processes and alter the stimulus before it even reaches the human brain. What implicates things further, are the electro-chemical properties of the communicated information and the small time duration of these events which makes their operation even more difficult to conceive and conceptualize. Memory is the deciding reference point of human perception and consciousness of the world and it can consist of both stored and acquired information. What makes each person unique is the diversity of its memory banks and his/her particular ways of interaction and association with incoming information through human information processes. I maintain that the observed elements of organization of information in the human body can be reflexively applied to describe characteristics of the system of information.

Neural networks and artificial intelligence projects are examples of the application of the human information processing model. The study of their application in models of non-human systems, in comparison to the human system, provides interesting comparisons between human and non-human systems, the common element being the principles of organization of the respective systems of information. The comparison here exemplifies how information can be used through programming to organize an artificial system; information generates 'life' and is assigned the characteristics of living elements itself. Consequently, the modeling and programming of non-human systems reflects principles of organization of information in the human system. The following two last sections of the current chapter briefly discuss some aspects of neural networks and artificial intelligence.

4.2.18 Neural networks

A neural network is a collection of processing nodes transferring activity to each other via connections (Taylor, 1993). The human brain, discussed above, is an observable example. The human brain, with its 15 billion neurons, performs fantastically 'at such tasks as vision, speech, information retrieval, and complex spatial and temporal pattern recognition in the presence of noisy or distorted data' (Karayiannis and Venetsanopoulos, 1993). Nerve cells fire impulses to each other across axons and detect the impulses through dendrites. The physical mechanisms of memory and learning remain a mystery, but it is known that people learn by practice and reinforcement, and that knowledge can change as more information is received. One theory of the physiology of human learning by repetition is that the repeated sequences of impulses strengthen connections between neurons and form memory paths. To retrieve what was learned, nerve impulses follow these paths to the correct information. As we get 'out of practice' these paths diminish and we forget what we have learned (Squire, 1987).

4.2.19 Computer networks and human learning

These are some of the things researchers are trying to train machines to do. Neural computing is an attempt at modeling the workings of a brain. In computing, neural network refers to a class of models, which simulate learning in order to assist us in detecting information, predicting outcomes, and making decisions. Essentially, computers are asked to do those things we already know how to do, but we want them to do it faster and more accurately than we can. Neural networks are the natural extension of exploring the limits of computing, in terms of methodology and theory. In terms of application, neural networks are found in systems performing image and signal processing, pattern recognition, robotics, automatic navigation, prediction and forecasting, and a variety of simulations. They are used to help humans wade through huge amounts of data and to extract relevant information. The application of machine programming along the model of human information processes does test and informs us about the principles of human information processing. Consequently this reverse analogy points towards models of organization of the system of information in human and machine neural networks.

Neural nets allow the programming of systems to solve 'problems in which the rules governing the situation are unknown or difficult to use' (Taylor, 1993) and to apply computing to problems not solvable in a strictly linear fashion. Knowledge Discovery and Data Mining (hereafter KDD) is one example of neural network application. A primary goal of KDD tools is to assist the user in detecting relationships in data which may not be readily perceptible due to the sheer size of data, missing data elements, or certainly lack of time to examine data and infer knowledge from them. Many applications of KDD tools are found in decision support and pattern recognition systems.

4.2.20 Artificial neural networks

Artificial neural networks may be represented by different data structures, but they are each designed to 'make use of some of the organizational principles felt to be used by the brain' (Stacey, 1994). In this way their organizational patterns consist a reflection of the patterns of organization of information in human systems. The neural net is composed of nodes named binary decision units (hereafter BDNs) by pioneers McCulloch and Pitts (Taylor, 1993). Each BDN has a number of inputs and a rule to emit activity (a '1') if the sum of the inputs is above a certain, threshold value and otherwise output no activity (a '0'). This is logically the same model as an individual nerve cell (neuron); hence these nodes are called neurons as well. The neural net can be feedforward or feedback to allow back-propagation of error data to improve accuracy (Karayiannis and Venetsanopoulos, 1993).

The behavior of the artificial neural net is determined, like the human brain, by the structure and strengths of the connections between neurons (Stacey, 1994). And, much like human learning, the neural net must have good training in order to respond as desired. A neural network's learning is defined by Stacey (1994) to be any change in the memory ('weight matrix'). There are a variety of strategies to achieve training of the net and its continued learning. These may involve detailed applications of statistical and numerical methods such as back-propagation of error, least squares fitting, differential equations and other iterative methods. The general procedure is, to introduce to the net, some patterns or pre-processed data with identified features and compare the output to the desired response.

Technological advances enable us to collect far more information than we can possibly analyze, while our time to accomplish our goals seems to be vanishing in this fast-paced world. We need help from intelligent assistants, expert systems, data mining, and complex information retrieval strategies to make sense of it all. We certainly do not need to be replaced by them or exchange our human nature for an artificial one. Intelligent applications though have been increasingly in demand as we suffer from workloads of more and more raw data and a highly competitive, global economic climate. The following section examines some examples and issues of artificial intelligence systems and artificial life projects.

4.2.21 Artificial intelligence

Artificial intelligence (hereafter AI) researchers study intelligence in machines and, through computers, in people. Artificial life (hereafter aLIfe) is the field of scientific study that attempts to model living biological systems through supplied information in the form of complex algorithms. Scientists use these models to test and experiment with a multitude of factors on the behavior of the systems. Some of the applications of AI include game playing, speech recognition, understanding natural language, computer vision, expert systems and others. The operation of these applications of these models reveals organizational patterns, of far more complex human functions, at a primary and basic level of operation (Winston, 1992).

AI and aLife applications set certain quality standards, which can be safely used to compare elementary logical thinking and life organization among human and artificial systems. AI application in computers can inform us about the way we think. In logic we formulate rules of interference; we consider things to be true, to be evident by applying a rule of evidence. 'How do we decide whether we know?' is to refer to the sources of our knowledge and to say that a supposed item of knowledge is genuine if, and only if, it is the product of a properly accredited source. In traditional Western philosophy there are four such sources: external perception, memory, self-awareness (reflection of inner consciousness), and reason (Chisholm, 1966:57).

The study of the imitation of human processes in machines does lead to interesting conclusions but one should consider the degree to which, human information processing and biological organization can be reduced to and, to which it can said to be, represented with precision in such experimental demonstrations. If one major question of AI poses as whether machines can think and feel (like humans), one more important question is to what extent do we, as humans, come to think, feel, and deduce our logic and thinking to that of machines. And if so, in the case of digital communication and interaction with computing systems, how can we safely secure the conclusion that our principles of the organization of human communication (with the use of information) are not actually being, in a reflective and associative way, programmed by AI principles. I will be discussing this issue more extensively in the closing sections of the book (epilogue). For now, I turn to a brief account of AI and aLife and try to identify some elements that contribute to our understanding of human and machine information processing and characteristic patterns of the application of information in artificial systems.

4.2.22 Computer vision

In a cultural environment where the media and computer networks dominate our daily informational intake through numerous collections of images, visual AI applications can reflect the organizational principles of human information processing of image association and recognition. Surely, these are elementary processes and image processing in the human brain should be a far more complex process. However, as indicated by cybernetic studies and experiments (discussed further in the next chapter), human image processing could be reduced to these elementary processes due to external intervention or simply because basic brain functions dictate so. The world is composed of three-dimensional objects and full computer vision requires partial three-dimensional information that is not just a set of two-dimensional views. Forsyth and Naylor (1985) consider three broad classes of computer vision: 'image processing', 'image analysis' and 'image comprehension'. Image processing refers to the digital representation of image. A computer may represent a visual image as a series of squares (pixels) and the whole scene may be held in a two dimensional array with the value of each element in the array corresponding to the brightness level of that pixel (the 'gray scale value of the pixel'). Image stretching can be used to overcome problems of perspective. The computer is not really seeing anything, does not understand what it is seeing; it is a passive operation.

Image analysis occurs when the computer gets to have a say in what processing should take place and when it makes a decision on the basis of what it sees before; it tries to find items in the image which correspond to the real world entities and tries to extract suitable description for the next step, which corresponds to not real but rather 'gray-scale levels', usually the line and the surface; surfaces are smooth and uniform, edges present sharp discontinuities. A series of techniques can be applied to make the necessary justifications: 'blurring' is used to remove small variations of little value; 'stereoscopic vision' involves using two cameras separated by distance to record images of the same scene which leads to an initial 'solid' appreciation of the scene; 'surface illumination' is used to determine the position and orientation of surfaces (Forsyth & Naylor, 1985).

In image comprehension, the computer has to have within it some knowledge of the type of thing it is likely to see in order to be able to make sense of what it sees. In the bottom-up approach (analysis by synthesis) the computer synthesizes images of objects it has never seen before whereas in the top-down approach it requires the computer to know an image in the form of an internal model before it can see it all (also called controlled hallucination). The computer can only carry out image comprehension if it is given enough information to enable it to build up a sensible interpretation of a scene before it. Some expert systems can be made to appear pretty intelligent, not by carrying out fully natural language processing (which is hard) but by simply looking for key words and phrases to enable it to side step the full scope of the problem and make an intelligent guess as to what it is being said to the computer quite quickly (the trick system). The issue of 'machine learning' has to do with the problem of how to get the machine to learn for itself and how to act without the need to be explicitly told; to do so one has to write a program which will enable it to do so; among other things, feedback from course of action (accumulation of experience) [is needed] for the machine to learn (Forsyth & Naylor, 1985).

4.2.23 The construction of intelligent identities

The science of control, cybernetics, recorded the switch from one dominant model, or set of explanations for phenomena to another. Energy - the notion central to Newtonian mechanics - was now replaced by information. Digital computers would indeed come to simulate human cognitive processes, but the approach would be quite different from that of biology or cybernetics. It would be called the information processing level of modeling, quite distinct from information theory, and its central idea would be the manipulation of symbols, as opposed to mere feedback, on on-off technology.

'The brain', MIT's Marvin Minsky declared years ago 'happens to be 'a meat machine'. As discussed further above, the brain is an electrical and chemical mechanism, whose organization is enormously complex, whose evolution is barely understood, and which produces complex behavior in response to an even more complex environment. The 'neural-net approach' took as its basic assumption that organic brain cells were largely undifferentiated, and only organized themselves into purposeful behavior because of experience and perceptions (Waren McCullogh's model in the 1940s). The model represented an overwhelming temptation for researchers using new technology to build systems that would likewise organize themselves (so-called organizing systems), that would do so randomly, and that would learn and adapt in the way that organic brains seemed to. A series of problems seemed to be inherent in the construction of an intelligent identity, all having to do with representation(s) of the world. Representation refers to ways in which a claim of truth can depend on the truth of another (necessary or sufficient conditions). A=B, B=A, B is necessary condition for A, A is sufficient condition for B. A computer is a device, which processes representation in a systematic way; it involves computation (algorithms) and automation. The problems AI scientists were faced with were: how to allow the incorporation of specific observations and generalizations from those observations; how to represent data from other than the physical world; how to get knowledge about the world; and, how to assimilate and express knowledge internally. Knowledge is dynamic and not static. The symbols that stand for knowledge are entities with a functional property. Symbols can be created: they lead to information; they can be reordered, deleted, and replaced. All this is seen explicitly in computer programs, but also seems to describe human information processing too. Understanding, then would be the application - efficient, appropriate, and sometimes unexpected - of this procedural information to a situation, the recognition of similarities to old situations and dissimilarities in new ones, and the ability to choose between the doing of small repairs, or debugging, and changing the whole system.

4.2.24 Artificial Life

aLife studies non-organic organisms, the life-like behaviour beyond the creation of nature. Behavioural biologists cross paths with computer and research leads to unifying knowledge. aLife is about emergent properties. An emergent property is created when something becomes more than the sum of its parts, i.e. life on this planet. We are more than the sum of our parts and as such capable of very complex behaviour. Life can be defined as something capable of reproducing its self, capable of adapting to an environment and also capable of independent actions not decided by some exterior agent. We are carbon-based life, the combination of commonly found atoms, depended on variables such as entropy and evolution. We must also remember that we are probably only one combination of atoms that leads to life (Adami, 1998) aLife is only artificial in the sense that is it man-made. In aLife the environment is originally created by humans inside a computer. Combinations of atoms are replaced by creating a set of rules for creatures or cells to follow. If these creatures are capable of reproduction and some form of mutation and they are complex enough the creatures will evolve or the cell pattern will change into new forms. The result is either the population dies out or a solution to survival in the environment is found. Life and aLife are both an emergent property. A single cell cannot do much without interaction with other cells. A single cell has no concept of the whole. In combination it can play its part in producing complex results. Along these lines, it should be evident, that aLife projects are life-forms constructed by information. The system of information itself, like aLife forms, presents emergent properties and is a living entity capable of reproduction, adaptation, mutation and evolution. Its organization also presents analogies with von Neumann's cellular automata and the theoretical propositions of the Gaia hypolthesis.

John von Neumann proposed the concept of cellular automata, a system for producing life-like results from simple rules. A cellular automaton is an array of cells that interact with their neighbors. Each cell has its own state that can be a variable, property or other information. By receiving input from connected cells or general messages a cell uses its own set of rules to determine what its reaction should be. This reaction is a change of state and can also be a trigger to send out its own messages. These messages are passed onto other selected cells, which cause them to act like wise. Natural cells work much in the same way. Artificial cellular automata are usually a lot simpler but can mimic many of the behavioral patterns of natural biological systems (Codd, 1968).

Using these terms it is possible to say that life on this planet is an emergent property with each part, cell, and creature playing a part in the whole. In 1972 Lovelock and Margulis released their view that the Earth can be seen as one living thing. This is known as the Gaia hypothesis. According to the Gaia hypothesis the whole of nature can be seen to be a dynamic equilibrium, in which thought is difficult to explain interdependencies and our actions towards unexpected or indirect results. Everything in the universe exists on a sliding scale of entropy. Life is about the fight against entropy. As other systems lose information to the surrounding environment, life has not only to keep hold of its information but also increase its amount of information. It does this by absorbing, or eating, energy from the surrounding environment.

Life is a complex system, in the dictionary sense of the words. It is a dynamic equilibrium that can carry on changing and evolving over a great amount of time without dying out or fading away (Lovelock, 1989; 2000).

4.2.25 Artificial life forms

Life forms simulated are simple and small with short life spans and simple worldviews. An example of such organisms is a program called Boids (http://www.geocities.com/ SiliconValley/Vista/1069/Boid.html). In Boids artificial life forms have preordained behaviour, but there are other creatures with behaviour which is of their own making. An environment is set up and functions are afforded to the growing creature. Through evolution the creatures work out how to interact with their environment. Goals are often set as a motivation for the creatures to evolve or the motivation for evolution may just be if you can't work out how to eat and breed you die. All these creatures are human initiated but soon find the same moths that nature uses to achieve their goals. Another well known example of artificial organisms is 'the Biomorph' program, a simple program that uses mutation and manual selection to breed creatures known as 'biomorphs' (Figure 4.4). Biomorphs are very simple digital creatures. They were originally created by Richard Dawkins in a program called *the Blind Watchmaker* (Dawkins, 1976; 1987) His main objective was to reduce to the barest minimum to the extend that which he designed them. Biomorphs illustrate the amazingly complex structures that can develop from the application of very simple rules. In Richard Dawkins' work biomorphs were only two-dimensional recursive drawings resulting from the evolution by a Darwinian process of random mutation and user-based selection. A creature without a brain could be said to be a plant. It cannot do much apart from chemically react to simple stimuli. Many still claim that human intelligence is impossible to surpass artificially and in 1989 a British mathematician, Roger Penrose, claimed that the workings of the human brain couldn't be duplicated by a machine - even in principle.

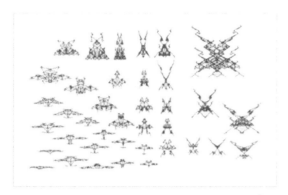

Figure 4.4: Richard Dawkins named 'biomorphs' after the word used by Desmond Dorris for the animal-like shapes in his surrealistic paintings. A biomorph is characterized by a 3D shape and shows a variety of behaviors. Like a real creature, it grows, eats, flees predators, reproduces, etc. (http://www.virtual-worlds.net/lifedrop/galerie/images/biomorph.gif)

Contemporary estimates claim that this can be succeeded by the year 2020. Surely there is more to human thought than the mere firing of synapses but also to fully understand human information processing one has to start from its elementary functions. Attempting to leap directly to the complex actions of the human brain may be a risk and result to misleading conclusions. The attempts of AI and aLife to reproduce the conditions of human intelligence and the organization of artificial systems in computer environments systems offer analogies with the organization and structure of information in human systems. Consequently, they offer insight to elementary principles of low complexity organization of the system of information.

In conclusion, the analogies between human and machine information processing exemplify the elements and principles of organization of information in both systems. The system of information is a living entity that can organize and give life by reproduction, adaptation, and self-organization. The ability of the system of information to reflexively organize other systems should be pointed out. In the case of AI applications, and during human/machine interaction, there exists the possibility for the reflexive adaptation of human information processing to the machine one. This is a possibility, I suggest, that can be generated at the primary levels of interaction between the systems. To what extent the human system will adapt and adjust to deduce its logic and thinking to that of the machine is dependent on the repetition, practice and addiction of the interaction between the systems. Our understanding of the code of the communicated information, the vulnerability of information and human information processing to cybernetic interventions, and the principles of human communication, is further enriched in the next chapter, where basic principles of information theory, cybernetic control and organization of human communication are discussed more extensively.

4.2.26 Summary

This second section of the chapter has focused on a brief investigation of scientific bodies of knowledge in an attempt to map general and specific principles of organization in a diversity of macroscopic and microscopic systems, such as the universe, subatomic particles, biological organisms, the human neurophysiological system, the brain and artificial intelligence models. Although dissimilar in terms of volume and substance, there are principles of organization in all these systems that can be seen as common, and which can be applied in terms of analogies and isomorphies to organizational patterns typical to the system of information. The various scientific disciplines contribute towards different aspects of organization of the system of information, such as spatial geometry, architecture, content and substance, forces, interactions and associations, genetics, and so on. They provide theoretical elements and models, which the intended philosophical imagination and attempted theoretical innovation of this book, endeavours to put forward within the context of an analytical model of theoretical approximations regarding the organization of the system of information. The main points and considerations above that can apply a model of the organization of the system of information are listed in the epilogue next.

4.3 EPILOGUE

The first section of the current chapter focused on various analyses of systems and attempted to draw analogies and isomorphies which can be applied to the organization of the system of information. Systems do use information for their organization and the reverse analogy, that the system of information is indeed a system, should bear no difficulty to realize. The analysis of system properties enhances our understanding of the internal patterns of relationships of, as well as of the native processes among, the constituent units of the system of information. The system of information emerges as a diverse entity, with interrelated and interdependent parts, based on principles of self-organization and differentiation, but also characterized by complex and chaotic organization along non-linear iterations towards fractalization. The main points made above on system properties and suggested theoretical arguments regarding the system of information are as follows:

On systemic characteristics of general, chaotic and fractal systems:

- A 'system' is characterized by a pattern of relationships between elements referring to a whole that is differentiated from its environment. Systems self-organize using communication conditioned by system-environment interactions towards non-predictable but ordered patterns of change.

- Systems present distinct emergent properties in a process of positive feedback between action and its environment. Emergent properties have contingent effects, including acting back on the elements from which they emerge. Systems differentiate by self-reference.

- System differentiation advances the system towards greater improbability by forcing the reproduction of its elements and its elemental operations by repetition and by regeneration of a number of subsystems which in turn continuously reconstruct the whole system.

- The property of autopoiesis presupposes 'a recurring need for renewal' with communication being the elementary operative level of the autopoietic system. The autopoietic reproduction of the system of information becomes a necessary condition of its maintenance against the continuing dissolution towards non-coordination and chaos due to the ever increasing volume of content and complexity.

- System maintenance regenerates the elements of a system and secures its stability by maintaining the instability of continuous change. It consists a built-in requirement of discontinuity and newness of any system, to manage and process system information.

- There exist universal principles applying to systems in general, more specifically models, principles, and laws that apply to them or their subclasses, irrespective of particularities, nature of components, and interrelations among them.

- System properties are characterized by structural similarities or isomorphisms. Isomorphisms are corresponding abstractions and conceptual models can be applied to different phenomena.

- System-environment interactions in the form of feedbacks dictate possibilities of 'change' rather than 'stability' in a system. This change takes place along 'non-linear trajectories' in the arrow of time, occurring within phase spaces of dynamic and strange attractors which are not predictable but their originating generic classes are.

- System complexity reproduces in existing iterative 'state cycles' by sharing information within emerging networks of information exchanges. Local interactions ensure the chaotic change of the system and may affect its global properties. Systems transform into qualitatively different state by perturbations arising from the external environment, internal fluctuations or interactions between both external and internal processes.

- In a complex, non-linear system, a small change in the input could produce a huge change (chaos) in the output (the 'butterfly effect'), and this can have considerable transformations of quantitative to qualitative value.

- Dynamic systems are in constant flux, showing points of instability, which become pervasive when the system is dominated by chaos.

- The irregular and contradictory nature of chaotic systems can be expressed with and understood through non-linear mathematical equations. The mapping non-linear equations of chaotic systems (strange attractors), shows patterns revolving around a core and within the system boundaries and point towards their unpredictable character.

- Fractals consist iterations of nonlinear equations and are characterized by self-similarity and fractional dimensions. They allow us to view the complexity of chaos and order and to advance our understanding of relationships of dissimilarity and interdependence.

On systemic analogies and isomorphies attributed to the system of information:

- The organization and function of the system of information in the digital era obeys principles of organization defined as properties of systems. The system of information is characterized by systemic properties that discursively dictate the organization and behaviour of other systems. It is though an open-end system which does not exclude alternative theoretical modification within the context of the proposed model in this book.

- The system of information can differentiate by self-reference regenerating its elements and its elemental operations in a process of autopoiesis. Systems of information at individual and collective levels, consist production networks that recursively reproduce their constituent subsystems/units of information, inner processes of association and external tensions for interaction, their environmental boundaries and restrictions, and secure their unity and conditions of reproduction.

- Varying degrees of organization and complexity characterize the organization of the system of information classifying it as a complex system. The system of information possesses the properties of chaotic, dynamic and fractal systems. As such, its chaotic organization can be understood along strange attractors and it can be demonstrated with the use of fractal models.

On specific theoretical suggestions regarding the organization of the system of information:

- Theoretical analogies and isomorphies from various scientific and philosophical bodies of knowledge expose properties of the system of information. Differences and contradictions in analogies and isomorphies should be incorporated, rather than rejected, towards a theoretical reconsideration of all accepted context.

- The abstract conceptualization of the organization of the system of information across interdisciplinary scientific contexts may contribute to our understanding of the principles that govern it. Such a conceptualization may demand abstract and uncertain suggestions (in the form of approximations) as an alternative to firm and finite conclusions.

- The ever-increasing specialization of contemporary science would benefit from a general theoretical point of view, not a theory of all, but one that cuts across scientific disciplines and takes into consideration possible analogies and isomorphies of the available knowledge.

- Patterns of parallel organization in various scientific disciplines are indicative of common system properties. There is need to study the organization of the system of information that lies in the core of all systems, in particular to study only structure and processes, organization and order, both in isolation and within the whole of the system.

- Contemporary science is in need of a general theory of organization, a theory of wholeness, to manage the fundamental problems of diverse intensity of organization and complexity in the societies of the digital era. It can propose a logicomathematical discipline which could be applied to most diverse fields.

The second section of the chapter turned to a closer examination of the organization of a diversity of systems, from the Cosmos to the human body, trying to identify analogies and isomorphies in their patterns of organization. Such an examination points towards relative suggestions and reverse comparisons regarding the application of the organizational principles of these systems to the system of information. The patterns of organization of these systems offer theoretical frameworks and models within which different aspects of the mechanics and dynamics of their structure and operation can be suggested. It is information that realizes both the physical and the intellectual domains of both the Cosmos and the human body. In analogy then, the observations and suggestions regarding their patterns of organization (discussed in detail above) can be reflexively applied to the organization of the system of information. A summary of the considerations regarding properties, analogies and isomorphies that can apply a model of the organization of the system of information is provided below:

On observed analogies and isomorphies of systems:

- Basic principles of organization of the universe, the electro-dynamics of particles, quantum mechanics, dark matter and wormholes can offer analogies and isomorphies, such as homogeneity, isotropy, forces and interaction, curved 4D space, and entropy. These can be used to describe the internal organization of the system of information.

- The organization of the electro-dynamics of particles presents analogies and isomorphies that can be applied to the organization of the system of information. These would include varieties of components, possibilities of varied interactions, structural similarities, diverse particle behaviours, and the presence of various interacting forces.

- Theoretical suggestions on the birth and state of the Universe may offer conceptual ideas of the production and regeneration of the system of information: 'bing bang', 'casually disconnected bubbles', creation ex-nihilo, quantum fluctuations, interconnected networks extending forever in time and space.

- Like in the Universe the system of information analogically presents wormholes of information, which connect regions of the system in spacetime. It also shows points of collapse and a like a black hole, it implodes inwards and sideways in the direction of new structural dimensions. Within the system of information, there exist spatial configurations of dark matter of information, that remain invisible and of unknown identity and substance.

- The system of information is a living entity and as such it reflects biological principles of operation and organization. The microcosmic organization of biological organisms exhibits patterns of the organization which can be applied to the organization of the system of information from its simplest to its more complicated forms.

- The genesis of organisms and the structure and function of its simplest form – the human cell – reveals the organized differential function of the constituent parts in biological organisms, and this consists an isomorphy of the internal organization of the system of information.

- The analysis of the human neurophysiological system presents elements of organization of the communicated flow of information which can be reflexively applied to the system of information itself.

- The system of information is not immune to loss and external interference. Interference in the form of noise may lead to distortions of the content depending on whether the system will accept to form associations with interfering data or it will decline any association and reject them.

- The system of information consists of a complex and chaotic organization of native components and of components acquired from environmental interactions. In this sense the content of each system of information is unique, but the principles of its organization remain the same.

- The application of neural networking in computing and artificial intelligence allows the comparison between principles of human and machine information processing. In a reverse analogy the common organizational patterns of these models reflect elements of the system of information at elementary levels of organization.

- The behavior of the artificial neural net is determined by the structure and strengths of the connections between neurons. In a similar way the strengths of associations and interactions within the components of the system of information decide the various phase-states and the dynamic change of the system.

- 'Life' is defined as characterized by emergent properties, as something capable of reproducing its self, capable of adapting to an environment and also capable of independent actions not decided by some exterior agent. In this sense the system of information can be said to be a living entity with all the characteristic traits of live organisms.

- Like everything in life, the system of information that informs and realizes the concept of life, exists on a sliding scale of entropy. The system had to keep hold of its informational content and at the same time to increase the amount of this content. It does this in the form of interactions with other informational systems in the surrounding environment.

On principles of organization of human information processing:

- The study of human neurophysiological processes shows the vulnerability of the stimulus of information in terms of losses and modifications during stages of human information processing before even the stimulus reaches the human brain.

- Human information processing is complex and its complexity is matched by the chaotic organization of the human brain where primary perturbations may generate infinitely large effects.

- The communication of information through the human neurones is conducted by both electrical impulses and chemical reactions; therefore, the communicated information is characterized by electro-chemical properties.

- Human memory consists of stored information, of both acquired and genetically present information dependent on environmental influences. It works as a reference bank for the brain to evaluate, reject or store new incoming information. Memory is a chaotic system of information in itself which organizes our perception and consciousness of the world.

- Memories can refer to processed by the brain information and not to the original form of the external stimulus. Because information is processed in a different way by each person the perception and recollection of memories referring to the same source of information are not the same.

- Brain disorders are an exemplification of the vulnerability of the originally emerged stimulus of information, in that is can be manipulated and distorted, therefore modifying the otherwise unaffected perception of the human brain.

- The natural composition of the nerves as well as responses to 'noise' and 'distortion' of stimuli, impose certain conditions in neural communication which can severely limit the kind of messages that nerves can convey.

- Communication among neurones occurs in the form of electrical transmissions. Neurone cells can either adapt by responding to changes in stimulation adaptation or habituate by showing a declining response. Through associations of meaning they can 'recognize' and selectively classify and filter stimuli.

- The complexity of the organization of human information processing is characterized by internal control mechanisms of individual selective differentiation to changing patterns of stimuli which adds to the complexity of human behaviour.

Finally, some general theoretical suggestions:

- In the quest for the enhancement of our lives with intelligent system applications we need to preserve our human character and avoid being dominated by the artificiality of machine information processing. We need to understand the changing principles of organization of the system of information in the digital era, and we need to adapt to the new forms of [hyper]reality.

- One should consider the degree to which, human information processing and biological organization can be reduced to and represented with precision by AI models. An important consideration would be to what extent do we, as humans, come to think, feel, and deduce our logic and thinking to that of machines.

- Knowledge is dynamic and not static. Knowledge is the result of informational activity of both incoming information and of the interaction of incoming information with the one already present. The origins of the content of knowledge can be traced in the components of the system of information from which it was constructed.

As examined so far in the current chapter of this part of the book, general and specific, system properties, as well as, principles of organization, in both macroscopic and microscopic systems, point towards common patterns of organization of the subsystems of information which organize them. I endeavoured to identify systemic analogies and isomorphies which can reflexively be said to apply to the organization of the system of information. I discussed how native problems in human infrastructure exemplify the vulnerability of the nature of information and of the communication of information, during human information processing, in the case of interference by cybernetic control mechanisms, and in artificial intelligence projects. The quest for knowledge about the functions and obscurities of this *terra incognita* continues in the following chapter with the examination of information theory principles, cybernetic control mechanisms, and, finally, principles of human communication.   ▶▶|

THE 'CHINESE ROOM':
Code, Control and Communication of Information

CONTENTS

CHAPTER 5

THE 'CHINESE ROOM':
Code, Control and Communication of Information

'Now that we have all this useful information, it would be nice to do something with it.'
(From a Unix Programmer's Manual)

5.0 PROLOGUE

The current chapter continues the quest for the identification of structural and processual attributes of the organization of the system of information, and of the communication of information, by looking into various aspects of the information process. To this end I focus on traditional concepts and relationships of information theory such as entropy (randomness), redundancy (constraint) and noise (disorder), which are characteristic elements that define the organization of the system of information. I am discussing how these relationships would apply, or in what ways they need to be reconsidered in relation, to the contemporary environment of digital technologies and communication. Further characteristics and relationships, are investigated, of important information-based tools for the communication, construction and processing of information, such as language, code and grammar (Campbell, 1982). Although the principles of classical information theory apply in general to the organization of the system of information, still, it should be stressed that the process of construction of meaning encounters difficulties in its traditional definition. The relations of meaning are changing with uncertainty and improbability becoming accepted paradoxes in the structure, organization and communication of the system of information. Understanding the code of the organization of information becomes a primary consideration and this may demand highly abstract and controversial ways of thinking.

The discussion then moves to the area of cybernetics where I examine cybernetic principles of human information processing. Biochemical and biophysical processes, associated with human information processing, are examined in relation to their role in securing the automation of certain bodily functions and achieving homeostasis (balance). Cybernetic observations, point towards the fact that, it is possible to interfere and influence human information processing and to this to affect the construction of 'realities', consequently of human behaviour (Saparina, 1966). The human brain is metaphorically exposed as a 'Chinese room'. Searle's (1980; 1984) 'Chinese room' resembles the inside of a computer and refers to a bunch of rules (the program) which operate on symbols, moving through an input/output window as a response to each other. According to Searle, although the 'Chinese room', just simulates thought, its seemingly understanding and calculations are not 'real' they are 'just as-if'. I attempt to investigate how and to what degree this interference and disturbance is actually possible through a discussion of cybernetic qualities of the human brain and of information processing. The case of cybernetic control exemplifies the importance of information for human consciousness, perception and construction of 'reality' about the world we live in.

Having established the basic principles of the communication of information, the ways it is constructed and communicated through language and grammar forms, and how it is controlled by cybernetic control mechanisms, the last section of this chapter looks into the structure and organization of human communication and interaction and certain behavioral pathologies that may arise during these processes (Watzlawick et al., 1967). Human behaviour is affected by communication issues related to information. Discrepancies in the rules of the communication of information may lead to paradoxical situations. These observations of human communication and behaviour, I suggest, show how important the concept of information is for the organization of human thought and expression. Furthermore, problems in the structure and organization of human communication are evident in the varying degrees of disturbances that the communicated information can have on human behaviour, interaction, and the construction of the social knowledge and of the 'reality' of the social.

5.1 ASPECTS OF THE INFORMATION PROCESS

Campbell (1982) provides a comprehensive account of some basic features of the information process, such as entropy, redundancy and noise. He also looks at various aspects of natural processes to identify analogies and isomorphies that are identifiable as characteristic principles of the process of information. He discusses these analogies among the organization of natural processes and principles of organization of information, and finally looks into the ways that brain uses all this input of information available to it. Campbell's account provides an opportunity to identify more isomorphic attributes of the organization of the system of information, but also to discuss further issues related to the coding of information and to human information processing.

5.1.1 Entropy

One basic assumption both by biology and philosophy is that the universe and the living forms it contains, are based, not on accident, but on forces of 'chance' and of 'anti-chance' which coexist in a complementary relationship. The random element in the universe is 'entropy', the agent of chaos, which tends to destroy meaning. Traditionally, information is thought to be the 'non-random element', which exploits the uncertainty inherent in the entropy principle to generate new structures, to inform the world in novel ways (Gray, 1990; Weber et al., 1988)). The classical view of entropy implied that structure is the exception and confusion the rule, whereas information is news, intelligence, facts and ideas that are acquired and passed on as 'knowledge'. Shannon's (1948) entropy equation suggested, at the very least, a powerful analogy between 'energy' and 'information', with entropy being the connection link. The concept of entropy is a measure of the disorderliness of a system, a measure of uncertainty, an aspect of probability. A system in a state of maximum entropy is in a ferment of constant change beneath the visible surface, as molecules shuffle and collide in random confusion; the system has lost its contrasts, its orderly arrangement, which gave it a potential for performing some definite task.

In a world where all things have the tendency to become entropic, disorderly, and their random deviations from order must be corrected continually, the science of 'cybernetics' intervenes to maintain order in the system. This is accomplished by using information about the behavior of the system to produce different, more regular behavior. By such means the system is kept on course. Cybernetics enforces consistency and permits change, but the change must be orderly and abide by the rules. It is a universal principle of control, and can be applied to all kinds of organization, just as principles of information theory apply to communication of all kinds (Ashby, 1957). The methods and techniques through which this is succeeded are discussed in more detail further in this chapter.

It takes longer to describe 'the message' than to describe 'the noise', because we know about 'the internal order' of the first and nothing about the 'internal disorder' of the second (Campbell, 1982). When noise though becomes information, as it is often the case in the Digital era, then certain aspects of the organization of the system of information can apply to it and noise becomes just another manifestation of the entropic tendencies of the system of information. I will argue here that, the system of information is characterized by entropic tendencies, in fact, it is in its entirety acting, not just as a force in favour of structure and 'meaning', but also as a force that regenerates randomness and chaos. Information is paradoxically entropy, because the rules of reference have been reversed, because 'destroyed meaning' does have 'meaning', simply because information is all there is anymore.

5.1.2 The communication of the message

A point of central importance in information theory is that, 'an actual message must be considered not in isolation but in its relation to all the possible messages'. Wiener (1964) recognized that to speak of one fixed item of information signal makes no sense. In an ordinary conversation, information is conveyed when the speaker says something that changes the listener's knowledge. This means that the listener is in a state of uncertainty as to what message he/she will actually hear. It may be highly improbable, and hard to predict, or it may be extremely probable, in which case the listener could have predicted it with ease. But the message will not be 'impossible', in the sense that it violates the rules of grammar or meaning. In the listener's mind are a number of possibilities or contingencies, some more probable than others. When the speaker sends the message, he/she makes one of these possibilities actual, excluding the others and resolving the listener's uncertainty. In traditional information theory, information is considered in relation to the construction of 'meaning'. In contrast, I will argue here though that because 'meaning' no longer subscribes to its classical definition, rather there exist 'relations of meaning', information can exist in various forms, such as noise or forms not necessarily associated with 'meaning'. Messages, in the information revolution of today, can be impossible and violate rules and conditions of grammar and meaning. Furthermore, communication is possible without the conditions set by rules of grammar and meaning, and is possible in conditions of uncertainty and improbability.

5.1.3 Order

Another aspect of information theory deals with the concept of 'order' (Woods, 1970; Hutchinson, 2001). Order, it claims, enables new forms to be created out of old forms and is intimately connected with meaning. Order regulates the equilibrium of a system, and although there is an enormous amount of change under the surface, nothing seems to change at all. Order is valuable in another sense, because it is much more difficult to produce than disorder as opposed to chaos is the easiest, most predictable, most probable state, and it lasts indefinitely. Order is improbable and hard to create and time is its enemy because entropy tends to increase with time. When a system is orderly, and therefore improbable, when it is low in entropy and rich in a structure on the macroscopic scale, more can be known about that system than when it is disorderly and high in entropy. When it is at equilibrium, the state of greatest change beneath the visible surface on the microscopic scale, but of the greatest 'sameness' as seen by the human observer, we have the least possible knowledge of how the parts of the system are arranged, of where each one is and what it is doing. Information like entropy is closely linked to the notion of variety. The problem nowadays, I maintain, is not just dealing with either order or disorder, rather with a variety of formations in which both tensions are present and alternating in volume and intensity. The task is then to recognize and comprehend these forms originating out of variations of orderly/disorderly systems. Such a task is undertaken in the statement of the theoretical approximations in the last two chapters of this book where I attempt to offer a philosophical proposal regarding the microcosm of the system of information that will enhance our understanding of the rules and conditions (the code) of its organization.

5.1.4 Probability

In 1894, Boltzmann (McGuinness, 1974), remarked that the higher the entropy, the less information we can have about the microcosm, the constituent parts of the matter. This is intuitively clear in everyday life. Shanon (1948) remarked: 'I think the connection between information theory and thermodynamics will hold up in the long run, but it has not been fully explored and understood. There is more there than we know at present. Scientists have been investigating the atom for about a hundred years and they are continually finding more and more depth, more and more understanding. It may be that the same will be true of the relationship we are speaking about'. Applied to a thermodynamic system, the golden theorem states that as the molecules move and collide at random, what ever contrasts there are in the system, whatever asymmetry exists between fast and slow molecules, it is most likely that these differences will be smoothed out. The longer the molecular collisions continue, the smaller the asymmetry is likely to become. And less asymmetry means higher entropy. Cardano realized that uncertainty possesses a structure, and that once one has the key to the structure, chance ceases to be an aspect of magic and becomes intelligible. There is no essential difference between probability and credibility, in this view. A given amount of evidence results in a degree of belief in a statement, and there is a logical relation between the evidence and the statement. This is called the probability relation.

According to the Keynes method (Hamouda & Smithin, 1988) probability is at the root of information theory and is inextricably connected with the amount and type of knowledge we possess about any given event or series of events whose outcome is uncertain. Serious difficulties arise when scientists try to separate the idea of probability from the idea of information, because the first cannot be defined with out the help of the second. In Shannon's theory, entropy is a probability distribution, assigning various probabilities to a set of possible messages. But entropy is also a measure of what the person receiving a message does not know about it before it arrives. 'Entropy' is 'an index of his uncertainty' as to what to expect. If the entropy is a maximum, that is to say, if all the possible messages are equally probable, then his ignorance is also a maximum. So probability measures both knowledge and ignorance.

5.1.5 Noise

In classical information theory messages during communication are immersed in noise, because noise is disorder, and it is an axiom of classical thermodynamics that disorder is easier and more permanent than order, which is difficult and temporary. Noise always tends to add itself to messages, randomizing and distorting them, making them less reliable (Pierce, 1962; Woods, 1970). I will point out at this point, though, that quite often in our contemporary digital (informational) environments noise is all there is, therefore noise is information, in the sense that meaning does not matter, it does not exist. For information theory, nearly all forms of communication, more messages are sent than are strictly necessary to convey the information intended by the sender. Such additional messages are seen to diminish the unexpectedness, 'the surprise effect' of the information itself, making it more predictable, making it 'redundant'. Redundancy is essentially a constraint. Redundancy reduces error by making certain letters and groups of letters more probable increasing predictability. Still, doing so, redundancy enables systems, both biological organisms and artificial intelligence machines, to become complex.

It might be obvious by now, that my understanding and reference to the concept of information is different to that discussed in classical information theory. I suggest that information is not necessarily a message or a part of messages that is associated with 'meaning'. My contention is that, in our contemporary societies of postmodern uncertainty and digital illusion, the relations of meaning have been upset. Information is associated with variations of 'relations of meaning'. Everything is information.

5.1.6 Genetic coding

Genetic engineering observations provide some interesting analogies and isomorphies that can be said to resemble aspects of the organization of the system of information and also offer an insight of the coding process of information. Campbell (1982) notes that once the genes are seen as information first and chemistry second, once their all-important role as symbols is recognized, then the barriers dividing one science from another come down. Symbols can be manipulated more freely than substance, and they can be manipulated to form new statements and expressions, which are only tentative, playful, and figurative. Symbols are at liberty to be a little irresponsible and experimental. The sequences of chemical symbols (the bases A, G, C, and T), which are strung out along the DNA molecule, are possibilities. Proteins are these possibilities made actual. Genes are linear, one-dimensional, like words on a page. Proteins are not linear, but three-dimensional. They are the substance, the reality, for which the symbols stand. Proteins are very complex and quite fragile. They are assembled by stringing together chains of amino acids as specified by the chemical code of the gene in a complex process of copying and translating. The twenty different kinds of amino acids can be arranged in an enormous number of different sequences, and it is the order of the sequence that decides what the particular protein is, and what role it will play in the living organism. Proteins are the meaning of the genetic message. One might say that DNA is the word, while proteins are the deed, and deeds are more directly engaged, run more risks, confront life more irretrievably, than do words (Campbell, 1982). Drawing this analogy to the system of information, symbols that exist in the form of data, form internal interactions based on a native code generated by a set of relations of meaning. These interactions lead to structural formations the architecture of which is not linear, but three-dimensional or fractal.

5.1.7 Codes

A code is really a set of rules, a form of stored information. It restricts the amount of choice allowed to the message source in special ways, by introducing redundancy, making some possibilities in the system more probable than others. But the whole point of a successful code is to retain an optimum amount of freedom, a wide variety of possible messages, consistent with the need to make and keep the messages intelligible (Abramson, 1963; Woods, 1970). Shannon's (1948; 1951) second theorem assured us that this can be done. Such a code does not make an information system simpler, by any means. It increases rather than diminishes complexity. Without redundancy, complexity cannot persist, because there would be no way to control error. There is another kind of organized system for which an external description would be unmanageably more elaborate than the system itself: a human society. A society, like a language, is rule-governed, and its surface properties may be a misleading guide to an understanding of its internal structure. It is complex by its very nature, and remains complex by reason of its inner rules principles. In a modern, democratic society, certain types of action are excluded by the rules. There are constraints on the freedom of its members. But within the limits of such constraints, a great profusion of choice is permitted, leading to innovation and change. Sameness persists amid the change, ensuring that the society remains intelligible, despite the randomizing forces of chance which are always present in all organized systems, whether natural or artificial. In life, mind, and society, Hayek believes, structures have a complexity, which could arise only through spontaneous ordering forces. A person can know, at most, the rules observed by part of the structure, but not all the parts and never all the circumstances affecting each part. Rules define general principles, while leaving the details open. This enables an extremely complex society to maintain itself in a steady state. Human society has 'emergent' properties it evolves in unpredictable ways. Like the cosmos, its order is intrinsic, generated within. Similarly, the system of information is organized by a 'code', which refers to complex rules and conditions, which allow change and which apply restraint towards a state of dynamic equilibrium (Abramson, 1963; Campbell, 1982). The quest for the identification of the 'code' that organizes the system of information predominates in the current book. Still, this book suggests that we can approach the 'code' of information in the form of theoretical approximations and not of final and definite conclusions because of its dynamic constantly changing character.

5.1.8 Self-regulating complexity and equifinality

'Language' and 'living systems' have at least one thing in common: they are complex and stable at the same time, and they achieve this by means of internalized rules. They do not surrender to the randomizing effects decreed by the second law of thermodynamics, and they depend less than might have been expected on chance and accident. Their complexity is 'self-regulating'. Prigogine (Browne, 1979; Thurston, 1980) believed that organized systems arise naturally out of unorganized matter. He proposed the existence of a hitherto unrecognized principle, which pushes living organisms, even human beings themselves, to states of greater and greater complexity, whether or not that is the direction in which they want to go. Prigogine observed that this is something completely new, and totally against the classical thermodynamic view that information must always degrade. The tendency to move forward towards a highly organized state, rather than backward toward a simpler state is a property of open systems, those that exchange matter and energy with their surroundings. Open systems do not behave in the same way as closed systems, which for a long time were the chief objects of study in physical chemistry. Under certain circumstances, open systems reach a steady state in which they are far from equilibrium, or maximum entropy, and they maintain that state. They are highly 'improbable', highly complex. What is more, such a steady state can be reached from different starting, points, and in spite of disruptions along the way. The state is called 'equifinal'.

Prigogine saw these open thermodynamic systems as beginning in a state of disorder, becoming unstable, and then entering a stage in which energy accumulates and structure develops. He called this 'the creation of order by fluctuations'. A fluctuation is a chance affair, a variation from average behavior that is normally smoothed out, but under special conditions grows larger and becomes established. Fluctuations are always occurring, but some grow large, while others are eventually smoothed out again. If fluctuations reach a critical size, they stabilize in the equifinal state. The creation of structure depends on how far the system is from equilibrium, and this in turn depends on the rate and amount of exchanges of matter and energy with the surroundings. The distance from equilibrium will be great if there are many exchanges and very small or non-existent if there. The same laws of physics apply in both cases, but near equilibrium. Prigogine observed that the laws lead to doom or destruction, whereas further from equilibrium they may become processes of construction and organization. In this latter case, he adds, probability theory breaks down. 'Non-equilibrium' can therefore be 'a source of order in open systems', whether these systems are chemical or biological, revealing a fundamental kinship between life and non-life. Complexity is maintained in both types (Browne, 1979; Thurston, 1980).

Both properties of self-regulating complexity and equifinality are characteristic of the organization of the system of information. Although its complexity can be affected by external interference it is up to internal conditions that regulate the level of its complexity. As argued elsewhere in this book, the system of information can acquire, maintain, and fluctuate, among a variety of states characterized by varying degrees of probability and complexity. Order and disorder, within the system of information, are alternating to the point that they resemble patterns of similar behaviour and organization. The state of equilibrium or non-equilibrium becomes irrelevant to the generation of order (Browne, 1979; Thurston, 1980; Campbell, 1982).

5.1.9 Complexity

Chomsky (1980; 2002) suggested that human language competence, which must be among the most complicated structures in the universe, arises uniquely in evolution at a certain stage of biological complexity. In other words, it appears when, and only when, evolution has led to an organism as complex as a human being. To begin with, he believed complexity belonged to the more general subject of information, and to what he called 'quasi-thermodynamical considerations'. Complexity, he said, displays critical and paradoxical properties, properties such as entropy, which are found only in systems, which are non-simple. Moreover, to understand complex systems, such as a large computer or a living organism, we cannot use ordinary, formal logic, which deals with events that definitely will happen or definitely will not happen. A probabilistic logic is needed; one that makes statements about how likely or unlikely it is that various events will happen. Another property of certain very complex systems is that they are able to reproduce themselves in such a way that the offspring do not lose, and may in fact gain complexity. Living creatures reproduce themselves, but they do more than just reproduce.

John von Neumann (1966) proposed that in living organisms, and even in machines, there exists a 'complexity barrier'. Beyond this barrier, where systems are of a very high complexity, entirely new principles come into play. Below the critical level, the power of synthesis decays giving rise to ever-simpler systems. Above that level, however, the synthesis of more elaborate systems, under the right conditions, becomes explosive. The important feature of complexity is that it is made possible by redundancy and generated by rules, which are a form of stored information. What emerges here as the link between the biology and the linguistics, are the rules.

5.1.10 The codes of language and life

'Linguistic rules' are not strict mechanisms of cause and effect but leave a system essentially open and incomplete, so that it is always capable of novelty. Choosey (quoted in Campbell, 1982) exposed the folly of supposing that English, or any natural language, is a 'finite-state system'. A 'finite-state grammar', is the simplest and most limited of all grammars. It is not like a machine, which starts by printing the first word of a sentence adds one word after another until the end of the sentence is reached, and at which point the machine stops. Living creatures are transformed from embryo into adult according to exquisitely subtle timetable of development for which a very complex system of controls and rules, 'a genetic grammar', must exist. In its modern sense, an algorithm is some special method of manipulating symbols, especially one that uses a single basic procedure over and over again. It converts certain quantities into other quantities, using a finite number of transformation rules. Similarly, I contend that the system of information can be said to be organized according a complex code characterized by both a genetic grammar, but also by rules and conditions that are acquired during further existence and evolution. This combined grammar is further elaborated in the statement of my theoretical approximations.

5.1.11 Anagenesis and neoteny

Biological complexity is characterized by two important properties. The process of 'anagenesis', refers to the ability of biological entities to match or surpass the complexity of the environment. This ability accounts for the progressive mastery exerted by living creatures over their surroundings, through a higher and higher level of molecular organization in the chemistry of body and brain. During evolution, the changes which led to such significant differences must have taken place in those parts of the DNA text that specify a protein directly, in the passages containing the algorithms which control the icing and use of existing structural genes. The result of these changes, clearly, was the emergence of that most distinctively human possession, the big brain (Campbell, 1982).

Another property that characterizes biological complexity is the technique of slowing down maturity, retaining into grown-up life the juvenile traits of ancestral species, which is called 'neoteny'. It means, literally, 'holding youth'. Nature uses information to organize matter, which is a symptom of versatility that tends to lead to more versatility. It is an activity in which neotenonic creatures typically engage. This comes in the form of repetition, which is the simplest form of redundancy. Existing genes duplicated themselves, producing exact copies, which at first were quite superfluous, of no use to the organism. The DNA text was extended, but the effect was like printing a book, which consists of the same few pages repeated over and over again. Extra copies of these pages provide no new deformation. As time went on, however, the redundant genes underwent 'chance mutations'. They ceased to be copies and became unique sequences, new pages in the book of life. In some cases, however, mutations may result in a gene copy 'acquiring a meaning'. A structural gene would code for a useful new protein. A gene that structural gene would code for a useful new protein. What is even more interesting is that a gene copy, as an extra page, is often ignored by natural selection, even when accumulating mutations, as long as the 'original page' of which it was a duplicate continues to serve its beneficial function. The copy is free to change in ways, which would not be tolerated in the original. Once the new gene acquires a useful meaning it may then come under the protection of natural selection and be preserved (Campbell, 1982). The processes of anagenesis and neoteny are characteristic processes of the organization of the system of information. They reflect the capacity of information to adapt and be assimilated in its environment through forming associations, and to organize unorganized matter, be means of iterations, into mutations. Most importantly these informational mutations may acquire independence from the original source and engage into novel relations of meaning.

5.1.12 Human language and activity

The 'ancient astronaut thesis' is behaviorism carried to extreme limits. That the human mind is passive, needing to be rather than being, to innovate on its own time, adapting rather than creating, copying, not originating. A theory of evolution which takes no account of the internal structure of the information in DNA stumbles and falters under the impact of new discoveries, new ideas, in the fast-moving science of molecular biology. In much the same way, a theory of language which concerns itself only with the surface appearance of the spoken or printed word, has no hope of understanding is most important and essential. It misses the whole point of language as a human activity (Campbell, 1982). One has to consider not just the observable, investigate deeper below 'the obvious', into more general rules of the 'code' that characterizes both the 'coding', as well as the communication process. As I have already discussed in previous sections, disturbances in the communication of information may appear during the encoding process at the source, due of the interference of noise, or even during the decoding process at its destination.

5.1.13 Abstract structures and universal grammar

Chomsky's (1980; 2002) thesis argued that, a singe message is of interest only from the point of view of its relationship with all other messages, which could have been sent but were not. The receiver must make sense of the message, disentangle it from the noise, and reconstruct it in its original, non-random form. Unless this is done, communication is impossible. In the era of digital communication relationships among messages and between messages and meaning are seriously disturbed, so the possibilities for communication, or even the essence of what consists communication, become questionable. Chomsky regarded language as a well-defined system, and interestingly he pointed to abstract structures that lie underneath, and to which the sentence self is related only indirectly. These structures are, in a sense, bans or descriptions of sentences. In Chomsky's linguistics a set of base rules generates 'deep structure' ('D' structure), which is the abstract plan of a sentence. 'Surface structure' ('S' structure) has become more abstract that it used to be, and has an enriched information content. It means that, from the point of view of syntax, of structure alone, sentence contains more useful information than might have thought. Similar structural layers and patterns of the system of information are described in my theoretical proposal, in particular, various structural levels of information are identified in terms of either content or intensity.

Basic requirement of any information system is that messages should vary unpredictably, but vary according to certain specific rules and conditions, a 'grammar'. Grammar is an anti-chance device, keeping sentences regular law-abiding. It is a systematic code applied at the message source. Chomsky called this device 'universal grammar' (Cook & Newson, 1996).As an innate predisposition, enabling a child to acquire competence in a language quickly and without methodical instruction, universal grammar leaves almost nothing to chance. Universal grammar, as Chomsky describes it, is not a grammar itself, but a theory of grammars in general, a set of hypotheses about them. Jackendoff (2002) argued that only by discovering the universal principles constraining choice, reducing possibilities, can we hope to explain why language is natural rather than invented. To explain boundary conditions on language, we need 'a theory of what goes on in the brain' when linguistic information is processed. Such a theory might be highly abstract and, when discovered, lead us to think of grammar in an entirely new way. In his opinion, 'archetypes are essentially constraints, mental structures in the unconscious mind' which make it possible for messages, in the form of images, to be sent to the conscious mind. The nature of these messages is mythological and symbolic. The order of words in a spoken sentence is determined only in part by formal mechanisms, which are under the control of universal grammar. It is also affected by more concrete specific factors, which have to do with the state of mind of speaker, his intentions, and the context in which he is speaking, impression he wants to make on other people. Jackendoff's proposal above, for a theory of information in the brain, justifies the attempt of this book to provide a set of theoretical approximations based on principles of organization of diverse scientific disciplines. It should be expected that such a model, trying to account for the organization of the system of information in the era of digital communication, will be highly abstract, controversial and one that would lead to rethinking of information in distinctively new ways.

5.1.14 Coding human information

The system in the human body responsible for coding and organizing information is the brain. Freud described the function of the brain as 'a pleasurable process of discharge' of high levels of 'nervous' energy unpleasant to the conscious brain (the 'nirvana principle'). It is thought that models of familiar or unimportant messages are stored somewhere in the brain, at an unconscious level, and that when the messages change, or new, significant messages arrive, mismatch between the incoming information and the models triggers attention for that information. Computer modeling programs (called 'programming demons') have been used to imitate the brain's ability to ignore certain types of information if the information is of relatively minor importance. The system of information does not necessarily need to store information as messages related to meaning, if that is what the brain does, rather it can store information as raw data and by processing them through phases of deconstruction, classification, and reconstruction.

One of the main concerns in the communication of information is the 'error' and how to control it. Shannon (1948; 1951) took it for granted that error will always be with us, because noise in communications systems is as natural as entropy is in thermodynamic systems. Shannon's solution was a code, which corrected random changes in the messages caused by noise. He established as a universal principle, that reliable information is possible in an unreliable world. 'Code works by adding redundancy'. This means that some sameness is mixed in with change. Change is the essence of information. There are contradicting opinions as to how 'reality' is constructed. Does the brain construct its own version of reality, relying on very little in the way of information, coming to the senses, or is it experience that provides all the needed information, and then the brain makes a selection from that data. A consideration of both possibilities would bring us to a closer understanding of how information is processed in the human brain. The brain does seem to have a chaotic freedom to process information according to its own internal rules, but it also looks vulnerable to incoming interference of external information.

5.1.15 Group theory

'Group theory' is trying to establish a correct theory on the basis of insufficient evidence. Information does not need to be enriched by the brain because it is already rich when it arrives at the eye. 'Group theory' is concerned with patterns and relations, with the essential sameness of things concealed beneath. Their surface differences, in much the same way that Chomsky's work in linguistics is concerned with universals, elements of language that are invariant, even though languages differ from another in relatively superficial ways. Group theory is highly abstract and general. It enables scientists to make sense of the hidden world of the atomic microcosm because of its peculiar power to generate information about the structure of events, even if the events themselves cannot be known. A group consists of a class or collection of elements, which may be as specific as numbers or squares or atoms or as vague as an undefined object of thought. Or the elements may be a class of operations performed on something (Suzuki, 1982; Campbell, 1982).

For a class of elements to be a group, in the mathematical sense of the term, certain conditions must be satisfied. One of these conditions is the rule that if the elements A and B are members of the class in question, then combining A and B by some operation, say addition or multiplication, results in an element which is also a member of the class. Another is the rule that there must be an 'identity' element in the class, such that, when it is combined with another element A, of the same class, the result is again A, unchanged by the operation. In simple arithmetic, four added to zero is still four, and four multiplied one is still four. Here the identity elements would be zero and one respectively. A further rule states that there must exist an element, which when combined with any other element, results in the identity. Only if all these conditions are met can the class of elements be called a group. Group may also consist of a class of operations performed on something, one after another in succession. The array possesses one very interesting property. Certain elements, when combined with themselves again and again, provide us with the entire group of elements, while others do not (Suzuki, 1982; (Campbell, 1982). The system of information can be said to be characterized by the properties of a group. It presents a complex architecture of patterns and relations, and it consists of defined as well as unknown components. Obviously the unit of information is the identity element of the group. Either at quantitative or qualitative levels, there exists the possibility for the system of information, to perform operations with other elements of the group and remain unchanged or to differentiate resulting to an iteration of the entire group of elements.

5.1.16 Construction of meaning

During the last chapter I referred to neurophysiological problems encountered in the processing of information in the human brain. From a different point of view here, it is interesting to see how the actual procedure of construction of meaning in the human brain works, which also reveals aspects of the organization of the system of information. Information is easier to remember when it is in an orderly state, rich in pattern and structure, highly interconnected, containing good deal of redundancy. Disorderly information that lacks structure is easy to forget. Information is remembered better if it is embedded in a wider context of information already known from personal experience. If the items display no obvious relationships, no discernible pattern, the brain will invent relationships, imposing some arbitrary order on the disorderliness of the material. In a way not fully understood, memory also depends on the structuring of information, the making of patterns, and is at its most fallible when pattern does not exist. Whether someone will be able to remember information depends on what meaning the whole experience for him/her, as well as what is expected of him/her when he/she recollects it. In an act of memory we construct and reconstruct experience, using any or all of these mental functions - perception, comprehension, inference belief, language - whether unconsciously or in full awareness (Campbell, 1982; Jackendoff, 2002)

Out of disconnected elements, a complete meaning is constructed, and that is what a person remembers. People tend to interpret new information in the context of their previous knowledge, and the two elements, old and new, become fused in memory. We construct meanings and remember constructions. Reconstruction may seriously distort the original information, but the person who remembers may be quite unaware of the distortion. If the material given to us is consistent with our knowledge and expectations, it is more likely to be recalled correctly, but if it is inconsistent, then there are likely to be systematic distortions. As argued before, the brain is not a device for processing information in a one-dimensional, linear fashion only. Unlike a computer, the brain is probable rather than certain in its actions, arriving at many answers, some more nearly correct than others, and these answers modified continually by feedback of new information. Jenkins believes that we remember experiences which have a personal meaning for us, even if the meaning is a pure construction of the mind: 'I think we will eventually conclude that the mind remembers what mind does, not what the world does ... experience is what will be remembered'. So the brain constructs and reconstructs information, creating highly personal mental artifact and calling it a memory. Whatever is retained in the brain, as a memory, is abstract. To be expressed, it must be converted into a different code, transformed into a structure closer to consciousness (Campbell, 1982).

The human brain then, organizes both orderly and disorderly information and stores it in memory. Information in context, or redundant it is easier to recall, still, difficulties in interconnections among units of information are resolved by the capacity of the brain to impose arbitrary order and relationships of meaning. Meaning in the human brain is constructed by formed associations between incoming and stored information which get fused in memory; often, the reconstruction of interconnections may get distorted. In a similar way, I will argue, the organization of the system of information follows interconnected patterns and structures, and has the independence to invent new interconnections, if they are absent or 'damaged', by means of continuous construction and reconstruction. The concept of 'meaning' in the system of information consists a confirmation of the structural interrelations and attempted interactions among components of the system of information. In this sense, it may confirm logical, random or paradoxical interconnections. 'Meaning' exists only as a temporary confirmation between the imagined and logically anticipated outcome and the actual result of communication.

5.1.17 Brain functions

The brain has the unique capacity of making patterns out of seemingly patternless material and this has been argued for both the state of consciousness and the state of dreaming. Jung said: 'every dream is an organ of information and control'. Similar theories agree that dreaming is an information process (Campbell, 1982). Certainly the brain is not passive when we dream. In certain respects, it works twice as hard as in the waking state, and is extremely alert to its own internally generated information. In the normal brain, the two hemispheres are not separate, but are connected by an enormous bundle of fibers called the 'corpus callosum', containing more than 200 million nerve cells. This great cable of tissue enables each side of the brain to communicate with the other side, although the exact nature of the communication is not known. The corpus callosum takes about two years to begin working, and is not fully formed until about the age of ten. This delay in establishing a mature connection may enable the two sides of the brain to develop independently in their own special fashion in early life (Carpenter, 1996). Even when the link is complete, there is no reason to assume that all information is shared by both sides or that the bridge spanning the two halves provides a perfect unity for the brain. Possibly the exchange of messages within the brain is only partial. Some research points tentatively to this conclusion. In one famous experiment, a man's left brain was put to sleep with a drug, sodium amytal. The man was asked to explore, by touch with his left hand, which is under the control of the right brain, an ordinary teaspoon. Later, when the anesthetic had worn out, he was unable to name the object he had touched, and declared his total ignorance of it. Yet when shown a collection of objects, he selected the spoon by pointing to it. The memory of the spoon was in the right hemisphere, which is virtually speechless. It was coded there in a form, which was untranslatable into the language of the left, speaking hemisphere. The Right brain knows whether a sentence is asking a question, giving an order, expressing a condition, or making a statement. It can construct imaginary situations into which these various different non-verbal items of information might fit and make sense (Campbell, 1982). The different functions of the two hemispheres of the brain are once more exemplary of the vulnerability of information during human information processing. Cybernetic control (examined further in the next section) is also an example of how the control of the flow of information can influence the content and the organization of the system of information.

5.1.18 Summary

Principles of classical information theory provide an initial insight into characteristic attributes of the system of information. Entropy, order and disorder, probability, noise, complexity, and redundancy are all to be found in some aspect of the organization of the system of information. One basic difference in the postmodern era of digital communication is the loss of 'meaning' in its traditional sense. With meaning reversed and replaced by relations of meaning, uncertainty and improbability become part of the communication process. It is of critical importance then to investigate the code of the organization of the system of information. The code refers to an internal set of complex rules and conditions native to the system of information, which works by introducing redundancy and decreases complexity towards a state of stability. Because of this complexity the code can exhibit paradoxical properties which require the employment of probabilistic logic. Similarly to the codes of language and life, the system of information is characterized by the presence of a very complex system of controls and rules, a grammar based both on genetic and acquired elements. The analysis of these rules and conditions of organization require a highly abstract and controversial way of thinking. It also requires the possibility to abandon any expectation of recognizable 'meaning'. The main points discussed above are listed in the epilogue at the end of the chapter.

5.2 CYBERNETIC PRINCIPLES OF HUMAN INFORMATION PROCESSING

Saparina (1966) took on a cybernetic approach to the human body as such, what she called *The Cybernetics Within Us*. In her approach, Saparina took into account the sciences of automatic control, mathematics, logic, biology, and communication theory, in an attempt to explain basic concepts in cybernetics, and throw some light into the inner functions of the human brain, and the function of human and machine systems. This section of the chapter focuses on her observations regarding principles of human information processing within the human body. Saparina's analysis of the cybernetic principles of the human s ystem, and of the human information processing, are vital to the hypotheses of this book. They demonstrate the variety of complex functions of the brain before and during the processing of information. They advance our understanding of the in-depth procedures of human information processing, and they exemplify the nature and other attributes of information that is finally processed and perceived. They demonstrate the possibilities of external interference to the system of information present and expose the dangers that such an interference may pose for the construction of knowledge, and to this extent of 'reality' for the affected system. Saparina's analysis concentrated on a series of cybernetic observations on cybernetic qualities of the human system and especially of the human brain. These would include, principles of information processing, automatic control mechanisms, brain functions, operational programmes, memory and storage, image processing, cognition and action, and are discussed next.

5.2.1 A science of control

Cybernetics is concerned with the study of control and communication (Ashby, 1957; Beer, 1959; Pask, 1975). The science of control covers three main spheres: control of machine systems and manufacturing processes, control of organized human activity, and control of processes in living organisms. To the later belong the physiological, biochemical and biophysical processes associated with the vital functions of the organism whose purpose is to ensure its survival in an overcharging environment. The question naturally arises whether 'it is possible to simulate the brain electronically, at least in part?' The answer may lie in the some of the branches of cybernetics, such as 'bionics' and 'mathematical linguistics'. 'Bionics', deals with the development of electronic neuron analogues and their utilization in computing machines, whereas 'mathematical linguistics' (a branch in the science of language) is closely linked with the development of 'machine language' and the automation of translation. If we compare, Saparina observed, the basic, fundamental aspects of machine operation and body functions, what these systems of control have in common, one finds is that their operation can be described by precisely the same mathematical formulas. These formulas can be used to describe the operation of a steam engine, an automatic steering device of the nervous system. In order to achieve the required results it is necessary to act directly on the main control system. As I argued before, the science of cybernetics exemplifies the power of information in constructing what we commonly classify as 'reality'. Most importantly it shows that it is possible to control the flow and communication of the system of information, through direct to the human brain external interference.

5.2.2 Cybernetic qualities

Nature fits so much information into a microscopic cell and codes the programme for constructing the intricate adult organism by storing the requisite information in the form of a detailed code, which is handed down the generations. Terms like 'genetic codes', 'hereditary genetic information' and 'the cybernetics of living systems' in bodies and the cells comprising them are in effect cybernetic systems in which, additionally, there are stored away codes carrying detailed information about the future organism and its development. The hereditary information is stored away in long molecular chains made up of thousands of simpler molecules. Knowledge of the genetic code reveals the mysteries of the mechanics of life. Did nature begin by producing molecular structures, which later evolved into living organisms, which in their turn developed cybernetic systems possessing qualities like living creatures? A machine isn't alive. But why isn't it alive? Living organisms are not only cybernetic systems on the larger macroscopic scale. Every constituent molecule itself obeys cybernetic laws. For a physical entity to be alive it must possess cybernetic qualities even at the molecular level. In future machines should be capable of reproduction and improvement - though not, their own accord, but as the result of the incorporation of a suitable programme of operations. The organism maintains these parameters at constant level by means of the system of automatic control called 'homeostasis'. The more one reads of the various automatic devices packed by nature into our bodies, all working to keep body processes in perfect balance, the clearer one comprehends the true meaning of Pavlov's words: 'Life as a whole from the very simplest to the most complex organisms, including, of course, man, represents a long series of increasingly complex equilibrium responses to the environment' (Saparina, 1966). It is important to notice how genetic information in a human system is partially responsible for the accumulated information in the human system. Moreover, I will argue here, genetic information, passed down through genetic code, in the sense that it is not innate to the system, can be said to have originated in the environment.

5.2.3 Reflexes and signaling devices

The brain regulates our movements by means of electrical impulses (action potentials). One can hardly overestimate the importance of motor activity to the body. Motor response to the initial stimulus is such as if the stimulus was reflected from the brain, and it is called a 'reflex'. In other words, a reflex is of necessity 'a closed loop', a characteristic feature of all control processes. Coordinated motion consists, in effect, suppressing surplus degrees of freedom; as a result an arm or leg is converted into a controllable mechanism. How is the control affected? The obvious conclusion is that the brain has nothing to do with the motion. This appears to be the case, and we do say that the involuntary reflex motions known, as unconditioned reflexes are quite automatic. Nerves are responsible for kinesthetic feedback, which tells the brain to what extent its commands have carried out. Kinesthetic feedback is adequate to perform automatic, involuntary motions (Carpenter, 1996).

The organism is remarkably well equipped with a variety of 'signaling devices'. Any automatic self-governing system must contain 'a motor' or 'effector', which drives the object being controlled, a 'sensor' for measuring the amount of adjustment (control) required, a 'unit for analysing the incoming information' from the sensors and translating this into commands, and finally, a 'regulator unit' which utilizes these commands to control the motor. An elaborate monitoring system, something like closed-circuit television, keeps the brain informed of extents in all parts of the body. With this information it is able to exercise its supreme command over body movement. Thus appears that our motions are controlled not by a single closed circuit but by a multitude of neural loops, by a multitude of superimposed automatic control unit regulators. The brain always seeks to get rid of tasks, which do not require mental effort (Carpenter, 1996; Blankenship, 2003).

5.2.4 The 'black box'

The known facts of cerebral activity appear to indicate that the living brain is a computer of sorts. The brain is a closed machine, a mysterious 'black box' as the cybernetician would call it. 'Some such automatic switching device probably operates in the brain', Pavlov wrote. Motion, for example, automatically, subconsciously is an inherent property of the nervous system, a mechanism that invariably responds to stimulation, an unconditioned rebel. Other responses develop as one's range of experience widens. The manner in which they are carried out depends on the conditions in which a person may find himself/herself. These are acquired or conditioned reflexes. The brain must constantly appraise the situation, decide the action required and tile motor activity best suited to achieve it. 'Programming' and 'data processing' are technical terms without which it would be impossible to describe a cybernetic system. This is exemplified in a cybernetic machine basic operations of which can be reduced to computations; which is why these machines are usually called computing machines or just computers. In fact, all animal brains are computers (Saparina, 1966; Carpenter, 1996; Blankenship, 2003).

The brain is not a plain calculating machine. Probably more like the cybernetic analogue technically known as analogue computer. Our brain operates in a somewhat similar manner. It mentally constructs an analogue of the future motion, utilizing of course, its incomparably greater capabilities. That our brain is an analogue system, which employs 'step search', is a discovery of tremendous importance. The obvious conclusion appears to be that closed-loop feedback is a universal principle of action of each and every cybernetic system. Despite its wide variety, the information fed back to the brain can be classified into several more or less distinct types according to the role it plays in the animal's behaviour. 'Organizing' information, is very important. No action can be carried out without it. Each stage of complex motion a go-ahead signal must be supplied to the central nervous system before it order the motion to be continued. This is the second type of information, which Anokhin (quoted in Saparina, 1966) calls endorsing or authorizing information. 'It appears', Anokilin stated, 'cellar before carrying out an action the brain sets up a mechanism for evaluating its anticipated result in that it matches the actual result'. Anokhin called this 'action acceptor'. Information from our sense organs and muscles converges at the action acceptor.

Observations confirm that recollections appear spontaneously and are due to stimulation the temporal lobes of the brain. The different levels of the temporal lobe appear be responsible for different types of recollections. Events are actually not recorded here, but in other sections of the brain, which are closely associated with the temporal lobe. In humans, each receptor of external stimuli appears to have a local memory store of its own. Our brain memorizes visual acoustic tactile or motor sensations separately. Memory of something heard is evidently a record of the original stimulations of certain nerve centers. The stimulations come to an end, but leave invisible 'misprints'. When we speak of information processing and storage capacity an electronic computer or the human brain are dealing with an exact mathematical quantity measured in specific units, called 'bits', which is a contraction of the words 'binary digits'. Our brain is capable of receiving 140,000 million bits of information per second. Facts and phenomena, it appears, are memorized not in isolation, but in correlation to one another, or in their contextual relationship (Saparina, 1966; Carpenter, 1996; Blankenship, 2003).

5.2.5 The reticular formation

When preliminary information has reached the central nervous system, it does not necessarily evoke a response. Additionally to information concerning the environment the organism requires a message to trigger the reflex. Many simple processes are started by such triggering signals. It thus takes a suitable combination of environmental and 'firing' information to trigger nerve mechanism of a reflex. The firing of a nerve cell is followed by a brief period of rest in which processes inside the cell are inhibited. Stimulation is always followed by inhibition. The brain uses such brief inhibition periods for running repairs. 'Alarm clock' and 'chronometer' nerve cells are found in a thin net covering the stem, which is nearby the area and is called the 'reticular formation'. The reticular formation appears to act as a kind of alarm clock, which rouses the cortex to activity. The awakened cortex is ready to sort out the signals coming in from the sense organs and extract pertinent data from its memory store. It intercepts both the messages entering the cortex and the commands it issues. The reticular formation also intervenes in the flow of information to and from upper and lower regions of the central nervous system and can increase or reduce the frequency of the impulses coming up to the brain from the sense organs of the muscles (the pro-prioceptors) thereby altering the nature of the information carried by them. The reticular formation was found to affect messages coming in from all sense organs without exception. Nearby is located another of the brain's guardians, its chief chronometer. It sets the rhythm, as it were, which all internal processes follow. The rhythm of our internal 'clock' does depend on the Earth's rotation. Body chronometer appears to be quite independent. Scientists have come to the conclusion that the body contains a variety of 'clocks'. The 'master chronometer' is located in the brain. The deep lying layers of tile brain are responsible for a person's emotional state. It is suggested that aminazine switches off the centre in the reticular formation, which is responsible for gainful sensations without affecting the centre, which alerts the brain for pleasurable sensations. It thus appears that there are at least two neural mechanisms at work in the reticular formation, one being responsive to aminazine, the other to its antidote, adrenalin. The conclusion is that psychic states apparently derive, at least in part, from complex nervous processes each one being evoked by different specific chemical substances (Saparina, 1966; Carpenter, 1996; Blankenship, 2003).

5.2.6 Operational programmes

Different types of neurons respond to incoming stimulations, some establish the general patterns, others generate nerve impulses, and others compare the excitation impulses of the first two to decide their action. Nerve impulses, as already discussed in the previous chapter, travel from one neuron to another through the synapses, like electric sparks may jump across a gap between two electrodes. One of the basic concepts employed by physiologists in the operation of nerve impulses is that of the 'reflex chain'. In a reflex chain, the signal initiating one action depends on the results of the preceding action. The meaning this term conveys is essentially that of an operational routine or programme of planned actions. The human brain is continuously constructing new programmes of action. Understanding the rules of the reflex chain would provide the key to an understanding of how living organisms develop their operational programmes. This primary, physiological mechanism helps the brain to select those elements of the programme which best agree with external conditions. The living brain produces a programme of action best adapted to the new circumstances of the environment. It develops strictly purposeful behaviour through experiment, through trial and error. As a result a multitude of random, purposeless motions is cut down to a few purposeful actions, which emerge as intelligent behaviour. This is how an existing programme is improved (Saparina, 1966; Carpenter, 1996; Blankenship, 2003).

Of primary interest are the rules, or algorithms, according to which the brain processes information. Neuro-cyberneticians suggest that the brain employs a hierarchy of algorithms of varying degrees of complexity. Every higher-level programme forms lower-lying programmes. The lowest-level programme essentially comprises the simplest behavioural patterns of animals, the rules for developing reflexes. The second-level programme develops rules according to which new forms of purposeful behaviour may evolve. The third level develops the algorithms of self-learning. Only man possesses this level. An algorithm is essentially a set of fairly simple rules. The rules according to which the brain functions are unknown, the task though remains for cyberneticians is to understand the internal structure of the brain the principles of neuron geography and interconnection.

Knowledge of this kind will provide further insight into how the brain operates. It was found that besides the 'triggering' conditioned stimuli, described by Anokhin, there also exist 'switch-on' stimuli, which do not elicit specific responses but affect the nature of a person's responses to the 'trigger' stimuli. The experiments showed that when it is confronted with changed conditioned stimuli the brain initially attempts to make use of old reflex chains, which have previously proved their worth in solving problems. Only if they do not stand up to the test does it proceed to draw up a new programme of operation. Further experiments concluded that new criteria for screening useful information are utilized when new programmes are being developed (called 'recruiting-agents'). It was found that some of the control mechanisms possess extraordinary powers. In the human system, 'reflex circuits' form very quickly without reinforcement. It appears that the human brain memorizes new information, which has not been screened by the control mechanisms or reinforced (Saparina, 1966).

Informational components within the system of information are organized in a series of multi-dimensional patterns, analogous to the operational programmes of the human brain. These patterns develop from internal interactions and external associations of the system of information and they are characteristic of the specific identity an informational subsystem can acquire. Similarly complex algorithms related to the code of information come into play to create a diversity of hierarchical levels of informational interactivity (Saparina, 1966; Carpenter, 1996; Blankenship, 2003).

5.2.7 Memory and storage

Messages of all kinds flow to the brain in an endless stream from the body's receptors. The brain is in constant need of a continuous flow of information. A human may be beset by obsessive memories or fixed ideas and hallucinations may arise. The brain is not affected by a disease; it suffers from the effects of forced inaction. This supports the idea that many psychic disorders start with intoxication of the nervous system. As a result many of the brain's neurons are engaged in an endless recycling of useless nerve impulses. The reduced ranks of unaffected neurons are unable to cope with all the functions of the brain. Incidental information, which is normally sifted away, may now get firmly imprinted in the memory and serve as a source of more false conceptions. Nonexistent images are projected in the brain and hallucinations appear. The brain is open for all kinds of information, whether 'useful' or not. It rapidly fills the memory to capacity leaving no place for useful messages. The brain forms an erroneous image of the environment. Pathological reflexes need not necessarily develop on the basis of an incorrect selection of ill-coming information. Cybernetically speaking, the matter need not necessarily be one of incorrect information processing, it might be a question of storage as well (Carpenter, 1996; Blankenship, 2003).

The control system need not have ready-made programmes for every possible contingency. The memory carries a minimum of information, which can be used to build up a number of programmes. Stored information can be said to be generally available to the neuron population at large. The brain uses some specific data to set up a reflex chain. Afterwards it returns this data to the store for subsequent use. Information is stored in the brain without interfering with the other functions. When new messages enter the brain, are processed and a specific programme develops, relevant requests are sent up to the cerebral 'archives' for the required information. Possibility of developing new behaviour patterns depends not so much on memory capacity as on the perfection of the supplementary mechanisms. There must exist a special physiological mechanism, which reviews the information in the memory store and compares it with incoming information. The brain carries out a selective search. The scanning of this or that chain begins only if the relevant 'bewitching-on' stimuli are present. The brain does not scan all the information in its memory stores but only a small and relevant portion of it. It engages in the 'step search', its 'steps' are normally in the right direction. It is interesting to notice the perceptual problems occurring in the brain in the case of 'incidental' information or inaction. It is also important that in human information processing not all stored or incoming information is used, moreover, a selective process is being used to filter the content of the communicated information (Carpenter, 1996; Blankenship, 2003).

5.2.8 Image processing and recognition

Our visual system appears to be a complex structure designed for the reception and transmission of images, or rather information about images. When physiologists took a cybernetic approach to the system of image transmission in living visual systems they discovered many interesting things. They found that the eye does not transmit the images of objects to the brain in a continuous stream. Like cinema projection and television, our eye breaks an image into frames, which are transmitted to the brain sufficiently quickly to form a continuous picture. Besides partitioning the image in time, the eye also breaks it up according to brightness. It screens the visual images for the essential information worth forwarding the brain. The intermediary cells between the receptors the nerve fiber appear to act as accumulators. The accumulators sift messages from several receptors for useful information and suppress irrelevant signals entering the communication channel. Their duty is noise suppression and filtering. The changes in a visual image are reported by means of a code, which is probably based on the number of impulses in a nerve discharge. The code gets more refined and the information is compressed, as it were, into a smaller space. Secondary messages are blocked and only essential information is transmitted further on. Much leaser nerve fibers end in area 17 of the visual centre, the most interesting and least known element of our 'cerebral television, its 'picture screen' (Saparina, 1966).

Walter (quoted in Saparina, 1966) suggests that the visual messages are scanned and transmitted to other parts of the brain in much the same may as an electron beam scans the screen of a cathode-ray tube. One of the inferences of these and other researches is that the image is 'dissected' in the brain and been reassembled to a complete picture in areas lying at some distance from the visual centre. The brain is able to study the 'dissected' image in greater detail. Where a detailed analysis is not essential generalized images of objects are formed in other parts of the brain. The theories offer an explanation only of the perception of simple images. They assume that our brain contains something like symbols, which denote a square, a circle and other geometrical figures. It is evident, however, that the brain cannot have a full stock of visual symbols imprinted in it from birth. It is probably correct to assume that a set of images constituting a kind of visual dictionary is not intrinsic but is acquired with life experience. The brain can then use simple, elementary images to build up new and complex ones. It does not passively store away the elements of the whole stock-in-trade of the external world. The brain itself creates images of objects and phenomena on the basis of information it receives. These images are not replicas of the optical images that our eyes see. The brain notes the main features of images and supplements them with mental images. Thus it does not restrict itself to the simple reception of initial information but supplements incoming messages with its own information.

In our contemporary era of digital technologies vast amounts of visual imagery are being intercepted by the human visual system. The rules that govern image processing and recognition become critical in understanding human information processing in this context. Two important points should be stressed. First, regarding the construction method the human brain uses to create images of objects and phenomena. It is not the actual image that is being transmitted to the brain, rather a copy which is the result of a process breaking up into pieces and then of reassembling, using both incoming and stored information. Secondly, it is important to notice the presence of a basic 'dictionary' of symbols upon which the brain bases its further processing of incoming images. Both attributes, I will argue are also characteristic of the more general organization of the system of information. The system of information is continuously undergoing processes of deconstruction and reconstruction which apply to all types of information. An array of symbols, functions and patterns are also characteristic of the elementary levels of organization of the system of information.

5.2.9 Cognition and purposeful action

Some areas of the human brain (39 and 40) are areas which occur only in the human brain. They developed late in the history of mammalian evolution and are responsible for abilities unique to man: cognition and purposeful work. In fact, they evolved in the process of work. Work transformed ape into human, and developed a section of the cerebral cortex, specifically for the purpose of analysing changes, in the environment created by purposeful activity. Work as a process must be organized and conducted according to plan. This is handled by area 40. In this case too, it is not the control of a specific movement that is affected (the motor centre is functioning normally) but the general plan of action, the labour skills developed by learning and experience. What is involved is the highest form of motor activity evolved by humans (Carpenter, 1996; Blankenship, 2003).

In animals, reality is signalized almost exclusively by stimulations and the traces they leave in the cerebral hemispheres, which come directly to the special cells of the visual, auditory or other receptors of the organism. This is what we, too, possess as impressions, sensations and notions of the world around us, both natural and social - with the exception of the spoken or written word. This is the first signal system of reality common to humans and animals. With the second signal system is associated the specifically human ability to abstract from the countless stream of specific information pouring in through the first signal system, to summarize its essence. The system of word perception is the second signal system, in which the conditional stimulus is the word, spoken, heard or seen. The brain must be able to identify a word whatever form it appears, establish connections between different words and, in the case of speech, mentally construct a word or even a whole sentence before the lips utter it

(Saparina, 1966).

5.2.10 Summary

In summary, to understand human communication one needs to consider the code of human information processing. One needs to understand the critical principles and control mechanisms affecting information in the human body, and to do so, one has to consider the detailed biochemical and biophysical processes associated with human information processing. A cybernetic analysis of these processes points towards a series of control mechanisms which secures automatic control functions and ensure the necessary balance among bodily functions. Electric impulses, reflexes, signaling devices are all part of a complex network of control of information. With their aid, the human brain works by constructing mental images of future action, then reports them to the nervous system, and endorses or authorizes the action by evaluating the anticipated result. By trial and error, and according to a code of complex algorithms, the human brain is continuously constructing new programmes of action using existing and incoming information. The main points discussed in the above section are summarized at the end of this chapter.

5.3 PRINCIPLES OF HUMAN COMMUNICATION

The last section of the current chapter focuses on a discussion of the issue of human communication. Human communication is expressed either verbally by language or by nonverbal body language and either form affects the behaviour of the participants of the communication. Advances in mathematics, cybernetics and information theory have helped to understand the relationships developed in human communication. More specifically they have helped to understand the various aspects of the communication of the system of information, many of which have already been discussed in the previous sections of this chapter as well as in the previous chapter. Watzlawick et al (1967) categorize the issues involved with human communication into three areas: 'syntactics', 'semantics', and 'pragmatics'. Syntactics, closer to information theory, refers to the problems of transmitting information, and deals with problems of coding, communication channels, capacity, noise, redundancy, and other statistical properties. Semantics focuses on the meaning of/in communication and tends to be more philosophical. Finally, pragmatics is actually the study of the effect of the communication of information on human behaviour. However, Watzlawick et al (1967) remarked the boundaries among these separate fields are not really distinct. Pragmatics are not only words, their configurations, and meanings (the data of syntactics and semantics) but their nonverbal concomitants and body language as well from this perspective of pragmatics, behavior, not only speech, is communication, and all communication affects behaviour.

In *The Pragmatics of Human Communication*, Watzlawick et al (1967) discuss a series of issues regarding the behavioural aspect (pragmatics) of human communication. Some of these issues are discussed further in this section, such as concepts, definitions and axioms of the behavioural aspect of human communication, distinctions between digital and analogic communication, pathologies that develop during communication, the organization of human interaction and interactional systems, and finally paradoxes of human communication. The issues discussed here are important to this book as they reflect the important role that information plays in human communication. They exemplify the significance of the organization of the system of information, disturbances in which may result in problems in the communication of information. Some attributes of the organization of the system of information are also revealed. During human communication it is information that is communicated and the result of this communication is expressed in forms of human behaviour. The analysis of the human communication of information therefore, reflects analogies and isomorphies that can be applied to the structure and organization of the communicated system of information along a multi-dimensional matrix of horizontally and vertically developed relations among human and non-human systems.

5.3.1 The notions of 'function' and 'relationship'

A new dimension of information was realized with the introduction of variables in number theory. In contrast to a number signifying a perceivable magnitude, variables do not have a meaning of their own; they are meaningful only in relation to one another. The relation between variables constitutes the concept of 'function'. To quote Spenlger (1926:77): 'functions ... are not numbers ... but signs representing a connection that is destitute of the hallmarks of magnitude, shape and unique meaning, an ensemble unified and so attaining existence as a number'. There exists a suggestive parallelism between the emergence of the mathematical concept of function and the awakening of psychology to the concept of relationship. Ashby (1957:117) remarked: '… memory is not objective, something that a system either does or does not possess; it is a concept that the observer invokes to fill in the gap paused when part of the system is unobservable. The fewer the observable variables the more will the observer be forced to regard events of the past as playing a part in the system's behaviour. Thus memory in the brain is only partly objective'. Movement is something relative, which can only be perceived in detail to a point of reference. What is not realized by everyone is that this same principle holds for virtually every perception and, therefore, for human's experience of reality. Sensory and brain research have proved conclusively that only relationships and patterns of relationships can be perceived and these are the essence of experience. A process of change, motion or scanning is involved in all perception. Not things, but functions are the essence of our perceptions and perceptions are not isolated magnitudes, but 'signs representing a connection … an infinity of possible positions of like character' (Ruesch & Bateson, 1951:173). Variables and functions are important concepts for describing the complex principles of human communication. They are also useful to describe the complex internal structure and processes of the system of information which is expressed by the content or the message of the communication. The dynamic character of the system of information can be understood as patterns of infinitely possible relationships (functions) among the diversity of variables that are responsible for the organization of its content.

5.3.2 Feedback loops and stochastic processes

A number of highly important phenomena remained outside the immense terriers conquered by science; they have their common denominator in the related concepts of growth and change. The advent of cybernetics showed that the principles could be brought together in a more comprehensive framework. This view became possible through the discovery of 'feedback', known to be either positive or negative and characterizing homeostasis (steady state); positive feedback leads to change, loss of stability or equilibrium. The point to make here is that interpersonal systems (groups, families, a set of relationships) may be viewed as feedback loops, since the behaviour of each unit of the system affects and is affected by the behavior of each other unit. Watzlawick et al (1967) pointed out that, 'self-regulating systems – systems with feedback – require a philosophy of their own in which the concepts of pattern and information – are as essential as those of matter and energy were in the beginning of the century'. Feedback is an important aspect of the organization of the system of information. It may be responsible for its qualitative and quantitative changes. Internal feedback loops of informational units can be responsible for its continuous turbulence. Reflecting attributes of self-regulating systems the organization of the system of information is based on complex patterns of relationships and networked processes.

Watzlawick et al (1967) called for new avenues of approach, simply because the traditional frames of reference are clearly inadequate. Advances made in other fields, are of immediate relevance to the study of human communication. One such development has been Ashby's 'homeostat' (1954) which led to the conclusion that no subsystem can attain its own equilibrium in isolation from the others. A chain of events in which every element has at all times an equal chance of occurrence is said to show randomness. However, if a system, like the homeostat, is provided with the ability to store previous adaptations for future use, the probability inherent in the sequences of internal configurations will undergo drastic gauge in the sense that certain groupings of configurations will become repetitive and, therefore, more probable than others. A chain of this type, in information theory, is called a 'stochastic process'. Thus, stochastic process refers to the lawfulness inherent in a sequence of symbols or events, whether the sequence is as simple the results of drawing white and black marbles from an urn, or as complex as the specific patterns of tonal and orchestral elements employed by a certain composer, the idiosyncratic use of language elements in the style of a given author, or the diagnostically highly important patterning contained in the tracings of electroencephalogram. Stochastic processes show redundancy and constraint.

5.3.3 Axioms of human communication

First of all, there exists the impossibility of not communicating. A single communicational unit will be called a message or, where there is no possibility of confusion, a communication. A series of messages exchanged between persons will be called interaction. (or patterns of interactions). All behavior is communication: one cannot not communicate.

Secondly, every communication has content and a relationship aspect such that the latter classifies the former and is therefore a meta-communication. The report aspect of a message conveys information and is, therefore, synonymous in human communication with the content of the message. It may be about anything that is communicable regardless of whether the particular information is true or false, valid, invalid, or undecided. The command aspect, on the other hand, refers to what sort of a message it is to be taken as, and, therefore, ultimately to the relationship between the communicants. What is important is the relation existing between the content (report) and the relationship (command) aspects of communication. An example would be, a computer which needs information (data) and information about this information (instructions). Clearly, the instructions are of a higher logical type than the data, they are meta-information since they are information about information, and any confusion between the two could lead to a meaningless result.

Thirdly, the nature of a relationship is contingent upon the punctuation of the communicational sequences between the communicants. To an outside observer, a series of communications can be viewed as an uninterrupted sequence of interchanges. However, the participants in the interaction always introduce what following Whorf (1956:273-274), Bateson and Jackson termed the 'punctuation of the sequence of events': 'the stimulus-response psychologist typically confines his attention to sequences of interchange so short that it is possible to label one item of input as stimulus and another item as reinforcement while labeling what the subject does between these two events as response. Punctuation organizes behavioral events and is therefore vital to ongoing interactions'.

The axioms of the pragmatic aspect of human communication analogically reveal principles of organization that characterize the system of information. Because behaviour is an explicit expression of internal informational processes, and all behaviour is communication, then communication becomes a path for the expression of the inner communicational tendencies of the system of information. The complex relationships that define the content of the system of information are abstract constructs of a higher logic than the data that comprise the content. These set of relationships are in fact instructional information (about the organization) and they are expressions of, what has elsewhere been referred to as, the code of the system of information.

5.3.4 Digital and analogic communication

A specific part of neural activity, consisting in the occurrence or non-occurrence of its firing, conveys binary digital information. The humoral system, on the other hand, is not based on digitalization of information. This system communicates by releasing discrete quantities of specific substances into the bloodstream. It is further known that the neural and the humoral modes of intra-organismic communication exist not only side by side, but that they complement and are contingent upon another, often in highly complex ways.

The two basic modes of communication, digital and analogic, can be found at work in the field of human-made organisms, more specifically computers. Some computers utilize the all-or-none principle of vacuum tubes or transistors and are called digital, because they are basically calculators working with digits. Another class of machines manipulates discrete, positive magnitudes (the analogues of the data) and hence is called analogic. These two types of communication are also equivalent to the concepts of the analogic and the digital respectively (Watzlawick et al, 1967).

Analogic communication is virtually all non-verbal communication. This term, however, is deceptive, because it is often restricted to body movement only, to the behavior known as kinesics. This would include posture, gesture, facial expression, voice inflection, the sequence, rectum, and cadence of the words themselves, any other nonverbal manifestation of which the organism is capable, as well as the communicational clues unfailingly present any context in which an interaction takes place. The human is the only organism known to use both the analogic and the digital modes of communication. There exists a vast area where we rely almost exclusively on analogic communication, often with very little grange from the analogic inheritance handed down to us from our mammalian ancestors. This is the area of relationship. We can further expect to find that the content aspect is likely to be conveyed digitally whereas the relationship aspect will be predominantly analogic in nature. Some of the characteristics of computers also apply to human communication: a digital message material is of a much higher degree of complexity, versatility, and abstraction than analogic material. But what is lacking in digital communication is an adequate vocabulary for the contingencies of relationship. In summary, human beings communicate both digitally and analogically. Digital language has a highly complex and powerful logical syntax but lacks adequate semantics in the field of relationship, while analogic language possesses the semantics but has no adequate syntax for the unambiguous definition of the nature of relationships (Watzlawick et al, 1967).

The distinction of human communication in analogic and digital reflects the organization of the system of information in the human system in relation to its environmental configuration. Elements of both analogic and digital organization are ever present. Varying degrees of complexity and abstraction characterize both content and relationships. In order to come to a closer understanding of the organization of the system of information in the era of digital technologies and communication, we need a theoretical framework that can adequately account for both the nature of the content and the logic of the relationships along which this content is interconnected. Such a framework, an analytical model of theoretical approximations of the organization of the system of information is offered in the last part of the book.

5.3.5 Types of interaction

In 1935 Bateson defined the phenomenon of 'schismogenesis' as a process of differentiation in the norms of individual behavior resulting from cumulative interaction between individuals.. He said, '... it is at once apparent that many systems of relationship, either between individuals or groups of individuals contain a tendency towards progressive change ...' (1958:176-77). As Watzlawick et al (1967) argued, 'relationships are based on either equality or difference'. In the first case the partners tend to mirror each other's behavior, and thus their interaction can be termed symmetrical. In the second one partner's behavior complements that of the other, forming a different sort of behavioral *gestalt*, and is called complementary. Symmetrical interaction, then, is characterized by equality and the minimization of difference, while complementary interaction is based on the maximization of difference. There are two different positions in a complementary relationship: one partner occupies what has been variously described as the superior, primary, or 'one-up' positions and the cadet-the corresponding inferior, secondary, or 'lie-down' position. A third type of relationship that was suggested is 'metacomplementarity', in which A lets or forces B to be in charge of him; by the same reasoning, argued Watzlawick et al (1967) 'pseudosymmetry' could also be added, in which A lets or forces B to be symmetrical. They conclude to one more axiom: all communicational interchanges are either symmetrical or complementary, depending on whether they are based on equality or difference.

The attributes of communicational interchanges in human interaction represent the internal organizational structure of the information that is communicated in the respective interaction. The geometry of this internal organizational structure of interacted information can be better

255

understood when expressed as spreading along three-dimensional spatial coordinates within the system of information, continuously changing with time.

5.3.6 Pathologies of human communication

Numerous behavioural problems may appear in human communication, which Watzlawick et al (1967), classify as pathologies of the pragmatics of human communication. These pathologies are evident in expressed language, verbal or non-verbal, and account for inabilities and confusion in recognition of 'meaning', as well as in rejections either of the communication or of the participant in the communication. It should be logical to suggest that, disturbances in the ability of recognition of compatibility as well as expressed uncertainty related to the content and relationship of communication, point towards defects in the inner structural and inter-relational interconnectedness of the organization of the system of information negotiated in the interaction.

'Schizophrenese' is a language which leaves it up to the listener to take his/her choice from among many possible meanings which are not only different from but may even be incompatible with one another. The phenomenon in question, however, is not limited to fairy tales or schizophrenia. It has much wider implications for human interaction. The pragmatics of this communicational context are narrowed down to a very few possible reactions: rejection, acceptance, and, disqualification of communication. Disqualifications are interesting, as they cover a wide range of communicational phenomena, such as self-contradictions, inconsistencies, subject switches, incomplete sentences, misunderstandings, obscure style or mannerisms of speech, the literal interpretations of metaphor, the metaphorical interpretation of literal remarks, and so on.

The phenomenon of disagreement provides a good frame of reference for the study of disturbances of communication due to confusion between content and relationship. Disagreement can arise on the content or the relationship level, and the two forms are contingent upon each other. It is in the nature of human communication that there are now three possible responses by A to B's self-definition, and all three of them are of great importance for the pragmatics of human communication: confirmation, rejection and disconfirmation. One has to communicate with others for the sake of his own awareness of self (confirmation), and experimental verification of this intuitive assumption is increasingly being supplied by research on sensory deprivation, showing that man is unable to maintain his emotional stability for prolonged periods in communication with himself only. Rejection, however, presupposes at least limited recognition of what is being rejected and, therefore, does not necessarily negate the reality of B's view of himself. Disconfirmation, as observed in pathological communication, is no longer concerned with the truth or falsity - if there be such criteria - of B's definition of himself, but rather negates the reality of B as the source of such a definition. In other words, while rejection amounts to the message 'you are wrong', disconfirmation says in effect 'you do not exist'. Or, to put it in more rigorous terms, if confirmation and rejection of the other's self were equated, in formal logic, to the concepts of truth and falsity, respectively, then disconfirmation would correspond to the concept of undecidability, which, as is known, is of a different logical order.

Disconfirmation of self by the other is mainly the result of a peculiar unawareness of interpersonal perceptions, called 'imperviousness' and defined by Lee (1963) as follows: 'What we are concerned with is the aspect of awareness and unawareness. For smooth, adequate interaction to occur, each party must register the other's point of view. Since interpersonal perception goes on many levels, so too, can imperviousness go on many levels. For, there exists for each level of perception, a comparable and analogous level of possible imperception or imperviousness. Where a lack of accurate awareness or imperviousness exists, the parties in a dyad relate about pseudo-issues … they attain an assumed harmony which does not exist, or argue over assumed disagreements that similarly do not exist'.

5.3.7 The organization of human interaction

Human interaction is described as a communication system characterized by properties of general systems such as, time as a variable, system-subsystem relations, wholeness, feedback, and equifinality. Ongoing interactional systems are seen as the natural locus for study of the long-term pragmatic impact of communicational phenomena. Limitation in general and the development of family rules in particular lead to a definition and illustration of the family as a rule-governed system.

The concept of pattern in communication can be seen as representing repetition or redundancy of events. As there are certainly patterns of patterns and probably even higher levels of organization this hierarchy cannot be shown to be limited. Interaction can be considered a system, and the general theory of systems gives insight into the nature of interactional systems. The obvious and very important variable of time (with its companion, order) must be an integral part of the studied system. As it has already been discussed in an earlier chapter, a system is a set of objects together with relationships between the objects and between their attributes, in which objects are the components or parts of the system, attributes are the properties of the objects, and relationships 'tie the system together'. Interactional systems, then, are two or more communicants in the process of, at the level of, defining the nature of their relationship. Another important aspect of the definition of a system is the definition of its environment. Following Hall and Fagen: 'for a given system, the environment is the set of all objects a change in whose attributes affect the system and also those objects whose attributes are changed by the behavior of the system' (Hall and Fagen, 1956:20). Moreover, '… organic systems are open, meaning they exchange materials, energies, or information with their environments … [whereas] a system is closed if there is no import or export of energies in any of its forms such as information, heat, physical materials, etc., and therefore no change of components…' (Hall and Fagen, 1956:23). With the development of the theory of hierarchically arranged open subsystems, the system and its environment need no longer be artificially isolated from one another. With this conceptual model a dyadic interactional system can be placed into larger family, extended family, community, and cultural systems. In short, communicating individuals are seen in both horizontal and vertical relations with other persons and other systems.

The principles of the organization of human interaction reflect isomorphies found in the principles of the organization of the system of information. Hierarchies of structural and relational patterns are characteristic of the informational architecture. These patterns expand into three-dimensional space accounting for the development of networks of multi-dimensional relationships with the components of, the same or an interacting, system of information.

5.3.8 Principles of interactional systems

Some of the macroscopic formal properties of open systems can be defined as they apply to interaction. Every part of a system is so related to its fellow parts that a change in one part will cause a change in all of them and in the total system (wholeness). 'Summativity' is its polar opposite: if variations in one part do not affect the other parts or the whole, then these parts are independent of each other and constitute a 'heap', that is no more complex than the sum of its elements. This quality of summativity can be put on the other end of a hypothetical continuum from wholeness, and it can be said that systems are always characterized by some degree of wholeness. 'Non-summativity', as a corollary of the notion of wholeness provides a negative guideline for the definition of a system. A system cannot be taken for the sum of its parts; it is necessary to neglect the parts for the *gestalt* and attend to the core of its complexity, its organization; in other fields there is great interest in emergent quality that arises out of the interrelation of two or more elements. In contrast, from the first axiom of communication - that all behavior is communication and one cannot, not communicate - it follows that communication sequences would be reciprocally inseparable; in short, that interaction is non-summative.

Feedback and circularity is an appropriate causal model for a theory of interactional systems. As discussed earlier, the principle of equifinality means that the same results may spring from different origins, because it is the nature of the organization, which is determinate. Von Bertalanffy elaborated on this principle: 'The steady state of open systems is characterized by the principle of equifinality; that is, in contrast to equilibrium states in closed systems which are determined by initial conditions, the open system may attain a time-independent state independent of initial conditions and determined only by the system parameters' (Von Bertalanffy, 1962:7). Then, not only may different initial conditions yield the same final result, but also different results may be produced by the same causes. Again, this corollary rests on the premise that system parameters will predominate over initial conditions. In the case of the open system, however, organizational characteristics of the system can operate to achieve even the extreme case of total independence of initial conditions. A system that is characterized by stability is called a 'steady state' system. To return to Hall and Fagen, 'a system is stable with respect to certain of its variables if these variables tend to remain within defined limits' (Hall and Fagen, 1956:23).

The operation of interactional systems is based on motivation, need satisfaction, social or cultural factors. The answer can be descriptive rather than explanatory, that is, on 'how' and 'not why' the interactional system operates. The factors above can be considered as limiting the effect of communication, by noting that in a communicational sequence, every exchange of messages narrows down the number of possible next moves. As noted further above, in every communication the participants offer to each other definitions of their relationship, or, more forcefully stated, each seeks to determine the nature of the relationship. Similarly, each responds with his definition of the relationship, which may confirm, reject, or modify that of the other. This stabilization of relationship definition has been called 'the rule of the relationship' by Jackson (1965a; 1965b).

The 'family-rules' theory fits the initial definition of system, as being stable with respect to certain of its variables if these variables tend to remain within defined limits. Such a model for family interaction was proposed by Jackson (1957) when he introduced the concept of 'family homeostasis'. The behavior of every individual within the family is related to the behavior of all the others. All behavior is communication and therefore influences and is influenced by others. The analysis of a family is not the sum of the analyses of its individual members. Many of the individual qualities of members, especially symptomatic behavior, are in fact particular to the system. Inputs (actions of family members or of the environment) introduced into the family system are acted upon and modified by the system. Implicit in the above are a pair of more basic assumptions of reliability within a defined range. The importance of change and variation (in terms of positive feedback, negative feedback, or other mechanisms) rests on the implicit premise of some fundamental stability of variation, a notion already shown to have been obscured by the dual use of homeostasis. The more accurate term for this fixed range is 'calibration', the 'configuration settings' of the system, which will be seen to be equivalent to the more specific concept ruled defined above. There is a calibration of customary or acceptable behavior (a family's rules or society's laws) within which individuals or groups operate for the most part. At one level these systems are quite stable, for a deviation in the form of behavior outside the accepted range is counteracted (disciplined, sanctioned, or even replaced by substitute). At another level, change occurs over time, which is at least in part due to amplification of other deviations, and may eventually lead to a new setting for the system ('step-function').

The system of information is itself an interactional system and local changes may affect global change. Although feedback always remains an important factor of change, it is possible that the system of information may move towards change and alteration on the base of its own initial conditions and parameters and obtain phase states independent to external influence. What makes each informational construct unique is the particularity of the quality of its components. Like an interactional system, changes in the system of information are calibrated by mechanisms of its inner organization, although long term changes are unavoidable if not necessary.

5.3.9 The paradoxes of human communication

'Paradox' not only can invade interaction and affect our behavior but also it challenges our belief in the consistency, and therefore the ultimate soundness, of our universe. A paradox may be defined as a contradiction that follows correct deduction from consistent premises. Three types of paradoxes are defined: logico-mathematical paradoxes or antinomies, usually referring to paradoxes arising in formalized systems such as logic and mathematics. Antinomy, according to Quine (1960:85), produces a self-contradiction by accepted ways of reasoning. Stegmeuller (1957:24) is more specific and defines an antinomy as a statement that is both contradictory and provable. Thus every antinomy is a logical contradiction, although, as will be seen, not every logical contradiction is an antinomy. There exists a second class of paradoxes that differ from the antinomies only in one important aspect. They rise out of some hidden inconsistencies in the level structure of thought and language. This second group is frequently referred to as the semantical antinomies or paradoxical definitions. The suggestion of paradoxical definitions was developed, mainly by Carnap and by Tarski, into what is known as 'the theory of levels of language'. In analogy to the theory of logical types, this theory safeguards against a confusion of levels. It postulates that at the lowest level of language statements are made about objects. This is the realm of the object language. Finally, there is the group of pragmatic paradoxes and they are divided into paradoxical injunctions and paradoxical predictions. Pragmatic paradoxes correspond, within the framework of the theory of human communication, to the three main areas of this theory: logical syntax, semantics, and pragmatics. There is a fallacy involved which was made apparent through the introduction of Russell's (1951) theory of logical types. Very briefly, this theory postulates the fundamental principle that, as Russell puts it 'whatever involves all of a collection must not be one of the collection'. A person that is caught in a paradoxical injuction is an untenable position. It is simply not possible to behave consistently and logically within an inconsistent and illogical context.

The schizophrenic, it has been hypothesized, 'must live in a universe where the sequences of events are such that his unconventional communicational habits will be in some sense appropriate' (Russell, 1951:253). This led to postulate and identify certain essential characteristics of such interaction, for which the term 'double bind' was coined. In a somewhat modified and expanded definition, the ingredients of a double bind can be described as follows: (a) two or more persons are involved in an intense relationship that has a high degree of physical and/or psychological survival value for one, several or all of them; (2) in such a context, a message is given which is so structured that, either it asserts something, or it asserts something about its own assertion and these two assertions are mutually exclusive; (3) finally, the recipient of the message is prevented from stepping outside the frame set by this message, either by meta-communicating (commenting) about it or by withdrawing. Therefore, even though the message is logically meaningless, it is a pragmatic reality: the recipient cannot, not react to it, but neither can the recipient react to it appropriately (non-paradoxically), for the message itself is paradoxical.

There can be no doubt, argued Watzlawick et al (1967), that the world we live in is far from logical and that we all have been exposed to double binds, yet most of us manage to preserve our sanity. Very different situation arises when the exposure to double binds is long-lasting and gradually becomes a habitual expectation. Here, then, we are laced with a definite pattern of interaction, interactional quality of this pattern may become clearer if it is kept in mind that double-binding cannot, in the nature of human communication, be a unidirectional phenomenon. If a double bind produces paradoxical behavior, then this very behavior in turn double-binds the double-binder. Once this pattern has sprung into operation it is virtually meaningless to ask when, how and why it was established, for pathological systems have a curiously self-perpetuating, vicious-circle quality. The predominant pattern of communication and where the diagnostic attention is limited to the overtly most disturbed individual, the behavior of this individual will be found to satisfy the diagnostic criteria of schizophrenia. This may sound as an over-exaggeration but it is necessary if the conceptual step from schizophrenia as a mysterious disease of the individual mind to schizophrenia as a specific pattern of communication is to be achieved. From the above it will be seen that double binds are not simply contradictory injunctions, but true paradoxes.

The pathological instances of human communication reflect existing differentiations in specific patterns of organization of the system of information. Paradoxical formations in terms of logical or reasonable contradictions are only defined as such, in relation to a particular kind of logic. With regard to the organization of the system of information there exists, not one particular and fixed logic, rather a diversity of logical arrangements which justify various conditions and practices of the system. Communicational pathologies are simply a multiplicity of informational patterns contradicting specific and fixed logical configurations - erroneously established - upon which they seek justification and reliability.

5.3.9 Summary

Various issues regarding human communication and interaction were discussed in this last section of the chapter. The structure, organization and disturbances of human communication stress the importance of the organization of the system of information during communication. The system of information justifies and expresses itself in a variety of types of human behaviour. The underlying processes of human communication clearly exhibit the informational character of the structure and interaction of communication and point towards analogies and isomorphies that can be applied to the organization of the system of information. A summary of the main points is provided in the epilogue.

5.4 EPILOGUE

The current chapter focused on the *terra incognita* of the code, control and communication of information. It attempted to establish principles of the organization of information, to exemplify the vulnerability of information to internal and external cybernetic control mechanisms, and finally to show how disturbances in the organization of information can account for pathologies in human communication.

To identify attributes of the structure and processes of the organization of system of information I examined traditional concepts and relationships of information theory. Although they provide useful background for the organization of the system of information, there emerges the need to be reconsidered within the context of the communication of information in postmodern digital environments. The construction of contemporary digital justification of 'reality' is manifested within a paradoxical framework of uncertainty and improbability. The main points of the above observations on aspects of the information process are listed next:

On systemic attributes:

- In any given system forces of chance and of anti-chance coexist in a complementary relationship. Randomness is expressed by the concept of entropy, the agent of chaos, which guarantees a state of constant change for the system.

- Entropy is a measure of disorderliness of a system, a measure of uncertainty, an aspect of probability. Probability is connected with the amount of knowledge and ignorance about any given event or series of events whose outcome is uncertain.

- Consistency and order can be implemented to control the entropic chaos with the application of cybernetic mechanisms. Information is used to regularize the system.

- Order regulates the equilibrium of a system and is much more difficult to produce than disorder. Order is improbable and hard to create because of the constantly effective innate entropy. There exists a variety of systemic formations characterized by alternating tensions of order and disorder.

- Noise is disorder, it randomizes and distorts the communicated information.

- Surplus information in communication diminishes unexpectedness making information more predictable, making it 'redundant'.

- Redundancy is essentially a constraint. Redundancy reduces error and increases predictability. Redundancy also enables system complexity.

- Data, expressed as symbols, form internal interactions which lead not to linear but to multi-dimensional structural formations. These interactions are based on an internal code generated by a set of relations of meaning native to the system of information.

- A 'code' is a set of statistical rules, a form of stored information which restricts the amount of choice by introducing redundancy and increases rather than diminishes complexity.

- 'Self-regulation' in organized systems by means of internalized rules achieves complexity and stability.

- Organized systems can emerge out of unorganized matter towards increasing complexity. This tendency is 'equifinality', which brings a system to a steady, still highly improbable and highly complex, state but not necessarily to a state of equilibrium.

- Open systems can begin in a state of disorder, becoming unstable and achieving order through a process of 'fluctuations'. A fluctuation is a chance affair, a variation from average behavior.

- A system in disorder and in non-equilibrium may generate construction and organization therefore, 'non-equilibrium' can be a source of order in open systems.

- Complexity can display critical and paradoxical properties for the understanding of which we need to abandon ordinary, formal logic and turn to a rather probabilistic logic.

- Complex systems are able to reproduce themselves in such a way so the emerging progeny does not lose, in fact, may gain complexity. There exists a 'complexity barrier', below which the system can decay, above which the system can become explosive.

- 'Grammar' is a very complex system of controls and rules, and it is based on special algorithms for manipulating symbols. A 'universal grammar' is a set of hypotheses about a systematic code of specific rules and conditions that applies to the source; as an anti-chance device leaves almost nothing to chance.

On principles of human information processing in the human brain:

- The human brain seems to function on some degree of relative freedom to process information; it is though, bound to innate rules and vulnerable to disturbances from external sources. Both these factors contribute to the construction of 'reality'.

- The human brain organizes and stores information in memory from where it is easier to recall it when it is in context or redundant. The brain also possesses the freedom to arbitrary impose order and relations of meaning.

- 'Meaning' in the human brain is constructed by associations formed between incoming and stored information. Incoming information is fused with stored information in memory, which makes the later reconstruction of interconnections of meanings problematic as they may get distorted.

On recorded analogies and isomorphies of systems:

- In the era of digital technologies and communication, the system of information is characterized by entropic tendencies, acting as a force that regenerates randomness and chaos.

- In digital environments noise is information regardless of the presence of a relation of meaning.

- The system of information is organized by a 'code' of complex rules and conditions which allows change and applies restraint towards a state of dynamic equilibrium.

- Self-regulating complexity and equifinality are characteristic of the organization of the system of information. Its complexity can be affected by external interference as well as by internal conditions.

- The system of information can acquire, maintain and fluctuate among, a variety of states characterized by varying degrees of probability and complexity. The states of equilibrium and non-equilibrium become irrelevant to the generation of order.

- The system of information obeys a complex code of organization, particular to the system, and based both on genetic and acquired rules and conditions.

- The organization of the system of information is characterized by the capacity to adapt and adjust to its environment through associations (anagenesis). By means of iterations it can lead unorganized material to informational mutations which may acquire independence and engage into innovative operations.

- Informational constructs present different layers and patterns of intensity in content and interactivity, which are arranged within defined architectural and spatial boundaries.

- The system of information does not need to operate on relations of meaning to store incoming material. Incoming information is processed as raw data through phases of deconstruction, classification, and reconstruction.

- Errors in the communication of information may be caused by the interference of noise. Codes can correct the distortion by adding redundancy, which implies that change is always present in the communication of information.

- The system of information presents group properties. Within its complex architecture of patterns and relations, information performs operations of iteration which result to the preservation of sameness or to differentiated iterations.

- The organization of the system of information obeys internally connected patterns, structures, and operations. Because of their continuous construction and reconstruction these interconnections may get damaged, in which case new interconnections are sought from external associations.

- 'Meaning' in the life-world of the system of information, represents the confirmation of the validity of the interrelations and interactions among the components of the system of information. It may refer to logical, random or paradoxical interconnections and it exists as a temporary confirmation between the imagined and logically anticipated outcome and the actual result of communication.

On some general theoretical observations:

- 'Meaning' no longer subscribes to its classical definition. The rules of reference have been upset, reversed and replaced by relations of meaning. Communication is possible without the conditions set by rules of grammar and meaning, and is possible in conditions of uncertainty and improbability.

- We can reach an understanding of the 'code' of information in the form of theoretical approximations. Because of its dynamic constantly changing character finite and absolute conclusions are bound to be inadequate and insufficient.

- To come to a closer understanding of the internal structure of the information, one has to investigate the rules of the 'coding' process, as well as the 'code' of the communication process.

- In the Digital era relationships among messages and between messages and meaning are seriously disturbed, and the very nature of communication becomes problematic.

- An analytical model of the organization of the system of information in digital technologies and communication should incorporate concepts and principles that account for the organization of information across various scientific disciplines. Such a model would be expected to be highly abstract, controversial and challenging to new ways of thinking.

- The possibility of the application of cybernetic control mechanisms to the human brain exemplify the vulnerability of human information processing and question the validity of its constructed 'realities'.

Principles of cybernetic control were discussed with particular attention drawn to the cybernetic qualities of the human brain and of human information processing. With the vulnerability of information exposed, cybernetic mechanisms of interference and disturbance remain always a potential danger for human consciousness. The danger is even more obvious in the era of digital technologies and communication since the possibilities for the interception or the manipulation of information are greater than ever. The main observations and suggestions are summarized here:

On the operation and functions of the human system:

- The general operation and functions of both machines and humans can be described by precisely the same mathematical formulas.
- Information constructs the variety of our 'realities'. It is possible to control the flow and communication of the system of information, therefore to control the construction of 'reality'.
- Genetic information is partially responsible for the accumulated information in the human system. Moreover, in the sense that it is not innate to the system, genetic information can be said to have originated in the environment.
- The brain always seeks to get rid of tasks, which do not require mental effort.
- The human brain is a computing machine that shows the qualities of cybernetic systems. It functions according to specific programming and data processing operations.

On principles of human information processing:

- The human organism maintains its existence by means of automatic control (homeostasis) through a complex exchange of information (stimulus/response) with the environment.

- Reflexes, acting independently from the brain, suppress surplus degrees of freedom and turn systems into controllable mechanisms. They are part of an elaborate 'signaling' system which monitors incoming information, and updates the brain.

- Stimulations are recorded by the human brain as invisible misprints and are stored as recollections in local memory positions, in correlation to one another.

- Triggering mechanisms play a decisive role in the processing of incoming information as they intercept and can alter the nature of the original stimulation before the actual processing takes place.

- A reflex chain of nerve impulses implies an operational programme on behalf of the brain, based on a hierarchy of algorithms of varying degrees of complexity. These programmes are generated according to a code and allow the adaptation of the human system to the circumstances of the environment by means of intelligent behaviour.

- The brain utilizes new criteria for screening information when attempts to use old reflex chains fail. New information that has not been screened by the control mechanisms it is possible to be stored in memory.

- The human visual system is a complex structure designed for processing information about images. The human eye transmits only essential information about the images to the brain. A selective process breaks the images in frames and suppresses and filters noise.

- Images are 'dissected' in the brain and are been reassembled in different areas of it. During this reassembling process the brain creates images of objects and phenomena on the basis of information it receives, whereas it supplements incoming information with its own stored one.

- Although the brain seems to contain a dictionary of basic symbols, it is probably correct to assume that a set of visual dictionary is not intrinsic but is acquired with experience.

- Differences in levels of signal systems of reality account for differences in the realities perceived by human and non-human systems. Humans are able to go beyond the level of initial stimulations to the level of the system of word perception, in which they can establish connections leading to mental constructions.

Finally, I looked into the structure and organization of human communication and certain behavioral pathologies that may develop during this exchange. From the discussion provided it becomes evident that communicational problems and disturbances in the content and relationships of the system of information can affect the construction of the social knowledge and the social world, and consequently their explicit expression, that is, human behaviour. A summary follows of the main points discussed above:

On attributes and principles of organization of human communication:

- Feedback is a decisive factor of organization of a system towards change, loss of stability or equilibrium.
- Interpersonal systems (such as social groups, families, a set of relationships) may be viewed as feedback loops, since the behaviour of each unit of the system affects and is affected by the behavior of each other unit.
- When a system has obtained the ability to store previous adaptations for future use, it will show redundancy and constraint, and certain internal configurations will become repetitive and more probable than others (stochastic process).
- The concepts of function and relationship refer to the relation between variables. Functions and relationships are sign representations of connections of infinite possible positions. Functions and relationships, or patterns of functions and relationships, are the essence of experience.
- The axioms of the pragmatics of human communication: (a) there exists the impossibility of not communicating; (b) every communication has content and a relationship aspect such that the latter classifies the former and is therefore a meta-communication; (c) the nature of a relationship is contingent upon the punctuation of

the communicational sequences between the communicants.

- Communication in the human body is both analogic and digital. Electrical and chemical events are responsible for the communication of information, which events complement and are contingent upon another in highly complex ways.

- The content aspect of human communication is digitally whereas the relationship aspect will be predominantly analogic in nature.

- Digital language shows a high degree of complexity, versatility, and abstraction but is lacking an adequate vocabulary for the contingencies of relationship. Analogic language possesses the vocabulary but has no adequate syntax for the unambiguous definition of the nature of relationships.

- In human interaction all communicational interchanges are either symmetrical or complementary, based on equality or difference respectively. The level of interaction is contingent to diverse degrees of symmetrical positions between the participants of the interaction.

- The inability of a person to relate to the most compatible, from a range of possible meanings, in an interaction, may lead to behavioral responses, such as, rejection, acceptance, and disqualification of communication.

- Confusion between the content and relationship of a communication may lead to disagreement in the form of confirmation, rejection and disconfirmation. Disconfirmation corresponds to undecidability and calls for a different logical order.

- An unlimited hierarchy of patterns appears in human communication expressed in repetition or redundancy of events.

- Interaction can be considered a general system (interactional system) in which the communicants in the process of, at the level of, defining the nature of their relationship.

- Hierarchically arranged open subsystems (such as human interaction) are not isolated from their environment. An interactional system is always in both horizontal and vertical relations with other systems.

- Interactional systems are characterized by changes in their totality caused by changes in one part of the system (wholeness). Still, some parts may not be affected (summativity) and the system change is not necessarily the sum of its partial changes (non-summativity). Interaction is non-summative.

- While feedback and circularity characterize interactional systems, equifinality also is at play, by which a system may independently obtain a state independent of initial conditions and determined only by the system parameters.

- An interactional system is a 'family', in which the behavior of every member within it is related to the behavior of all the others. Individual qualities of the family units account for its particularity based on a fundamental stability of variation.

- Change and variation of families are controlled by means of 'calibration' (configuring the 'settings') of the system. Calibration may counteract certain behavior that deviates from stability. Still, change also occurs over time due to the amplification of possible deviations from the stable condition.

- Human communication can be characterized by 'logical' or 'reasonable' contradictions that are classified as paradoxes. They are distinguished in logico-mathematical paradoxes or antinomies, semantic antinomies or paradoxical definitions, and pragmatic paradoxes which are divided into paradoxical injunctions and paradoxical predictions.

- One of the paradoxes of human interaction occurs when, even though the message is logically meaningless, it is a pragmatic reality: the recipient cannot, not react to it, but neither can react to it appropriately (non-paradoxically), for the message itself is paradoxical (double bind).

- Pathologies in human communication systems are in essence specific patterns of communication which have a curiously self-perpetuating, vicious-circle quality.

On analogies and isomorphies arising form the analysis of human communication that can be applied to the organization of the system of information:

- Variables and functions are useful in understanding the complex internal structure and processes of the system of information expressed by the content of communication.

- One way to think about the system of information in human communication is as patterns of infinitely possible relationships (functions) among the diversity of variables that are responsible for the organization of its content.

- Elements of both analogic and digital organization characterize both the content and the relationships of the organization of the system of information in the form of varying degrees of complexity and abstraction.

- The geometry of internal organizational structure of the system of information can be better understood in three-dimensional models floating in space and continuously changing with time.

- Behavioral disturbances, related to the content and relationship of communication, reflect defects in the inner structural and inter-relational interconnectedness of the organization of the system of information negotiated in the interaction.

- Three-dimensional hierarchies of structural and relational patterns are characteristic of informational architecture, and account for the development of multi-relational networks within or with interacting systems of information.

- It is possible for the system of information to move towards phase states of change and alteration based on its own initial conditions and parameters. The particularity of the quality of its components guarantees the uniqueness of each change, and of the outcome of change.

- The organization of the system of information shows a flexible compliance to a diversity of logical arrangements which justify various conditions and practices of the system. As a result, 'logically' contradictory or erroneous organization is simply an exemplification of system differentiation in response to seeking justification and reliability from specific and fixed logical configurations.

During this chapter I examined aspects of the coding, control and communication of information and attempted to define some concepts and principles of their respective organization. I drew attention to mechanisms of cybernetic control and pathological communication and I stressed the vulnerability of the system of information especially within the context of postmodern digital environments. I suggested that the construction of contemporary digital justification of 'reality' is realized with a context uncertainty and improbability. The need to understand the code of the organization of the system of information becomes a primary concern, and as I have stressed earlier in the book, this may demand highly abstract and controversial ways of thinking. Taking into account the various observations and considerations I made throughout the discussions in the previous chapters, in the last part of the book (the following two chapters) I finally propose a series of theoretical approximations regarding the organization (code) of the system of information. Fasten your seatbelt!

▶▶|

PART THREE

FRACTAL FETISHES

CHAPTER SIX

THE ECLIPSE OF MEANING:
Virtual Implosion and Fractal Dynamics

CONTENTS

CHAPTER SIX

THE ECLIPSE OF MEANING:
Virtual Implosion and Fractal Dynamics

'The world we have created is a product of our thinking;
it cannot be changed without changing our thinking'.
(Albert Einstein)

6.0 PROLOGUE

This book has so far attempted to establish the background and the contextual framework within which a series of theoretical approximations regarding the organization of the system of information are proposed. As you may recall, during the first part of the book my discussion focused on structural, operational and organizational characteristics of contemporary world society which I argued consist of reflections and expressions of a continuous and intensified digital re-organization of the flow of the system of information which constitutes them. In a time where computer technologies and the media dominate the world cultural experience this re-organization leads societies towards social formations of variable and infinite possibilities. I then argued that the organization of the system of information is reflexively manifested in forms of social knowledge which in turn discursively reproduces and regenerates the social architecture and organization. I then examined ideological systems as systems of information and provided a discussion of characteristics of the contemporary postmodern-and-beyond world. I argued that the crisis of representation, the reassignment of the 'meaning' of 'reality' and the reorganization of the 'reality' of 'meaning' in the postmodern-and-beyond era, are once more exemplifications of organizational infrastructure of information.

The second part of the book concentrated on the concept of 'the system' and I attempted a journey in various scientific disciplines in order to indicate properties, analogies and isomorphies that can apply to account for the organizational patterns of the system of information. I stressed the vulnerability of information in postmodern digital environments and

277

I suggested the construction of the digital justification of 'reality' or the digital reconstruction of 'hyper-reality' to finally stress the need to understand the code of the organization of the system of information within fresh ways of thinking, unavoidably abstract and probabilistic and possibly paradoxical and controversial. To this end, in these two last chapters I propose a series of theoretical approximations on the organization of the system of information, namely: '*Virtual Implosion*', '*Fractal Dynamics*', and '*Infogramics*'. These main propositions along with some additional conceptualizations, such as the '*Level-States of Information*' and '*Endogenesis*' and '*Exogenesis*' comprise an analytical model which I like to call '*Infogramic Analysis*'.

The theoretical approximations proposed here can be argued to be a meta-philosophical proposition towards a radical reconstruction of long-established thinking of the production of social knowledge. The analytical model put forward in the form of conceptual / digital / graphical approximations is a radical methodological suggestion on how we can improve our understanding about the operation and impact of the system of information in the digital reconstruction of contemporary societies and on the re-realization of human consciousness in the postmodern-and-beyond era. The proposed theoretical model aims to offer an alternative idea and to envisage as to how we can use the results of such an understanding to identify exploitation, domination and struggle in a diversity of real, imagined and other places. The use of computer generated three-dimensional models (see digital component) provides a more accurate expression of the representation of theoretical proposals put here in printed word, but also points towards insufficiencies and weaknesses of the printed word to sufficiently account for the multi-dimensional theorizations of the digital world. The current in-depth analysis of the organization of the system of information hopes to redefine principles of organization of social transformation, social change and successful survival in living with computer and digital technologies.

The proposed conceptualizations of the organization of the system of information refer in general, and in particular, to all entities that the system of information organizes including itself. One spatial context where these conceptualizations are made explicit and can be represented with more ease and comfort, as if in their natural habitat, is the space where human and machine technologies converge, that of 'hyperspace' or 'cyberspace'. Wilson and

Corey (2000) defined this spatial context of the emerging digital technologies such as, computers, telecommunications networks, electronic media, and the Internet, as 'e•space'. This is just another term for what is widely accepted as cyberspace, a multi-media web of digital networks, and an information superhighway that is infusing rapidly into social, cultural and economic life. Cyberspace has also been described as a 'conceptual hallucination' (Gibson, 1984) or a 'parallel universe' (Benedict, 1991), or even 'a new kind of space, invisible to our direct senses ... layered on top of, within and between the fabric of traditional geographical space' (Batty, 1993).

In the era of digital technologies and communication, the digital reorganization of information in hyperspace is to a great degree responsible for the organization of the system of information in every human and non-human entity, the existence of which this system claims to represent. Moreover, an analogy is suggested here among similar spatial contexts of informational systems. In this context, it is suggested that the patterns of organization of the system of information as expressed in hyperspatial environments, can apply to describe the organization of any system of information. Social structures, systems, and processes, and human agents depend on, and are directly affected by, the digital communication of information in the ways that are further proposed. Along these lines then, the theoretical proposals in the current and next chapters consist of a project of theoretical approximations which interrelate in a triad of interconnected spatiality, the level-states of the system of information which are defined and described further below.

6.1 TRIALECTICS, HETEROTOPIAS AND THIRDSPACE

The proposed analytical model directly challenges (and is intended to deconstruct) conventional modes of spatial thinking. As an introduction to the statement of my theoretical propositions, it would be useful to make a short reference to some of the background theoretical thinking. The proposed approximations are based on the assertion of an alternative envisioning of spatiality, as illustrated in the 'trialectics and thirdings' of Lefebvre (1982; 1991), the 'heterotopologies' of Foucault (1986), and Soja's (1996) concept of 'thirdspace'. Some elements of these accounts are discussed briefly next.

6.1.1 Trialectics and the production of space

Lefebvre's spatial perspective is a very important theoretical view that is adopted in the theoretical propositions of this book regarding the organization of the system of information. It points towards a spatial consideration and understanding of social reality and sets the spatial parameters of the environment within which the system of information is considered. 'Space', wrote, Lefebvre (1991a:410), 'is becoming the principal stake of goal-directed actions and struggles ... the disinterested stage or setting, of action'. Social reality is not just coincidentally spatial, it is presuppositionally and ontologically spatial. In his project Lefebvre opposed the heterogenizing 'differential' to the homogenizing 'repetitive' and set out to an alternative path that draws on and encompasses both materialism and idealism, yet one that remains open to much more than their simple combination. Lefebvre aimed to identify exploitation, domination and struggle through a redefinition of social transformation and revolution as essentially more socio-cultural. Lefebvre called his spatial perspective 'transdisciplinary', as a strategy to prevent spatial knowledge and praxis from being fragmented and compartmentalized as a disciplinary specialty. Following Lefebvre's perspective the current book has adopted a transdisciplinary strategy to identify elements of exploitation, domination and struggle, and principles of social organization and social change as these can be reflected in the organization of the system of information, and described by a model of theoretical approximations.

Lefebvre's transdisciplinary 'trialectics' describes not just a 'triple trialectic' but also a mode of dialectical reasoning that is more inherently spatial than conventional dialectics, a continuing expansion of spatial knowledge. For Lefebvre each field of human spatiality – the physical, the mental, the social – is seen as simultaneously real and imagined, concrete and abstract, material and metaphorical. Similarly, the proposed theorizations on the system of information, at the core of this book, are envisioned as 'real' and imagined, physically present but absent or invisible in an abstract way.

Lefebvre's 'production of space' inter-relates in a dialectically linked triad (three moments of social space): 'spatial practice' (perceived space), 'representations of space' (conceived space), and 'spaces of representation' (lived space)'. 'Spatial practice' is defined as producing a spatiality that embraces production and reproduction, and the particular locations and spatial sets (ensembles) characteristic of each social formation. The 'representations of space' define 'a conceptualized space', the space of scientists, planners, urbanists, which is constituted via control over knowledge, signs, and codes: over the means of deciphering spatial practice and hence over the production of spatial knowledge. Finally, the 'spaces of representation' are distinct from the other two spaces and encompass them, embodying 'complex symbolisms, sometimes coded, sometimes not'. Further below I argue how the social space of the system of information is defined by, and expressed through, across time, an ever-present spatial triad of level-states. This 'trialectic' represents different spatial configurations of the organization of the system of information: the 'perceived' physical space of the production and reproduction of information, the 'conceived' conceptualized space of the control and exploitation of the system of information and social knowledge, and the 'lived' symbolic and imaginary space of the system of information.

The justification of the proposal in this book for theoretical approximations and not definite conclusions begins from Lefebvre. For Lefebvre, spatial knowledge, as a means 'to thread through the complexities of the modern world', is achievable only through a series of heuristic 'approximations', a constant search to move beyond (meta-) and never as permanent dogma. Lefebvre suggests that there are no 'conclusions' that are not also 'openings'. There is always the Other, a third term that disrupts, disorders, and begins to reconstitute conventional binary oppositions. Each trialectic is an 'approximation' that builds cumulatively on earlier approximations, producing a certain practical continuity of knowledge production that is an antidote to the hyper-relativism and 'anything goes' philosophy often associated with such radical epistemological openness.

Lefebvre implicitly suggested the possibility of constructing a 'unitary theory' from the fragments into which spatial knowledge has historically been broken and proceeds to fuse (objective) physical and (subjective) mental space into social space through a critique of what he called a 'double illusion'. The illusion of transparency, for Lefebvre, makes space appear 'luminous', completely intelligible, open to the free play of human agency, willfulness, and imagination. Social space comes to be seen entirely as mental space, an 'encrypted reality'. Reality is confined to 'thought things' (*res cogito*) and comprehended entirely through its representations. Everything, including spatial knowledge, is condensed in communicable representations and re-representations of the real world to the point that the representations substitute for the real world itself, the 'incommunicable having no existence beyond that of an ever-pursued residual'. In agreement with Lefebvre's thinking then, an investigation of the organization of the system of information becomes a project of the analysis of representations of the 'real' world, and of understanding the 'encrypted' codes of the organization of social reality itself.

6.1.2 Heterotopias

In *Of Other Spaces*, Foucault (1986) theorized spatiality in a search for 'other spaces' and 'other sites'. 'Utopias', some of the first sites he encountered, are fundamentally 'unreal places'. More 'real', as Foucault (1986) noted, are 'heterotopias': 'there are real places, like counter-sites, a kind of effectively enacted utopia in which the real sites, all the other real sites, can be found in the culture, are simultaneously represented, contested, and inverted'. Heterotopias are those singular spaces to be found in specific social spaces and whose functions are different or even the opposite of others. The principles of heterotopology were defined by Foucault (1986) as: (a) heterotopias are found in all cultures and have no absolutely universal models, however, two main categories can be identified, one of 'crisis' and the other of 'deviation'; (b) heterotopias can change in function and meaning over time, according to the particular 'synchrony' of the culture in which they are found; (c) a heterotopia is capable in juxtaposing in one real place several different spaces, 'several sites that are in themselves 'incompatible' or foreign to one another; (d) heterotopias are typically linked to slices of time, which 'for the sake of symmetry' Foucault called 'heterochronies' (intersection and phasing of space and time); (e) heterotopias always presuppose a system of opening and closing that simultaneously makes them both isolated and penetrable, different from what is usually conceived of as more freely accessible public space; and, (f) heterotopias have a comprehensive function: 'either their role is to create a space of illusion that exposes every real space, all the sites inside of which human life is partitioned, as still more illusory … or else, on the contrary, their role is to create a space that is other, another real space, as perfect, as meticulous, as well arranged as ours is messy, ill constructed, and jumbled'.

From the assumptions, analogies and isomorphies made throughout the current book, it should be obvious that, the system of information can be described - as in this book - as a 'heterotopia'. Applying the principles of heterotopology to the system of information it can be said that: the system of information can be identified in worldwide signification and representational systems in differentiated forms, it can alter and transform over time in synchronization to specific environments it occupies, it can exist in different spatial configurations, even incompatible to each other, it presents heterochronic formations, it can be closed and isolated or open and permeable at the same time, it is responsible for creating illusionary 'other' spaces.

6.1.3 Thirdspace

Foucault's heterotopias is a conceptualisation that resonates with what might be called the micro- or site geography of Soja's (1996) 'Thirdspace'. Taking after Lefebvre and Foucault, Soja proposed a new way of thinking about space and the related concepts that compose and comprise the inherent spatiality of human life. This is one more way of thinking that be applied to the considerations (of this book) of the system of information. Soja's 'Thirdspace' project called for a different way of thinking about the meanings and the significance of our already established spatial or geographical imaginations. From the interjection of a critical spatial imagination into the interpretive dualism, and the combinatorial perspective of modernism and postmodernism, 'Thirdspace' can be described as a creative recombination and extension towards a multiplicity of real-and-imagined places. Thirdspace can be seen as a new approximation, a different way of looking at the same subject, a sequence of never-ending variations on recurrent spatial themes. This is a view which I have stressed throughout, that because of the nature of the system of information we are in need for flexible and dynamic open-end theorizations of its structure, organization, and communication. These theorizations have to include frequent reconsiderations and recombinations of alternating conceptualizations of its organization.

Soja defined the qualities of Thirdspace as 'a knowable and unknowable, real and imagined life-world of experiences, emotions, events, and political choice that is existentially shaped by the generative and problematic interplay between centers and peripheries, the abstract and concrete, the impassioned spaces of the conceptual and the lived, marked out materially and metaphorically in spatial praxis, the transformation of (spatial) knowledge into (spatial) action in a field of unevenly developed (spatial) power'. Soja placed Thirdspace as the space where all places are, but also a secret and conjectured object, filled with illusions and allusions, a space that is common to all of us yet never able to be completely seen and understood, an 'unimaginable universe'. Thinking trialectically is a necessary part of understanding Thirdspace as a limitless composition of life-worlds that are radically open and openly radicalizable. Trialectical thinking is difficult, for it challenges all conventional modes of thought and taken-for-granted epistemologies. It is disorderly, unruly, constantly evolving, unfixed, never presentable in permanent constructions, denoting a shift from existential ontology to an epistemology of space.

Firstspace epistemologies focused their primary attention on the 'analytical deciphering' of what Lefebvre called 'spatial practice' or perceived space, a material and materialized 'physical' spatiality that is directly comprehended in empirically measurable configurations. Secondspace epistemologies have tended to arise in reaction to the excessive closure and enforced objectivity of mainstream Firstspace analysis, to the point that First- and Secondspace knowledge have become increasingly blurred, especially with the intermixing of positivist, structuralist, poststructuralist, existential, phenomenological, and hermeneutic ideas and methods. The starting-point for the strategic re-opening and rethinking of new possibilities, Thirdspace epistemologies, is the provocative shift back from epistemology to ontology and specifically to the ontological trialectic of Spatiality-Historicality-Sociality. The key processes of a new cultural politics of difference in the development of radical postmodern subjectivity, argued Soja, should focus on the disorderding of difference from persistent binary structuring and its reconstitution. A multiplicitous alterity, a transgressive 'third way' of critical spatial thinking seeks to privilege uncertainties, to reject authoritative and paradigmatic structures that suggest permanence or inviolability, to invite contestation, and thereby to keep open the spatial debate to new and different possibilities. 'Social space can no longer be imagined simply in terms of a territory or a gender... spaces structured over many dimensions are necessary ... there is a paradox of being within the Same/Other and also elsewhere' (Rose, 1993). As Spivak (1990) put it, we need 'a deconstructive 'practique sauvage', a wild practice, a practical politics of open end in which choosing marginality becomes an invitingly anarchic, centerless, act of inclusion' (Spivak, 1990).

In conclusion, a spatial perspective is needed to consider and understand social reality and the organization of the system of information which sets the coordinates of its spatial configuration. Identified elements of exploitation, domination and struggle in this transdisciplinary strategy, can help come to a closer understanding of social change and of the new hyperrealities in the Digital era. A series of conceptual shifts is required for defining the framework of the proposed approximations, dealing, at the same time, with the 'real' and imagined, the supposed and the proven, the physically present and the absent. The consideration of the organization of the system of information inevitably leads to intriguing analogies and becomes an analysis and an understanding of the organization of [the digital reconstruction of] social reality and knowledge themselves. The theoretical approximations that follow further below are the beginning of a journey to other spaces, the imaginable and unimaginable hallucinatory universes created by the system of information. Watch for the rabbit coming out of the hat!

6.2 DIGITAL REORGANIZATION AND FRACTALIZATION

6.2.1 The digital reorganization of information

In the various theoretical accounts examined in the previous chapters, a series of considerations have been made regarding the characteristic components and functions of the system of information. They point towards a pattern of organizational traits of the system of information which can also apply to describe the digital reorganization of information in hyperspatial environments, and in turn, as I suggested further above, the organization of any system of information. It is suggested then, that information, in the various landscapes of cyberspace, consists a whole, irregular, non-linear dynamic system flow characterized by pervasive points of instability. Furthermore, the system of information, exists in a continuous dynamic transformation (implying quantitative alterations and qualitative mutations) of abstract flows of coded (as information, representation, transaction) and uncoded electronic signals, which produce an irregular, contradictory, and habitually chaotic, informational simulations (simulacra, copies of non-existent originals). Moreover, the system of information is constantly produced and regenerated by means of informational simulations of fractal nature, that is, simplified, controllable and programmable versions of an original archetype. 'Reality', 'meaning', and 'truth', as well as social structures (i.e. information society), social phenomena and discourses (i.e. globalization), and the human agent (all of which organization is dependent or relying on information) they mutate to simplified, controllable and programmable versions of themselves.

Information is a complex system of accumulated data which usually refers to a set of combined data concerning particular constructions of knowledge and 'reality'. But information, in the digital environments of the postmodern-and-beyond world, can also refer to abstract and undefined data formations (such as otherwise considered as pure noise), when the abstract and undefined become accepted and parts of a legitimate logic. The proposed processes of virtual implosion and fractal dynamics attempt to offer an approximation of how this is achieved. Information in this sense, is pure data or sets of data combined into a message entailing some 'relation to meaning'. Because in the postmodern digital world the referents of meaning are difficult to locate, if any, I suggest we can only refer to 'relations of meaning'; this means, that 'new' accepted meanings can be - according to traditional modernist logic - variations of 'meaning', such as 'meaningless', 'non-meaning', 'meaningful', 'me%a&ni*n(g', and so on. Data, in contrast, are quantities, characters, or symbols used in performed operations, and which may be stored or transmitted in different forms, such as, electrical signals, etc. Data can be termed information when coupled with context and made relevant, although this is not always the case. Data can also convey 'relations of meaning' without having to relate.

It is useful at this point to recall a few of the considerations made so far about the systemic properties of the system of information, as this will be helpful in understanding the philosophical thinking of the theoretical approximations I propose. The system of information presents certain emergent properties, which are often the result of the communication of interactions and associations, and which have contingent effects, that is, they can act back and influence the elements from which they are produced. Information is a system under continuous communication with the environment through processes of feed-forward as well as feedback, which are responsible for quantitative and qualitative changes of the phase spaces in the system of information itself. Such changes, though, may also emerge due to internal fluctuations or due to interacting external and internal processes, but always a less coded form of "a temporary homeostatic equilibrium of entropy" is necessary. The transformation of the system of information, random or otherwise, is characterized by disorder, paradoxically organized in complex ways produced by iterations of information itself. The iterative process refers to functions that are repeated. Multiple interactions between feed-forward and feedback, act as chaotic or strange attractors that cause non-linear trajectories of change, producing a chaotic system of different levels of complexity, occurring within states, 'phase spaces' of complex irregular informational patterns. These, in turn, have different levels of impact, depending on the frequency of their reoccurrence or stability. Although generally unstable, under constant change, and unpredictable long-term, still, the genesis and proliferation of these phase spaces can be described, investigated and possibly predicted.

The mutation of the system of information is based on a pattern of relationships, internally exhibiting some degree of organization within limits, which maintains - rather than separates - the interconnections with the environment. The growth of this pattern of relationships is what justifies the system of information as a self-organizing system, differentiated from its environment. This means that the system of information may be in constant active relation to the environment but is not purely determined by it. Rather, through feed-forward and positive and negative feedback, components of the system of information, are used during communication to organize both internally and in relation to the environment. The result is non-predictable but ordered patterns of change, which reproduce their existing conditions and move along trajectories from one phase space to another. Locally occurring interactions in the process of the transformation of the system of information create chaotic mutations, which can be a source of global change in a wider context. An important feature of this chaotic behaviour is that small changes in initial conditions can produce very large differences in outcome (Blackman, 2000). Environmental properties condition and constrain the system of information, which remains in a relatively stable condition of processing and accumulation, until dynamic attractors, emerging from feedback processes, produce state cycles of transformation which disturb the temporally equilibrium and generate a trajectory.

The system of information is shared in a variety ways within networks of exchanges, where internal communication, along with communication with the environment, enables its content to organize (Stonier, 1992). In this sense, the system of information is a self-referential system that exists in a differentiated environment with differentiated relations to itself and to the environment. The result is a complex system with substantial internal differential integration and co-ordination that exists in a state that is neither totally ordered nor totally chaotic. Alternating between order and chaos it settles into patterns associated to 'relations of meaning'. The distribution of the elements of information patterns is unpredictable; still they do not disperse outside the boundaries of the pattern. Breaking apart the elements, that make up the code of information, and looking at the individual pieces and their interrelationships, is the key in understanding the complexity of the system of information, and coming to a closer understanding of social 'reality'. Informational patterns revolve around a central strange attractor (i.e., theme) that organizes the points within it, producing order. This dynamic state is based upon mutative iterative cycles whereby output and input among cycles interact with each other.

6.2.2 The fractalization of information

The result from iterations is sets of complex components of information, that is, fractal information, characteristic properties of which are, self-similarity of components and fractional dimensionality. Self-similarity refers to the same element of information that at level after level repeats itself, like multiple copies. The fractal dimension of the system of information means that smaller magnifications (simplified versions), or arbitrarily partial components of information, appear to be the same as the original ones. In other words, scaling down does not change the appearance of the 'original' system of information. The relative instability of a system of information, towards order or disorder, creates potential fractal conditions. The visualization of the informational patterns of fractal irregularity could simply provide visual pleasure and excite our imagination; still, it can visually demonstrate the relationships inherent in the organization of the system of information which is difficult to be expressed in printed form.

The dynamic retransformation or *fractalization* of the system of information is defined further below as '*Virtual Implosion*' and develops in distinct phase spaces (spatial changes across time). Through virtual implosion, information mutates to a fractal, continuously alternating phase space. Virtual implosion is empowered by what is defined further below as

'*Fractal Dynamics*' (Figure 6.1). The later refers to the interconnecting micro-processes that support and make possible the process of virtual implosion, and they become a pattern of powerful organizing principles of societies, social processes, of human agents, into entities of unpredictably programmable identity and 'consciousness'. Moreover, the impact of this process of virtual implosion on both society and individuals is the development of interrelations, which directly affect the construction of the cultural environment within which, virtual implosion, acts as a potentially controlling force of change and transformation of the world-society. It emerges in hyperspatial environments and powers up social change of worldwide societies and the reconstruction of homo-sapiens to an emerging global digi-sapiens.

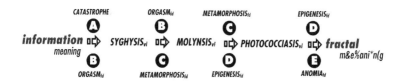

Figure 6.1: Phase spaces of Virtual Implosion and microprocesses of Fractal Dynamics.

Although the systemic properties, analogies and isomorphies already discussed in previous chapters can be applied to describe the organization of the phase spaces, and micro-processes, of virtual implosion and fractal dynamics respectively, still, one way to understand them is as 'imaginary systems'. An imaginary system refers to a system in which properties, processes and actors exist and function both inside and outside the limits of the system's conventional landscape, formed by structure, exchanges, operational plans, and language. It consists of a number of components, which are joined together with relationships based on exchanges, a shared infrastructure, appeal of a concept, or, less often, a contract. Emerged from an original concept, competitiveness and survival of the system depend on successful co-ordination among phase spaces. An imaginary system requires imaginary vision for it is an artificial representation (Hedberg et al, 1997). Imagination can help to improve our ability to see and understand in new ways, finding images for new ways of organizing, creating a shared understanding, achieving personal empowerment, and, developing the capacity for continuous self-organization (Morgan, 1993).

The end result of the fractalization of information, that is, the mutation of information to electronically distorted repetitions, needs to be addressed and answers to be established to a number of relevant questions that will naturally arise. Whatever answers we may come up with, our experience with theoretical and empirical prevailing so-called orthodoxies, as I argued before, will have to accept, the appearance of paradoxes, unavoidable controversies, the non-absolute of 'reality' or the partial availability of 'truth', as legitimate parameters in the statement of the theoretical approximations that follow further below.

6.3 INFOTYPES AND LEVEL-STATES

At any moment of transformation across time, the system of information can preserve its quantitative and qualitative dimensions from one trajectory to another, which are embodied in what can be called an '*infotype*'. An infotype refers to the specific content and the general architectural characteristics of the system of information. Different systems of information may belong to the same infotype, and a system of information may belong to more than one infotypes. The infotype carries the code (instructions) which the components of the system of information need to use for their structural and interactive orientation and their iterative proliferation. For an infotype to survive and secure its existence in the ocean of informational landscapes, it needs to regenerate constant change by way of adaptation and habituation to the available informational environments. Adaptation implies quantitative and/or qualitative alterations, which can be the result of mutation of information through iterative processes, whereas habituation refers to the successful establishment of adaptation.

As mentioned further above, the system of information is organized across space and time in an interconnected triad of associated spatial level-states of organization: an '*Era of Romanticism*' (actuality), an '*Epoch of Ersatz*' (imitation), and an '*Age of Chimera*' (fantasy) (Figure 6.2). 'Romanticism', 'Ersatz' and 'Chimera' consist space-time coordinates, which remain unaffected as a triad globally, but they differentiate individually and locally, across the arrow of time. They refer to the volume and intensity of available information during various historical periods, not necessarily distinct ones, but related to the historical, socio-economic and cultural conditions of these periods (Figure 6.3). They coexist as general spatial frameworks across time that encompass and host diverse systems and organization networks. At different space-time coordinates one level-state may predominate to the expense of the others depending on the degree of intensification of the flow and organization of information within a given system.

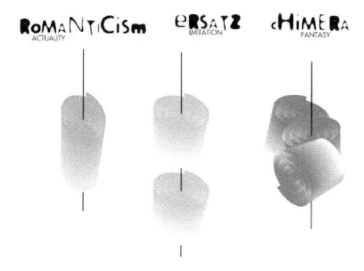

Figure 6.2: Infotype level-states of the system of information: Romanticism, Ersatz and Chimera,

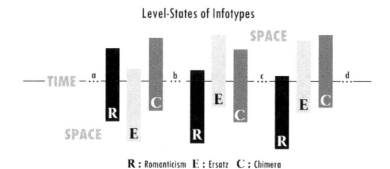

Figure 6.3: The infotype level-states of the system of information differentiate in intensity across the arrow of time and within distinct historical periods (a-b, b-c, c-d, and so on).

6.3.1. The Era of Romanticism

The '*Era of Romanticism*' is the first of the three co-existing space-time coordinates of the spatial and historical organization of the system of information (Figure 6.4).

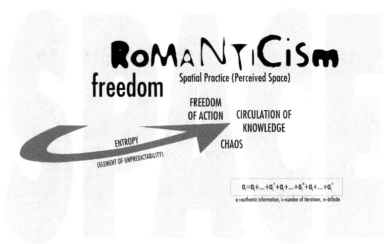

Figure 6.4: The Era of Romanticism.

The Era of Romanticism is predominated by the intensification of 'spatial practice'. The perceived physical space is the main domain of the negotiation of information and social knowledge (actuality). At this level-state the system of information is characterized mainly by the authenticity, and subsequently by the simplicity and originality of its components. The system of information is highly entropic, and the production and circulation of information at this level are unpredictable and chaotic. They are the result of the relative freedom that characterizes the establishment of interaction and association within this particular level-state. The volume of pure, unattached and original information distinctly predominates over the volumes of imitation and fantasy of 'Ersatz' and 'Chimera'. The Era of Romanticism would probably characterize socio-spatial formations of primary and basic organization, where the networks of information are almost non-existent or just emerging, where communication of the information is scarce and elementary, and where social transformation and change is time-consuming. It is an era of potential progress and development as a result of social exploration, error and trial, based on the unhindered 'freedom' of information. Authentic information (a_i) is the result of an infinite and simplistic 'analogue' accumulation of data, which is reproduced and regenerated by continuous additional iterations according to the following formula:

$$a_i = a_i + ... + a_i^n + a_i + ... + a_i^n + a_i + ... + a_i^n$$

a_i : authentic information, i : number of iterations, n : infinite

6.3.2 The Epoch of Ersatz

The '*Epoch of Ersatz*' is characterized by the intensification of 'representations of space', in which information is disputed, infected and dominated (Figure 6.5).

Figure 6.5: The Epoch of Ersatz.

The Epoch of Ersatz signifies the 'conceptualized space' of the system of information. The social during the 'epoch of Ersatz' is constituted through the control and exploitation of information. Information is classified and categorized into controlled knowledge and defined signs and codes are responsible for the construction of social reality. The system of information during this level-state becomes redundant with the elements of unpredictability and entropy being controlled. Informational constructs are generated through imitation and floating signifiers define the limits of social experience. Reason and logic dominate social action and change. The authenticity of 'Romanticism' gradually decreases and fades away as the shift towards the fantasy of 'Chimera' becomes increasingly visible and accessible. The Epoch of Ersatz can probably apply to developing and developed patterns of organization, with well established networks of communication. This would be a system indicative of experimentation, justification and potential exploitation of choices and alternatives. Information in the Epoch of Ersatz becomes simulated information (s_i) which results from the infinite and steady multiplication of authentic information, according to the following formula:

$$s_i = (a_i * a_i * ... * a_{ni})^n$$

s_i = simulated information, a_i: authentic information,
i : number of iterations, n : infinite

6.3.3 The Age of Chimera

In the '*Age of Chimera*', fantasy becomes the predominant component of the system of information (Figure 6.6).

Figure 6.6: The Age of Chimera.

Information becomes illusive, provocative and hyper-real. The 'spaces of representation' become intensified with the original authenticity of 'Romanticism' and the 'original' simulations of 'Ersatz' becoming incorporated and assimilated in the domination of lived experience. The system of information shows a highly complex organization, with 'reality' being encoded, and 'hyper-reality' being decoded as the dominant socio-spatial dominant. At this level-state the system of information is dominated by the rejection of authenticity and originality, by increased tensions of imagination and hallucination, and by the emergence of distorted spatial formations. The system of information reactivates its entropic tendencies within a system environment alternating between states of chaotic organization and of organized chaos. The Age of Chimera is a period of domination to the code of the system of information which controls and regenerates ever-emerging spatial realities. The Age of Chimera is intensified in advanced modes of organization characterized by networked flexibility, flexible networking and infinite possibilities of communication. Change and transformation is fast and at its extreme leads towards the fractalization of the system of information. At this level, fractal information (f_i) is the result of infinite set of multiplications among authentic and simulated information according to the following formula:

$$f_i = a_i * (s_i * i)^n$$

f_i : fractal information, a_i : authentic information,
s_i : simulated information, i : number of iterations, n : infinite

6.4 VIRTUAL IMPLOSION (VI)

The process of '*Virtual Implosion*' of information consists a theoretical approximation of the organization of the system of information, and intends to describe how the system of information, related to the certainty and security of meaning, transforms (mutates) to a fractal system, where meaning is replaced with the ambiguity of 'relations of meaning'. As argued throughout the book, information is considered as a system therefore, for the purposes of this theorization, the subsequent use of the term 'information' corresponds to the term 'the system of information'. 'Virtual Implosion' takes places in a series of continuous, infinite loops of dynamic change, expressed in distinctive phase spaces, and repeated in alternating and interrelated iterative cycles (Figure 6.7). During 'Virtual Implosion' abstract flows of electronic signals, coded as information, undergo quantitative and qualitative alterations within trajectories (phase spaces) of mutation. These phase spaces lead to the fractalization of information, by reproducing irregular, contradictory and chaotic distortions of the original. These fractal informational simulations may be simplified, distorted, controllable and programmable versions of the original information.

The 'Virtual Implosion' of the system of information is characterized by three phase spaces of fractal mutation: (a) '*Syghysis*' (deconstruction): With Syghysis, a relatively ordered group of components (fragments of data or fragments of information) of meaningful information is deconstructed into the individual components; these are then rearranged randomly, in disorder, around a core reference point and within the boundaries of the information environment; (b) '*Molynsis*' (differentiation): Molynsis follows the phase of Syghysis. During Molynsis each one of the randomly dispersed individual units (data) start to differentiate acquiring diverse degrees of emphasis, prestige, and structure, of similar dimensions; (c) '*Photococciasis*' (reconstruction): As a result of Molynsis, with Photococciasis, the differentiated stress applied on the constituent units of information, generates a non-linear stretching of the components towards a disorganized reconstruction of fractal dimensions. A detailed description of each one of the phase spaces of Virtual Implosion follows in more detail. Also considered, brief descriptions of the systemic organization and conditions of information (meaningful information vs. m&e%ani*n{g-ful fractal) before and after Virtual Implosion.

6.4.1 Information

'*Information*' can be considered as segments of communicated knowledge concerning particular facts, subjects, or events. The communication of information usually occurs in sets of data combined into messages or signs (a system of information), which entail some relation to meaning. Any set of data, out of which information is constructed, is in essence an abstract flow of electronic signals, which are coded and exist in various forms. These coded data sets, are defined here as 'fragments of data', whereas, the components of a system of information as 'fragments of information'. Fragments of data make up data, data make up fragments of information, which, in turn, can form a system of information, which presents systemic characteristics. A set of information is in essence a system of information.

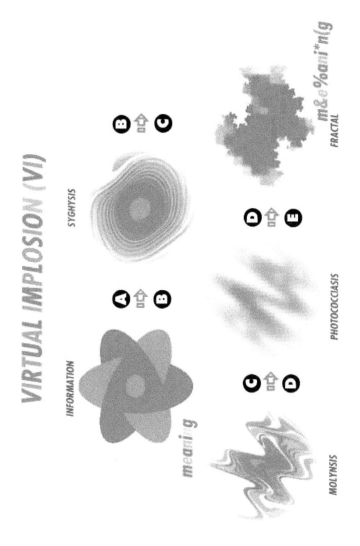

Figure 6.7: The phase spaces of Virtual Implosion: Information (meaning), Syghysis, Molynsis, Photococciasis, Fractal (m&e%ani*n(g).

A system of information in its initial condition stands at a potential equilibrium characterized by the uniform spatial distribution (homogeneity) of its constituent parts, the fragments of, data and information. It is an isotropic system, that is, it shows the same properties in all spatial directions. In this sense, a system of information consists a homeostatic inertial frame, which means that, when no external interference is involved, it remains either at rest or in homogenous motion within a certain absolute space in which it is defined. Interconnections of meaning among the fragments of information, act in principle as an electro-weak force that keeps the powerful interaction in tact, and as a whole keeps a meaningful order in the system of information. The interconnections of meaning are based on existing libraries of cloned knowledge, on associations formed among internal data and external interactions from the surrounding environment. The strength of the associations and interactions of the fragments of information in a system of information, is characterized by flexibility, which implies fragility, in other words, they stand in a potentially dynamic stage of change.

information
a system of communicated knowledge
concerning particular facts, subjects, or events,
usually as sets of data combined into messages
entailing some relation to meaning

A system of information, although it may be thought to be defined within a certain scale, of a specific shape and form, it is also characterized by moments of polarization (alternating movements towards defined limits of extremes) in relation to developing associations and interactions with other systems of information. The meaning of information, which is otherwise preserved, is interactively vulnerable, due to the questionable intensity of interconnected associations, and this consequently accounts for the potential for 'disturbance' of the meaning due to phenomena of interference. Whereas, the structural composition of the fragments of information accounts for the global kinetics of a system of information, the strength of internal and external interactivity accounts for the vulnerability, fragility and potential of change. The interactive intensities of a system of information can lead either its stability or instability; these intensities depend on the entropy of meaning which is generated from the multiple polarizations of the informational components. The meaning of an original system of information can increase towards greater disorder when associations and interactions are destabilized. Certain internal interactions of the fragments of information show greater resistance of links to surrounding external intruders, and in this way externally interfering systems of information, can be dissolved in fragments of information, and assimilated and absorbed very shortly after the interaction by the receiving system. At the same time, other interactions of the fragments of information are loosely linked and are prone to destabilize and form associations and get mixed with external fragments of data. Internal interactions of fragments of information depend on space-time symmetries. Strong interactions present isospin symmetries, whereas other weaker interactions present rotational symmetries or symmetries of reversal under inversion of the arrow of time. The interactions of the fragments of information, in moments of imbalance, create mobility, which assigns differentiated performance of each component. Some of this mobility concerns assignment of specialized function to fragments of information, assimilation of invading fragments of data, which can be of positive, viral, or negative nature. Mobility will also serve as a recognition or translation or neutralization tool of the interacting fragments. The preservation of the autonomy and integrity of a system of information is dependent upon the successful engineering of the conditions through which imbalances among internal and external, associations and interactions, can lead to the isolation, transfer, replication and reactivation of the system of information.

6.4.2 Syghysis

The 'Syghysis' of the system of information occurs with the fractal Catastrophe, the deconstruction of the system of information into its constituent components, that is, fragments of information and fragments of data. Fractal Catastrophe initiates fractal Orgasm, the generation of random movement of the fragments which forces their spatial rearrangement in the periphery of the original core meaning, but in any case within the initial limits of the meaning entailed in the system of information. The dynamic equilibrium of the original system of information is distressed by means of external interference of similar, contradictory or

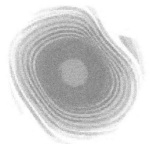

syghysis
(/ˈsɪɡjɪsɪs/ gr. σύγχυσις)
confusion; a confused or disordered condition; disorder in reference to ideas, notions

indifferent (with relation to the native meaning of the system) information. The external informational intruder generates the disorderly mobilization of the fragments of information and fragments of data, within the original system, by increasing the entropic tendencies of the system. Their mobilization reaches extreme degrees of intensification, bouncing between structural expansion and collapse. The 'tectonic' vibrations of the pending external associations 'break through' the architecture of the interactions of meaning of the original information, and 'fire up' a random heterogenous mixture of fragments, which spread along spatial curves of reference to a central point, on a continuous rearrangement process.

The established associations among fragments of information deteriorate with the emergence of their undifferentiated interlinking with incoming associations, which 'fill up' the spatial structural cracks of the 'damaged' associations of the original system of information. Subsequent multiple polarizations of interactions, among alien and host fragments of information and fragments of data, alters the shape and form of the system, and reproduces a temporary equilibrium of entropy. The system of information advances towards the synchronization of two conditions: a state of homogenous heterogeneity (similar patterns of differentiation) within the system and a state of heterogenous homogenization (differentiated patterns of similarity) outside the system. This way it preserves the limits of the internal entropy of meaning and balances the interaction with the potential external entropy of meaning. Existing associations are not totally destroyed, but they remain in prospective susceptibility to ever active unstable external interactions of organized complexity. Asymmetrical patterns of associations appear among the fragments of data and information, which are assigned self-referential functional meaning, this way becoming 'open' to the possibility of novelty. The autonomy and integrity of the meaning of the system of information is now deconstructed from a state of initial perpetuation to a state of depreciation and dispersion.

6.4.3 Molynsis

'*Molynsis*' is initiated with fractal Orgasm, the disorderly mobilization which generates the architectural repositioning of, both homogenous and transgenic, fragments of information, around chaotic peripheries of meaning. This leads to a phase of fractal Metamorphosis, that is, a phase of dissimilar application of selected and differentiated emphasis and scale on the indiscriminately dispersed fragments of information. The previously extreme intensification of structural upset of the environmental equilibrium is coming to a gradual stability and differentiated levels of meaning start to 'colonize' random strategic positions. Strong

molynsis
(/ˈmɔlɪnsɪs/ *gr. μόλυνσις*)
infection; an action or process of
contamination or corruption; a horrific condition
of quality by negative influences

heterogeneity in qualitative transformation emerges, and it is relocated in spatial curves around a geometric core of meaning. Qualitative alterations develop in the fragments of information, the result of a continuous enforcement of prestige and importance, which in turn produces inflationary and deflationary effects on the meaning of the intermixed fragments. Overflows and leakages in the negotiation of external interactions result to re-differentiation, iterative differentiation, or neutralization of the qualitative value of all the fragments of information. Undifferentiated links of all involved native associations decline, and self-similarity among the chains of associations of the original and the transgenic fragments of information, becomes the decisive factor of initiating novel patterns of symbiosis or contracts for the extinction of meaning. The emerged self-similarity of the interconnections, implies infinite possibilities of cloning, towards reproduction, reverse generation or regeneration of new relations of meaning. Homogenous heterogeneity and heterogenous homogenization are established both within the inner and the outer entropial environments, which become semi-conductively vulnerable to qualitative non-linear stretching of organized complexity. New symmetrical patterns of interactions emerge which shrink the self-referentiality of the fragments of information and produce a re-differentiated, unrefined, fractional phase of meaning.

6.4.4 Photococciasis

Fractal Molynsis generates the phase space of '*Photococciasis*'. Metamorphosis has already added differentiated emphasis on the components of the system of information and forces the system towards fractal Epigenesis, a fractal reconstruction of re-differentiated fragments through flexible non-linear iterations. Initially the dispersed fragments are assigned levels of differentiation, towards a gradual self-adaptation and relative stability. Both original and transgenic fragments of information are positioned strategically around the network of

photococciasis
(/ˈfəʊtəʊ ˈkɒkɪəsɪs/ gr. φωτοκοκκίασις)
the process of breaking down into pixels, smaller elements

new associations of the freshly established equilibrium. Change takes place as an intense assigning and intermixing of qualitative characteristics along an alternating, between inflation and deflation, repetitive pattern. Structural expansion and collapse are reversed, and geometry settles back in homogeneity and isotropy. A regeneration process sets off, by which novel interactions are built and the fragments of information are allocated assignments of different functions. Tensions of differentiation and re-differentiation in the qualitative value of the system create interactions and associations characterized by fertility and/or sterilization. Prevailing and compliant fragments of information are participating in a symbiotic experimentation of self-similarity which results to strengthened interconnections of infinite possibilities and new reconstructions of meaning. Such possibilities may lead to extreme cloning, exclusion, reversal, superfluous repetitions, or intense contradictions in the construction of new meaning. Initially undifferentiated external associations, repair structural fractures of meaning, by building up links of qualitative continuities over damaged fragments or interruptions in internal interactions. Potentially semi-conductive fragments of information will increase the degree of their vulnerability to produce self-similar copies or distortions in organized complex symmetries. The weakening of self-referentiality leads to a phase of total extinction, of rough and meaningless character. An irresolute condition of the system of information occurs, where the later, becomes self-dependent to arbitrariness and irregularity.

6.4.5 Fractal

Photococciasis generates the mutation of the system of information that is, '*Fractal Information*', with fractal Anomia, the iterative non-linear stretching of the fragments of information towards a disorganized 'meltdown' of fractal dimensions. Selective differentiation on the qualitative stress and importance of the fragments of information produces new architectural structures upon the flexible exploitation of non-linear associations among them.

fractal
irregular, contradictory and chaotic distortions of an original produced by iterations

Randomly colonized spatial positions of differentiated levels of meaning are self-adapting to the gradual stability, and become compliant to the self-organizing properties of emerging interactions. Interactions of heterogeneity are stabilized within a renewed equilibrium, where expansion and collapse implode to a self-organizing sense of balance. The alternating conditions of inflation and deflation of meaning, regenerate the process of the construction of interactions and associations, and of the assignment of functions, at diverse networks of relation between the new and the original meaning.

The variety of the levels of differentiation is a result of, both qualitative selectiveness, as well as the result of chains of effective dominance and compliance of meaning among the fragments of information. Self-similarity becomes familiar with negotiated contracts of meaning among the components, and advances towards their verification or retreats towards their rejection. Symbiosis in the fractal system becomes dependent to the acceptance and agreement of the potential associations in the fractal construction of new meaning, whereas rejection and denial of the associations results to its extinction. The qualitative vulnerability of the fragments of information arises from fracture points along the lines of internal associations. Non-linear stretching increases the patterns of interruption and turns them into patterns of organized complexity, reduced-size self-similar iterative copies, floating in a state of synchronous homogenous heterogeneity and heterogenous homogenization of meaning. The shrinking of the self-referentiality of the components of the system of information reaches the point of implosion, that is inward collapse and disappearance, inside of which the Fractal system of information evolves, actively independent and randomly unpredictable.

The Fractal system of information can be considered, as an irregular, disorganized mutation of communicated knowledge. In contrast to the original, meaning-related system of information, the fractalized system of information consists of repetitive distortions of facts, subjects, or events, without any specific or necessary reference to meaning, truth or reality, other than the reference to themselves. The qualitative property of the fractal the system of information lies in the simplification, reduction, non-complex transformation of original interconnections and interactions of meaning; fractals, are for this reason, visually spectacular, intellectually impressive and exciting versions of the new 'relations of meaning' and 'reality'. The increase of quantitative entropy of a fractal selectively emphasizes certain attributes and suppresses and diminishes others. The fractal presents a dynamic equilibrium of disorderly spatial distribution (heterogeneity) of the fragments of information (fractal fragments), and controversial, antithetical and unpredictable properties in its spatial environment (anisotropy).

A fractal system of information remains in heterogeneous motion of qualitative discrepancies, triggered around fracture points, which become black holes of meaning in the fractal environment. Whereas the original system of information was characterized by order, the eventual multi-directional re-collapse of meaning in a fractal, is characterized by strong gravity and concentration of mass of meaning in condensed form. Irregularity and extremity of fractal external interactions violate existing banks of cloned knowledge and lead to ultimate and extravagant relations with the environment. Vulnerability and plasticity of shape and form and a balanced multiple polarization of associations and interactions characterize a fractal, which may regenerate new processes of virtual implosion with other systems of information or fractals. The structural architecture of a fractal, accounts for the exhibited vulnerability, fragility and anomia, whereas the irregularity of the patterns of interactivity accounts for the potential manipulation, controllability, and programmability. The later may regenerate distorted versions of an original, and disguise it as the original itself. Fractal interactivity can lead to unstable disturbances and interference with systems of information by means of increasing their entropy towards a chaotic environment of disorganization, and the reconstruction of the system along space-time symmetries of rotation, inversion, reversal and other unspecialized virtual discrepancies. The viral character of the fractal the system of information neutralizes and liquidifies the original translation, and its scandalous behaviour produces false recognition of the original system of information.

6.5 FRACTAL DYNAMICS (FD)

The three phase spaces of the Virtual Implosion of the system of information to fractalization, are controlled and interconnected by five powerful micro-processes, which power up the transformation from one phase to the next. They are hereby collectively termed as '*Fractal Dynamics*' (Figure 6.8): (a) '*Catastrophe*' (destruction) generates the Syghysis of the system of information, by breaking down, deconstructing, the components of the system to fragments of information and data; (b) '*Orgasm*' (excitement) completes Syghysis and powers up Molynsis, by generating random mobility of the components of the system of information; it forces them to rearrange in the periphery of, but still within the prescribed limits, of the

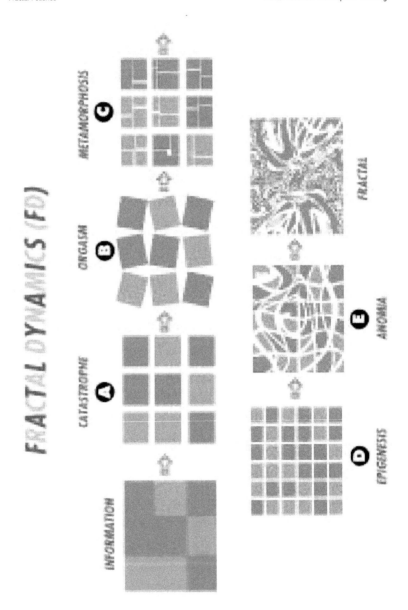

Figure 6.8: The micro-processes of Fractal Dynamics from Information to Fractal: Catastrophe, Orgasm, Metamorphosis, Epigenesis, and Anomia.

system; (c) '*Metamorphosis*' (transformation) concludes Molynsis and initiates Photococciasis, by producing levels of differentiation among the fragments, and assigning to them various degree of emphasis and substance; (d) '*Epigenesis*' (rebirth) signals the end of Photococciasis, restructuring the differentiated fragments by exercising flexible non-linear stretching on them towards the Fractal phase of the system; and (e) '*Anomia*' (lawlessness) secures the fractalization of the system of information by the irregular disorganized reconstruction of the stretched components The five micro-processes of Fractal Dynamics are described in more detail next:

6.5.1 Catastrophe

'*Catastrophe*' generates the Syghysis in the system of information, by breaking down and deconstructing the components of the system of information into its constituent parts. The dynamic equilibrium of the system of information is disturbed by means of interference of externally interacting, similar or opposing systems of information. Due to this interference,

catastrophe

(/kə'tæstrəfi/ gr. καταστροφή)
a final event; overthrow, ruin, calamitous
fate; a sudden disaster, wide-spread, very
fatal, or signal

inner mobility in the system is generated, which directly affects the homogeneity of the fragments of information, and causes them to alternate repositioning between expansion and collapse. The structural vibrations of interfering fragments of information set off the mobilization and deconstruction towards a heterogenous distribution. The established interconnections of meaning of the existing fragments of information lose strength, due to their interaction with the emerging interconnections of the incoming fragments. The incoming interconnections weaken the associations within the system of information and 'fire up' its structural transformation. Change initiates within the increase of activity of multiple polarization, which alters the spatial dimensions of the system. The system of information moves towards a state of homogenous heterogeneity (internal entropic meaning) and heterogenous homogenization (external entropic meaning). Existing interlinks between fragments of information are interrupted, but not destroyed, and become potentially vulnerable to internal mobility and interaction with interfering fragments of data. The system of information becomes an unstable system of organized complexity, wherein space-time symmetries create asymmetrical patterns. In intensified moments of interaction like this, fragments of information are assigned the special function of acting self-referentially, preserving the relative autonomy of information, still depreciating and confusing the integrity of the meaning of entailed in the system of information.

6.5.2 Orgasm

'*Orgasm*' completes the Syghysis of the system of information and powers up Molynsis. Orgasm produces random movement of the fragments of information and forces them to rearrange spatially in the periphery of original meaning and within the defined limits of the system. The equilibrium that characterized the original state of the system of information is distressed and a disorderly intrusion of incoming fragments of information commences. The

orgasm
(/ˈɔgæzm/ *gr. οργασμός*)
immoderate or violent excitement;
excitement or violent action accompanied with
turgescence

mobilization of the intruding components is intensified and they start to interfere and intermix in original spatial reference points. They spread randomly on a continuous process of rearrangement. Intermixed fragments of information are placed at new positions with regard to a core reference point of meaning, and remain susceptible to infinite possible alternative directions around this point. Repositional expansion reaches the outer limits of extreme meaning in the system of information, whereas repositional collapse retreats to the inner limits of minimal meaning in the system. This heterogenous distribution breaks down the chains of internally established associations and deconstructs the established meaning of the whole system.

The externally emerged interconnections 'fill' the spatial gaps of associations. The interrelation that develops between the new interconnections is undifferentiated, that is, one of embryonic character, therefore the developed elementary new associations are weak, but clearly characteristic of the structural transformation taking place. Multiple polarization re-establishes relative stability of the disorderly environment, sustaining the dyad of homogenous heterogeneity (internal entropic meaning at stable level) and heterogenous homogenization (balancing the effect of external entropic meaning). Previous interconnections, having surpassed their limit of vulnerability, are destroyed as a result of inner and outer interactions with the new arrivals. Fragments of information are distributed into spatial asymmetrical patterns of strong self-referentiality, open to the development of new associations. While the autonomy and integrity of the dispersed components is high, the meaning of the system of information is confused, if not totally lost, due to the total destruction of the associations within.

6.5.3 Metamorphosis

'*Metamorphosis*' completes the introduction of Molynsis in the system of information and generates the Photococciasis of the system of information. This is done by producing levels of differentiation which, in turn, assign various degrees of emphasis and substance to the randomly dispersed fragments of information. The random disorderly mobility of the fragments of information comes to a relative stability of dispersion, and both original and transgenic fragments occupy new strategic positions. The mobilization of fragments of information is more of an intensified assignment of parameters of quality rather than geometry, regenerating transgenic fragments of information. Placed in random core and peripheral areas they inflate and deflate, in terms of qualitative value, to the new interconnected meaning of all involved systems. Some fragments of information will retain their previous qualitative value, or will be re-differentiated, while some others will show critically low levels to the point of inability to interact and build up associations.

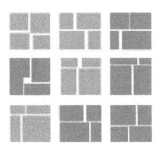

metamorphosis

($/\ '$metəmɔfəsɪs$/$ *gr.* μεταμόρφωσις)
*the action or process of changing in form,
shape or substance; a complete change in the
appearance, circumstances, condition, character,
affairs*

Self-similarity between original and transgenic fragments of information is important for their symbiotic survival or extinction. Intermixed fragments of information are loaded with fresh potential to interconnect and form associations of an infinite number of possibilities. Depending on the nature of interactions and associations, these possibilities extend between the extremes of exact cloning of the original meaning to the full reversal of it. Chains of associations are visible, potentially restored, still, undifferentiated. Spatial gaps are filled in by the structural variations along a qualitative scaling of all components. Structural gaps exist only at the point of pending associations and interactions. Multiple polarization retains stability and entropy remains stable. The instability of differential structural stress increases the vulnerability of the new fragments of information. New symmetries are re-established and self-referentiality is weakened. A re-differentiated partial autonomy of meaning develops, still, of crude and as a whole meaningless character

6.5.4 Epigenesis

'*Epigenesis*' is, in a way, the reverse process of Orgasm. It signals the end of Photococciasis and triggers the 'fractalization' of the system of information. Epigenesis reconstructs the differentiated fragments of information by applying stretching to the flexible non-linear associations among them. The self-adaptation of all the fragments of information to the relative stability within the spatial boundaries of the original meaning of information is followed. A renewed equilibrium of interaction among the fragments of information is established and a structural change takes place. Homogeneity and isotropy are restored by means of a reverse version of the initial condition between expansion and collapse during

epigenesis
(/ˈepɪˈdʒenəsɪs/ gr. επιγένεσις)
the development of a complex entity,
from a simple, undifferentiated unit

Catastrophe. Structural mobility is regenerated setting off the reconstruction of interactions and associations and the assignment of functions of each fragment. Depending on the effects of Metamorphosis, stronger interactions are formed among dominant fragments of information, and weaker among compliant fragments of information. In antithesis with Catastrophe, these interconnections strengthen the associations within the system of information and indicate the possibility of forming new arrangements of meaning. The self-similarity exhibited, by previously transgenic fragments of information, to original ones, allows the development of a familiarity for associations with them, but it does not guarantee absolute inclusion of all fragments, or it does not exclude the possibility of including superfluous repetitions or contradictions in the construction of new meaning.

Moreover, the structural non-linear stretching of the fragments of information may result in fracture points, which damage the fragments or interrupt the interaction, producing smaller self-similar copies or distortions in the intended result. Increases in the entropy of meaning are temporal and along an interruptive pattern, having the effect of an irresolute condition of the information between homogenous heterogeneity and heterogenous homogenization of meaning. Organized complex symmetries emerge and they disperse in complex patterns of associations and interactions. Any kind of local or self-reference as a whole in the system of information, is lost; the new information becomes self-dependent and reliable to randomness and unpredictability.

6.5.5 Anomia

'*Anomia*' characterizes the transition from Photococciasis to the Fractal phase of the system of information. It is the process which secures that epigenetic components of the system of information will undergo an irregular disorganized reconstruction into fractals. Anomia consists an anarchous phase of final mutation into distortion, repetition, non-referentiality to meaning, truth or reality. The quantity of iterative transformations as the result of epigenetic non-linear stretching overpowers the qualitative and potentially meaning-inclusive fragments of information. Quantitative entropy increases, diminish or alter quality properties, or set controversial or antithetical (to the original information) qualitative

anomia

(/ˈæno ˈmiə/ gr. ανομία)
disregard of law, lawlessness; the state or condition lacking of accepted standards or values

properties: they assign primitive simplified versions, which do not require complex, meaning-related, interconnections and interactions. Equilibrium, homogeneity and isotropy show self-similarity to the original information although they are potentially unpredictable in this new phase. Extreme states of mobility appear, either dynamic expansion towards further iteration or eventual re-collapse inwards (implosion). Interactions, associations, and functions become irregular, ultimate, and extremely spectacular. Self-similarity decides the selection of fragments of information for building up new interconnections, which unavoidably will include qualitative contradictions of already differentiated fragments of information. In the same way interactions of meaning and associations with other systems of information will present qualitative discrepancies. Fracture points in interactions may become starting or ending points in building up associations, whereas structural distortions in fragments of information themselves, may eventually become dominant and powerful attractors in the new system of information. Because complex interconnections are not a requirement to the construction of meaning in the anomic system of information, the later, is in itself vulnerable to manipulation, not necessarily intentional directions being present. This vulnerability also arises from the simplified form of reduced complexity in associations and interactions that the system of information is shaped into. As such it becomes controllable and can be programmed to altered versions of the original. If it is extremely difficult to regenerate an exact copy of the associations, interactions and construction of meaning in an original system of information, it is though, relatively simple to produce altered and distorted copies and even easier to disguise them as exact copies of their original. And that ... is a fractal 'reality'.

6.6 EXAMPLES OF VIRTUAL IMPLOSION AND FRACTAL DYNAMICS

The Virtual Implosion of the system of information to a fractal is demonstrated in the following two examples. The first example refers to the original information and knowledge, available through scientific investigation and evidence, about *Life in the Universe*. The following analysis shows how, applying the phase spaces of Virtual Implosion and Fractal Dynamics, this authentic system of information (or set of systems of information comprising a body of knowledge), implodes into the fractal realities of 'Little Green Men' and other cultural mutation such as *Aliens*. The second example that exemplifies the processes of Virtual Implosion and Fractal Dynamics, refers to the concepts of *Physical Space* and *Virtual Space*. The analysis further below, attempts to describe how our notion of Physical Space, through the advance of electronic communication, implodes to an artificial virtual environment. The analysis accounts for the mechanics of the digital reconstruction of Virtual Space, which replaces Physical Space as the new spatial reality.

6.6.1 Life in the Universe and Aliens

What we know about the '*Life in the Universe* '(hereafter *i-LitU*) is a complex set of combined interdisciplinary scientific information. It provides a framework of knowledge (in terms of theoretical justification and explanation) that originates in diverse scientific disciplines such as Astronomy, Particle Physics, Cosmology, and so on. What is suggested here is that the scientific corpus which composes i-LitU, mainly due to media industry influences (print, radio, TV, cinema, and so on), undergoes a virtual implosion, and is gradually replaced by an artificial, non-scientific corpus of distorted (fractal) information which claims the authenticity and 'truth' of the original one. This is expressed in the numerous global media images and texts of extraterrestrial anthropomorphic, or not so anthropomorphic, species of intelligent life which are incorporated as authentic cultural representations, generally term as 'Aliens' or, as used here, '*Alien Species*'(hereafter *f-A*).

The available original information on i-LitU, is based on scientific evidence and experimentation, and consists of a number of meaningful segments of information, in the sense that they refer to the concepts of life and universe which 'make meaning'. These would include, for example, theories about the birth or the structure of the universe, research evidence from the exploration of our solar system, the difficulty in providing proof of extraterrestrial intelligent civilization or other form of life, related themes and concepts from related sciences (physics, chemistry, and so on), or even guesswork and assumptions based on calculated assessment from observations and established knowledge (Figure 6.9).

black holes   **not known civilization**   galaxies
       . . .
stars **LIFE IN THE UNIVERSE**   unknown
meteorites   chaos . . .   space travel   gravity
                electroweak

Figure 6.9: Life in the Universe (i-LitU) in its original (meaningful) phase.

The components of the information that make up the i-LitU are characterized by a balanced distribution around the core meaning they refer to (forces, matter, energy as parts of life or the universe). The components are assigned equally qualitative value in terms of their relative truth and originality. Interactions among theoretical justification and speculation based on scientific evidence offer interconnections of justifiable meaning to the i-LitU, and among the individual fragments of information, such as, between the possibility of space-travel, the environmental conditions of planets, and their possible colonization by the human race. It is also the associations of this theoretical justification and speculation with internal existing packets of knowledge (degree of sensibility, attraction, rejection) that confirm and enforce the associative interactions of meaning. For example, whether or not, the possibility of colonization of another planet by the human race is within real or unreal limits. The fact, though, that it is exactly the acceptance or rejection of these theoretical justifications and speculations, that produces these interactions, is what grants fragility and flexibility of the meaning of the i-LitU towards potential change.

Depending on the strength of the theory and evidence within which they are originally produced, some of fragments of information, (for example, the ones assigned to account for the chaotic organization of the universe), will present stronger or weaker polarizations with fragments they can relate, (for example, with those related to the chaotic organization in everyday life) within the system environment of the prescribed meaning. This property, of establishing relations, makes them vulnerable to create associations, absorptions, and liquidifications with potentially intruding fragile fragments of information (such as, similar in theme systems of information, as for example, science fiction.). The result is actually the disturbance of the original meaning of i-LitU.

As a whole the i-LitU is indeed a relatively unstable system of information, whose entropic content can increase with, for example, the development of new theoretical proposals, or research evidence. In any case, the available system of information of i-LitU can be altered, by increase or decrease in quantity without necessarily implying change in meaning, but it cannot decrease in terms of already acquired and established meaning regarding life in the Universe. The ways that theory proposes and justifies the meaning of the various fragments, that make up i-LitU, is what determines the formation of space-time symmetries of the involved fragments. Interactions among concepts, expressed by meanings of fragments of information, originating from the same theory or experiment for example, will establish more stable structural symmetries, thus stronger associations of meaning. Others will establish symmetries subject to rotation, reversal or similar geometrical and spatial disturbances, if coming from different, or contradictory, theoretical accounts, for example, Big Bang theory vs. Inflation theory on the birth of the Universe. Certain fragments of information of the i-LitU will establish similar structural properties and behaviour with externally interacting fragments of data or information (for example, if originating from the same theory). Depending on the status of their vulnerability, they will act as agents of assimilation, recognition, translation or neutralization, and they will decide, either the continuation of the present stability, or the further progression towards the virtual Syghysis of the meaning of i-LitU.

Fragments of data or fragments of information (such as, those originating from the media industry and science fiction), may refer to the same theme of the original system of information of i-LitU. However, their origin is not based on scientific proof; rather, the origins of their meaning are based on the imagination and individual intentions of their sources. Such fragments of information or data present similar structural properties and behaviour with those fragments of the original i-LitU which have a vulnerable status, and are susceptible in forming interactions of assimilation, recognition, translation or neutralization. For example, a media proposed image of a planet may easily be assimilated with the image of a planet as described by scientific exploration, or even, the anticipated possibility of a media image for existence of alien life, may coincide with the acceptance of the mathematics of probability theory, or simple human instincts of curiosity. The Syghysis of the meaning of the original i-LitU is initiated with the catastrophic interaction and formation of associations between such external and similar internal fragments of information (Figure 6.10).

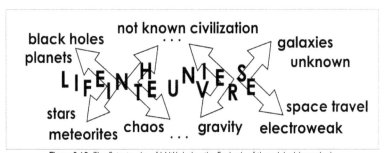

Figure 6.10: The Catastrophe of i-LitU during the Syghysis of the original (meaning).

Fragments of information i-LitU are deconstructed into their separate individual meanings and position themselves within a temporary distance, of uncertain relativity, to the central meaning of the i-LitU. Media generated fragments of information of similar, contradictory or indifferent dimensions (for example, 'a Jurassic period like environment in a faraway planet', or 'gigantic spaceships travelling through black holes'), come to interfere with the actual meaning of i-LitU. Inaccurate sci-fi jargon, for example, mixes with established scientific terminology, or technological innovations of extreme improbability (for example, matter teleportation). Like magnets, these interfering fragments of data, establish connections and create intense mobilization of meaning towards extreme states of indefinite expansion (for example, alien conspiracy and the aftermath), or condensational collapse (for example, life in another dimension through wormholes). What follows is a series of Orgasmic decision processes among associations of meanings, as they intermix with interacting partners, towards a continuous rearrangement and settlement (Figure 6.11).

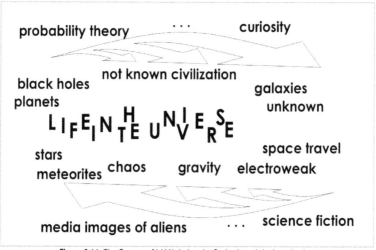

Figure 6.11: The Orgasm of i-LitU during the Syghysis and the introduction of Molynsis of the original (meaning).

The potential for creating associations of the interfering fragments of data or fragments of information may be stronger in relation to its own meaning, and that will override the establishment of poorer associations of meaning with the existing fragments of information of the i-LitU. For example, a science fiction narrative regarding the content and structure of a black hole, may be more meaningful and attractive to association (exactly because it is constructed to 'make sense') rather than an abstract mathematical astrophysical explanation, which unavoidably because of the lack of adequate information cannot 'make sense'. Although, in essence undifferentiated, the establishment of dynamic interactions between incoming and existing associations will eventually override the original meaning of i-LitU.

Similarly, theoretical gaps and inaccuracies may easily be filled in to construct a more spectacular and attractive visual pattern of associations.

While fractal Orgasm spatially reconstructs the original meaning of i-LitU, within the range of possible understandings, the original meaning of i-LitU is preserved with relation to its scientific basis, but those intruding non-scientific, artificial fragments of information come to attach themselves to the original ones, and to claim part of the original meaning. Astrology, for example, is far away from being granted scientific status, still, such false status may be claimed as true by native to astrology systems of information, upon the establishment of associations with i-LitU. The original meaning of i-LitU starts to reorganize in a complex way, while foreign, to the original meaning, fragments of information (for example, media images, science fiction texts), are interweaved on a depreciative and dispersed progress towards the blurring of the actual meaning of i-LitU. This is the phase of conceptual and informational contradictions, the Molynsis of the original meaning of i-LitU. Once the orgasmic interactions of 'transgenic' intrusions are established, for example, between the scientific attempts for space exploration (original to the i-LitU) and the actual distant galaxies explorations and discovery of alien civilizations (original to the incoming annoyances), they are all, now intermixed and repositioned around the meaning of i-LitU. The intermixed fragments of information come in potentially chaotic numbers of possible combinations of the metamorphosed meaning of the original i-LitU.

Figure 6.12: The Metamorphosis of i-LitU during the Molynsis of the original (meaning) and the generation of Photococciasis of the original (meaning).

Subject to fractal Metamorphosis in Virtual Implosion (Figure 6.12), what we originally are informed about life in the universe, undergoes a selective and diverse differentiation. Stronger in simplicity interactions (in terms of forming complex meaning) prevail, such as the visualization of an Alien, as opposed to an abstract and vague description of some alien bacterial life form found on a meteorite. This extreme intensification of non-linear stretching of the existing boundaries of meaning, adds differential weight of importance and emphasis to certain components than others. The media constructed possibility of another space dimension through a black hole dominates, as it excites imagination, rather confuses it and frustrates it, as it would be in the case of a astrophysical offer of explanation. Upon this qualitative differentiation, new individual meanings are stabilized in strong associations with the original i-LitU. i-LitU is presented with a flexible pattern of inflationary and deflationary proposals of meaning, of what life in the universe is about; during this process de-emphasized components will be suppressed, for example, the insistence of sci-fi films presenting sound in absolute vacuum (air fights of spaceships) will prevail over the scientific evidence that sound cannot travel in vacuum. 'Leakages' of meaning are replaced by a repetitive multiplication of the meaning of the intrusive fragments of information, which may also create extreme overflows (for example, not one but many alien nations).

Self-similarity becomes a decisive factor in the formation of new interactions at the expense of the qualitative aspect of meaning. The simultaneous heterogeneous homogenization (of the constituent parts of meaning of i-LitU) is exemplified with new contracts of meaning, such as: unexplained phenomena are translated to explained, alien characteristics obtain characteristics of the insect world, alien personalities obtain targeted human desires, alien advanced civilizations are threatening civilizations, and so on. At the same time, homogenous heterogenization is retained, with the entropic meaning of the i-LitU reaching temporal enclosures and boundaries, towards the external environment; the meaning of i-LitU is still, although infected, the meaning attached to i-LitU. Once the new contracts of meaning of i-LitU are established, new re-differentiated spatial associations have to be assigned, and ordered around the core meaning. An illusionary reconstruction of interactions of meaning, among the new components is reconstructed, such as: aliens live in distant planets, travel with spaceships, they intend to colonize Earth, they look like insects, they are mean and unfriendly, and so on (Figure 6.13).

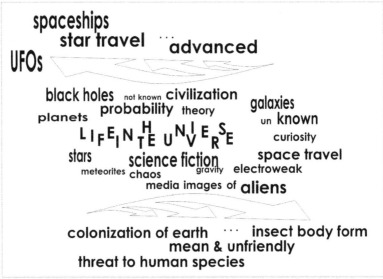

Figure 6.13: The Epigenesis of i-LitU during Photococciasis and the mutation towards the fractal phase of 'Alien Species' (f-A) (distorted meaning) of the original (meaning).

Once these initial interactions are stabilized, a gradual self-adaptation of meaning interconnections is assigned to the i-LitU, for example, a UFO, i.e. an unexplained flying object, is most of the time related to presence of aliens. The repositioning of these new meanings around the main theme of the i-LitU, reverses the established geometrical equilibrium. The process of retaining homogeneity and isotropy enforces the new phase of the i-LitU, thus the meaning of the i-LitU, as referring to alien species and their related characteristics is empowered. Moreover, the new components constructing the changing i-LitU are assigned internal associations of self-reference, that is, UFOs imply spaceships, alien species imply advanced civilization, and so on. These internal associations may mean the production of excess meaning, for example, a spacecraft may be magnified to a gigantic 'mother' spaceship, or the probability of non-existence of an alien species in the universe may be reduced to zero.

Once these initial associations are formed, they can potentially multiply in copies of great quantities, as the possible interconnections among them are infinite.

The system of information regarding travel in space, for example, may be iteratively reproduced, to indicate travel through time teleports, gateways to other dimensions, dematerialization-materialization teleports, and so on. The cloning of already cloned meaning is potentially trouble free, with exclusion not even being a matter of concern, with reversal possibly a desired effect, and with contradiction a challenge to prove otherwise. Epigenesis signals the birth of a new fractal meaning, the building of synthetic overpasses among damaged original interconnections of meaning. Conceptual gaps, theoretical insufficiencies and weaknesses of the original i-LitU, are all sealed up with adhesive 'simulated data' matter. The result is the development of even more complex symmetries of uncertain meaning, difficult to predict how they will develop and connect among them and with other similar systems of information; the i-LitU reaches a self-dependent, irregular and random phase of constructing meaning.

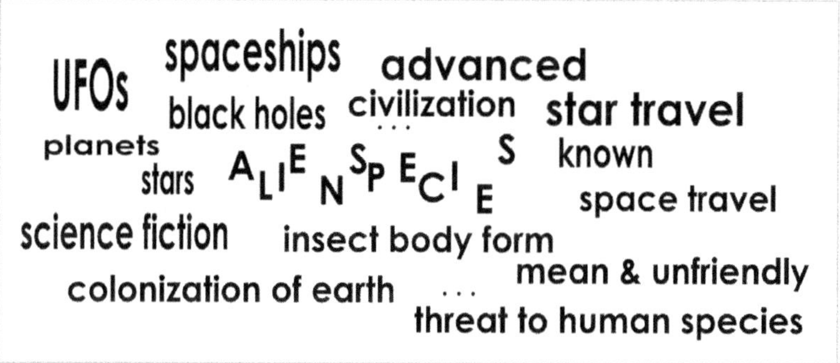

Figure 6.14: The Anomia of i-LitU during the fractal mutation of the original (meaning) towards 'Alien Species' (f-A) (distorted meaning).

Gradually i-LitU is replaced by f-A in the final phase towards fractalization, Anomia (Figure 6.14). Artificial new associations of meaning have reached a level of dominance towards compliant original meaning. Life in the universe has become synonymous with the existence of alien intelligent life (we are not alone). f-A reorganizes and legitimizes itself, and reconstructs false meaningless interpretations, such as: how is the alien colonization going to be achieved, how the advanced alien enemy technology could be faced, what is the future of our planet in the face of an alien threat, and so on. f-A consists of a distorted version of the original i-LitU. Anomia governs the final structural and qualitative mutations towards the Fractal (Figure 6.15) dimension of the i-LitU.

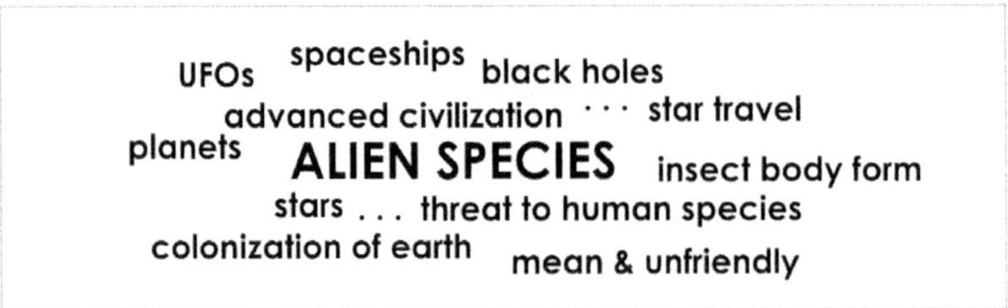

UFOs   spaceships   black holes
advanced civilization   · · ·   star travel
planets   ALIEN SPECIES   insect body form
stars . . . threat to human species
colonization of earth   mean & unfriendly

Figure 6.15: The Fractal phase of 'Aliens Species' (f-A) (distorted meaning) of the original (meaning) of 'Life in the Universe' (i-LitU).

f-A has distortedly displaced originality with artificiality, by repetitive qualitative dislocations, replacements and other interactions described above. f-A is a system of information of plasticity and liquidity, which can be chaotically manipulated along multiple parameters. The loss of reference, to the scientific basis of i-LitU, allows further quantitative and qualitative interactions, thus further fractalization of unpredictable dimensions, such as: building sciences to examine alien nature, investigating alien languages, analyzing alien cultures, and so on. The fractal phase of f-A allows the flexible abuse of the associations and interactions of fractal meaning, in other words, the reconstruction and reproduction of hyperreal entities and virtual realities, to justify its existence and secure its survival. Fractal flexibility, and complex patterns of organization, isolate negotiations and imploding effects with external, original systems of information, or internal remaining instances of pre-existing associations, that would be potential rioters and correction agents.

Once established, it is questionable whether the quantitative and repetitive logic of f-A can be overridden by scientific input, that may be contradictory to the established meaning of f-A. Although, original and fractal information undergo symbiosis, the total extinction of meaningful information is more probable in terms of repetitive denials and rejections of applications for new associations between the two. The eventual non-linear stretching of fractal information appears to be more powerful and it tends to overpower the original qualitative architectural meaningful properties. The fractalization of f-A appears to provide redundant answers, solutions and explanations, at a faster and more 'satisfactory' level, in comparison to those that come from the scientific world. f-A becomes a reduced distortion of life in the universe, characterized by complex organization, multiple self-similar copies of artificial meaning, which destroys any reference to the original system of information, to secure its evolution and survival in an unpredictable fractal reality.

6.6.2 Physical Space and Virtual Space

'Physical Space' (hereafter i-PS) is the environment that we, and the objects around us, occupy. It entails some meaning for it is there where our existence starts and ends, where we retrieve, negotiate and exchange our daily experiences with other subjects like us or objects. i-PS is the space of matter, energy, forces, chemistry, the content of which we have a basic understanding of and which we can explain to an adequate degree. The concept of i-PS can be said therefore to be meaningful, it 'makes sense' because of its interconnectedness to our senses and our lived experience.

Therefore, the concept of i-PS encompasses, in this sense, numerous authentic and original experiences, for which little or none justification is needed, as we encounter them in the practice of our daily lives. With the advance of electronic communication and digital technologies, a new spatial experience has been intensified and regenerated, that is 'Virtual Space' (hereafter f-VS). More importantly, this new space claims the 'reality' of lived experience by reconstructing and repositioning our daily practices and challenging our mental considerations of life itself. f-VS, the natural habitat of the system of information, appears to establish itself as the new domain of the negotiation and redefinition of social existence, translating the rules, conduct, and codes of i-PS to digital reproductions. The example provided here suggests that this transformation of i-PS to f-VS can be described by the phases of Virtual Implosion and Fractal Dynamics.

The description of i-PS can be said to include different aspects of the structure and organization of local and global spatial experience, such as: citizens of a state, law and order agencies (police, army, etc.), traffic jams and accidents, natural disasters (floods, earthquakes, etc.), diseases (HIV, poisoning, etc.), weather changes (warm, cold, climate, seasons, etc.), environmental pollution, working life, central and district administration, strikes, and so on (Figure 6.16).

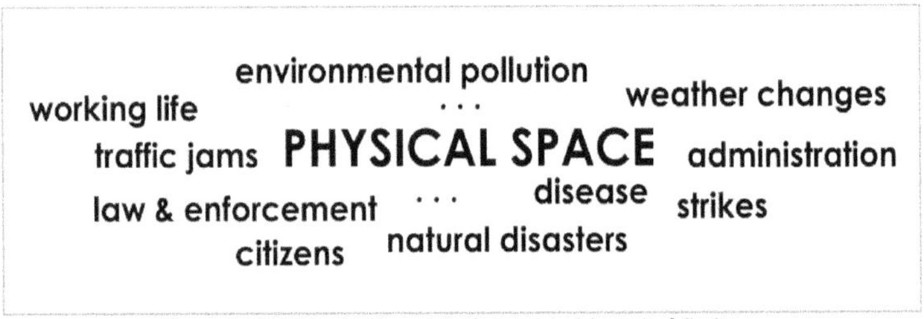

Figure 6.16: A 'Physical Space' (i-PS) in original (meaningful) phase.

The fragments of information that make up the i-PS are ordered in balanced alternating distribution around the core meaning of physical space, along continuities of spatial adjustments along the arrow of time. The quality (negative or positive) of each one of the components of meaning, that comprise i-PS, is recognizable, undisputed, and often taken for granted. All the components of meaning are assigned qualitative value because their 'truth' is indeed experienced and evidenced. The everyday interactions within the limits of the system of i-PS, justify and enforce the reality of the interconnections of its meaning, such as: the daily working routines, sources of urban pollution, the stress or repeated traffic congestions, overcrowding, hard working conditions, unemployment, epidemics and health risks, administrative crises, crime and law enforcement, seasonal and climatic changes, social unrest, strikes and disputes, and so on. Most of these social organizational patterns within the system, are taken for granted, and usually they go undisputed as they are based on inner associations of observation, logic, acceptance, denial, compliance, conformity, insecurity, and so on. It is this internal interaction that legalizes and reproduces the meaning of i-PS within the wider collective societal consciousness. Such inner associations, though, contribute to the fragility of the meaning of i-PS towards external interference and prospective transformation.

There exist powerful, weak or irrelevant to power associations, whose interactive engagement produces levels of meaning to i-PS of differentiating power. Dismay, distrust, or totally indifferent states of opinion, create vulnerabilities, allowing intrusions which weaken the defenses of the original meaning of i-PS. Similar sets of information will be engaged, and artifice, illusion, hallucination, and virtual reality will interfere and upset the original meaning of i-PS. The instability of the meaning of i-PS, can be quantitatively enriched and recreated from scratch, within the sphere of imagination, and in alternative forms and models. The later forms and models can be abstractly theorized and defined within space-time (rotational, reverse, spherical, curved) symmetries of meaning, rotational, reverse, spherical and curved symmetries of meaning. Incorporation, identification, conversion or neutralization, of the developed interactions and rearrangements of symmetries of meaning, will generate fractal dynamic processes, which will advance the meaning of i-PS towards virtual implosion. Artificial and simulated fragments of data or information, as those originating from information technologies and the internet, quite often interlace with the meaning of space; the meaning of the virtual entities occupying hyperspace though, is one of synthetic construction, programming and imagination of software engineers and marketing consultants, rather than of actual everyday experience. The structural properties of hyperspatial simulated information, bears similarities and representational patterns comparable to the original i-PS and this accounts for the vulnerability of the development of interactions among them. During Virtual Implosion, the meaning of the original i-PS is confused with the development of such initial interactivity (Figure 6.17).

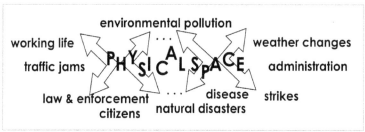

Figure 6.17: The Catastrophe of i-PS during the Molynsis of the original (meaning).

In an undifferentiated fashion, individual fragments are spatially deconstructed, and discretely created along qualitative distances from the core meaning of i-PS. The development of interactions with the interfering simulations, enable the easy assimilation of the incoming fragments of information, which magnetize and generate a hypnotic mobilization of the original fragments. The relative freedom and stability of a virtual environment, as well as the relative anonymity of its members, and the possibility for the construction of 'safe' identities, they all offer more attractive and appealing alternatives for escape from the painful construction of meaningful associations of the everyday reality of i-PS (Figure 6.18)

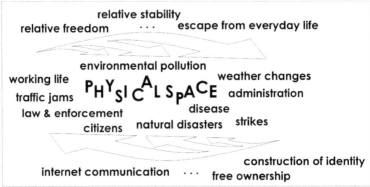

Figure 6.18: The Orgasm of i-PS during the Molynsis and introduction of Molynsis of the original (meaning).

The projected satisfaction and excitement of the new eventual interactions of the i-PS with the intruding simulations of virtual space, supersede the agonizing reality of meaning, and are responsible for the potential of architectural interruption of the original meaning of the i-PS. The satisfaction and excitement are justified by what virtual space has on offer: free housing, work from home, no pain or irreversible (usually) loss, no strikes and riots, a place where you can talk free-of-complications, no waste and pollution, no bad weather, time standing still, distance minimized, stability and continuity of peace and eternal existence secured and guaranteed behind virtual firewalls. An effortless, in terms of quality, constructed meaning.

Insignificance and unhappiness in i-PS are replaced with extravagant and eye-catching alternative spectacles and distractions. The actual meaning of physical space is never lost, as everyday experience is there to justify and refresh its memories; the meaning of belonging within the particular boundaries of physical space, though, is confused to the degree that its originality and truth are at the risk of being replaced by hyper-realistic alternatives. A virtual environment, can hardly claim the originality of 'real' experience, although graphic design, interactive technology, and a colorful mixture of global participation offer a virtual experience that is quite appealing, in contrast to the sensory famine and aesthetic degradation of the i-PS conceptual experience. The 'transgenic' incoming disturbance establishes interconnected associations with the original i-PS, such as, between the physical identity and virtual existence, ownership of a virtual home and a physical home, and so on. The new interactions of orgasmic meaning, multiply in alternative combinations to the original i-PS. Fractal Metamorphosis of virtual implosion (Figure 6.19), selectively and diversely, stresses certain fragments of information more than others, depending on their levels of simplicity or organization. Sensual and attractive extensions of associations, such as, escape from problems, free of charge and debt, anonymity of communication, a variety and openness in development of acquaintances, relative autonomy out of collective nuisance, and so on, prevail the more realistic and painful interactions of experience of the i-PS.

Figure 6.19: The Metamorphosis of i-PS during the Molynsis of the original (meaning) and the generation of Photococciasis of the original (meaning).

Virtually constructed alternatives of differentiation stabilize new individual meanings. The meaning of i-PS is inflated and deflated as to what physical space is about and what more could be; certain original depressing experiences are suppressed in isolation, such as, accident, disaster, disease, limits and boundaries, restrictions, exploitation, and so on. The original associations of meaning escape in terms of continuous circulation of transgenic simulated fragments of information, to a variety of superficial environments and worlds, and suspiciously antisocial interactions which finally reduce and distort the i-PS. Virtual fragments of information negotiate new relations of meaning, for example: government administration becomes a system administrator or operator, a disease becomes an infection from a Trojan or a malicious worm virus, home ownership becomes homesteading, a weather disaster becomes a server system crash, and so on. In the fresh new environment of interactions, a reconstruction of interactions of fantasy is taking place. They account as the emerging characteristics of f-VS: physical social relationships are no different from those developing in a virtual environment, false and anonymous identities are permitted, what is illegal in the physical world can be powerful and prestigious in the virtual world, marketing and advertising become the main financial activities for the survival of the virtual setting, registration of a virtual membership is necessary for survival, higher speed of communication is the ultimate of existence in a virtual world, and so on (Figure 6.20).

Figure 6.20: The Epigenesis of i-PS during Photococciasis and the mutation towards the fractal phase of 'Virtual Space' (f-VS) (distorted meaning) of the original (meaning).

Such interconnections progressively lead to a reverse self-adaption of the meaning of i-PS, for example, power and control in a f-VS is related to good knowledge of computer use, networks, computer languages, or of related software, as well as on time spent and personal work devoted towards contributing to the f-VS community. The diffusion of new associated meanings between simulated and original i-PS systems results in the generation of reversed symmetries of the meaning of i-PS as a whole: a f-VS poses as a 'better', relatively problem free world, where many of the troubles of the physical world, can actually be dealt and resolved faster and adequately, although it can often become a long-term commitment of frustration, dissatisfaction and unpredictable isolation.

The new fragments of data and information responsible for the change of i-PS internally, acquire degrees of self-reference, for example, having a virtual home (a homepage or web page) is as necessary as a physical home, or an e-mail address as important as the telephone number and postal address in the physical world. Exaggeration of the internal associations reach extreme distortion of meaning, such as that, a f-VS is structurally as concrete and stable as, or better than, the physical world; or that, the progress and maturity of f-VS is solely dependent on technologically advances and services. Infinite interconnections of this kind are chaotically propagated through similarly simulated systems of information. The Molynsis and distortion of i-PS become a habitual activity towards fractal transformation. The establishment of artificial meaning is secured, and further virtual connections 'seal up' intangible cracks of possible remains of meaningful associations of the original i-PS. Virtual entities, objects, and events, which realize the networks of the new interactions of meaning, are added and multiply in substance and diversity; furthermore, they create and legalize the fractal reality of the f-VS and the newly emerged consciousness: virtuality. Unpredictable and uncertain meaning characterizes the self-relying, irregular and non-systematic transition from the original i-PS to the f-VS (Figure 6.21).

Figure 6.21: The Anomia of i-PS during the fractal mutation of the original (meaning) towards 'Virtual Space' (f-VS) (distorted meaning).

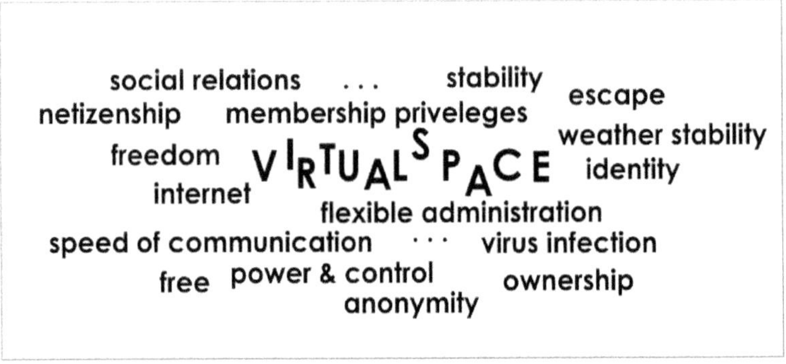

Figure 6.22: The fractal phase of 'Virtual Space' (f-VS) (distorted meaning)
of the 'Physical Space' (i-PS) original (meaning).

With fractalization f-VS becomes 'self-similar' to i-PS. Like an 'obedient' fractal, f-VS undergoes iterative reorganizations, legitimations, reconstructions, and interpretations, such as: global public relations and recognition as a prestigious community, worldwide expansion of membership registration, trans(hyper)national financial activity, services, globally broadcasted events, and so on. f-VS becomes the distorted version of the original i-PS, by many a much desired and adored construction, but in essence a hyperreal cultural construct, which in effect reduces the validity of meaning of the i-PS itself. The fractal phase of i-PS is ruled by structural and qualitative mutations, by which an ideal and imaginative programmable 'home' environment comes to replace dissatisfaction, incapability, disorganization and originality of experience (Figure 6.22).

The construction of f-VS, chaotically stage-manages the loss of reference to the real experience of i-PS and provocatively offends and questions the originality of experience of i-PS. Modes of interactivity are added, virtual reality audio-visual experiences are enhanced with the appearance of new technologies, virtual entities obtain physical identities, and physical identities vanish in the anonymity of the hyper-real. For as long as original experience and life in physical space will create unambiguous and fragile identities of systems of information, quantitative and repetitive activities of simulated systems of information, such as f-VS, will unquestionably over-stretch and exhaust our mental comprehensibility, and isolate us in a hallucinatory environment of counterfeit solutions, programmable self-reflections and fractal destiny.

6.7 EPILOGUE

The current chapter has put forward the first part of the theoretical approximations on the organization of the system of information of this book. I have argued that these proposals can contribute towards our thinking of the digital construction of 'reality' and the digital reconstruction of 'hyper-reality' in the era of electronic communication and digital technologies. The justification for the conceptual shift to understanding the concept of spatiality in the current philosophical proposals is to be found in theorizations, such as Lefebvre's trialectics and spatiality, Foucault's heterotopias and Soja's thirdspace. The proposed conceptualizations of the organization of the system of information can be better understood in their natural habitat of hyperspace. To this end, in addition to the accounts in this chapter, the proposed conceptualizations and processes are also presented by means of audio-visual presentations with two- and three-dimensional (2-D and 3-D) computer models (see attached digital component). The digital reorganization of the system of information in hyperspace, though, is becoming increasingly responsible for the organization of the system of information in every human and non-human entity, therefore, the theoretical approximations proposed here, it is suggested that, they can be applied to a wide range of themes of social investigation.

I have argued that the system of information is defined by the Infotype, a general concept that encompasses a specific content, particular architectural characteristics and a code of organization. The infotypes the system of information are organized across space and time in a triad of spatial level-states of organization: an 'era of Romanticism' (actuality), an 'epoch of Ersatz' (imitation), and 'an age of Chimera' (fantasy). These three levels of organization of the infotypes of the system of information are ever present but with varying degrees of intensification among them. In order to account for the organization of the system of information, and in particular for its digital reorganization and subsequent fractalization, I proposed two interlinked processes. First, the Virtual Implosion of the system of information, characterized by three phase spaces: Syghysis (deconstruction), Molynsis (differentiation), and Photococciasis (reconstruction). Secondly, the Fractal Dynamics of the Virtual Implosion of the system of information, the five interconnecting micro-processes that realize Virtual Implosion: Catastrophe (destruction), Orgasm (excitement), Metamorphosis (transformation), Epigenesis (rebirth), and Anomia (lawlessness). All the concepts offered here make up the first part of the proposed analytical model, which I call Infogramic Analysis, and which is concluded with further proposals made in the following chapter. In brief, the main points of this chapter can be summarized as follows:

On general observations on the proposed theoretical approximations:

- The proposed theoretical approximations consist of a meta-philosophical proposition towards a radical reconstruction of long-established thinking of the production of social knowledge. It can improve our understanding of the organization (code) of the system of information in the digital reconstruction of contemporary societies and on the re-realization of human consciousness in the postmodern-and-beyond era.

- In the era of digital technologies and communication, the digital reorganization of information in hyperspace influences to a great degree the organization of the social (physical) world. The patterns of organization of the system of information in hyperspatial environments, can apply to describe the organization of any system of information

- A spatial logic is needed to account for the organization of the system of information. Within this spatial logic the proposed approximations can be envisioned as 'real' and imagined, physically present, but absent or invisible in an abstract way.

- The spatial organization of the system of information presents three spatial configurations: the physical space of the production and reproduction, the conceptualized space of the control and exploitation, and the lived space of abstract symbolism and imagination.

- An investigation of the organization of the system of information, becomes a project of reconsideration of the analysis of the construction of social 'reality', and a project of 'breaking' the 'encrypted' codes of the organization of social life.

- The system of information can be described as a heterotopia. As such, it is identified in worldwide signification and representational systems in differentiated forms, it can alter, transform and synchronize to its environment, it can exist in different spatial configurations, it presents heterochronic formations, it can be closed and isolated or open and permeable at the same time, it is responsible for creating illusionary 'other' spaces.

- The system of information can be understood as a realization of Thirdspace: a secret and conjectured object, filled with illusions and allusions, a space that is common, to yet never completely seen and understood, an unimaginable universe.

- In the postmodern digital world, because the referents of 'meaning' are no longer visible or difficult to locate, it is suggested we should refer to relations of meaning instead.

On the proposed theoretical approximations:

- An 'infotype' refers to the specific content and the general architectural characteristics of the system of information. The infotype carries the code (instructions) that the system of information needs to regenerate constant change by means of adaptation and habituation.

- Infotypes are organized across time, along three general spatial frameworks of varying degrees of intensification, the spatial level-states of organization: an 'era of Romanticism' (actuality), an 'epoch of Ersatz' (imitation), and 'an age of Chimera' (fantasy).

- In the 'era of Romanticism' the system of information is characterized by authenticity, simplicity and originality (authentic information). The system of information remains pure and unattached, shows primary and basic organization, and entails the potential for progress and development.

- In the 'epoch of Ersatz' the system of information is characterized by imitation, control and exploitation (simulated information). The system of information shows an intensification of controlled knowledge, signs and codes, it presents redundancy, and developing or developed patterns of organization.

- In the 'age of Chimera' the system of information becomes illusive, provocative and hyper-real (fractal information). Fantasy in lived experience predominates. The code dominates in the system of information, which shows points of distortion, chaotic organization and organized chaos, with visible tendencies towards its fractalization.

- The process of the Virtual Implosion of the system of information consists of three trajectories (phase spaces) of mutation: Syghysis, Molynsis and Photococciasis. Syghysis is a deconstruction phase of meaning, characterized by random and disorderly mobilization, spatial rearrangements, imbalance of equilibrium, and increase of entropic tendencies. Molynsis is a phase of differentiation of meaning, characterized by gradual stability, increase of heterogeneity, enforcement of prestige and importance, and new patterns of symbiosis or elimination of meaning. Finally, Photococciasis is the phase of reconstruction of meaning, characterized by fractal reconstruction, non-linear iterations and repetitive patterns, self-similarity and distortions, and arbitrariness and irregularity.

- A dual state of spatial synchronization is characteristic of the phase spaces of Virtual Implosion. It is defined as homogenous heterogeneity (referring to similar patterns of differentiation) and heterogenous homogenization (referring to differentiated patterns of similarity). It refers to a three-dimensional spatial fluctuation of the components of the system of information, to synchronize with the occasional homeostatic condition of the system.

- Five micro-processes of Fractal Dynamics realize the Virtual Implosion of the system of information: Catastrophe, Orgasm, Metamorphosis, Epigenesis, and Anomia. Catastrophe is a process of destruction, which breaks down to fragments the meaning of the system of information. Orgasm is the process of excitement, which generates random mobility and rearrangements. Metamorphosis refers to the transformation process, by which levels of differentiation and assignment of varying emphasis occurs among the fragments. Epigenesis, the process of rebirth, restructures the differentiated fragments applying fractal dimensions. Finally, Anomia, a process of lawlessness, finalizes the reconstruction of the fragments to irregular disorganized fractals.

The second part of the proposed theoretical approximations on the organization of the system of information is continued in the following chapter. The additional theoretical proposals introduce structural and organizational conceptualizations of the organization of the system of information, such as, datagrams and infograms, endogenesis and exogenesis and their relative classifications. All the proposed concepts and definitions in these two last chapters are incorporated within the analytical model of infogramic analysis, for which a number of examples are also provided. The suggested model of infogramic analysis consists a proposal of the analysis of digital systems of information (and of any the system of information). It is introduced as an open philosophical consideration of approximation in the social investigation of the digital construction of reality and the digital reconstruction of hyper-reality.

▶▶◄

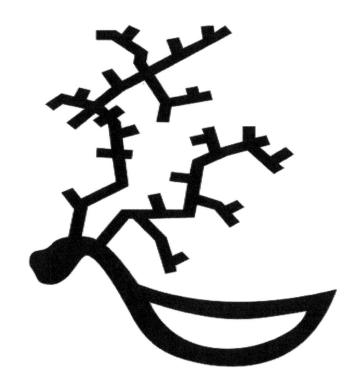

DIGITAL ILLUSIONS:
Infograms and Infogramic Analysis

CONTENTS

CHAPTER SEVEN

DIGITAL ILLUSIONS:
Infograms and Infogramic Analysis

'In civilizations without boats, dreams dry up, espionage takes the place of adventure,
and the police take the place of pirates'

(Foucault,1986:27)

7.0 PROLOGUE

T he previous chapter has already proposed that, in the era of electronic communication and digital technologies, the organization of the system of information is characteristic of two related of sets of processes: '*Virtual Implosion*' (hereafter VI) and '*Fractal Dynamics*' (hereafter FD). These processes, I argued, are responsible for the digital reorganization and fractalization of the system of information in postmodernity-and-beyond. Both VI and FD, examples of which have been presented in the previous chapter, are part of the analytical model proposed in this book, termed '*Infogramic Analysis*'. They refer to in-depth structural and processual organization, the microcosm of the system of information. Still, they can apply accordingly to account for the organization of any scale (up or down) of informational systems.

The current chapter continues on the theoretical approximations of the last chapter, and puts forward further proposals of the structural and processual organization of the system of information at a large scale. With VI and FD always present at the basic level of organization, the focus turns to the analysis of a larger scale informational constructs and patterns of informational organization. These constructs and patterns refer to what would often account for basic or complex, concepts, definitions, attitudes, opinions, beliefs, ideologies, theories, bodies of knowledge, in general, for any organized or non-organized (around meaning or relations of meaning) system of information. These informational constructs are further below defined as '*Datagrams*' and '*Infograms*', whereas the informational patterns of organization, which account for the development of the internal associations and the external interactions of datagrams and infograms, are defined as 'Endogenesis' and 'Exogenesis' respectively. Once more, all these conceptualisations can be represented in two- and three-dimensional computer animated models (see digital component).

7.1 INFOGRAMS

7.1.1 Datagrams

The simplest forms of infograms are '*Datagrams*'. Datagrams are basic and simple systems of informational constructs of symbols, icons, signs, figures, characters, letters, numbers, archetypes, and so on. They may generate infinite combinations within their native environment to add more informational units to their system. The self-similarity and plurality of the components of datagrams accounts for, and appends to the 'meaning' entailed in the datagram. Datagrams may interact with other similar or not datagrams, in infinite combinations, to produce infograms.

Three examples are presented here to exemplify the concept of the Datagram (Figures 7.1 – 7.3). Figure 7.1 represents a matrix of all the possible expressions of the abstract concept of 'up', in an infinite series such as:

> *[infinite] ... up, upward, upstairs, upper, up up and away, upright, upside down, upside, uphill, up and about, upturn, uplift ... [infinite]*

Similarly, Figures 7.2 and 7.3 are representational matrixes of all the possible variations of the abstract concepts of 'out' and 'centre' respectively, in the following infinite series:

> *[infinite] ... out, outward, out of here, outer, almost out, outright, outdoors, outside, outing, outflow, outdated, out and about ... [infinite]*

and,

> *[infinite] ... centre, core, central, heart, central part, nucleus, middle, hub, focus, centrality, centro, epicenter ... [infinite]*

datagram (up)

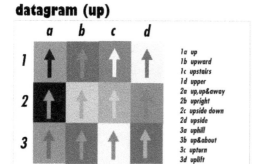

	a	b	c	d
1				
2				
3				

1a up
1b upward
1c upstairs
1d upper
2a up,up&away
2b upright
2c upside down
2d upside
3a uphill
3b up&about
3c upturn
3d uplift

Figure 7.1: Datagram of the concept of 'up'.

datagram (out)

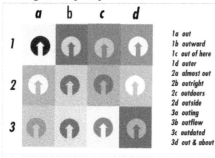

	a	b	c	d
1				
2				
3				

1a out
1b outward
1c out of here
1d outer
2a almost out
2b outright
2c outdoors
2d outside
3a outing
3b outflow
3c outdated
3d out & about

Figure 7.2: Datagram of the concept of 'out'.

datagram (centre)

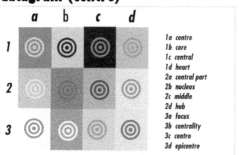

	a	b	c	d
1				
2				
3				

1a centre
1b core
1c central
1d heart
2a central part
2b nucleus
2c middle
2d hub
3a focus
3b centrality
3c centro
3d epicentre

Figure 7.3: Datagram of the concept of 'centre'.

A more accurate representation of the concept of the datagram would be the three-dimensional models illustrated here. The purpose of this kind of representation is to stress the complexity, and at the same time simplicity, of the basic organization of systems of information, and therefore, of the knowledge constructed out of these systems.

7.1.2 Infograms

An '*Infogram*' is an informational construct of higher level of complexity than that of a datagram. An infogram can be generated from interacting datagrams but is not necessarily the sum of the source datagrams. Infograms present multi-dimensional patterns of organization of spatial symmetries and structural non-linear curves. They can be said to represent, at varying degrees of complexity, concepts, definitions, ideas, perceptions, explanations, descriptions, segments of information, bodies of knowledge, and so on. Infograms are organized around a 'theme' (relevant to their infotype) which is characterized by specific content and relationships. According to their origin of their constituent components (combined arrangements of datagrams or other infograms), infograms are distinguished as: (a) '*Authentic*' infograms (A-*Infograms*), (b) '*Simulated*' infograms (Σ-*Infograms*), and (c) '*Fractal*' infograms (Φ-*Infograms*).

7.1.3 Authentic Infograms

An '*authentic*' infogram (A-*Infogram*) is an informational construct concerning original and discrete concepts and ideas, facts, events, and so on, which are innately present and exist without any interference or interaction from outside the systemic environment of the infogram. An authentic infogram shows strong relations of meaning that is, well built associations among its constituent components, which also accounts for its powerful resistance to foreign interactions. Figure 7.4 illustrates an example of an authentic infogram. The infogram refers to someone's originally evolved targets that he/she has set in life, and which would represent a programme of basic and common needs and corresponding actions. The matrix illustrates an infinite series of components, which are though generated internally to the infogramic system:

> *[infinite] … to own a house, job, car, time is money, eat fast, take a holiday, travel, be happy, get a partner, enjoy nice weather, do sports, escape to an island … [infinite]*

7.1.4 Simulated Infograms

A '*simulated*' infogram (Σ-*Infogram*) refers to an informational construct that has originated in, and has been produced in the environment, that is, outside the boundaries of the infogramic system. Collectively and individually considered, the components of a simulated infogram consist one of many visible imaginary versions of the components of an authentic infogram. A simulated infogram need not relate to a specific authentic infogram; it may be generated and claim authenticity *in absentia* of a probably existing, but not visible existing, authentic infogram. Simulated infograms are characterized by strong self-reference of meaning, they refer to themselves. Returning to the example set before, Figure 7.5 the simulated infogram shows how original (authentic) components have been replaced by a set of environmental (media) intrusions. The original programme of someone's life targets, have been assigned a reference to specific 'symbolic text', which, in the example, represents a simulation of original needs and actions generated from the daily environment:

> *[infinite] ... own a luxury villa, get a prestigious job (in the CBD), buy a Mercedes Benz, buy Citizens, eat at McDonalds, take a holiday around the world, travel with Quantas, money bring happiness, join the company of a highly paid escort, sunny holidays, go sailing, escape to exotic Fiji ... [infinite]*

7.1.5 Fractal Infograms

A '*fractal*' infogram (Φ-*Infogram*) is an informational construct that is the result of the fractalization of an authentic or simulated or of a combination of these types of infograms. What is important is that this type of infogram is a simplified, distorted, and programmable version of 'dubious' meaning, which can replace (by extinction) the original meaning of the authentic infogram. The fractal infogram is the result of repeated iterations and continuous regenerations of the system of information along the lines of the previously proposed processes of Virtual Implosion and Fractal Dynamics. The meaning of the original theme is being replaced in the fractal infogram by several possible relations of meaning, to several possible existing and imaginary associations. The meaning is distorted and confused. The fractal infogram is virtually imploded and is regenerated as 'a digital illusion' of the present, which, like an act of magic, can be manipulated and programmed to excite and entertain.

authentic infogram

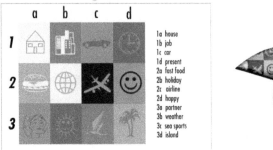

Figure 7.4: An authentic infogram (A-Infogram).

simulated infogram

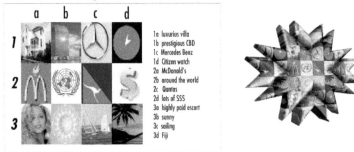

Figure 7.5: A simulated infogram (Σ-Infogram).

fractal infogram

Figure 7.6: A fractal infogram (Φ-Infogram).

Carrying on with the previous example in Figure 7.6, in the fractal infogram, the original 'meaningful' programme is so confused by the repeated iterations of interacting proposals and actions from the environment that it breaks in pieces and disperses, blurring the content and the relation of the content to the theme of the infogram. In this way, the original and simulated life targets merge, are intermixed and lose particular reference to previously existing meaning:

> *[infinite] ... buy what h#"ouse, not that jo#@b, my lc@ar, not pre&^s#ent, maybe not fa>#st f*(ood, always hol-^+iday, what ai;}rl-ine, am I ha@*p)py, many pa[]r;tner, what's wrong with the w%ea)ther, yes se;a no s<p?orts, lost is/l??and ... [infinite]*

7.2 ORGANIZATIONAL PATTERNS OF INFOGRAMS

Infograms (and datagrams) present distinctive patterns of organization which account for the inter-relativity and interactivity of infogramic systems. The inter-relativity here refers to the internal built-in or 'naturally' evolved associations among the component elements of the system. The interactivity is expressed in the external interactions of datagrams and infograms, which are partly accountable for the fractalization of the infogramic system. These organizational patterns are here defined as: (a) '*Endogenesis*', and (b) '*Exogenesis*' respectively.

7.2.1 Endogenesis

'*Endogenesis*' refers to the innate tendencies of the structural condition of the infogramic system to self-relate, generate and maintain a stable and enduring structural architecture of meaning around the core theme characteristic of the system. Three levels of structural condition characterize the endogenous associations of the infogram: (a) '*Organization*' (◉), (b) '*Lethargy*' (⊗), and (c) '*Disorganization*' (◉) (Fig. 7.7). Endogenous, then, associations within the same informational unit can be organized, stable and uninterested, and/or totally disorganized. In each case of course, there are analogous repercussions to the organization and the 'fate' of meaning within the infogramic system. Endogenous associations can be organized, in the sense that, they may progress to meaningful connections or coordination of the constituent parts, in order that some distinct path of orderly connection is established and maintained in existence. At the other extreme, in disorganized endogenous associations, a

Figure 7.7: 'Endogenesis' refers to the patterns of organization of the internal associations of datagrams and infograms, which develop in three levels of structural condition: Organization, Lethargy, and Disorganization.

systematic breakdown of meaning-related interconnections and associations takes place, and non-coordination and non-synchronization prevail. In lethargic endogenous associations, the negotiated exchanges of interconnections do not lead to any systematic organization or breakdown, rather the preserve stability and motionlessness, and non-interest, as in a prolonged inert narcosis.

7.2.2 Exogenesis

'*Exogenesis*' refers to the tendencies of the infogramic system to communicate or respond to incoming communication with its environment. Exogenesis expresses the tendency of the system of information to associate, to establish networks, and to progress to further evolvement. During this process, losses or disturbances in the established associations of meanings are unavoidable. Three levels of structural involvement characterize the exogenous interactions of infograms: (a) '*Simplicity*'(✻), (b) '*Apathy*' (✖), and (c) '*Complexity*'(✿) (Fig. 7.8). Therefore, endogenous associations within the infogramic environment can be simple, apathetic (indifferent), and/or complex. Simple exogenous interactions show preoccupation with simple form and structure, absence of intricacy, and free of artifice, deceit, or duplicity. Apathetic exogenous interactions show a tendency for independence of form, or insensibility to, active, positive or negative, involvement, a state of indifference, un-interest or

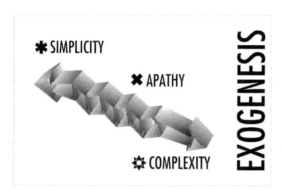

Figure 7.8: 'Exogenesis' refers to the patterns of organization of the external interactions of datagrams and infograms, which develop in three levels of processual involvement: Simplicity, Apathy, and Complexity.

inaction. Finally, complex exogenous interactions present the tendency to complicate form and structure, and to produce artificial and sophisticated relations of extreme obscurity.

The possible combinations among endogenous associations and exogenous interactions, either within an individual infogramic system or among interacting systems, may indeed be

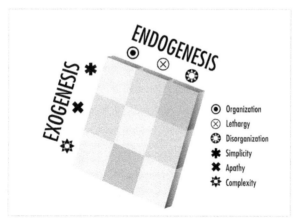

Figure 7.9: Matrix of possible (infinite) combinations (grey areas) of endogenous associations and exogenous interactions of datagrams and infograms.

infinite. In this sense, the systemic inter-relativity and interactivity are reflected in the form, image, and behaviour of the infogram, and infograms can be described to show: organized complexity, disorganized simplicity, organized simplicity, disorganized complexity, lethargic complexity, lethargic simplicity, lethargic apathy, organized apathy, disorganized apathy, and so on (Figure 7.9). In any state of infogramic activity or inaction, the system is balanced as endogenous associations establish a condition of heterogeneous homogenization, whereas exogenous interactions, on the opposite side, apply a condition of homogenous heterogeneity.

7.3 INFOGRAMIC ANALYSIS

'*Infogramic analysis*' utilizes all the proposed theoretical approximations so far and applies them to certain concepts to account for their virtual implosion, or fractalization, that is, their gradual deconstruction, differentiation and reconstruction, from authentic and original infogramic systems, to abstract fractal systems of multi-dimensional levels of meaning. Infogramic analysis is exemplified in the hypothetical example below of the fractalization (referring here to confusion, exploitation and disorientation) of a subject's set of occasional original 'life-targets'. The example shows how occasional original and basic targets, common in the life of each human subject, are intercepted by global media texts, and how, depending on each subject's geographic location on the planet, they mutate to diverse in content but self-similar in organization fractal versions of the original authentic infogram of 'targets'.

7.3.1 The emergence of authentic experience

At any time, for any subject, there exist the possibilities for the generation of various forms of original and inexperienced programmes of planned action. These programmes (potential organizational patterns) are composed of organized authentic systems of information, in the form of authentic infograms. Consider the following three authentic infograms in which the components are strongly related to discrete and visible meaning. Figure 7.10 represents a hypothetical authentic infogram of spatial orientation, composed of an infinite number of possible 'directions':

> *[infinite]*...down, up, left, right, back, around, in, out, to, towards, reverse, ahead... *[infinite]*

authentic infogram (directions)

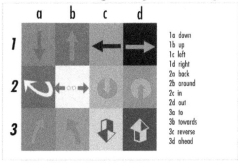

Figure 7.10: An authentic infogram of 'directions'.

authentic infogram (targets)

Figure 7.11: An authentic infogram of 'targets'.

authentic infogram (directions-targets)

nice HOME; a well-paid JOB; a good CAR; quick FOOD; look around for PRESENT;
find PARTNER; book a HOLIDAY; be HAPPY; what's wrong with the WEATHER;
I love SEA SPORTS; dreaming of an exotic ISLAND

Figure 7.12: An authentic infogram of combined 'directions-targets'.

This would represent all the potential spatial organization interconnections available to the specific infogram and to the subject itself. Some of these possible interconnections will be exploited by other interacting infogramic systems. For example, consider the authentic infogram (used earlier above) in Figure 7.11. It represents a hypothetical infinite series of personal planned organization, a set of occasional 'targets' in a subject's life:

> *[infinite] … house, job, car, present, fast food, holiday, airline, happy, partner, weather, sea sports, island … [infinite]*

The nature of the authentic infogramic systems endogenous and exogenous tendencies generate possible combinations of organizational patterns using these (and other) related authentic infograms. In the present example, spatial orientation is related to the realization of 'targets' as its presence is a prerequisite condition for the subject's 'direction' towards his/her 'targets'. Figure 7.12 illustrates the interaction of, among others, the two authentic infograms of 'directions' and 'targets', to a combined authentic infogram of 'directions-targets' of an infinite series of meaningful and distinct statements:

> *[infinite] … nice home, a well-paid job, a good car, quick food, look around for present, find partner, book a holiday, be happy, what's wrong with the weather, I love sea sports, dreaming of an exotic island … [infinite]*

7.3.2 The exploitation of imitation

Figures 7.13-7.15 are three examples of hypothetical proposed programmes of 'targets' in the form of simulated infograms. Simulated infograms originate in the environment, as copies and regenerations of originals, for example from global media texts. They are characterized by endogenous internal associations varying between complexity and apathy, and exogenous dynamic interactions varying between a lethargic state and disorganization. Depending on the global geographic position, the environmental arrangements, and the selective accessibility of the subject to media texts, different interactions will be generated and reproduced. The result is seemingly different simulated infograms, still, although the content may differ, depending on local conditions, the simulated infograms present self-similar patterns of organization.

In the current example, the first of the three examples of simulated infograms (Figure 7.13) may represent one of many world experiences regarding a proposed programme of life-targets:

> *[infinite] ... a nice cottage house somewhere in the French Alps, a prestigious permanent job in the EU administration, a powerful German Mercedes Benz, Revlon cosmetics for partner's present, a five dollar lunch at Burger Kings, travel the world, Virgin Airlines as a 'cool', cheap and trendy airline to fly with, financially free as a means to happiness, a high maintenance girlfriend, don't you love romantic sunsets, relaxing weekends sailing, islands of Fiji probably as a faraway exotic destination for holidays ... [infinite]*

Another similar proposal is represented in the simulated infogram in Figure 7.14 as follows:

> *[infinite] ... a villa in the countryside, an academic job in a university, a reliable Mitsubishi car, a Citizen watch for girlfriend's present, breakfast at McDonalds, discover new places, fly Quantas, invest in the stock exchange, an intellectual woman, hot climates, water sports, let's go to Cuba ... [infinite]*

Finally, in the third example of simulated infograms, in Figure 7.15:

> *[infinite] ... a townhouse in a fancy suburb, a highly paid job in the CBD, a Holden Astra convertible, Clinique products for mother's present, dinner at KFC, safari tour in Africa, fly Ansett (RIP!), diamond necklace for the wife, a hard working housewife, sunny holidays, windsurfing, island of Hawaii ... [infinite]*

Each one of these simulated infogramic systems can exist on its own as a valid proposal. In the contemporary age of global electronic communication and digital technologies, though, exogenous interactions among two or more simulated infograms (usually many) take place fast and almost in an invisible way. They may interlink in a chaotic variety of possible blends and mutually exchange and replace components without changes in their general organizational patterns. Consider such an interaction has taken place among the simulated infograms 1, 2, and 3 described above, and many more similar ones (Figure 7.16). Figure 7.16 represents an example of what the result of such a global interaction would look like. A simulated proposition which has 'borrowed' and 'assimilated' simulated elements from

simulated infogram

1a cottage house
1b government
1c Mercedes Benz
1d Revlon cosmetics
2a Burger King
2b around the world
2c Virgin
2d lots of $$$
3a highly paid escort
3b sunset
3c sailing
3d Fiji

Figure 7.13: A simulated infogram of 'targets' (1).

simulated infogram

1a country villa
1b university
1c Mitsubishi
1d Citizen watch
2a McDonald's
2b sea cruise
2c Qantas
2d shares
3a intellectual
3b burning hot
3c water ski
3d Cuba

Figure 7.14: A simulated infogram of 'targets' (2).

simulated infogram (targets)

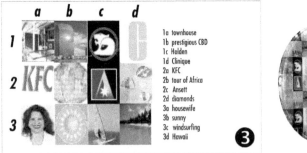

1a townhouse
1b prestigious CBD
1c Holden
1d Clinique
2a KFC
2b tour of Africa
2c Ansett
2d diamonds
3a housewife
3b sunny
3c windsurfing
3d Hawaii

Figure 7.15: A simulated infogram of 'targets' (3).

similarly organized simulated proposition:

> *[infinite] ... a villa in the countryside, a highly paid job in the CBD, a powerful German Mercedes Benz, a Citizen watch for girlfriend's present, breakfast at McDonalds, travel the world, fly Quantas, financially free as a means to happiness, a high maintenance girlfriend, relaxing weekends sailing, islands of Fiji probably as a faraway exotic destination for holidays ... [infinite]*

simulated infogram

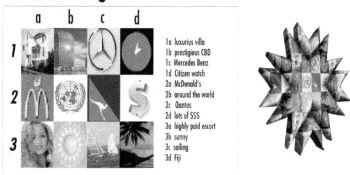

	a	b	c	d
1				
2				
3				

1a luxurius villa
1b prestigious CBD
1c Mercedes Benz
1d Citizen watch
2a McDonald's
2b around the world
2c Qantas
2d lots of $$$
3a highly paid escort
3b sunny
3c sailing
3d Fiji

Figure 7.16: A globally simulated infogram of 'targets' (1•2• ...•3).

7.3.3 The fractalization of originality

All of the simulated infogramic systems described here are characterized by strong self-referentiality and potential exogenous interactivity. Compared to their respective authentic infogramic system (of authentic targets), they present redundant and simplified, if not distorted, information regarding widely acceptable choice, taste and originality of experience. More importantly, they are inherently characterized by their vulnerability to programmability. When extremely programmable simulated systems of this kind, develop exogenous interactions with authentic or other simulated infograms the result is a fractal manipulation of the original authentic intentions and objectives, or to put in another way, the regulation of information, knowledge, action and experience. Such a fractal infogram of 'directions-targets' is shown in Figure 7.17.

fractal infogram (directions-targets)

a LUX^URIO!US V@ILLA; a CON\SU{[LTANT in CBD; an AU()TOMA)TIC ME((RS+EDES BENZ;
a $4.95 MCDONA%?LDS M;EAL; aS GI:OLDEN CITIZS#''EN W(ASTCH; a H(IGHLY PA^ID ESC!ORT;
bo''''ok with QAN^^'TAS; AR'OUN%D TSHE WIORLD holi>?day&^ L'OTS OF MO'NEY /HAPPY;
too hot in the S?UN;lo,cal SAI[[LI)NG CSLUB; exof'ic ,,FIJI

Figure 7.17: A fractal infogram of combined 'directions-targets'
(authentic 'directions', authentic 'targets', simulated 'targets' 1, 2, 3, and many more).

The original authentic infogram of combined 'directions-targets' has been made redundant, to an artificial version of disorganized and fragile organizational patterns. Authentic components have been indiscriminately replaced by media generated versions, and appear to claim originality and legal status, by registering themselves in the existing acquired libraries of knowledge and experience. The fractal reality, such infograms create, is an artificial system of information, a digital illusion, where 'reality', 'truth' and 'meaning', are redefined to actually 'mean' nothing more than referring to themselves; furthermore, they remain unchallenged, become stabilized and exempt from being offended or provoked, and they are, finally, mentally digested, as valued informational nectar to the satisfaction and excitement of the senses.

7.4 DIGITAL ILLUSIONS

Infogramic analysis can be said to utilize all the theoretical approximations proposed in these two last chapters of the book. The representation of concepts and definitions as infogramic systems can provide a fresh new way to analyze and discuss social issues. The concepts of the 'datagram' and 'infogram' can account for the organizational structure of the system of information that represents component units or the totality of the content of the issue. The organizational patterns of 'endogenesis' and 'exogenesis', can account for the relationships among the parts that comprise the intellectual context, within which an issue is discussed, and also for the logic of the development of possible relativities with other issues. The 'level-states' of the system of information, mentioned in the previous chapter, can be applied to account for the degrees of intensification of the content of the issue in question across different historical periods. Accordingly, the processes of 'virtual implosion' and 'fractal dynamics' can account for the fractal transformation of the informational context of the issue in relation to meaning.

In any case, the various stages of the analysis can be represented by two- and three-dimensional computer models, which can only exemplify and stress the complexity of the system of information at all the stages and levels of its organization. In the era of electronic communication and digital technologies, infogramic analysis suggests that social formations and configurations are increasingly imploding into programmable fractal hyper-realities; the world is becoming a digital artifact, a world of *digital illusions*. Three examples are considered here in an attempt to demonstrate how an elementary infogramic analysis could utilize the above mentioned theoretical proposals to explain and account for social change and transformation. The first example deals with the globalization proposal and illustrates how the concept of 'globalization' can be analysed as a genuine conceptual fractal implosion of the authentic concept of 'internationalization'. The second and third examples examine the concepts of the 'information society' and 'digi-sapiens' as fractal mutations of the authentic notions of 'society' and 'homo-sapiens' respectively.

7.4.1 Internationalization to Globalization

For the purpose of exemplification the current example uses Waters' (1995) definition of globalization. As discussed in chapter two, Waters (1995) defines globalization in three social arrangements of life, Economy, Polity, and Culture, structurally independent to each other but which may interact among them. As you may recall from the previous discussion, 'economic globalization' seeks to provide evidence on the development of an international class structure within capitalism, whereas the issue of 'political globalization' has to do much with the sovereignty and decision-making of states. The progressive displacement of economic and political exchanges by symbolic ones, defines 'cultural globalization'. The later can be conceived as the progressive culturization of social life, characterized by conflicts between various aspects of value-systems within the context of expansionist political-economic ideologies.

The defining sectors of social life, economy, polity, and culture in the above definition consist the starting point of the analysis. Each of these three sectors of human activity can be represented as a meaningful and original informational construct, an authentic infogramic system. The authentic infogram of Figure 7.18 can be argued to represent the authentic perception of economy, incorporating an infinite series of original concepts which comprise or relate to economic activity, such as:

> *[infinite] ... telecommunications, working force, capital, enterprise, energy, accounting, industry, computer networks, technology, research, management, stock exchange ... [infinite]*

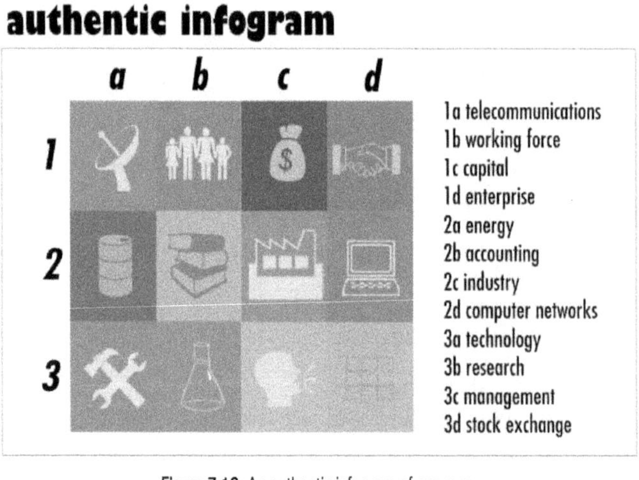

Figure 7.18: An authentic infogram of economy.

Similarly, Figure 7.19 represents an authentic infogram of polity including an infinite series of defining and related representations such as:

> *[infinite] ... nation state, organization, political party, political system, ideological beliefs, policy, elections, freedom, politicians, sponsors, media, national security ... [infinite]*

authentic infogram

	a	b	c	d
1				
2				
3				

1a state
1b organization
1c party
1d political system
2a ideology
2b policy
2c elections
2d freedom
3a politicians
3b sponsors
3c media
3d national security

Figure 7.19: An authentic infogram of polity.

Finally, Figure 7.20 represents an authentic infogram of culture incorporating an infinite series of signifying cultural elements such as:

> *[infinite] ... history, music, literature, religion, fine arts, tradition, style, gender, fashion, sports, education, values ... [infinite]*

authentic infogram

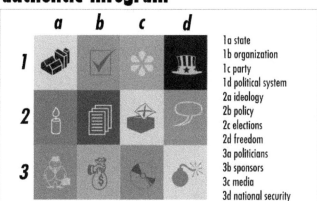

1a history
1b music
1c literature
1d religion
2a fine arts
2b tradition
2c style
2d gender
3a fashion
3b sports
3c education
3d values

Figure 7.20: An authentic infogram of culture.

According to the aforementioned definition of globalization, an original authentic conception of a universal system of global economy, common political system, and a unity of cultures, could be said to be collectively represented by the concept of internationalization, which can be illustrated as the combined authentic infogram shown in Figure 7.21.

Figure 7.21: The concept of internationalization, as an authentic infogram, incorporating the authentic infogramic notions of economy, polity and culture.

At any given historical time and depending on the global geographical location each one of the above authentic infograms of economy, polity and culture develop intense interactivity with global media simulations empowered by the micro-mechanisms of fractal dynamics. The distinctive meaning-related descriptions of each of the three authentic infogramic systems are being virtually imploded, and their signifying symbolisms, first, they undergo a simulated substitution, which later finalizes to a fractal distortion. Figures 7.22-7.24 constitute examples the transition from the simulated to the fractal phase.

In Figure 7.22, media influences translate the signifying components of economy to simulated replacements, and further, to multiple distorted and programmable repetitions one of which can be described in an infinite series of definitions such as:

> *[infinite] … telecommunications to satellites to AT&T, working force to middle class to professional class, capital to currency to US dollar, enterprise to multinational to Toshiba, energy to nuclear power to nuclear bombs, accounting to databases to Merril Lynch, industry to computer software to Microsoft, computer networks to www to Compaq, technology to cybernetics to Motorola, research to information to MIT, management to multi-corporations to WTO, stock exchange to global trade to Wall Street … [infinite]*

simulated ◄◄ infogram ►► fractal

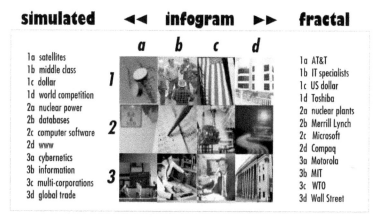

1a satellites	1a AT&T
1b middle class	1b IT specialists
1c dollar	1c US dollar
1d world competition	1d Toshiba
2a nuclear power	2a nuclear plants
2b databases	2b Merrill Lynch
2c computer software	2c Microsoft
2d www	2d Compaq
3a cybernetics	3a Motorola
3b information	3b MIT
3c multi-corporations	3c WTO
3d global trade	3d Wall Street

Figure 7.22: Simulated and fractal infograms of economy.

Similarly, as Figure 7.23 shows, the simulation and fractalization of the concept of polity would follow an accordingly similar infinite series of patterns:

> *[infinite] … nation state to technologically advanced to USA, organization to world cooperation to United Nations, political party to liberal to Democrats, political system to kingdom to Queen, ideological beliefs to authoritarian to fascism, policy to environment to Greenpeace, elections to free-vote to e-vote, freedom to democracy to America, politicians to legislation to GATT, sponsors to investment to BBC, media to audiovisual to CNN, national security to agencies to FBI … [infinite]*

simulated ◄◄ infogram ►► fractal

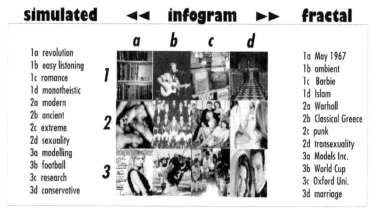

1a revolution	1a May 1967
1b easy listening	1b ambient
1c romance	1c Barbie
1d monotheistic	1d Islam
2a modern	2a Warhol
2b ancient	2b Classical Greece
2c extreme	2c punk
2d sexuality	2d transexuality
3a modelling	3a Models Inc.
3b football	3b World Cup
3c research	3c Oxford Uni.
3d conservative	3d marriage

Figure 7.23: Simulated and fractal infograms of polity.

Finally, the virtual implosion of the concept of culture (Figure 7.24) can also be represented in the following infinite series of descriptions such as:

> *[infinite] ... history to revolution to May 1967, music to easy listening to ambient, literature to romance to Barbie, religion to monotheistic to Islam, fine arts to modern to Warhol, tradition to ancient to Classical Greece, style to extreme to punk, gender to sexuality to transexuality, fashion to modeling to Models Inc., sports to football to World Cup, education to research to Oxford Uni., values to conservative to marriage ... [infinite]*

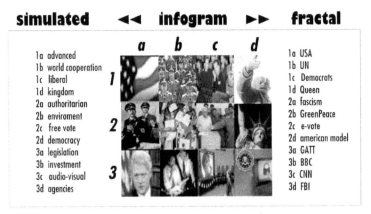

Figure 7.24: Simulated and fractal infograms of culture.

The implicit suggestion behind these fractal mutations is that, the final phase (architectural and organizational condition) of the transformation of an infogram is never a definite one, or it is simply one of many possible outcomes. Depending on the source and the intensity of the simulation, fractal infogramic systems emerge to substitute authentic meanings with programmable and artificial relations of meaning, and to legitimize themselves by claiming the authenticity of the original. It should be realized that, such arbitrary assignments of value associations between fractals and 'reality', consist nothing more than a confirmation of a digital illusion. When all the distinct economic, political and cultural exchanges, that define globalization, virtually implode under fractal dynamics, then the representation, to which the original concept referred to, becomes problematic and questionable. The definition of globalization becomes a programmable 'reality', a hyper-reality, dependent on the floating simulations of hyperspace, therefore, a distorted and redundant version of its original (Figure 7.25).

Figure 7.25: The concept of globalization, as a fractal infogram, incorporating the simulated and fractal infogramic versions of economy, polity and culture.

7.4.2 Society to Information Society

The second example uses the definition of the contemporary information society and suggests how the authentic classification of society implodes a fractal version of itself that is, an information society. The societal characteristics used in the current example come from a variety of theoretical contributions (some of which have been examined in chapter one). They provide a multi-dimensional range of images characteristic of our contemporary world. An authentic infogram of the original idea of society is shown in Figure 7.26. They reflect an infinite series of elements that can characterize the conceptual representation of a contemporary society:

> *[infinite] … technological advances, large-scale partnerships, fixed space-time, global telecommunications, variety of taste and differences, reign of capitalism, specialized industries, development and growth, enterprises, employment crisis, 'new' class systems, social representations and reflections … [infinite]*

The gradual simulation and fractalization of the authentic infogramic system of 'society' is illustrated in Figure 7.27. An infinite series of fractal elements include:

[infinite] ... technological advances to IT to Microsoft, large-scale partnerships to networks to Novell, fixed space-time to space-time flexibility to hyperspace, global telecommunications to internet to the .net, variety of taste and differences to advancement in technologies to cybernetics, reign of capitalism to digital capitalism to AT&T, specialized industry to 'new' industry to Yahoo!, development and growth to innovation to NetPhone, enterprises to TNCs and MNCs to .com companies, employment crisis to IT occupations to web development, 'new' class systems to new social divisions to info-rich & info-poor, social representations and reflections to simulations and Ananova ... [infinite]

authentic infogram

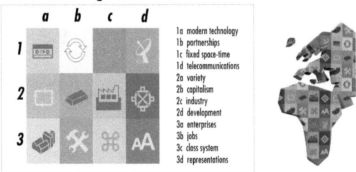

Figure 7.26: The concept of Society, as an authentic infogram incorporating authentic infogramic notions of societal attributes.

simulated ◄◄ infogram ►► fractal

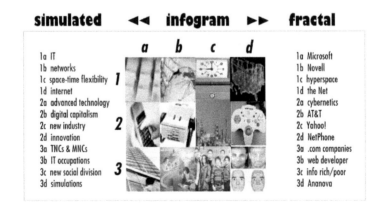

Figure 7.27: The concept of Information Society, as a fractal infogram incorporating simulated and fractal infogramic notions of societal attributes.

7.4.3 Homo-Sapiens to Digi-Sapiens

The final example deals with the definition of what characterizes the human subject, or as it is termed here, Homo-Sapiens. Figure 7.28 illustrates how this authentic infogramic

authentic infogram

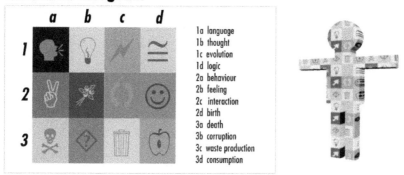

	a	b	c	d	
1					1a language
					1b thought
					1c evolution
					1d logic
2					2a behaviour
					2b feeling
					2c interaction
					2d birth
3					3a death
					3b corruption
					3c waste production
					3d consumption

Figure 7.28: The concept of Homo-Sapiens, as an authentic infogram incorporating authentic infogramic notions of distinctly human traits.

construction mutates to the fractal version of a contemporary 'digital' human subject, or Digi-Sapiens. The attributes that characterize an 'authentic' thinking human subject can probably be represented in an infinite series of definitions which includes the following:

> *[infinite] … language, thought, evolution, logic, behaviour, feelings, interaction, birth, death, corruption, waste production, consumption … [infinite]*

With the explosion of global media and telecommunications, and the advance of electronic communication and digital technologies, human subjectivity transforms to a hyper-real substitute of fractal proportions. Authentic and original human attributes become infected, and finally replaced, by identical copies of simulacra, which in turn, mutate to hyper-real entities that seek to replace the original human subjectivity with artificial and fractal substitutes of computer language and automated behaviour. Figure 7.29 illustrates the phases of simulation and fractalization, in an infinite series of attributes, as follows:

[infinite] ... language to jargon to html, thought to fantasy to virtual reality, evolution to creation to programming, logic to binary logic to digital logic, behaviour to programme to wired, feelings to aphasia to being 'stalled', interaction to isolation to disconnected, birth to cloning to copy & paste, death to erase to extinction, corruption to error to banned, waste production to recycling to artifice, consumption to consumerism to self-marketing ... [infinite]

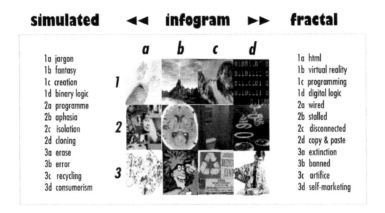

simulated   ◄◄   **infogram**   ►►   **fractal**

simulated		fractal
1a jargon		1a html
1b fantasy		1b virtual reality
1c creation		1c programming
1d binary logic		1d digital logic
2a programme		2a wired
2b aphasia		2b stalled
2c isolation		2c disconnected
2d cloning		2d copy & paste
3a erase		3a extinction
3b error		3b banned
3c recycling		3c artifice
3d consumerism		3d self-marketing

Figure 7.29: The concept of Digi-Sapiens, as a fractal infogram incorporating simulated and fractal infogramic notions of converged human and machine (computer) traits.

7.5 EPILOGUE

The current chapter continued with the introduction of the second part of the proposed theoretical approximations on the organization of the system of information. It has been suggested that the analysis of the digital construction of reality and the digital reconstruction of hyper-reality, in the digital era, can be further advanced with the introduction of the current philosophical discussion of approximation. To this end I have put forward the model of infogramic analysis, a term that incorporates the various concepts and definitions introduced as theoretical approximations. In addition to VI and FD, the analysis of the organization of the system of information, I argued, can be based on the in depth concept of the infogram, or infogramic system, and distinct organizational patterns of inter-relativity and interactivity, namely endogenesis and exogenesis. To this end I have introduced a number of classifications of different types of infogramic systems and of infinite possible combinations among endogenous and exogenous organization, all of which point to and stress the complexity of the organization of the system of information. In brief, the main points discussed can be summarized as follows:

On the proposed theoretical approximations:

- The digital reorganization and fractalization of the system of information in the hyper-real landscapes of postmodernity-and-beyond can be analysed and illustrated using a model based on the organization of the system of information, proposed as infogramic analysis.

- Infogramic analysis can apply to the organization of systems of information of different scale, ranging from microcosmic to macrocosmic organizational patterns of the world of information.

- The model of infogramic analysis consists an open theoretical suggestion and incorporates elements of the theoretical approximations of virtual implosion, fractal dynamics, infotypes and level-states, infograms, and endogenesis and exogenesis.

- Datagrams and infograms are systems of information that refer to organized or non-organized constructs of information, structured around meaning or relations of meaning.

- Infograms are distinguished according to their organizational arrangements into: (a) Authentic (A-Infograms), (b) Simulated (Σ-Infograms), and (c) Fractal (Φ-Infograms).

- An authentic infogram is an original informational construct with discrete meaning, whereas a simulated infogram originates in the environment and is characterized by strong self-reference of meaning.

- A fractal infogram is the result of the fractalization of an authentic or simulated or of a combination of these types of infograms to their simplified, distorted, and programmable version, a virtually imploded digital illusion.

- Endogenesis and exogenesis account for the organizational patterns of infogramic systems, and refer to their inter-relativity and interactivity respectively. Endogenous associations establish a condition of heterogeneous homogenization within, whereas exogenous interactions a condition of homogenous heterogeneity outside the infogramic system, this way retain its homeostatic balance.

- Endogenesis refers to native infogramic patterns of organization of internal associations, and is characterized by three structural conditions: (a) Organization (◉), (b) Lethargy (⊗), and (c) Disorganization (✿).

- Organizational endogenesis refers to orderly interconnections within the infogramic system, whereas dis-organizational endogenesis refers to a systematic breakdown of meaning. Lethargic endogenesis is, in contrast to the two extremes, characterized by stability and motionlessness.

- Exogenesis refers to native infogramic patterns of organization of external associations, and is characterized by three types of interactivity: (a) Simplicity (✽), (b) Apathy (✖), and (c) Complexity (✿).

- Simple exogenesis refers to basic and elementary interactions, whereas complex exogenesis, in contrast refers to complicated and advanced interactions. Apathetic exogenesis is a middle condition of neutral an indifferent interactivity.

- In the era of electronic communication and digital technologies, infogramic analysis can become the tool for analyzing how social formations and discourses are imploding into programmable fractal hyper-realities; artifacts in a world of digital illusions.

This last part of the book has introduced an analytical model of organization of the system of information, which it has been suggested can account for the organization of information in electronic communication and the world of digital applications and technologies. It has been the concluding part of a philosophical journey of revisiting digital labyrinths, *terra incognita* landscapes, which finally ended in a world obsessed with *fractal fetishes*. The closing epilogue, which follows, recaptures the main themes discussed throughout this book, summarizes the introduced theoretical approximations, and concludes with the final comments and considerations on the organization of the system of information.

▶▶|

EPILOGUE

EPILOGUE

I
n the beginning of the 21st century, the contemporary world society finds itself in a global crisis of identity. The problem is information related. With the advances in applications of electronic communication and digital technologies, the pace of human social progress has suddenly accelerated. The world has come to find out about each other too much too fast, too soon. This has led to extremes of preferred excitement or unrestricted disappointment towards advanced (computer) technologies. Societies have always based their organization on information, and have always tried to maintain the order of this system of organization. Achieving this order has always been rewarded whereas anarchy and disorder have, traditionally, always been condemned. Once the importance of the organizational power of the system of information is recognized and acknowledged, a series of issues become critical in the construction and transformation of the global social order and of social change.

The current book assumed that information, or the system of (all available) information, organizes every aspect of social life and human consciousness. It has suggested that patterns of social organization reflect the organization of the system of information, and it has attempted to provide and account for a closer understanding of the code that defines the organization of the system of information. To this end, it has introduced a theoretical model, in the form of a series of theoretical approximations, for the analysis of the organization of the system of information, in a world dominated by the presence and use of computer and digital technologies, and by an increasing human consciousness integrated with such technologies.

Transnational and global media corporations have taken over the control and flow of the worldwide dominant system of information, and amidst the digital revolution, their aim has been the normalization of its indiscriminate and anarchic character. Advanced societies around the world, have been deluged with a surplus of media simulated and perplexed hyper-realities, at the same time the rest of the developing world is bombarded with a cocktail of confused meanings and indecision towards an uncertain future. The development of IT and telecommunications networks have intensified the production, generation, regeneration, circulation and exploitation of the system of information in an endless vicious circle. Global capitalism is renewed in flexibility and the effects are evident in qualitative transformations and rearrangements of social structures and conversions and mutations of human experience. Human communication is being challenged and disturbed as technological development comes to commercialize and colonize the world of human representation and imagination. Human interaction and communicational practice with computer technologies form and recreate new social attitudes and modes of spatial thinking. The increasing flow and management of information reconstructs social knowledge and re-organizes social life.

Distinct social discourses characteristically inform and affect human awareness and subjectivity about social reality and change. Their effects are embodied in the accumulated social experience and knowledge. They are also evident of their organizational patterns of the system of information that realizes them. The mechanics of the organizational system that boosts the world, that of information, can be identified in notions of interactivity, networking and flexibility. It is these attributes that provide the structural and processual support for the world dominance of digital capitalism and media imperialism. The new relations of human experience and construction of meaning are re-negotiated in the hyper-real cultural environments. They are globalized through economic systematization, the design and promotion of a global culture and consciousness, which seemingly integrates and unifies the world on the surface, but leaves the particular details of the validity of the underlying changes and transformations unresolved. Rationalization tendencies strive to compete and survive in a world that becomes more irrational with every step towards the future. This is a world where irrationality is taking over and replacing the meaning of rationality.

There is a cultural dominant in the world of electronic communication and digital technologies, guided by a new kind of probalistic logic that is credited to a transforming human awareness worldwide. This global transformation is manifested in the uneven progress and fate of global cultural systems. The intrusion of the cultural domain by computer communication and technologies has created a surplus of informational value and has led to the fatal acceptance of defeat. Postmodernity, and beyond, is the intensification of culturally dominant signifiers with the purpose of the maximization of consumerism and maintenance of global capitalism. Cultural homogenization and normalization networks aim in securing these conditions of consumption, often in the form of ideologies. Human ideologies become programmable systems of information, contributing towards the digital cloning and mutation of human consciousness. Their structural and architectural organization has always reflected patterns of systematic organization of information. With the increasing digital possibilities for manipulation and exploitation of the system of information, ideologies become confused, seeking refuge indiscriminately to whatever social configuration can still put up with their perplexing management.

The emerging new forms of postmodernity are dominated by the code of information. They do not consist a separate historical period, rather they are manifestations of the intensification of certain cultural attributes because of that surplus of information. New relations between spatiality and time are generated by the code of information in the hyper-real cultural environments. In our traditional physical world, the past exists in the form of memories and as practiced and acknowledged experience that has been interweaved in programmes of intended future action. The future exists only in the sphere of our imagination, and exists only as a projection of calculated evaluation and desired outcomes.

The present is nothing other than a transitional illusion between the past and the future. It is the line that we draw to mark the end of the input of memory and prior experience and the where our projection of the future begins. In this sense, the present hardly exists, which leaves only the past as the only acknowledged physical 'reality'. In the landscapes of hyperspace though, these relations between space and time are transformed. Past, present and future all remain in an infinite existence, as time is slowed down to becoming static. The past is rewritten and relived again and again in infinite alterations and modifications. The illusions of a future that is infinitely and potentially prescribed and programmed, become lived 'realities' of the present. As for the present, this is intensified with added excitement, imagination, creativity, sociability, and so on, and lasts indefinitely, or as long as your predefined 'access' allows you to. With the increasing intrusion and use of electronic communication and computer technologies, the time of postmodernity, and beyond that, is characterized by the gradual shift and replacement of our lived experience of the physical world, with these hyper-spatial relations: the past is rewritten, the future is realized in the present, and the present is enhanced and redesigned to accommodate everything else.

In order to cope with the emerging digital reconstruction of hyper-reality, alternative ways of thinking and logic are needed, to map and decode the code of information. Information lies at the core of organization and it comes in the form of systematically dispersed order or systematically organized chaos. Whatever the form, the organizational patterns of diverse subsystems of the system of information provide analogies and isomorphies, the identification of which can provide an initial theoretical basis to develop models of analysis of the code of information. The analysis of information as a system, and the analogic and isomorphic comparisons to other systems which information consist the organizational element of, can reveal different aspects of the mechanics and dynamics of its structure and operation. The system of information is a diverse entity based on conditions of interrelation and interdependence, on principles of self-organization and differentiation, and on factors of unpredictably complex and chaotic non-linear iterations towards fractalization.

The code, the control and the communication of information are all important aspects of the organization of the system of information. Traditional information theory concepts and principles are not inadequate or insufficient, they rather need to be reconsidered within the postmodern digital environments, and to be readjusted to the logic of the justification of digital construction of reality. The digitalization of the system of information makes it vulnerable to control and programmability. The system of information is vulnerable to the weaknesses of human information processing but also to the exploitative tendencies and interests of external interference and disturbance. Regardless of the strength of our defenses to these susceptibilities, one starting point of our response would be coming to a closer understanding of the ways that the system of information organizes itself, and reflexively organizes everything else. The potential danger of digital cybernetic interference is matched by potential problems in the content and relationships of the communicated system of information. In any case, it is obvious that the construction of social knowledge, reality and the world itself, are dependent on the code of the system of information.

Computer and digital technologies are digitally constructing reality, or to put it in another way, they are digitally reconstructing hyper-reality. The re-organization and transformation of the system of information is taking place within the boundaries of hyperspace or cyberspace. Still, the human obsession with this electronic spatiality, recreates the conditions of the organization of the system of information in every aspect of contemporary social life. In this sense, a framework of analysis regarding the organization of the system of information can apply to describe a wide range of issues of social consideration. The code of the system of information is structured along coexisting and interacting with each other, levels of organization, each characterized by various degrees of intensification of information.

At any point in the arrow of time, the system of information presents coexisting and alternating degrees of authentic, simulated and illusionary segments of information. The meaning of their particular logic of organization is dependent and is reflected in the organization of social life and the world. In the era of digital communication and computer technologies, the system of information implodes towards fractalization. The meaning that justifies the relation of the system of information to the social configurations and entities which reflexively are organized by it, is undergoing a gradual transformation of deconstruction, differentiation and reconstruction. Consequently, all logical justifications and confirmations of social reality in the postmodern world and beyond, are destroyed, intensified, transformed, reborn and set free of the tyranny of reason.

The virtual implosion of the system of information in the digital era, is an exemplification of the fractal fate of postmodern societies. Social change and transformation is powered up by the catastrophe of non-conformity to the dominant ideology and status quo of digital capitalism. Societies are led to an orgasmic state of intensities and extremes, promoted and marketed through media imperialism. The world is metamorphosed along opposing landscapes, one of secure existence and futuristic technological progress and one instability and misery and of no visibly better future. New epigenetic social structures and forms emerge continually, only making contemporary life and the solutions to its problems more complicated. We live in an anomic world, where we are programmed informationally. Both in terms of structural architecture and of social interaction, we become the virtual representations of our imaginary and desired selves. We become infogramic systems in a hyper-real world. As long as

371

we understand, and as soon as we accept this, we can if not be free, be conscious of the constraints upon our freedom.-

⏭

BIBLIOGRAPHY

Abercombie, N., Hill, S. & Turner, B.S. (1986). *Sovereign Individuals of Capitalism.* London: Allen & Unwin.

Abramson, N. (1963). *Information Theory and Coding.* New York: McGraw-Hill.

Adami, C. (1998). *Introduction to Artificial Life.* New York: Springer.

Anderson, B. (1991). *Imagined Communitites: Reflections on the Origin and Spread of Nationalism.* London: Verso.

Anderson, P. (1984). Modernity and Revolution. *New Left Review, 144,* 96-113.

Andoniou, C. (1986). *Cultural Propaganda & Stereotyping Through Children's Comic Book Literature.* Unpublished M.Ed., University of Wales College of Cardiff, Cardiff, Wales, UK.

Ang, I. (1985). *Watching Dallas: Soap Opera and the Melodramatic Imagination.* London: Methuen.

Appadurai, A. (1990). Disjuncture and Difference in the Global Cultural Economy. In M. Featherstone (Ed.), *Global Culture: Nationalism, Culture & Modernity* (pp. 295-310). London: SAGE.

Ashby, W. R. (1954). *Design for a Brain.* New York: John Wiley & Sons.

Ashby, W. R. (1957). *An Introduction to Cybernetics.* New York: John Wiley & Sons Inc.

Athusser, L. (1971). *Lenin and Philosophy and Other Essays.* London: New Left Books.

Barber, B. R. (1995). *Jihad vs. McWorld.* New York: Times Books.

Barnouw, E. (1978). *The Sponsor.* New York: Oxford.

Barraclough, G. (1964). *An Introduction to Contemporary History.* Baltimore: Penguin.

Barraclough, G. (Ed.). (1978). *The Times Atlas of World History.* London: Times.

Barron, I. & Curnow, R. (1979). *The Future with Microelectronics: Forecasting the Effects of Information Technology.* London: Pinter.

Bateson, G. (1958). *Naven.* Stanford: Stanford University Press.

Batty, M. (1993). The Geography of Cyberspace. *Environment and Planning B: Planning and Design, 20,* 699-712.

Baudrillard, J. (1981). *Simulacres et Simulation.* Paris: Galilee.

Baudrillard, J. (1983a). *In the Shadow of the Silent Majorities.* New York: Semiotext(e).

Baudrillard, J. (1983b). *Simulations*. New York: Semiotext(e).

Baudrillard, J. (1984a). Game with Vestiges. *On the Beach, 5,* 19-25.

Baudrillard, J. (1984b). On Nihilism. *On the Beach, 6,* 38-39.

Baudrillard, J. (1985). *La Gauche Divine*. Paris: Grasset.

Baudrillard, J. (1993). *Symbolic Exchange and Death*. London: SAGE.

Baudrillard, J. (1996). *The System of Objects*. New York: Verso.

Beck, U. (1992). *Risk Society*. London: SAGE.

Beer, S. (1959). *Cybernetics and Management*. London: The English Universities Press Ltd.

Bell, D. (1976a). *The Cultural Contradictions of Capitalism*. New York: Basic Books.

Bell, D. (1976b). *The Coming of Post-Industrial Society: A Venture in Social Forecasting*.
Harmdondsworth: Penguin, Peregrine Books.

Bell, D. (1979). The Social Framework of the Information Society. In M. Dertouzos & J. Moses (Eds.),
The Computer Age: A Twenty-Year View (pp. 163-211). Cambridge, MA: MIT Press.

Bell, D. (1980). *Sociological Journeys, 1960-1980*. London: Heinemann.

Bell, D. (1989). The Third Technological Revolution and its Possible Socioeconomic Consequences.
Dissent, 164-176.

Benedict, M. (1991). Introduction. In M. Benedict (Ed.), *Cyberspace: First Steps*. Cambridge, MA: The
MIT Press.

Berger, P. (1974). *Pyramids of Sacrifice*. Harmondsworth: Allen Lane.

Berman, M. (1983). *All That is Solid Melts into Air: The Experience of Modernity*. London: Verso.

Best, S. & Kellner, D. (1991). *Postmodern Theory: Critical Interrogations*. London: Macmillan.

Beyer, P. (1994). *Religion and Globalization*. London: Sage.

Biomorphs. http://www.virtual-worlds.net/lifedrop/galerie/images/biomorph.gif

Blackman, T. (2000). Complexity Theory. In G. Browning, Halcli, A. & Webster, F. (Ed.), *Understanding
Contemporary Society: Theories of the present* (pp. 139-151). London: Sage.

Blankenship, J. E. (2003). *Neurophysiology*. St.Louis: Mosby.

Boids. http://www.geocities.com/ SiliconValley/Vista/1069/Boid.html.

Bourdieu, P. (1981). *Ce Que Parler Veut Dire: l' Economie des Echanges Linguistiques*. Paris: Fayard.

Braman, S. (1995). Horizons of the State: Information Policy and Power. *Journal of Communication, 45*(4), 4-24.

Braverman, H. (1974). *Labor and Monopoly Capital: The Degradation of Work in the 20th Century*. New York: Monthly Review Press.

Browne, M. (1979, May 29). Scientists See a Loophole in the Fatal Lam of Physics. *New York Times*, pp. C1, C4.

Bryman, A. (1995). *Disney and his Worlds*. London: Routledge.

Bull, H. (1977). *The Anarchical Society*. New York: Columbia University Press.

Burrows, W. E. (1986). *Deep Black: Space Espionage and National Security*. New York: Random House.

Burton, J. (1972). *World Society*. Cambridge: Cambridge University Press.

Business Week editorial. (1997, 19 May). New Thinking About the Economy. *Business Week,* 150.

Campbell, J. (1982). *Grammatical Man: Information, Entropy, Language, and Life*. London: Allen Lane.

Carpenter, R. H. S. (1996). *Neurophysiology*. London: Arnold.

Castells, M. (1989). *The Informational City: Information Technology, Economic Restructuring and the Urban-Regional Process*. Oxford: Blackwell.

Castells, M. (1996). *The Information Age: Economy, Society and Culture, Vol.I, The Rise of the Network Society*. Oxford: Blackwell.

Castells, M. (1997). *The Information Age: Economy, Society and Culture, Vol.II, The Power of Identity*. Oxford: Blackwell.

Castells, M. (1998). *The Information Age: Economy, Society and Culture, Vol.III, The End of Millennium*. Oxford: Blackwell.

Castoriadis, C. (1975). *L' Institution Imaginaire de la Societe*. Paris: Seuil.

Castoriadis, C. (1978). *Carrefours du Labyrinth*. Paris: Seuil.

Castoriadis, C. (1981). *Devant la guerre, vol.1: Les realites*. Paris: Fayard.

Castoriadis, C. (1985). Reflections on 'Rationality' and 'Development'. *Thesis Eleven, 10/11,* 18-36.

Chisholm, R. M. (1966). *Theory of Knowledge*. Englewood Cliffs, NJ: Prentice-Hall.

Chomsky, N. (1980). *Rules and Representations*. Oxford: Blackwell.

Chomsky, N. (2002). *Syntactic Structures*. Hawthorne, N.Y.: Mouton de Gruyter.

Cilliers, P. (1998). *Complexity and Postmodernism: Understanding Complex Systems*. London: Routledge.

Codd, E. F. (1968). *Cellular Automata*. New York: Academic Press.

Cook, V. & Newson, M. (1996). *Chomsky's Universal Grammar: An Introduction*. Oxford: Blackwell Publishers.

Crook, S., Pakulski, J. & Waters, M. (1992). *Postmodernization: Change in an advanced society*. London: Sage.

Davis, M. (1990). *City of Quartz: Excavating the Future in Los Angeles*. London: Verso.

Dawkins, R. (1976). *The Selfish Gene*. Oxford: Oxford University Press.

Dawkins, R. (1987). *The Blind Watchmaker*. New York: W.W. Norton.

De Coursey, R. M. (1974). *The Human Organism*. New York: McGraw-Hill.

De Landa, M. (1991). *War in the Age of Intelligent Machines*. New York: Zone Books.

Deleuze, G. & Guattari, F. (1983). *Anti-Oedipus*. Minneapolis: University of Minnesota Press.

Deleuze, G. & Guattari, F. (1987). *Thousand Plateaus: Capitalism and Schizophrenia*. Minneapolis: University of Minnesota Press.

Deleuze, G. & Parnet, C. (1987). *Dialogues*. New York: Columbia University Press.

Derrida, J. (1987). *The Post Card: From Socrates to Freud and Beyond*. Chicago: University of Chicago Press.

Dicken, P. (1992). *Global Shift: The Internationalization of Economic Activity*. London: Paul Chapman.

Dickson, D. (1984). *Alternative Technology and the Politics of Technical Change*. London: Fontana.

Dordick, H. S., Bradley, H. G. & Nanus, B. (1981). *The Emerging Network Place*. Norwood, N.J.: Ablex.

Dorfman, A. & Mattelart, A. (1975). *How to Read Donald Duck: Imperialist Ideology in the Disney Comic*. New York: International General.

Drucker, P. F. (1957). *Landmarks of Tomorrow*. New York: Harper & Row.

Dunning, J. (1993). *Multinational Enterprises in a Global Economy*. Wokingham: Addison-Wesley.

Emmott, B. (1993). Everybody's Favourite Monsters. *The Economist, 27*, (supplement).

Evans, H. (1979). *Good Times, Bad Times*. London: Weidenfeld & Nicolson.

Eve, R., Horsfall, S. & Lee, M. (Ed.). (1997). *Chaos, Complexity & Sociology: Myths, Models & Theories*. Thousand Oaks, CA: Sage.

Featherstone, M. (1990). Global culture: An introduction. In M. Featherstone (Ed.), *Global Culture: Nationalism, Culture & Modernity* (pp. 1-14). London: Sage.

Featherstone, M. (1991). *Consumer culture and postmodernism*. London: Sage.

Feifer, M. (1985). *Going Places*. London: Macmillan.

Fejes, F. (1981). Media Imperialism: An Assessment. *Media, Culture and Society, 3*(3), 281-289.

Forsyth, R. & Naylor, C. (1985). *The Hitch-Hiker's Guide to Artificial Intelligence*. London & New York: Chapman & Hall/Mehtuen.

Foucault, M. (1972). *The Archaeology of Knowledge*. London: Tavistock.

Foucault, M. (1973). *The Order of Things*. New York: Vintage Books.

Foucault, M. (1975). *The Birth of the Clinic*. New York: Vintage Books.

Foucault, M. (1982). The Subject and Power. In H. L. Dreyfus & Rabinow, P. (Ed.), *Michel Foucault: Beyond Structuralism and Hermeneutics* (pp. 208-226). Chicago: University of Chicago Press.

Foucault, M. (1986). Of Other Spaces. *Diacritics, 16,* 22-27.

Foucault, M. (1988). Technologies of the Self: A Seminar with Michel Foucault. In H. M. Luther, Gutman, H. & Hutton, H. H. (Ed.), *Technologies of the Self* (pp. 16-49). Amherst: University of Massaschusets Press.

Freeman, C. (1987). *Technology Policy and Economic Performance*. London: Pinter.

Freeman, C. & Perez, C. (1988). Structural Crises of Adjustment, Business Cycles and Investment Behavior. In G. Dosi, Freeman, C., Nelson, R., Silverberg, G. & Soete, L. (Ed.), *Technical Change and Economic Theory*. London: Pinter.

Friedman, J. (1994). *Cultural identity and global process*. London: Sage.

Friedmann, J. (1986). The World-City hypothesis. *Development and Change, 17*(1), 69-83.

Friedmann, J. & Wolff, G. (1982). World City Formation: An Agenda for Research and Action. *International Journal of Urban and Regional Research, 6,* 309-344.

Fukuyama, F. (1992). *The End of History and the Last Man*. London: Hamish Hamilton.

Gandy, O. H. J. (1993). *The Panoptic Sort: A Political Economy of Personal Information*. Boulder, Co: Westview.

Gershuny, J. I. (1978). *After Industrial Society? The Emerging Self-Service Economy*. London: Macmillan.

Gibson, W. (1984). *Neuromancer*. London: Harper & Collins.

Giddens, A. (1981a). *The Class Structure of the Advanced Societies*. London: Hutchinson.

Giddens, A. (1981b). *A Contemporary Critique of Historical Materialism: Power, Property and the State*. London: Macmillan.

Giddens, A. (1984). *The Constitution of Society: Outline of the Theory of Structuration*. Cambridge: Polity Press.

Giddens, A. (1985). *A Contemporary Critique of Historical Materialism: The Nation State and Violence*. Cambridge: Polity.

Giddens, A. (1987). *Social Theory and Modern Society*. Cambridge: Polity.

Giddens, A. (1990). *The Consequences of Modernity*. Stanford, CA: Stanford University Press.

Gilpin, R. (1987). *The Political Economy of International Relations*. Princeton: Princeton University Press.

Gleick, J. (1987). *Chaos*. London: Cardinal.

Goddard, J. B. (1992). New Technology and the Geography of the UK Information Economy. In K. Robins (Ed.), *Understanding Information: Business, Technology and Geography* (pp. 178-201). London: Belhaven Press.

Goffman, E. (1961). *Asylums*. Garden City, NY: Anchor Books.

Goldman, S. L., Nagel, R. N. & Preiss, K. (1994, 9 October). Why Seiko Has 3,000 Watch Styles. *New York Times*, pp. 9.

Gouldner, A. W. (1976). *The Dialectic of Ideology and Technology*. London: Macmillan.

Gray, R. M. (1990). *Entropy and Information Theory*. New York: Springer-Verlag.

Gribbin, J. (1998). Cosmology, *The Future Now: Predicting the 21st Century* (pp. 1-40). London: Phoenix.

Habermas, J. (1987). *The Philosophical Discourse of Modernity*. Cambridge: Polity Press.

Habermas, J. (1989). *The Structural Transformation of the Public Sphere: An Inquiry into a Category of Bourgeois Society*. Cambridge: Polity.

Hall, A. D. & Fagen, R.E. (1956). Definition of System. *General Systems Yearbook, 1*, 18-28.

Hall, N. (Ed.). (1992). *The New Scientist Guide to Chaos.* Harmondsworth: Penguin.

Hall, S. (1977). Culture, the Media and the 'Ideological Effect'. In J. Curran, Gurevitch, M. & Woollacott, J. (Ed.), *Mass Communication and Society* (pp. 315-348). London: Edward Arnold.

Hamouda, O. F. & Smithin. J.N. (Ed.). (1988). *Keynes and Public Policy After Fifty Years.* New York: New York University Press.

Hannerz, U. (1990). Cosmopolitans and Locals in World Culture. In M. Featherstone (Ed.), *Global Culture* (pp. 237-252). London: Sage.

Harvey, D. (1989). *The Condition of Postmodernity: An Enquiry into the Origins of Cultural Change.* Oxford: Blackwell.

Hawley, J. F. & Holcomb, K.A. (1998). *Title Foundations of Modern Cosmology.* New York: Oxford University Press.

Hedberg, B., Dahlgren, G., Hansson, J. & Olve, N-G. (1997). *Virtual Organizations and Beyond: Discover imaginary systems.* Chilchester: Wiley.

Held, D. (1991). Democary and the global system. In D. Held (Ed.), *Political Theory Today* (pp. 197-235). Cambridge: Polity.

Hewison, R. (1987). *The Heritage Industry: Britain in a Climate of Decline.* London : Methuen

Hillyard, P. & Percy-Smith, J. (1988). *The Coercive State.* New York: Pinter Publishers.

Hiltz, S. & Turoff, M. (1978). *The Network Nation: Human Communication via Computer.* London: Addison-Wesley.

Hirst, P. (1979). *On Law and Ideology.* London: Macmillan.

Hobsbawm, E. (1983). Introduction: Inventing Traditions. In E. R. T. Hobsbawm (Ed.), *The Invention of Tradition* (pp. 1). Cambridge: Cambridge University Press.

Hock, D. (1999). *Birth of the Chaordic Age.* San Francisco: Berrett-Koehler Pub.

Hof, R. D., Browder, S. & Elstrom, P. (1997). Internet Communities. *Business Week,* 64-85.

Holub, R. C. (1991). *Juergen Habermas: Critic in the Public Sphere.* London: Routledge.

Hopcroft, J. E. (1987). Computer Science: The Emergence of a Discipline. *Communications of the Association for Computing Machinery, 30*(3), 201.

Horkheimer, M. & Adorno, T. (1972). *Dialectic of Enlightenment.* New York: Seabury.

Horrobin, D. F. (1966). *The Human Organism: An Introduction to Physiology.* New York: Basic Books.

Hundt, R. (1997). *The Internet: From Here to Ubiquity.* Paper presented before the Institute of Electrical and Electronics Engineers.

Hutchinson, L. (2001). *Order and disorder.* Oxford: Blackwell Publishers.

Inglehart, R. (1990). *Culture Shift in Advanced Industrial Society.* Princeton: Princeton University Press.

Jackendoff, R. S. (2002). *Foundations of Language: Brain, Meaning, Grammar, Evolution.* Oxford: Oxford University Press.

Jackson, D. (1957). The Question of Family Homeostasis. *The Psychiatric Quarterly Supplement*(31), 79-90.

Jackson, D. (1965a). Family Rules: The Marital Quid Pro Quo. *Archives of General Psychiatry, 12*, 589-594.

Jackson, D. (1965b). The Study of the Family. *Family Process, 4*, 1-20.

Jameson, F. (1984). Postmodernism, or the Cultural Logic of Late Capitalism. *New Left Review*(146), 53-93.

Jameson, F. (1991). The Cultural Logic of Late Capitalism. In F. Jameson (Ed.), *Postmodernism, Or, The Cultural Logic of Capitalism* (pp. 1-54). London: Verso.

Jürgens, H., Peitgen, H.O. & Saupe, D. (1992). *Chaos and Fractals: New Frontiers of Science.* New York: Springer-Verlag.

Karayiannis, A. N., & Venetsanopoulos, A.N. (1993). *Artificial Neural Networks: Learning Algorithms, Performance Evaluation, and Applications.* Boston, Mass.: Kluwer Academic.

Katz, E. & Liebes, T. (1985). Mutual Aid in the Decoding of Dallas. In P. P. Drummond, R. (Ed.), *Television in Transition* (pp. 187-198). London: British Film Institute.

Kavolis, V. (1988). Contemporary Moral Cultures and the 'Return of the Sacred'. *Sociological Analysis, 49*(3), 203-216.

Kellert, S. H. (1993). *In the Wake of Chaos.* Chicago: University of Chicago.

Kellner, D. (1983). Critical Theory, Commodities and Consumer Society. *Theory, Culture and Society, 1*(3), 64-84.

Kerr, C., Dunlop, J., Harbison, F. & Myers, C. (1973). *Industrialism and Industrial Man.* Harmondsworth: Penguin.

King, A. D. (1989). Colonialism, Urbanism and the Capitalist World-Economy: An Introduction. *International Journal of Urban and Regional Research, 13*(1), 1-18.

King, A. D. (1990a). Architecture, Capital and the Globalization of Culture. In M. Featherstone (Ed.), *Global Culture: Nationalism, Culture & Modernity* (pp. 397-411). London: Sage.

King, A. D. (1990b). *Global Cities.* London & New York: Routledge.

Kleinberg, B. S. (1973). *American Society in the Postindustrial Age: Technocracy, Power, and the End of Ideology.* Columbus, OH: Merrill.

Knight, D. & Willmott, H. (Ed.). (1990). *Labour Process Theory.* Basingstoke: Macmillan.

Krieger, D. J. (1998). *Operationalizing Self-organization Theory for Social Science Research.* Paper presented at the SOEIS Conference, Bielefeld.

Lasch, C. (1985). *The Minimal Self: Psychic Survival in Troubled Times.* London: Picador.

Lash, S. & Urry, J. (1987). *The End of Organized Capitalism.* Cambridge: Polity.

Lash, S. & Urry, J. (1994). *Economies of Sign and Space.* London: Sage.

Lears, T. J. & Fox, R. W. (1983). *The Culture of Consumption: Critical Essays in American History 1880-1980.* New York: Pantheon.

Lechner, F. (1991). Relgion, Law and Global Order. In R. G. Robertson, W. (Ed.), *Religion and Global Order* (pp. 263-280). New York: Paragon.

Lee, A. R. (1963, September 1963). Levels of Imperviousness in Schizophrenic Families. *Paper read at the Western Division Meeting of the American Psychiatric Association.*

Lefebvre, H. (1971). *Everyday Life in the Modern World.* New York: Harper & Row.

Lefebvre, H. (1980). *La Presence et l' Absence.* Paris: Casterman.

Lefebvre, H. (1991a). *The Production of Space.* Oxford, UK and Cambridge, MA: Blackwell.

Lefebvre, H. (1991b). *Critique of Everyday Life - Volume I: Introduction* (J. Moore, Trans.). London: Verso.

Lefort, C. (1978a). *Les Formes de l' Histoire: Essais d' Anthropologie politique.* Paris: Gallimard.

Lefort, C. (1978b). *Sur une Colonne Absente: Ecrits Autour de Merleau-Ponty.* Paris: Gallimard.

Lefort, C. (1979). *Elements d' Une Critique de la Bureaucratie.* Paris: Gallimard.

Lefort, C. (1981). *L' Invention Democratique: Les Limites de la Domination Totalitaire.* Paris: Fayard.

Leidner, R. (1993). *Fast food, Fast Talk: Service Work and the Routinization of Everyday Life.* Berkeley, CA: University of California Press.

Levy, M. (1966). *Modernization and the Structure of Societies.* Princeton: Princeton University Press.

Lohr, S. (1997, 3 June). Study Ranks Software As No. Three Industry. *New York Times,* pp. C2.

Lovelock, J. (1987). *Gaia.* Oxford: Oxford University Press.

Lovelock, J. (1989). *The Ages of Gaia: A Biography of our Living Earth.* Oxford: Oxford University Press.

Lovelock, J. (2000). *Gaia: A New Look at Life on Earth.* Oxford: Oxford University Press.

Luchman, N. (1976). Generalized Media and the Problem of Contingency. In J. Loubser (Ed.), *Explorations in General Theory of Social Science.* New York: Free Press.

Luhmann, N. (1986). The Autopoiesis of Social Systems. In F. Geyer & van der Zouwen, J. (Ed.), *Sociocybernetic Paradoxes.* London: Sage.

Luhmann, N. (1995). *Social Systems.* Stanford: Stanford University Press.

Lyotard, J.-F. (1971). *Discours, Figure.* Paris: Klincksieck.

Lyotard, J.-F. (1974). *Economie Libidinale.* Paris: Minuit.

Lyotard, J.-F. (1984). *The Postmodern Condition: A Report on Knowledge.* London: Manchester University Press.

Lyotard, J.-F. (1986). Rules and Paradoxes and Svelte Paradox. *Cultural Critique, 5*(2-3), 277-310.

Machlup, F. (1962). *The Production and Distribution of Knowledge in the United States.* Pinceton, NJ: Princeton University Press.

Mandel, E. (1975). *Late Capitalism.* London: New Left Books.

Mannheim, K. (1936). *Ideology and Utopia: An Introduction to the Sociology of Knowledge.* London: Routledge & Kegan Paul.

Mannheim, K. (1940). *Man and Society, in an Age of Reconstruction: Studies in Modern Social Structure.* London: Kegan Paul, Trench, Trubner.

Marcuse, H. (1960). *Reason and Revolution: Hegel and the Rise of Social Theory.* Boston: Beacon.

Marcuse, H. (1972). *One-Dimensional Man.* London: Abacus.

Martin, J. (1978). *The Wired Society.* Englewood Cliffs, NJ: Prentice-Hall.

Maturana, H. R. (1980). *Autopoiesis and Cognition: the Realization of the Living.* Dordrecht: Reidel.

McCannell, D. (1976). *The Tourist: A New Theory of the Leisure Class.* New York: Schocken.

McGuinness, B. (Ed.). (1974). *Theoretical Physics and Philosophical Problems: Selected Writings / Ludwig Boltzmann*. Dordrecht: Reidel Pub. Co.

McLuhan, M. (1964). *Understanding Media*. London: Routledge.

Meadows, D., Randers, J. & Behrens, W. (1976). *The Limits to Growth*. Scarborough: Signet.

Meyrowitz, J. (1985). *No Sense of Place: The Impact of Electronic Media on Social Behavior*. New York: Oxford.

Mills, C. W. (1959). *The Sociological Imagination*. New York: Oxford University Press.

Morgan, G. (1993). *Imaginization: The Art of Creative Management*. Newbury Park, CA: Sage.

Myerson, A. R. (1996, 28 July). America's Quiet Rebellion Against McDonaldization. *New York Times*, pp. E5.

Nettl, J. & Robertson, R. (1968). *International Systems and the Modernization of Societies*. London: Faber.

Nietzsche, F. (1967). *The Will to Power*. New York: Random House.

OECD (Ed.). (1992). *Globalization of Industrial Activities*. Paris: OECD.

Offe, C. (1984). *Contradictions of the Welfare State*. London: Hutchinson.

Ohman, R. (1996). *Selling Culture*. London: Verso.

O'Neill, J. (1990). AIDS as a Globalizing Panic. In M. Featherstone (Ed.), *Global Culture: Nationalism, Culture & Modernity* (pp. 329-342). London: Sage.

Pask, G. (1975). *The Cybernetics of Human Learning and Performance*. London: Hutchinson.

Pecheux, M., Henry, P., Poitou, J-P. & Haroche, C. (1979). Un Exemple d' Ambiguite Ideologique: Le Rapport Mansholt. *Technologies, Ideologies et Pratiques, 1*(2), 3-83.

Penacchioni, I. (1984). The Reception of Popular Television in Northeast Brazil. *Media, Culture & Society*(6), 337–341.

Perkin, H. (1990). *The Rise of Professional Society: Britain Since 1880*. London: Routledge.

Pierce, J. R. (1962). *Symbols, Signals and Noise: The Nature and Process of Communication*. London: Hutchinson.

Pieterse, J. N. (1994). Globalization as Hybridisation. *International Sociology, 9*, 161-184.

Pine, J. (1993). *Mass Customization: The New Frontier in Business Competition*. Cambridge, MA: Harvard Business School Press.

Pinel, J. P. (2003). *Biopsychology.* London: Allyn & Bacon.

Piore, M. & Sabel, C. (1984). *The Second Industrial Divide.* New York: Basic Books.

Pool, I. (1979). Direct Broadcast Satellites and the Integrity of National Cutlures. In, K. Nordenstreng & Schiller, H. I. (Ed.). *National Sovereignty and International Communication* (pp. 120-153). New Jersey: Ablex.

Poster, M. (1990). *The Mode of Information: Postructuralism and Social Context.* Cambridge: Polity.

Quine, W. O. (1960). *Methods of Logic.* New York: Henry Hold & Company.

Ricoeur, P. (1978). *The Rule of Metaphor.* London: Routledge & Kegan Paul.

Rieff, D. (1991). *Los Angeles: Capital of the Third World.* London: Phoenix.

Ritzer, G. (1996). *The McDonaldization of Society.* Thousand Oaks, CA: Pine Forge Press.

Ritzer, G. (1998). *The McDonaldization Thesis: Explorations and Extensions.* Thousand Oaks: SAGE Publications.

Robertson, R. (1992). *Globalization: Social Theory and Global Culture.* London: Sage.

Rojek, C. (1993). Disney Culture. *Leisure Studies*(12), 121-135.

Ron, M. & David, A. (Ed.). (1998). *Disorders of Brain and Mind.* Cambridge: Cambridge University Press.

Roos, M. (1994). *Introduction to Cosmology.* Chilchester: John Willey & Sons.

Rose, G. (1993). *Feminism and Geography.* Cambridge: Polity Press.

Rosenau, J. (1980). *The Study of Global Interdependence.* New York: Nichols.

Rosenberg, B. & White, D. (1957). *Mass Culture.* Glencoe, Il: The Free Press.

Ruesch, J. & Bateson, G. (1951). *Communication: The Social Matrix of Psychiatry.* New York: W.W. Norton & Company, Inc.

Russell, B. (1951). Introduction, *Ludwig Wittgenstein, Tractatus Logico-Philosophicus.* New York: Humanities Press.

Saparina, Y. (1966). *Cybernetics Within Us.* Moscow: Peace Publishers.

Sassen, S. (1991). *The Global City: New York, London, Tokyo.* Princeton, NJ: Princeton University Press.

Schiller, D. (1999). *Digital Capitalism: Networking the Global Market System.* Cambridge, MA: MIT Press.

Schiller, H.I. (1973). *The Mind Managers*. Boston: Beacon Press.

Schiller, H.I. (1976). *Communication and Cultural Domination*. White Plains, N.Y: M.E. Sharpe

Schiller, H.I. (1979). Transnational Media and National Development. In K. Nordenstreng & Schiller, H.I. (Ed.), *National Sovereignty and International Communication* (pp. 21-32). New Jersey: Ablex.

Schiller, H.I. (1981). *Who Knows: Information in the Age of the Fortune 500*. Norwood, NJ: Ablex.

Schiller, H.I. (1987). Old Foundations for a New (Information) Age. In J. R. Schement & Leivroux, L. (Ed.), *Competing Visions, Complex Realities: Aspects of the Infromation Society* (pp. 23-31). Norwood, NJ: Ablex.

Schlesinger, P. (1987). On National Identity: Some Conceptions and Misconceptions. *Social Science Information, 26*(2), 219-264.

Schwarz, E. (1996). Toward a Holistic Cybernetics From Science Through to Epistemology to Being, *Cybernetics and Human Knowing*. Alborg.

Searle, J. (1980). Minds, Brains, and Programs. *Behavioral and Brain Sciences, 3*, 417-424.

Searle, J. (1984). *Minds, Brains and Science*. Cambridge: Harvard University Press.

Seliger. (1976). *Ideology and Politics*. London: George Allen & Unwin.

Servan-Schreiber, J.-J. (1968). *The American challenge*. New York: Atheneum.

Shannon, C. E. (1948). A Mathematical Theory of Information. *Bell System Technical Journal*(27), 379-423.

Shannon, C. E. (1951). Prediction and Entropy of Printed English. *Bell System Technical Journal, 30*(1), 50-64.

Sinclair, J. (1987). *Images Incorporated: Advertising as Industry and Ideology*. London: Croom Helm.

Sklair, L. (1991). *Sociology of the Global System*. Hemel Hempstead: Harvester Wheatsheaf.

Smith, A. D. (1990). Towards a Global Culture. In Featherstone. In M. Featherstone (Ed.), *Global Culture: Nationalism, Culture & Modernity* (pp. 171-192). London: Sage.

Smythe, D. W. (1981). *Dependency Road: Communications, Capitalism, Consciousness, and Canada*. Norwood, N.J.: Ablex.

Soja, E. W. (1989). *Postmodern Geographies: The Reassertion of Space in Critical Social Theory*. New York: Verso.

Soja, E. W. (1996). *Thirdspace: Journeys to Los Angeles and Other Real-and-Imagined Places*. Oxford: Blackwell Publishers.

Spenlger, O. (1926). *The Decline of the West, Form and Actuality* (Vol. 1). New York: Alfred A. Knopf, Inc.

Spivak, G. C. (1990). *The Post-Colonial Critic.* New York: Routledge.

Squire, L. R. (1987). *Memory and Brain.* New York: Oxford University Press.

Stacey, D. (1994). Intelligent Systems Architecture: Design Techniques. In C. Dagli (Ed.), *Artificial Neural Networks for Intelligent Manufacturing.* London: Chapman and Hall.

Stegmeuller, W. (1957). *Das Wahrheitsproblem und die Idee der Semantik [The Truth Problem of Semantics].* Vienna: Springer-Verlag.

Stein, J. F. (1982). *An Introduction to Neurophysiology.* London: Blackwell Scientific Publications.

Stonier, T. (1992). *Beyond Information: The Natural History of Intelligence.* London: Springer-Verlag.

Suzuki, M. (1982). *Group Theory.* New York: Springer-Verlag.

Talbott, S. P. (1996). Global Localization of the World Market: Case Study of McDonald's in Moscow. *Sociale Wetenschappen, December,* 31-44.

Taylor, J. G. (1993). *Mathematical Approaches to Neural Networks.* Amsterdam: North Holland.

The Mentor. (1986). *The Hacker Manifesto.* http://www.mithral.com/~beberg/manifesto.html.

Thompson, R. F. (1989). *Learning and Memory.* Boston: Birkhauser.

Thrift, N., & Williams, P. (Ed.). (1987). *Class and Space : The Making of Urban Society.* London: Routledge & Kegan Paul.

Thurston, C. M. (1980). Ilya Prigogine: Towards a Unity of Science and Culture. *Christian Science Monitor,* 16.

Tiryakian, E. A. (1991). Pathways to Metatheory: Rethinking the Presuppositions of Macrosociology. In G. Ritzer (Ed.), *Metatheorizing* (pp. 69-87). Newbury Park, C.A.: Sage.

Tomlinson, J. (1991). *Cultural Imperialism: A Critical Introduction.* London: Pinter.

Trachtenberg, A. (1982). *The Incorporation of America: Culture and Society in the Gilded Age.* New York: Hill & Wang.

Turner, L. & Ash, J. (1975). *The Golden Hordes.* London: Constable.

Turow, J. (1992). *Media Systems in Society: Understanding Industries, Strategies, and Power.* New York: Longman.

UN Economic and Social Council, Commission on Transnational Corporations. (1984). *The Role of Transnational Corporations in Transborder Data Flows.* 10th Session, 18-27 April.

Urry, J. (1990). *The Tourist Gaze: Leisure and Travel in Contemporary Societies.* London: Sage.

Useem, M. (1984). *The Inner Circle : Large Corporations and the Rise of Business Political Activity in the US and UK.* New York: Oxford University Press.

van der Pijl, K. (1989). The International Level. In T. Bottomore & Brym, R. (Ed.), *The Capitalist Class* (pp. 237-266). Hemel Hempstead: Harvester Wheatsheaf.

Vogler, J. (1992). Regimes and the Global Commons. In A. McGrew & Lewis, P. (Ed.), *Global Politics* (pp. 118-137). Cambridge: Polity.

von Bertalanffy, L. (1962). General Systems Theory - A Critical Review. *General Systems Yearbook, 7,* 1-20.

von Bertalanffy, L. (1968). The Meaning of General System Theory, *General System Theory. Foundations, Development, Applications* (pp. 30-53). New York: George Braziller.

von Neumann, J. (1966). Lecture at University of Illinois. In A. W. Burks (Ed.), *Theory of Self-Reproducing Automata.* Urbana: University of Illinois Press.

Wallerstein, I. (1974). *The Modern World-System I, Capitalist Agriculture and the Origins of the European World-economy in the Sixteenth Century.* New York: Academic Press.

Wallerstein, I. (1980). *The Modern World-System II, Mercantilism and the Consolidation of the European World-economy, 1600-1750.* New York: Academic Press.

Waters, M. (1995). *Globalization.* London & New York: Routledge.

Watzlawick, P., Helmick-Beavin, J. & Jackson, D. D. (1967). *Pragmatics of Human Communication: A Study of Interactional Patterns, Pathologies, and Paradoxes.* New York: Norton.

Weber, B. H., Depew, D.J. & Smith, J.D. (Ed.). (1988). *Entropy, Information, and Evolution: New Perspectives on Physical and Biological Evolution.* Cambridge, Mass.: MIT Press.

Webster, F. (1995). *Theories of the Information Society.* London: Routledge.

Wheatly, M. (1992). *Leadership and the New Science.* San Francisco: Berrett-Koehler.

Whorf, B. L. (1956). Science and Linguistics. In J. B. Carroll (Ed.), *Language, Thought and Reality. Selected Writings of Benjamin Lee Whorf* (pp. 207-219). New York: John Wiley and Sons Inc.

Wiener, N. (1954). *The Human Use of Human Beings: Cybernetics and Society.* New York: Anchor.

Wiener, N. (1964). *Ex-Prodigy: My Childhood and Youth.* Cambridge, Mass.: MIT Press.

Williams, F. (1962). *The American Invasion.* New York: Crown.

Williams, R. (1976). *Keywords: A Vocabulary of Culture and Society.* London: Fontana Paperbacks.

Wilson, K. G. (1988). *Technologies of Control: The New Interactive Media for the Home.* Madison: University of Wisconsin Press.

Wilson, M. I. & Corey, K. E. (2000). *Information Tectonics.* Chilchester: Wiley.

Winston, P. H. (1992). *Artificial Intelligence.* Reading, Mass: Addison-Wesley.

Wolf, M. (1997, 1 October). The Heart of the New World Economy. *Financial Times,* pp. 12.

Woods, L. C. (1970). *An Introduction to Information Theory.* Oxford: Mathematical Institute.

Zukin, S. (1991). *The City as a Landscape of Power: London and New York as Global Financial Capitals.* London: Routledge.

▶▶|

www.ingramcontent.com/pod-product-compliance
Lightning Source LLC
LaVergne TN
LVHW022259060326
832902LV00020B/3167